BEFORE THE SECOND WAVE

Gender in the Sociological Tradition

BARBARA FINLAY
Texas A&M University

PEARSON

Prentice Hall

Upper Saddle River, New Jersey 07458

Library of Congress Cataloging-in-Publication Data

Finlay, Barbara.
  Before the second wave : Gender in the Sociological Tradition / Barbara Finlay. — 1st ed.
     p. cm.
     ISBN-0-13-184803-8
  1. Women—United States—Sociological aspects—History.   2. Sex role—United States—History.
3. Social role—United States—History.   4. Sociologists—United States—Attitudes—History.
5. Sociology—United States—History.   I. Title.

  HQ1181.U5F56 2006
  305.4072'073—dc22

                                                                      2006009283

*To the Founding Sisters
of American Sociology*

Editorial Director: Leah Jewell
Publisher: Nancy Roberts
Editorial Assistant: Lee Peterson
Executive Marketing Manager: Marissa Feliberty
Marketing Assistant: Anthony DeCosta
Production Liaison: Marianne Peters-Riordan
Manufacturing Buyer: Brian Mackey
Cover Art Director: Jayne Conte
Cover Design: Kiwi Design
Cover Illustration: Kaadaa/Stock Illustration Source/Images.com.
Manager, Cover Visual Research & Permissions: Karen Sanatar
Composition/Full-Service Project Management: Sarvesh Mehrotra/Techbooks
Printer/Binder and Cover Printer: R.R. Donnelley & Sons

Credits and acknowledgments borrowed from other sources and reproduced, with permission, in this textbook
appear on appropriate page within text.

Pearson Education LTD.   Pearson Education North Asia Ltd
Pearson Education Singapore, Pte. Ltd   Pearson Educación de Mexico, S.A. de C.V.
Pearson Education, Canada, Ltd   Pearson Education Malaysia, Pte. Ltd
Pearson Education–Japan   Pearson Education, Upper Saddle River, New Jersey
Pearson Education Australia PTY, Limited

10 9 8 7 6 5 4 3 2 1
ISBN: 0-13-184803-8

CONTENTS

PREFACE

For many years I have been fascinated by the discovery of sociological statements about women and gender-related topics by the classical giants in the field and by others whose work has been neglected or forgotten by subsequent generations. As a student of sociology in the late 1960s and early 1970s, I focused my studies on theory and family, the latter of which was the location of practically all discussion of gender. In my educational experience, I had almost no contact with women writers or male-authored writings about women. The topic seemed to be of no concern to "serious scholarly thinking" about human society.

My love of books and the history of ideas, however, frequently took me to the remote stacks of libraries, where I browsed through old editions of works by some of the early sociologists—authors such as Auguste Comte, Lester Frank Ward, E. A. Ross, Albion Small, and Herbert Spencer. I began to notice that these writers often gave some attention to the status of women in their theoretical expositions of human society, and the question arose as to why these parts of their work were never included in contemporary discussions of their work.

Over the years, this question has remained with me, as I have moved further into the study of gender and its profound intersection with other aspects of human societal structure. In my career I have observed the birth and flourishing of the sociology of gender, with its gradual integration into other subfields of the discipline. In the field of theory, however, the new thinking about gender has been slow to have an impact. Many textbooks on theory still include few women thinkers, and most discussions of the "masters" curiously ignore their discussions of women or their explanations of sex differences and their social implications. One would assume that these discussions did not exist, or that they are irrelevant to legitimate theory. Yet, if Comte, Durkheim, Simmel, Spencer, and other classical thinkers thought these topics were important enough to include in their major works on the nature of human societies, why have we ignored them as a discipline? I believe the neglect of classical discussions of women and the gendered nature of society is rooted in the academic and sexual politics during the period in which sociology became institutionalized in American universities. The details of this process are now being uncovered by many scholars, and this book is my attempt to contribute to this process.

I thank Nancy Roberts of Prentice Hall for her encouragement in my decision to attempt this project. I would also like to thank the following reviewers: Daniel D. Cervi, California State–Fresno; Emily S. Kearns, Emerson College; and Diane Baxter, University of Oregon. Any anthology must be selective, this one included. I could have selected different writers or different portions of the writings of the scholars whose work I have included. Making these decisions was difficult, and I am sure that there are works that may have deserved to be included but are absent. However, at some point, one must bring a project to a close, and I believe that the readings I have chosen fairly represent the history of sociology on these issues. I hope the reader finds the work excerpted here as fascinating as I have, and that these readings stimulate the desire to learn more about the history of sociological thought about women and gender.

INTRODUCTION

When questioned by a student, "Why are we not covering any women thinkers?" a sociologist I know responded, "This is classical theory. There *were* no women theorists." That was a few years ago. Even at that time, such a response was unwarranted, but today it would reveal ignorance of recent developments in the field. Indeed, one of the most rapidly expanding subfields in sociology is the history of the theory, especially as it relates to issues of class, race, and gender. Currently, there are a number of books that document the contributions of women to the origins and development of sociological theory, casting a more inclusive net than before across the writings of the past and revising the notion of the sociological canon (e.g., Camic, 1997; Deegan, 1987, 1991, 2002; Lengermann and Niebrugge-Brantley, 1997; McDonald, 1996).

In a parallel development, some recent research has also brought to light the work by both female and male scholars who analyzed gender and women's issues, long before the rise of the sociology of gender and women's studies in the late 1960s (e.g., Coser, 1977; Finlay, 1998; Kandal, 1988; Lehmann, 1994; Pickering, 1994; Sydie, 1994; Peterson, 2001). It turns out that scholars from Comte, to Spencer, to Durkheim in the nineteenth century, and Ward, Simmel, and Parsons in the twentieth century, all wrote about sex roles, women's status, sex conflict, or similar issues. Nevertheless, to read traditional discussions of the history of sociology, one would think that none of the classical writers or later leading thinkers of the field ever thought about women, gender, or sexuality. If we turn to the *actual writings* of historically important sociologists, on the other hand, we find that many—perhaps most—of them did think, and write, about these topics. The explanation for the virtual erasure of their work from the official histories of the discipline is a question that has only recently been raised. In this introductory chapter, I briefly address this question and present an overview of the history of sociological attention to women and gender as I have come to discover it. I conclude with a description of the plan and contents of the remainder of the book, which presents a series of articles and book excerpts that document the history of sociological thinking about women and gender, focusing primarily on American sociology.

THE POLITICS OF COLLECTIVE MEMORY IN AMERICAN SOCIOLOGY

It has become a truism that our reading of the past is a function of where we are today—historically, culturally, and socially. As our understanding of what is important in the present has evolved, our view of the significance of historical events has changed as well. What was once deemed irrelevant may now be seen to be of signal importance. Thus, since the rebirth of feminism in the second wave of the 1960s and 1970s, many academic disciplines have felt the need to rethink their histories with gender in mind, to discover what might have been unjustly excluded owing to the male bias of the canonizers.

Recent years have witnessed a growing sense in sociology specifically that we need to rewrite our disciplinary history to recover work that was excluded from our collective memory that might be worth preserving. Feagin and Vera (2001), for example, make a strong case that many early sociologists were critical and reform-oriented—in their terms *liberationists*. They document an alternative history of the discipline, showing how individuals with such perspectives tended to be ignored, neglected, and excluded by mainstream chroniclers of the field. Similarly, Adams and Sydie (2001), in their recent textbook on theory, include a number of formerly excluded thinkers and present an insightful discussion of how the political and ideological assumptions of mainstream sociologists distorted and introduced bias into our official history. Lengermann and Niebrugge-Brantley (1997) present a strong case for the role of sexism in erasing women's work from the canon. These writers take up the question of how women scholars and nonwhite men were marginalized in the discipline, and their work and issues devalued.

One of the most important scholars doing the work of recovery is Mary Jo Deegan. Her *Women in Sociology* (1991) contains the biographies of 51 women sociologists, many of them "founding sisters" who were writing in the early twentieth century. Deegan's description of her surprise in discovering these women and their work is poignant.

> I first discovered the vast work done by early women sociologists when I was standing in the basement stacks at Regenstein Library at the University of Chicago in 1975. In front of me were row upon row, from floor to ceiling, of dozens and dozens of books written on women's work in the marketplace, and almost all were written before 1925. Who were these female authors? Were they sociologists? Why had I been led to believe that feminists raised similar questions only since 1965 or 1970? (Deegan 1991: xiii)

The neglect of classical sociological discussions of women and the gendered nature of society is rooted in the history of the discipline itself, especially in the academic and sexual politics during the period in which sociology became institutionalized in American universities. The story of this process has been better told elsewhere (Connell, 1990; Deegan, 1987, 1991; Feagin and Lengermann and Niebrugge-Brantley, 1997; Vera, 2001), but its basic plot is briefly sketched here.

During the nineteenth and early twentieth centuries, sociology was in the process of forming, in reaction to the disruption of European societies by various revolutions—political, social, and economic—which together created widescale dislocation, displacement, and social unrest. The disruptions of the time led to social movements, violence, and major social problems in the rapidly growing cities. In response, a number of scholars sought to use the models of other scientific approaches, attempting to observe human societies with a view toward understanding and perhaps developing better approaches to politics and social planning, so as to solve some of these problems. Over time, a community of scholars developed who knew each other's work and who came to view themselves as leaders of the development of a new human science, sociology. In the United States, by the late nineteenth century, a few courses had been organized at some universities in the new field (the first being taught at Yale by W. G. Sumner), and sociological work was being published (Lester Ward's *Dynamic Sociology* appeared in 1883, and the *American Journal of Sociology* was inaugurated in 1895). By the turn of the century, sociology was a developing discipline with centers in academic institutions such as the University of Chicago, Yale, and Stanford, and in urban institutions such as Jane Addams's Hull House settlement in Chicago.

In the period 1890–1920, sociology was a lively field, with many scholars trained in other disciplines writing and teaching in the field. Many of these scholars were also "applied" thinkers, actively criticizing various aspects of their societies and, through their efforts, seeking ways to improve conditions. The Progressive Era in politics had its corresponding progressive developments in social sciences. Among the important writers who published in the field of sociology (e.g., in the *American Journal of Sociology*) during this period were Jane Addams, Charlotte Perkins Gilman, E. A. Ross, and W. I. Thomas. These thinkers saw no contradiction between good scholarship and social critique and calls for reform. Many were working in Chicago and were connected with the University of Chicago sociology department (Deegan, 1987; Feagin and Vera, 2001).

By the 1920s, however, a new era of academic sociology arose, focusing more on objectivity and scientific legitimacy—a focus many recent observers have challenged as "scientistic." As part of this new move to become a respected part of the university/academic environment, many works of previous scholars were discarded or dismissed as being nonscientific or biased, including several works by and about women. Meanwhile at the leading department (the University of Chicago), women were increasingly marginalized from the Department of Sociology (Deegan, 1987; Seigfried, 1996). Although the 1920s saw a few progressive thinkers continuing, the mainstream of the field gave up social criticism and social-problems work in favor of "value-free" empirical studies. During this period, some women continued to write successfully, including Anna Garlin Spencer and Sophonisba Breckenridge, but their work was not as well preserved by later sociologists as that of the more conservative male writers. For most of sociology, the 1920s were a time of retrenchment, of concern with being scientific and objective, leading to an expansion of empirical work and statistical expertise but a neglect of feminist or activist work by the mainstream. It was during this phase that the canon of sociology was defined, and it began to be defined primarily by the men who dominated the field during this conservative period.

The decades of the 1930s through the 1950s were dominated by two perspectives inconsistent with feminist or critical sociology. First, the emphasis on empiricism and quantitative measurement and analysis continued to grow, fostering a focus on methodology and precision without much attention to the larger questions of where society should be going or how sociologists might contribute to that process. Although there were dissenters, the dominant group was represented by George A. Lundberg, whose *Can Science Save Us?* (1947) argued that science was (and should be) neutral, an objective tool that could be used by citizens for good or evil.

There were, of course, opponents, among them Robert S. Lynd, whose *Knowledge for What?* (1948) was in part an answer to Lundberg. C. Wright Mills (1959), likewise, was strongly critical of what he called *abstracted empiricism* in sociology, as was Pitirim Sorokin (1956) of Harvard. However, the dominant style, as represented by the major journals, was still more on the side of Lundberg. Thus, social problems such as inequality, sexism, or racism did not receive as much attention in these decades as we find later (Karides et al., 2001). This in turn meant that studies of the status of women tended to be "objective" and were not oriented to critically questioning their status.

The second characteristic of American sociology in the decades prior to 1960, led by Talcott Parsons of Harvard, was the dominance of theoretical functionalism. This approach tends to accept the status quo of society as given, because all parts of society are assumed to have evolved to perform some function and exist in balanced relation to the whole. Differentiation of roles is seen as serving a function for society; otherwise it would not have developed, nor would it persist. Hence, the status and roles of women and men were rarely questioned by functionalist scholars; instead, there were attempts to explain why they must be so, in terms of how such role distinctions contributed to the well-being of society. Even those who questioned aspects of sex roles did so on the basis that the current role definitions contained "strains" that needed to be resolved by various means—but rarely were there suggestions for actual changes in the basic roles. Much less common was any analysis of gender as a basis of inequality or unfairness. These types of questions were not in the purview of functionalists, whose assumptions defined *what is* as serving important social/societal needs.

Because of the relatively conservative and nonengaged approach of the statistical empiricists and the functionalists, a revolt occurred in the early 1950s, led by Alfred McClung Lee, Elizabeth Briant Lee, Ernest Burgess, Arnold Rose, and others who objected to the elitist and conservative nature of the American Sociological Association. This group formed the Society for the Study of Social Problems (SSSP) and inaugurated a

new journal, *Social Problems,* as an alternative to the less critical *American Sociological Review* (Bernard, 1973). The SSSP's focus on social issues and problems created a professional vehicle for the increased social criticism of the 1960s, a decade that saw the demise of functionalist dominance and the rise of conflict theories, including antiracist and feminist work.

Thus, the positivistic emphasis on quantification, empiricism, objectivity, and value neutrality, combined with a functionalist theoretical approach, made it difficult for sociologists to do critical work during the decades of the 1920s through the 1950s. Unfortunately, these decades were the ones that saw the field becoming established in universities, and proponents of these views were primarily responsible for developing the canon of important classical works. This canon turned out to be much different from that which earlier sociologists had studied, raising to foundational prominence the more conservative thinkers such as Comte, Spencer, Durkheim, and Sumner, and downplaying (or even ignoring) the work of Marx, Ward, and many women sociologists.

PURPOSE OF THIS COLLECTION

The purpose of the current anthology is to bring to the attention of a wider audience some of the key works on gender and women throughout the history of the discipline by both recognized male scholars and their (often unrecognized) female counterparts. Many of the selections in this volume are written by scholars who are well known for their contributions in other areas, especially in sociological theory, but whose work on women has been virtually invisible to later generations. Other selections are written by sociologists who focus on women or gender but who are not as well recognized because their topics were viewed as secondary to the mainstream of theory or because of their own marginal status in the field (women, men of color, more critical thinkers). Some are feminist, some are not, but all demonstrate that the question of the status of women and related questions of gender have been with us since the beginning of the field. They show us that the sociology of gender has a history, that many classical and contemporary thinkers have paid attention to the impacts of sex differences and gendered structures on social relations.

Some of these thinkers were written out of the discipline because their work was not considered objective enough by the sociologists who dominated the discipline from the 1920s to the 1960s. In addition, we cannot rule out the role of simple sexist prejudice and discrimination among many of the early academic sociologists in discounting much of this work. Deegan's description of the manner in which women were eliminated by Robert Park and others from the preeminent Department of Sociology at the University of Chicago is a case in point (Deegan, 1987; also see Bernard, 1973; Feagin and Vera, 2001). Nevertheless, at all times during the history of American sociology there were some scholars who were thinking about, researching, and writing about women and gender.

One might wonder why it is important to recover these writings now. There are many reasons, but I will mention only three in this context. First, we need to correct the record—these writings constitute an important part of our history that has been suppressed, and we need to know the full story of our past. Second, we can still learn something from reading their arguments and insights into the questions they address, even if we disagree with the author, or if their language is archaic. One finds that in many cases the arguments are all too relevant to our contemporary situation. Third, the study of these writers allows us to better understand how history and the social sciences are influenced by social, cultural, and historical contexts, allowing certain questions to take priority over others. Through this insight, we learn the importance of diversity and of listening to various readings of history. We see that those who set the agenda for sociology represented specific social locations and standpoints, while ignoring or even suppressing others. From a review of these documents, what we see in the past depends in large part on who and where we are in the present. By recovering their work, and by appreciating the long history of the sociological debate about women and their place in society, we can gain a better appreciation for our forebears and reflect on their lessons for the present.

ORGANIZATION OF THE BOOK

I have organized the readings more or less chronologically, beginning with the nineteenth century and moving through the twentieth century up to the end of the 1950s. I chose a chronological perspective mainly because I am interested in the historical development (or in some ways the lack of continuity) of the ideas about women and gender in our discipline. I also believe that this allows us to analyze the impact of broader changes in the discipline on the general attitude toward feminism and gender issues. For each selection, I have given a brief biographical sketch of the author and his or her place in the history of sociology, followed by a brief introduction to and analysis of the reading itself.

I also emphasize American thinkers, although I include a few Europeans whose work had an influence here. Inevitably, however, an anthology must be selective, so I have focused primarily on the United States and on pieces that represent the period they come from or that stand out as especially insightful or illustrative. Some of the authors will be very familiar to sociology students, such as Auguste Comte, Talcott Parsons, and

Herbert Spencer. Others will be less so, but I include them because I believe their work should be recognized for their contributions to later thought, to show why it should have been given attention by later scholars, or to illustrate the perspectives of the time.

I begin with excerpts from some of the giants of the field of nineteenth-century sociology—Comte, Spencer, Durkheim, and Veblen, with other selections from the lesser-known Harriet Martineau, August Bebel, and Lester Frank Ward. I then look at the sociological writing around the turn of the century up to 1920 in the United States: work energized and inspired by the Progressive movement. In that era—the beginnings of American sociology—there were a number of active women sociologists who published in the major journals of the field, women such as Mary Roberts Coolidge, Edith Abbott, Charlotte Perkins Gilman, Leta Hollingsworth, and Anna Garlin Spencer, whose work I include here. I also include a brief excerpt from Alexandra Kollontai, the Russian social theorist of Marxism.

It was with the rise of the Chicago School—especially the accession of Robert E. Park to its leadership—that attention to women and gender declined. The dominant message in the 1920s seemed to be that sex differences were inevitable, biologically given categories, and that feminist attempts to change these "natural" social categories were dangerous to the welfare of society. Of course, this was also the period following the ratification of the Nineteenth Amendment when feminist activism was diminished; the time of the Red Scare and rampant nativism; and the era of presidents Coolidge and Hoover. Sociologists were not immune to the conservatism of the general culture. In this book, I present an excerpt from Park and Burgess's famous *Introduction to the Science of Society* (a short essay by the German author Albert Moll) and part of a chapter from Sumner and Keller's three-volume *Introduction*

to the Science of Society to illustrate the conservative side. To show that not all male sociologists of the time supported this tendency, I also include excerpts from W. E. B. Du Bois's 1920 book *Darkwater* and E. A. Ross's *Principles of Sociology,* published in the same year. By this time Du Bois had left academic sociology, but his outsider status (as an African American and as a nonacademic) gave him a unique perspective. Ross was at the University of Wisconsin, perhaps far enough away from Chicago to escape its dominance.

The 1930s gave us a number of truly groundbreaking works, some of which are excerpted here. These include Margaret Mead's 1935 book *Sex and Temperament in Three Primitive Societies,* demonstrating the culturally diverse nature of gender and countering biologistic theories. Sophonisba Breckenridge, founder of Social Work at Chicago, published a major study on *Women in the Twentieth Century,* whose conclusion I reprint. I also include Willard W. Waller's famous "rating and dating" description of campus dating patterns in the 1930s a study that still resonates among undergraduates.

The 1940s and the war sent women into the labor market at higher rates than previously, and this brought renewed questions about women's proper roles. I have included Alva Myrdal's "One Sex a Social Problem" from her *Nation and Family;* and her husband Gunnar Myrdal's appendix to his major study of race in the United States, which analyzes women's status as a "parallel to the Negro problem." I also include a selection from a 1940 book by E. A. Ross, whose mild feminism and conflict approach are still apparent. Joseph Folsom, an important family sociologist of the time, discusses changes in marital roles as a result of economic changes and argues strongly for equality for women as a prerequisite for true democracy in the excerpt reprinted here. I also include portions of Talcott Parsons's essay on age and sex in the U.S. social structure (one of his more accessible analyses) and a small section of Robert Lynd's *Knowledge for What?* Mirra Komarovsky's influential article on the cultural contradictions of sex roles for women was also published in the 1940s. Overall, there seems to have been more attention by sociologists to women in this decade (though still very little), perhaps because of their increased participation in the national economy.

The 1950s are recognized as a conservative period in American history, especially in terms of family roles. Most family sociology books in this era were uncritical of middle-class gender role prescriptions and sought ways to help women (and men) adjust to their roles as defined by society. Parsons and Bales's work in this decade exemplifies this attitude as well as the shortcomings of a functionalist approach. Still, there were new voices of protest and criticism. One significant publication early in the decade was Helen Mayer Hacker's article comparing women's status to that of a minority group. About the same time, Mirra Komarovsky updated her earlier study to show that contradictions in sex roles for women still existed. Viola Klein, a student of Karl Mannheim, published a critique of feminine stereotypes. All three of these articles are included in this collection. A second selection by Margaret Mead shows the influence of the times, this one being more cautious about women's role changes than her 1935 book. I have also included a piece by William H. Whyte, author of *The Organization Man,* on the problematic status of corporate wives, from an article that appeared in *Fortune* magazine. His was also a voice of dissent raised to protest the conformity of middle-class life and the trivialization of women by corporate leaders. The final entry for the decade is a second piece by Helen Mayer Hacker, on the new "burdens of masculinity." Although this article contains assumptions that would not be accepted today, it is perhaps the first in the sociological literature to address the problems of masculinity.

With the Hacker article, I close the volume. The 1960s and 1970s were a time of immense change, both in the society and in sociology as a field. The story of the rise of the sociology of gender has been amply documented and told elsewhere, notably in the collection sponsored by Sociologists for Women in Society, *Feminist Foundations: Toward Transforming Sociology* (Myers, Anderson, and Risman, 1998), and in numerous articles and anthologies. My purpose has been to focus on the earlier decades.

REFERENCES

Adams, Bert N., and R. A. Sydie. 2001, *Sociological theory.* Sage.

Bernard, Jessie. 1973. My four revolutions: An autobiographical history of the ASA. *American Sociological Review* 78 (4): 773–91.

Camic, Charles. 1997. *Reclaiming the sociological classics.* Malden, MA: Blackwell.

Connell, R. W. 1990. The wrong stuff: Reflections on the place of gender in American sociology. In *Sociology in America,* ed., H. J. Gans. Newbury Park, CA: Sage. pp 156–166.

Coser, Lewis. 1977. George Simmel's neglected contributions to the sociology of women. *Signs: Journal of Women in Culture and Society* 2 (4): 869–76.

Deegan, Mary Jo. 1987. *Jane Addams and the men of the Chicago School, 1892–1918.* New Brunswick, NJ: Transaction.

———. 1991. *Women in sociology: A bio-bibliographical introduction.* Westport, CT: Greenwood.

———. 2002. *Race, Hull-House, and the University of Chicago: A new conscience against ancient evils.* Westport, CT: Greenwood.

Feagin, Joe R., and Hernan Vera. 2001. *Liberation sociology.* Boulder, CO: Westview.

Finlay, Barbara. 1998. "Lester Frank Ward as a Sociologist of Gender: A new look at his sociological work." *Gender & Society* 13 (2): 251–265.

Kandal, Terry R. 1988. *The woman question in classical sociological theory.* Gainesville, FL: University Presses of Florida.

Karides, Marina, Joya Misra, Ivy Kennelly, and Stephanie Moller. 2001. Representing the discipline: *Social Problems* compared to *ASR* and *AJS.* *Social Problems* 48 (1, February): 111–28.

Lehmann, Jennifer M. 1994. *Durkheim and Women.* Lincoln: University of Nebraska Press.

Lengermann, Patricia Madoo, and Jill Niebrugge-Brantley. 1997. *The women founders: Sociology and social theory, 1830–1930, a text with readings.* Columbus, OH: McGraw-Hill.

Lundberg, George A. 1947. *Can science save us?* New York: Longmans, Green.

Lynd, Robert S. 1948. *Knowledge for What? The Place of Social Science in American Culture.* Princeton, NJ: Princeton University Press.

McDonald, Lynn. 1996. *Women founders of the social sciences.* Ottawa, Canada: Carleton University Press.

Mills, C. Wright. 1959. *The sociological imagination.* New York: Oxford University Press.

Myers, Kristen A., Cynthia D. Anderson, and Barbara J. Risman, eds. 1998. *Feminist foundations: Toward transforming sociology.* Thousand Oaks, CA: Sage.

Pedersen, Jean Elisabeth. 2001. Sexual politics in Comte and Durkheim: Feminism, history, and the French sociological tradition. *Signs: Journal of Women in Culture and Society* 27 (1): 229–63.

Pickering, Mary, 1994. Angels and demons in the moral vision of August Comte. *Journal of Women's History* 6 (2): 10–40.

Siegfried, Charlene H. 1996. *Pragmatism and feminism: Reweaving the social fabric.* Chicago: University of Chicago Press.

Sorokin, Pitirim. 1956. *Fads and foibles in modern sociology and related sciences.* Chicago, IL: Henry Regnery.

Sydie, R. A. 1994. *Natural women, cultured men.* Vancouver, BC: University of British Columbia Press.

The Classical Period
Nineteenth-Century Sociology

Auguste Comte (1798–1857) on Women in Positivist Society

Auguste Comte, often called the father of sociology, was an influential social thinker of early nineteenth-century France. Raised as a devout Catholic, Comte came to reject his original faith in favor of a more secular, but still strongly moralistic, set of beliefs. As a young man, he was a supporter of the goals of the French Revolution, but as he aged he became more conservative and concerned with social order. Educated at the École Polytechnique in Paris, Comte was dismissed for unruly (political) behavior. As a young man he served as secretary to Henri Saint-Simon, an early utopian liberal thinker. The relationship broke apart in a dispute over intellectual ownership of ideas. According to Coser (1977:18), Comte's adult life was always characterized by neglect and isolation, but he further isolated himself by his practice of "cerebral hygiene," in which he refused to read the work of other writers for fear of being wrongly influenced by their ideas.

Mary Pickering's essay on Comte includes a section on "the problem of Comte's attitude toward women." She notes that his views changed over his lifetime. His early work tended toward feminism, following Condorcet and Mary Wollstonecraft. After his marriage to Caroline Massin in 1825, his attitude changed as he came to oppose the egalitarianism of John Stuart Mill, Saint-Simon, and others. Comte developed his "positive philosophy," which he began to promote through lectures in 1826. His ideas attracted a fairly large following in France and later in England and beyond. After 17 years of unhappy marriage, he separated permanently from his wife. Two years later, in 1844, he met and fell in love with a young woman, Clothilde de Vaux, whom he idealized in spite of her apparent indifference. Comte's devotion became even more obsessive after her death a few months later (in 1846). After this tragic event in his life, he devoted much of the remainder of his days to the memory of "his angel," at the same time coming to praise the feminine virtues of morality and compassion. His dedication of the *System of Positive Polity* is an amazingly romantic paean to his lost love.

Comte's late thinking about women was, in contemporary terms, *essentialist* when it came to sex differences. He believed that men and women were by nature different and that society must be organized in such a way as to be consistent with (and take advantage of) those differences. Otherwise, certain chaos would develop. The social mission of woman, for Comte, is rooted in her nature, especially her moral superiority over man. More than man, he believed, woman has the capacity to put social interests above personal ones, thus playing a critical role in the future positive society.

Comte's early work, *Course in Positive Philosophy,* was very influential in the origin and development of nineteenth-century sociology, introducing his "law of the three stages" of societal development and his "hierarchy of the sciences." His later work, *System of Positive Polity,* was less well received, with its tendency toward the development of an essentially secular religion. In that book, he envisions a society organized and led by social scientists according to scientific principles, and he develops his "religion of humanity." His thoughts about women, their unique character, and their proper role in society are to be found in this work.

MAJOR WORKS

Comte, Auguste. *Cours de philosophie positive* (Course in positive philosophy): 6 vols. Paris: J. B. Bailliére et Fils, 1864.

Système de politique positive (System of positive polity): 4 vols. Paris: Carilion-Goeury et Vor Dalmont, 1851.

SOURCES

Coser, Lewis A. 1977. *Masters of sociological thought.* New York: Harcourt, Brace, Jovanovich.

Pickering, Mary. 1997. A new look at Auguste Comte. In *Reclaiming the sociological classics: The state of the scholarship,* ed. Charles Camic, 11–44. Malden, MA: Blackwell.

THE SELECTION

Auguste Comte placed the family and domesticity for women at the center of a well-ordered society, referring to scientific arguments of the day that "proved" women's intellectual inferiority to men. He balanced this stance by holding up woman as a key to the success of positive society. In the following excerpt, Comte presents his essentialist argument, which defined the sexes as having very different characters: women being more moral, nurturant, and emotional than men. For Comte, the influence of women was indispensable to the well-being of society, providing a necessary balance to the overly rational and aggressive character of male leadership. Although he believed in the importance of sex difference, he nevertheless believed in equal education of women and men, except for professional education, and recommended the provision of public spaces for discourse between the sexes to enhance the influence women have on men. Conservative that he was, Comte did not favor individual rights for either sex, preferring instead an orderly society in which each person knew and played his or her role for the good of the whole.

From Auguste Comte, "The Influence of Positivism on Women," in *System of Positive Polity, Vol. 1* (1875, orig. pub. 1851), trans. John Henry Bridges (London: Longmans, Green), 164–202.

THE INFLUENCE OF POSITIVISM UPON WOMEN

In the alliance which has been here proposed as necessary for social reorganisation, Feeling, the most influential part of human nature, has not been adequately represented. . . . On this, as well as on other grounds, it is indispensable that Women be associated in the work of regeneration as soon as its tendencies and conditions can be explained to them. With the addition of this third element, the constructive movement at last assumes its true character. We may then feel confident that our intellectual and practical faculties will be kept in due subordination to universal Love. The digressions of intellect, and the subversive tendencies of our active powers will be as far as possible prevented.

Indispensable to Positivism as the co-operation of women is, it involves one essential condition. Modern progress must rise above its present imperfect character, before women can thoroughly sympathise with it.

At present the general feeling amongst them is antipathy to the Revolution. They dislike the destructive character which the Revolution necessarily exhibited in its first phase. . . . Nor is this merely due, as is supposed, to a natural regret for the decline of chivalry, although they cannot but feel that the Middle Ages are the only period in which the feeling of reverence for women has been properly cultivated. . . .

However this may be, the feelings of women upon these subjects are a very plain and simple demonstration of the first condition of social regeneration, which is, that Politics must again be subordinated to Morality; and this upon a more intelligible, more comprehensive, and more permanent basis than Catholicism could supply. A system

which supplied such a basis would naturally involve reverence for women as one of its characteristic results. Such, then, are the terms on which women will cordially co-operate in the progressive movement.

Women will gladly associate themselves with the Revolution as soon as its work of reconstruction is fairly begun. Its negative phase must not be prolonged too far. . . . Women will feel enthusiasm for the second phase of the Revolution, when they see republicanism in the light in which Positivism presents it, modified by the spirit of ancient chivalry.

Then, and not till then, will the movement of social regeneration be fairly begun. The movement can have no great force until women give cordial support to it; for it is they who are the best representatives of the fundamental principle on which Positivism rests, the victory of social over selfish affections. . . .

The social mission of Woman in the Positive system follows as a natural consequence from the qualities peculiar to her nature.

In the most essential attribute of the human race, the tendency to place social above personal feeling, she is undoubtedly superior to man. Morally, therefore, and apart from all material considerations, she merits always our loving veneration, as the purest and simplest impersonation of Humanity, who can never be adequately represented in any masculine form. But these qualities do not involve the possession of political power, which some visionaries have claimed for women, though without their own consent. In that which is the great object of human life, they are superior to men; but in the various means of attaining that object they are undoubtedly inferior. In all kinds of *force,* whether physical, intellectual, or practical, it is certain that Man surpasses Woman, in accordance with the general law prevailing throughout the animal kingdom. Now practical life is necessarily governed by force rather than by affection, because it requires unremitting and laborious activity. If there were nothing else to do but to love, as in the Christian utopia of a future life in which there are no material wants, Woman would be supreme. But we have above everything else to think and to act, in order to carry on the struggle against a rigorous destiny; therefore Man takes the command, notwithstanding his inferiority in goodness. Success in all great undertakings depends more upon energy and talent than upon goodwill, although this last condition reacts strongly upon the others.

Thus the three elements of our moral constitution do not act in perfect harmony. Force is naturally supreme, and all that women can do is to modify it by affection. Justly conscious of their superiority in strength of feeling, they endeavour to assert their influence in a way which is too often attributed by superficial observers to the mere love of power. But experience always teaches them that in a world where the simplest necessaries of life are scarce and difficult to procure, power must belong to the strongest, not to the most affectionate, even though the latter may deserve it best. With all their efforts they can never do more than modify the harshness with which men exercise their authority. And men submit more readily to this modifying influence, from feeling that in the highest attributes of Humanity women are their superiors. They see that their own supremacy is due principally to the material necessities of life, provision for which calls into play the self-regarding rather than the social instincts. Hence we find it the case in every phase of human society that women's life is essentially domestic, public life being confined to men. Civilisation, so far from effacing this natural distinction, tends, as I shall afterwards show, to develop it, while remedying its abuses.

Thus the social position of women is in this respect very similar to that of philosophers and of the working classes. And we now see why these three elements should be united. It is their combined action which constitutes the modifying force of society. . . .

Spiritual power, as interpreted by Positivism, begins with the influence of women in the family; it is afterwards moulded into a system by thinkers, while the people are the guarantee for its political efficiency. Although it is the intellectual class that institutes the union, yet its own part in it, as it should never forget, is less direct than that of women, less practical than that of the people. The thinker is socially powerless except so far as he is supported by feminine sympathy and popular energy.

Thus the necessity of associating women in the movement of social regeneration creates no obstacle whatever to the philosophy by which that movement is to be directed. On the contrary, it aids its progress by showing the true character of the moral force which is destined to control all the other forces of man. It involves as perfect an inauguration of the normal state as our times of transition admit. For the chief characteristic of that state will be a more complete and more harmonious union of the same three classes to whom we are now looking for the first impulse of reform. Already we can see how perfectly adapted to the constitution of man this final condition of Humanity will be. Feeling, Reason, Activity, whether viewed separately or in combination, correspond exactly to the three elements of the regenerative movement, Women, Philosophers, and People.

Women's minds no doubt are less capable than ours of *generalising* very widely, or of carrying on long processes of deduction.

They are, that is, less capable than men of abstract intellectual exertion. On the other hand, they are generally more alive to that combination of reality with utility which is one of the characteristics of Positive speculation. In this respect they have much in common intellectually with the working classes; and fortunately they have also the same advantage of being untrammelled by the present absurd system of education. . . .

Women therefore may, like the people, be counted among the future supporters of the new philosophy. Without their combined aid it could never hope to surmount the strong repugnance to it which is felt by our cultivated classes, especially in France, where the question of its success has first to be decided. . . .

Thus the part to be played by woman in public life is not merely passive. Not only will they give their sanction individually and collectively to the verdicts of public opinion as formed by philosophers and by the people; but they will themselves interfere actively in moral questions. It will be their part to maintain the primary principle of Positivism, which originated with themselves, and of which they will always be the most natural representatives.

But how, it may be asked, can this be reconciled with my previous remark that women's life should still be essentially domestic?

For the ancients, and for the greater part of the human race at the present time, it would be irreconcileable. But in Western Europe the solution has long ago been found. From the time when Women acquired in the Middle Ages their proper freedom in the household, opportunities for social intercourse arose which combined most happily the advantages of private and of public life; and in these women presided. The practice afterwards extended, especially in France, and these meetings became the laboratories of public opinion. It seems now as if they

had died out, or had lost their character in the intellectual and moral anarchy of our times which is so unfavourable to free interchange of thoughts and feelings. But a custom so social, and which did such good service in the philosophical movement preceding the Revolution, is assuredly not destined to perish. In the more perfect social state to which we are tending, it will be developed more fully than ever, when men's minds and hearts have accepted the rallying-point offered by the new philosophy.

This is, then, the mode in which women can with propriety participate in public life. Here all classes will recognise their authority as paramount. Under the new system these meetings will entirely lose their old aristocratic character, which is now simply obstructive. The Positivist *salon* placed under feminine influence completes the series of social meetings, in which the three elements of the spiritual power will be able to act in concert. First, there is the religious assemblage in the Temple of Humanity. Here the philosopher will naturally preside, the other two classes taking only a secondary part. In the Club again it is the people who will take the active part; women and philosophers supporting them by their presence, but not joining in the debate. Lastly, women in their *salons* will promote active and friendly intercourse between all three classes; and here all who may be qualified to take a leading part will find their influence cordially accepted. Gently and without effort a moral control will thus be established, by which misguided or violent movements will be checked in their source. Kind advice, given indirectly but seasonably, will often save the philosopher from being blinded by ambition, or from deviating, through intellectual conceit, into useless digressions. Working men at these meetings will learn to repress the spirit of violence or envy that frequently arises in them, recognising the sacredness of the care thus manifested for their interests.

And the great and the wealthy will be taught from the manner in which praise and blame is given by those whose opinion is most valued, that the only justifiable use of power or talent is to devote it to the service of the weak. . . .

[I]n the Positivist theory of marriage and of the family the principal service to be rendered by Woman is one quite unconnected with the function of procreation. It is directly based upon the highest attributes of our nature.

Vast as is the moral importance of maternity, yet the position of wife has always been considered even *more* characteristic of woman's nature; as shown by the fact that the words woman and wife are in many languages synonymous. Marriage is not always followed by children; and besides this, a bad wife is very seldom indeed a good mother. The first aspect then under which Positivism considers Woman, is simply as the companion of Man, irrespective of her maternal duties.

Viewed thus, Marriage is the most elementary and yet the most perfect mode of social life. It is the only association in which entire identity of interests is possible. In this union, to the moral completeness of which the language of all civilised nations bears testimony, the noblest aim of human life is realised, as far as it ever can be. For the object of human existence, as shown in the second chapter, is progress of every kind; progress in morality, that is to say, in the subjection of Self-interest to Social Feeling, holding the first rank. Now this unquestionable principle, which has been already indicated in the second chapter, leads us by a very sure and direct path to the true theory of marriage.

Different as the two sexes are by nature, and increased as that difference is by the diversity which happily exists in their social position, each is consequently necessary to the moral development of the other. In practical energy and in the mental capacity connected with it, Man is evidently superior to Woman. Woman's strength, on the other hand, lies in Feeling. She excels Man in love, as Man excels her in all kinds of force. It is impossible to conceive of a closer union than that which binds these two beings to the mutual service and perfection of each other, saving them from all danger of rivalry. The voluntary character too of this union gives it a still further charm, when the choice has been on both sides a happy one. In the Positive theory, then, of marriage, its principal object is considered to be that of completing and confirming the education of the heart by calling out the purest and strongest of human sympathies.

It is true that sexual instinct, which, in man's case at all events, was the origin of conjugal attachment, is a feeling purely selfish. It is also true that its absence would, in the majority of cases, diminish the energy of affection. But woman, with her more loving heart, has usually far less need of this coarse stimulus than man. The influence of her purity reacts on man, and ennobles his affection. And affection is in itself so sweet, that when once it has been aroused by whatever agency, its own charm is sufficient to maintain it in activity. When this is the case, conjugal union becomes a perfect ideal of friendship; yet still more beautiful than friendship, because each possesses and is possessed by the other. For perfect friendship, difference of sex is essential, as excluding the possibility of rivalry. No other voluntary tie can admit of such full and unrestrained confidence. It is the source of the most unalloyed happiness that man can enjoy; for there can be no greater happiness than to live for another.

But independently of the intrinsic value of this sacred union, we have to consider its importance from the social point of view. It is the first stage in our progress towards that which is the final object of moral education, namely, universal Love. Many writers of the so-called socialist school, look upon conjugal love and universal benevolence, the two extreme terms in the scale of affections, as opposed to each other. In the second chapter, I pointed out the falseness and danger of this view. The man who is incapable of deep affection for one whom he has chosen as his partner in the most intimate relations of life, can hardly expect to be believed when he professes devotion to a mass of human beings of whom he knows nothing. The heart cannot throw off its original selfishness without the aid of that affection which, by virtue of its concentration on one object, is the most complete and enduring. From personal experience of strong love we rise by degrees to sincere affection to all mankind, strong enough to modify conduct: although, as the scope of feeling widens, its energy must decrease.

The purpose of marriage once clearly understood, it becomes easy to define its conditions. The intervention of society is necessary; but its only object is to confirm and to develop the order of things which exists naturally.

It is essential in the first place to the high purposes for which marriage has been instituted, that the union shall be both exclusive and indissoluble. So essential indeed are both conditions, that we frequently find them even when the connection is illegal. That any one should have ventured to propound the doctrine that human happiness is to be secured by levity and inconstancy in love, is a fact which nothing but the utter deficiency of social and moral principles can explain. Love cannot be deep unless it remains constant to a fixed object; for the very possibility of change is a temptation to it. So differently constituted as man and woman are, is our short life too much for perfect knowledge and love of one another? Yet the versatility to which most human affection is liable makes the intervention of society

necessary. Without some check upon indecision and caprice, life might degenerate into a miserable series of experiments, ending in failure and degradation. Sexual love may become a powerful engine for good: but only on the condition of placing it under rigorous and permanent discipline. . . .

Thus the theory of marriage, as set forward by the Positivist, becomes totally independent of any physical motive. It is regarded by him as the most powerful instrument of moral education; and therefore as the basis of public or individual welfare. It is no overstrained enthusiasm which leads us to elevate the moral purity of marriage. We do so from rigorous examination of the facts of human nature. All the best results, whether personal or social, of marriage may follow when the union, though more impassioned, is as chaste as that of brother and sister. The sexual instinct has no doubt something to do in most cases with the first formation of the passion; but it is not necessary in all cases to gratify the instinct. Abstinence, in cases where there is real ground for it on both sides, will but serve to strengthen mutual affection. . . .

The continuous progress of Humanity in this respect, as in every other, is but a more complete development of the preexisting order. Equality in the position of the two sexes is contrary to their nature, and no tendency to it has at any time been exhibited. All history assures us that with the growth of society the peculiar features of each sex have become not less but more distinct. Catholic Feudalism, while raising the social condition of women in Western Europe to a far higher level, took away from them the priestly functions which they had held under Polytheism; a religion in which the priesthood was more occupied with art than with science. So too, with the gradual decline of the principle of caste, women have been excluded more and more rigidly from royalty and from every other kind of political authority. Again, there is a visible tendency towards the removal of women from all industrial occupations, even from those which might seem best suited to them. And thus female life, instead of becoming independent of the Family, is being more and more concentrated in it; while at the same time their proper sphere of moral influence is constantly extending. The two tendencies, so far from being opposed, are on the contrary inseparably connected.

Without discussing the absurd and retrograde schemes which have been recently put forward on the subject, there is one remark which may serve to illustrate the value of the order which now exists. If women were to obtain that equality in the affairs of life which their so-called champions are claiming for them without their wish, not only would they suffer morally, but their social position would be endangered. They would be subject in almost every occupation to a degree of competition which they would not be able to sustain; while in the meantime by rivalry in the pursuits of life mutual affection between the sexes would be corrupted at its source.

Leaving these subversive dreams, we find a natural principle which, by determining the practical obligations of the active to the sympathetic sex, averts this danger. It is one which no philosophy but Positivism has been sufficiently real and practical to bring forward systematically for general acceptance. It is no new invention, however, but a universal tendency, confirmed by careful study of the whole past history of Man. The principle is, that Man should provide for Woman. It is a natural law of the human race; a law connected with the essentially domestic character of female life. We find it in the rudest forms of social life; and with every step in the progress of society its adoption becomes more extensive and complete. A still larger application of this fundamental principle will meet all the material difficulties under which women are now labouring. All social relations, and especially the question of wages, will be affected by it. The tendency to it is spontaneous; but it also follows from the high position which Positivism has assigned to Woman as the sympathetic element in the spiritual power. The intellectual class, in the same way, has to be supported by the practical class, in order to have its whole time available for the special duties imposed upon it. But in the case of women, the obligation of the other sex is still more sacred, because the sphere of duty in which protection for them is required is the home. The obligation to provide for the intellectual class affects society as a whole; but the maintenance of women is, with few exceptions, a personal obligation. Each individual should consider himself bound to maintain the woman he has chosen to be his partner in life. Apart from this, however, men must consider themselves as collectively responsible in an indirect way for the support of the other sex. Women who are without husbands or parents should have their maintenance guaranteed by society; and this not merely as a compensation for their dependent position, but with the view of enabling them to render public service of the greatest moral value.

The direction, then, of progress in the social condition of woman is this: to render her life more and more domestic; to diminish as far as possible the burden of out-door labour; and so to fit her more completely for her special office of educating our moral nature. . . .

Coming now to the subject of female education, we have only to make a further application of the theory which has guided us hitherto.

Since the vocation assigned by our theory to women is that of educating others, it is clear that the educational system which we have proposed in the last chapter for the working classes, applies to them as well as to the other sex with very slight alterations. Unencumbered as it is with specialities, it will be found, even in its more scientific parts, as suitable for the sympathetic element of the moderating power, as to the synergic element. We have spoken of the necessity of diffusing sound historical views among the working classes; and the same necessity applies to women; for social sympathy can never be perfectly developed, without a sense of the continuity of the Past, as well as the solidarity of the Present. Since then both sexes alike need historical instruction as a basis for the systematisation of moral truth, both should alike pass through the scientific training which prepares the way for social studies, and which moreover has as intrinsic value for women as for men. Again, since the period of spontaneous education is entirely to be left to women, it is most desirable that they should themselves have passed through the systematic education which is its necessary complement. The only department with which they need not concern themselves, is what is called professional education. This, as I have before observed, is not susceptible of regular organisation, and can only be acquired by careful practice and experience, resting upon a sound basis of theory. In all other respects women, philosophers, and working men will receive the same education.

But while I would place the sexes on a level in this respect, I do not take the view of my eminent predecessor Condorcet, that they should be taught together. On moral grounds, which of course are the most important consideration, it is obvious that such a plan would be equally prejudicial to both. In the church, in the club, in the *salon,* they may associate freely at every period of life. But at school such intercourse would be premature; it would check the natural development of character, not to say that it

would obviously have an unsettling influence upon study. Until the feelings on both sides are sufficiently matured, it is of the greatest importance that the relations of the two sexes should not be too intimate, and that they should be superintended by the watchful eye of their mothers. . . .

It appears, then, that the primary principle laid down at the beginning of this chapter enables us to solve all the problems that offer themselves on the subject of Woman. Her function in society is determined by the constitution of her nature. As the spontaneous organ of Feeling, on which the unity of human nature entirely depends, she constitutes the purest and most natural element of the moderating power; which, while avowing its own subordination to the material forces of society, purposes to direct them to higher uses. First as mother, afterwards as wife, it is her office to conduct the moral education of Humanity. In order the more perfectly to fulfil this mission, her life must be connected even more closely than it has been with the Family. At the same time she must participate to a more and more complete extent in the general system of instruction. . . .

Women's mission is a striking illustration of the truth that happiness consists in doing the work for which we are naturally fitted. Their mission is in reality always the same; it is summed up in one word, Love. It is the only work in which there can never be too many workers; it grows by co-operation; it has nothing to fear from competition. Women are charged with the education of Sympathy, the source of human unity; and their highest happiness is reached when they have the full consciousness of their vocation, and are free to follow it. It is the admirable feature of their social mission, that it invites them to cultivate qualities which are natural to them; to call into exercise emotions which all allow to be the most pleasurable. All that is required for them in a better organisation of society is a better adaptation of their circumstances to their vocation, and improvements in their internal condition. They must be relieved from outdoor labour; and other means must be taken to secure due weight to their moral influence. Both objects are contemplated in the material, intellectual, and moral ameliorations which Positivism is destined to effect in the life of women.

Harriett Martineau (1802–1876) on American Women

Harriett Martineau was born in Norwich, England, to middle-class parents, the sixth of eight children. Martineau's formal education was limited, but she studied independently at home in a wide variety of topics. After the death of her father in the 1820s, the resulting economic hardship forced Martineau to make her way on her own: a situation that she described as liberating. Although engaged to be married at one time, her fiancé died and she never again came close to marrying, preferring the relative freedom of single life, which allowed her to study, travel, and write. She supported herself through writing, publishing in a wide range of genres, both fiction and nonfiction, for a variety of audiences. While living in London in the 1830s, Martineau had friends such as intellectual giants Charles Babbage, Thomas Malthus, Charles Darwin, Charles Dickens, George Eliot, Florence Nightingale, Charlotte Brontë, and William Wordsworth. In the mid-1830s she traveled to the United States, publishing her observations in *Society in America*. During this time, Martineau also wrote *How to Observe Manners and Morals,* which is considered the first systematic methods book in sociology. Martineau was also important in bringing the work of Auguste Comte to the attention of the English-speaking world, with her translation and condensation of his *Course in Positive Philosophy.* Rossi (1973) calls Martineau the first woman sociologist, not without reason. Martineau retired to the Lake District in northern England in her later years and died in 1876 after a long illness.

Harriett Martineau was a prolific author, with several books and many essays, tracts, newspaper columns, journal articles, and other publications to her credit. Her *Illustrations of Political Economy* was an attempt to explain to a popular audience the complexities of sociopolitical realities. Her *Society in America* was a serious study of American culture and society, comparable in some ways to the earlier work of de Tocqueville. Her translation of Comte was a key moment in his influence in the Western world. In recent years, Martineau's contributions to classical sociology have been recognized by her inclusion in a number of textbooks, including those of Adams and Sydie (2001) and Zeitlin (2001). Martineau's discussions of women are found in a number of essays and books.

MAJOR WORKS

Martineau Harriet *Illustrations of Political Economy.* 6 vols. London: Charles Fox, 1832/1834.
———. *Society in America.* 3 vols. London: Saunders & Otley, 1837. Abridged edition by Seymour M. Lipset, Anchor Books, 1962.
———. *Retrospect of Western Travel.* 2 vols. London: Lea & Blanchard, 1838.
———. *How to Observe Morals and Manners.* Philadelphia: Lea & Blanchard, 1838.
———. *The Positive Philosophy of Auguste Comte.* Translated and edited by Harriett Martineau. New York: Blanchard, 1853.
———. *Harriet Martineau's Autobiography.* Edited by Maria Weston Chapman. 2 vols. Boston: James Osgood, 1877.

SOURCES

Hill, Michael R. 1991. Harriet Martineau. In *Women in sociology: A bio-bibliographical sourcebook,* ed. Mary Jo Deegan, 290–97. Westport, CT: Greenwood.
Rossi, Alice. 1973. The first woman sociologist: Harriet Martineau (1802–1876). In *The feminist papers,* 119–24. New York: Columbia University Press.
Yates, Gayle G., ed. 1985. *Harriet Martineau: On women.* New Brunswick, NJ: Rutgers University Press.
Zeitlin, Irving M. Harriet Martineau. 2000. 109–124. In *Ideology and the development of sociological theory,* 7th ed. Upper Saddle River, NJ: Prentice Hall.

THE SELECTION

Printed below are excerpts from Harriet Martineau's *Society in America,* "Woman" and "Occupation," in which she records her observations during her travels in the United States. Martineau is disappointed in the conditions of the women she comes across, noting that this implies a failure of Americans to live up to the promise of democracy in this regard. She claims that, notwithstanding their lip service to special treatment via "chivalry," American women are treated unjustly in access to education and serious professions, leaving marriage as the only option. Instead of intellectual development, they are overly involved in religion of a shallow sort. The lack of independence and intellectual development of women stunts their moral sense as well: When women attempt to speak out on issues such as slavery, they are suppressed and accused of immodesty. Martineau expresses disappointment on finding that American men are "ungentle and tyrannical," while women are "weak, ignorant, and subservient."

In the discussion of occupations, Martineau observes that American women are often active in charity work, but they have problems gaining access to employment. Also, she notes that the lot of poor women is sad. Overall, she thought that American women were given too few opportunities to pursue their own interests and develop their own talents by a restrictive system of attitudes about women's proper roles.

From Harriet Martineau, *Society in America,* 2nd ed. (London: Saunders & Otley, 1837), 3:105–12, 115–18, 144–51.

WOMAN

"The vale best discovereth the hill. There is little friendship in the world, and least of all between equals, which was wont to be magnified. That that is, is between superior and inferior, whose fortunes may comprehend this one the other."

BACON

If a test of civilisation be sought, none can be so sure as the condition of that half of society over which the other half has power,—from the exercise of the right of the strongest. Tried by this test, the American civilisation appears to be of a lower order than might have been expected from some other symptoms of its social state. The Americans have, in the treatment of women, fallen below, not only their own democratic principles, but the practice of some parts of the Old World.

The unconsciousness of both parties as to the injuries suffered by women at the hands of those who hold the power is a sufficient proof of the low degree of civilisation in this important particular at which they rest. While woman's intellect is confined, her morals crushed, her health ruined, her weaknesses encouraged, and her strength punished, she is told that her lot is cast in the paradise of women: and there is no country in the world where there is so much boasting of the "chivalrous" treatment she enjoys. That is to say,—she has the best place in stage-coaches: when there are not chairs enough for everybody, the gentlemen stand: she hears oratorical flourishes on public occasions about wives and home, and apostrophes to woman: her husband's hair stands on end at the idea of her working, and he toils to indulge her with money: she has liberty to get her brain turned by religious excitements, that her attention may be diverted from morals, politics, and philosophy; and, especially, her morals are guarded by the strictest observance of propriety in her presence. In short, indulgence is given her as a substitute for justice.

The intellect of woman is confined by an unjustifiable restriction of both methods of education,—by express teaching, and by the discipline of circumstance. The former, though prior in the chronology of each individual, is a direct consequence of the latter, as regards the whole of the sex. As women have none of the objects in life for which an enlarged education is considered requisite, the education is not given. Female education in America is much what it is in England. There is a profession of some things being taught which are supposed necessary because everybody learns them. They serve to fill up time, to occupy attention harmlessly, to improve conversation, and to make women something like companions to their husbands, and able to teach their children somewhat. But what is given is, for the most part, passively received; and what is obtained is, chiefly, by means of the memory. There is rarely or never a careful ordering of influences for the promotion of clear intellectual activity. . . .

Accordingly, marriage is the only object left open to woman. Philosophy she may pursue only fancifully, and under pain of ridicule: science only as a pastime, and under a similar penalty. Art is declared to be left open: but the necessary learning, and, yet more, the indispensable experience of reality, are denied to her. Literature is also said to be permitted: but under what penalties and restrictions? . . .

Nothing is thus left for women but marriage.—Yes; Religion, is the reply.—Religion is a temper, not a pursuit. It is the moral atmosphere in which human beings are to live and move. Men do not live to breathe: they breathe to live. A German lady of extraordinary powers and endowments, remarked to me with amazement on all the knowledge of the American women being based on theology. She observed that in her own country theology had its turn with other sciences, as a pursuit: but nowhere, but with the American women, had she known it make the foundation of all other knowledge. Even while thus complaining, this lady stated the case too favourably. American women have not the requisites for the study of theology. The difference between theology and religion, the science and the temper, is yet scarcely known among them. It is religion which they pursue as an occupation; and hence its small results upon the conduct, as well as upon the intellect. We are driven back upon marriage as the only appointed object in life: and upon the conviction that the sum and substance of female education in America, as in England, is training women to consider marriage as the sole object in life, and to pretend that they do not think so.

The morals of women are crushed. If there be any human power and business and privilege which is absolutely universal, it is the discovery and adoption of the principle and laws of duty. As every individual, whether man or woman, has a reason and a conscience, this is a work which each is thereby authorised to do for him or herself. But it is not only virtually prohibited to beings who, like the American women, have scarcely any objects in life proposed to them; but the whole apparatus of opinion is brought to bear offensively upon individuals among women who exercise freedom of mind in deciding upon what duty is, and the methods by which it is to be pursued. There is nothing extraordinary to the disinterested observer in women being so grieved at the case of slaves,—slave wives and mothers, as well as spirit-broken men,—as to wish to do what they could for their relief: there is nothing but what is natural in their being ashamed of the cowardice of such white slaves of the north as are deterred by intimidation from using their rights of speech and of the press, in behalf of the suffering race, and in their resolving not to do likewise: there is nothing but what is justifiable in their using their moral freedom, each for herself, in neglect of the threats of punishment: yet there were no bounds to the efforts made to crush the actions of women who thus used their human powers in the abolition question, and the convictions of those who looked on, and who might possibly be warmed into free action by the beauty of what they saw. . . .

One lady, of high talents and character, whose books were very popular before she did a deed greater than that of writing any book, in acting upon an unusual conviction of duty, and becoming an abolitionist, has been almost excommunicated since. A family of ladies, whose talents and conscientiousness had placed them high in the estimation of society as teachers, have lost all their pupils since they declared their anti-slavery opinions. The reproach in all the many similar cases that I know is, not that the ladies hold anti-slavery opinions, but that they act upon them. The incessant outcry about the retiring modesty of the sex proves the opinion of the censors to be, that fidelity to conscience is inconsistent with retiring modesty. . . .

How fearfully the morals of woman are crushed, appears from the prevalent persuasion that there are virtues which are peculiarly masculine, and others which are peculiarly feminine. It is amazing that a society which makes a most emphatic profession of its Christianity, should almost universally entertain such a fallacy: and not see that, in the case they suppose, instead of the character of Christ being the meeting point of all virtues, there would have been a separate gospel for women, and a second company of agents for its diffusion. It is not only that masculine and feminine employments are supposed to be properly different. No one in the world, I believe, questions this. But it is actually supposed that what are called the hardy virtues are more appropriate to men, and the gentler to women. As all virtues nourish each other, and can no otherwise be nourished, the consequence of the admitted fallacy is that men are, after all, not nearly so brave as they ought to be; nor women so gentle. But what is the manly character till it be gentle? The very word magnanimity cannot be thought of in relation to it till it becomes mild—Christ-like. Again, what can a woman be, or do, without bravery? Has she not to struggle with the toils and difficulties which follow upon the mere possession of a mind? Must she not face physical and moral pain—physical and moral danger? Is there a day of her life in which there are not conflicts wherein no one can help her—perilous work to be done, in which she can have neither sympathy nor aid? Let her lean upon man as much as he will, how much is it that he can do for her?—from how much can he protect her? From a few physical perils, and from a very few social evils. This is all. Over the moral world he has no control, except on his own account; and it is the moral life of human beings which is all in all. He can neither secure any woman from pain and grief, nor rescue her from the strife of emotions, nor prevent the film of life from cracking under her feet with every step she treads, nor hide from her the abyss which is beneath, nor save her from sinking into it at last alone. While it is so, while woman is human, men should beware how they deprive her of any of the strength which is all needed for the strife and burden of humanity. Let them beware how they put her off her watch and defence, by promises which they cannot fulfil;—promises of a guardianship which

can arise only from within; of support which can be derived only from the freest moral action,—from the self-reliance which can be generated by no other means.

But, it may be asked, how does society get on,—what does it do? for it acts on the supposition of there being masculine and feminine virtues,—upon the fallacy just exposed.

It does so; and the consequences are what might be looked for. Men are ungentle, tyrannical. They abuse the right of the strongest, however they may veil the abuse with indulgence. They want the magnanimity to discern woman's human rights; and they crush her morals rather than allow them. Women are, as might be anticipated, weak, ignorant and subservient, in as far as they exchange self-reliance for reliance on anything out of themselves. Those who will not submit to such a suspension of their moral functions, (for the work of self-perfection remains to be done, sooner or later,) have to suffer for their allegiance to duty. They have all the need of bravery that the few heroic men who assert the highest rights of women have of gentleness, to guard them from the encroachment to which power, custom, and education, incessantly conduce.

Such brave women and such just men there are in the United States, scattered among the multitude, whose false apprehension of rights leads to an enormous failure of duties. There are enough of such to commend the true understanding and practice to the simplest minds and most faithful hearts of the community, under whose testimony the right principle will spread and flourish. If it were not for the external prosperity of the country, the injured half of its society would probably obtain justice sooner than in any country of Europe. But the prosperity of America is a circumstance unfavourable to its women. It will be long before they are put to the proof as to what they are capable of thinking and doing: a proof to which hundreds, perhaps thousands of Englishwomen have been put by adversity, and the result of which is a remarkable improvement in their social condition, even within the space of ten years. Persecution for opinion, punishment for all manifestations of intellectual and moral strength, are still as common as women who have opinions and who manifest strength: but some things are easy, and many are possible of achievement, to women of ordinary powers, which it would have required genius to accomplish but a few years ago.

OCCUPATION

As for the occupations with which American ladies fill up their leisure; what has been already said will show that there is no great weight or diversity of occupation. Many are largely engaged in charities, doing good or harm according to the enlightenment of mind which is carried to the work. In New England, a vast deal of time is spent in attending preachings, and other religious meetings: and in paying visits, for religious purposes, to the poor and sorrowful. The same results follow from this practice that may be witnessed wherever it is much pursued. In as far as sympathy is kept up, and acquaintanceship between different classes in society is occasioned, the practice is good. In as far as it unsettles the minds of the visitors, encourages a false craving for religious excitement, tempts to spiritual interference on the one hand, and cant on the other, and humours or oppresses those who need such offices least, while it alienates those who want them most, the practice is bad. I am disposed to think that much good is done, and much harm: and that, whenever women have a greater charge of indispensable business on their hands, so as to do good and reciprocate religious sympathy by laying hold of opportunities, instead of by making occupation, more than the present good will be done, without any of the harm.

All American ladies are more or less literary: and some are so to excellent purpose: to the saving of their minds from vacuity. Readers are plentiful: thinkers are rare. Minds are of a very passive character: and it follows that languages are much cultivated. If ever a woman was pointed out to me as distinguished for information, I might be sure beforehand that she was a linguist. I met with a great number of ladies who read Latin; some Greek; some Hebrew; some German. With the exception of the last, the learning did not seem to be of much use to them, except as a harmless exercise. I met with more intellectual activity, more general power, among many ladies who gave little time to books, than among those who are distinguished as being literary. I did not meet with a good artist among all the ladies in the States. I never had the pleasure of seeing a good drawing, except in one instance; or, except in two, of hearing good music. The entire failure of all attempts to draw is still a mystery to me. The attempts are incessant; but the results are below criticism. Natural philosophy is not pursued to any extent by women. There is some pretension to mental and moral philosophy; but the less that is said on that head the better.

This is a sad account of things. It may tempt some to ask 'what then are the American women?' They are better educated by Providence than by men. The lot of humanity is theirs: they have labour, probation, joy, and sorrow. They are good wives; and, under the teaching of nature, good mothers. They have, within the range of their activity, good sense, good temper, and good manners. Their beauty is very remarkable; and, I think, their wit no less. Their charity is overflowing, if it were but more enlightened: and it may be supposed that they could not exist without religion. It appears to superabound; but it is not usually of a healthy character. It may seem harsh to say this: but is it not the fact that religion emanates from the nature, from the moral state of the individual? Is it not therefore true that unless the nature be completely exercised, the moral state harmonised, the religion cannot be healthy?

One consequence, mournful and injurious, of the 'chivalrous' taste and temper of a country with regard to its women is that it is difficult, where it is not impossible, for women to earn their bread. Where it is a boast that women do not labour, the encouragement and rewards of labour are not provided. It is so in America. In some parts, there are now so many women dependent on their own exertions for a maintenance, that the evil will give way before the force of circumstances. In the meantime, the lot of poor women is sad. Before the opening of the factories, there were but three resources; teaching, needle-work, and keeping boarding-houses or hotels. Now, there are the mills; and women are employed in printing-offices; as compositors, as well as folders and stitchers.

I dare not trust myself to do more than touch on this topic. There would be little use in dwelling upon it; for the mischief lies in the system by which women are depressed, so as to have the greater number of objects of pursuit placed beyond their reach, more than in any minor arrangements which might be rectified by an exposure of particular evils. I would only ask of philanthropists of all countries to inquire of physicians what is the state of health of sempstresses; and to judge thence whether it is not inconsistent with common humanity that women should depend for bread upon such employment. Let them inquire what is the recompense of this kind of labour, and then wonder if they can that the pleasures of the licentious are chiefly supplied from that class. Let them reverence the strength of such as keep their virtue, when the toil which they know is slowly and surely destroying them will barely afford them bread, while the wages of sin are luxury and idleness. During the present interval between the feudal age and the coming time, when life and its occupations will be freely thrown open to women as to men, the condition of the female working classes is such that if its sufferings were but made known, emotions of horror and shame would tremble through the whole of society.

For women who shrink from the lot of the needle-woman,—almost equally dreadful, from the fashionable milliner down to the humble stocking-darner,—for those who shrink through pride, or fear of sickness, poverty, or temptation, there is little resource but pretension to teach. What office is there which involves more responsibility, which requires more qualifications, and which ought, therefore, to be more honourable, than that of teaching? What work is there for which a decided bent, not to say a genius, is more requisite? Yet are governesses furnished, in America as elsewhere, from among those who teach because they want bread; and who certainly would not teach for any other reason. Teaching and training children is, to a few, a very few, a delightful employment, notwithstanding all its toils and cares. Except to these few it is irksome; and, when accompanied with poverty and mortification, intolerable. Let philanthropists inquire into the proportion of governesses among the inmates of lunatic asylums. The answer to this question will be found to involve a world of rebuke and instruction. What can be the condition of the sex when such an occupation is overcrowded with candidates, qualified and unqualified? What is to be hoped from the generation of children confided to the cares of a class, conscientious perhaps beyond most, but reluctant, harassed, and depressed?

The most accomplished governesses in the United States may obtain 600 dollars a-year in the families of southern planters; provided they will promise to teach everything. In the north they are paid less; and in neither case, is there a possibility of making provision for sickness and old age. Ladies who fully deserve the confidence of society may realise an independence in a few years by school-keeping in the north: but, on the whole, the scanty reward of female labour in America remains the reproach to the country which its philanthropists have for some years proclaimed it to be. I hope they will persevere in their proclamation, though special methods of charity will not avail to cure the evil. It lies deep; it lies in the subordination of the sex: and upon this the exposures and remonstrances of philanthropists may ultimately succeed in fixing the attention of society; particularly of women. The progression or emancipation of any class usually, if not always, takes place through the efforts of individuals of that class: and so it must be here. All women should inform themselves of the condition of their sex, and of their own position. It must necessarily follow that the noblest of them will, sooner or later, put forth a moral power which shall prostrate cant, and burst asunder the bonds, (silken to some, but cold iron to others,) of feudal prejudices and usages. In the meantime, is it to be understood that the principles of the Declaration of Independence bear no relation to half of the human race? If so, what is the ground of the limitation? If not so, how is the restricted and dependent state of women to be reconciled with the proclamation that "all are endowed by their Creator with certain inalienable rights; that among these are life, liberty, and the pursuit of happiness?"

Herbert Spencer (1820–1903) on the Rights and Status of Women

Herbert Spencer was a leading English sociologist and a philosopher of individualism and utilitarian moralism. His role in the development of sociology was immense, perhaps especially in the United States, primarily because of his noninterventionist and libertarian laissez-faire economics based on a Social Darwinist theory. Spencer developed a unitary evolutionary approach to all scientific knowledge, which he applied in his theory of society. Born in Derby in 1820 to nonconformist parents, he was largely educated at home in science, mathematics, and radical religious, political, and social theories. Spencer never completely abandoned his parents' iconoclastic rejection of popular British culture, although he did give up his religious leanings in favor of a more secular, scientific approach.

Spencer worked as an engineer for several years in his early adult life, at the same time reading widely in the sciences, from which he developed his evolutionary ideas. Later he worked as a journalist for an important free-enterprise economics periodical, *The Economist,* until he received an inheri-

tance in 1853 that allowed him to work as a private scholar for the rest of his life. During his tenure at *The Economist* he wrote his first substantial book, *Social Statics,* which he would later consider his weakest work. Spencer suffered a number of nervous illnesses during his life, but he was able to publish prolifically and gained an international reputation. As he grew older, his individualism and disdain for social interventionism and welfare became entrenched, which led to a loss of public support as attitudes began to change.

In *Social Statics,* Spencer made a strong argument for equal rights for women. He mitigated this stance in some of his later work, however. In his *Principles of Ethics* (1896) and *Principles of Sociology* (1898), Spencer adds two qualifications to his general support of equality: (1) Since men are more responsible for the property and upkeep of families, and women are "naturally" constituted for maternity and childrearing, husbands should have more rights to property (including the right to control a wife's property); and (2) women should have fewer political rights than men as long as only men are required to serve in the military because voting and other rights of citizenship can influence military decisions. On the other hand, even in this later work, Spencer in general opposes the notion that women are by nature inferior to men, and he makes an effort to justify women's equality in other matters.

MAJOR WORKS

Spencer, Herbert. *Social Statics: Or The Conditions Essential to Human Happiness Specified, and the First of the Developed.* London: Appleton, 1888 (Orig. Pub. 1850).

———. *The Principles of Ethics.* London: Appleton, 1896.

———. *Principles of Sociology.* London: Appleton, 1898.

SOURCES

Adams, Bert N., and R. A. Sydie. 2001. *Sociological theory.* Thousand Oaks, CA: Pine Forge Press.

Coser, Lewis A. 1977. *Masters of sociological thought.* New York: Harcourt, Brace, Jovanovich.

THE SELECTION

"The Rights of Women" is from Herbert Spencer's first major book, *Social Statics* (1850), published while he was a journalist for *The Economist*. Here he makes a strong argument for sex equality in terms of basic rights. He counters many of the common claims of his day that sought to justify differential treatment of women: for example, their supposed mental inferiority. He likewise opposes the arbitrary authority of husbands over wives as signs of "barbarity" that will eventually be recognized as such. He points out that love is inconsistent with command, and marriage will benefit when relationships are based on mutual concessions instead of authoritarian rule. Finally Spencer promotes the idea of political rights for women, in spite of the fact that custom—which is "variable and evanescent"—seems to oppose this.

The second selection, "The Status of Women," is from a chapter in *Principles of Sociology* (1898) that contains much anthropological evidence for his argument. Here Spencer is less concerned with the ethics of equality than with the sociological explanation of variation in the status of women. In the earlier portion of the chapter, his evolutionary assumptions led him to examine changes from "primitive" or "inferior," simple societies to the situation in modern, industrial societies. He sees the earliest societies as being more "savage" with respect to the treatment of women, owing to men's greater physical strength and the lack of the development of altruism. As societies progress, they come to rely more on industry and less on conquest and hunting for survival, and these characteristics are positive for the status of women.

Spencer's most important observations in this chapter, however, have nothing to do with the evolutionary sequence. In the brief excerpt presented here he examines causes

---

The first selection, on women's rights, is from Herbert Spencer, *Social Statics* (New York: Appleton, 1850/1888), 172–90. The second is from his later *Principles of Sociology* (New York: Appleton, 1898), 742–44.

of variation in the status of women, regardless of stage of development. This he explains in two ways: (1) Where men and women have similar occupations, there is more equality of status between the sexes; and (2) to the extent that a society is militaristic rather than industrial (i.e., focused on war and aggression instead of commerce and production of goods for domestic and peaceful uses), women's status will be low. Even in advanced societies, during times of war, women's status often declines. These observations are very important, representing one of the earliest statements of such principles—notions often cited as explanations of gender inequality.

THE RIGHTS OF WOMEN

I. Equity knows no difference of sex. In its vocabulary the word man must be understood in a generic, and not in a specific sense. The law of equal freedom manifestly applies to the whole race—female as well as male. The same *a priori* reasoning which establishes that law for men may be used with equal cogency on behalf of women. The Moral Sense, by virtue of which the masculine mind responds to that law, exists in the feminine mind as well. Hence the several rights deducible from that law must appertain equally to both sexes.

This might have been thought a self-evident truth, needing only to be stated to meet with universal acceptation. There are many, however, who either tacitly, or in so many words, express their dissent from it. For what reasons they do so, does not appear. They admit the axiom, that human happiness is the Divine will; from which axiom, what we call rights are primarily derived. And why the differences of bodily organization, and those trifling mental variations which distinguish female from male, should exclude one-half of the race from the benefits of this ordination, remains to be shown. *The onus of proof lies on those who affirm that such is the fact; and it would be perfectly in order to assume that the law of equal freedom comprehends both sexes, until*

the contrary has been demonstrated. But without taking advantage of this, suppose we go at once into the controversy.

Three positions only are open to us. It may be said that women have no rights at all—that their rights are not so great as those of men—or that they are equal to those of men.

Whoever maintains the first of these dogmas, that women have no rights at all, must show that the Creator intended women to be wholly at the mercy of men—their happiness, their liberties, their lives, at men's disposal; or, in other words, that they were meant to be treated as creatures of an inferior order. Few will have hardihood to assert this.

From the second proposition, that the rights of women are not so great as those of men, there immediately arise such queries as—If they are not so great, by how much are they less? What is the exact ratio between the legitimate claims of the two sexes? How shall we tell which rights are common to both, and where those of the male exceed those of the female? Who can show us a scale that will serve for the apportionment? . . . [W]hether the rights of women were violated by that Athenian law, which allowed a citizen under certain circumstances to sell his daughter or sister? whether our own statute, which permits a man to beat his wife in moderation, and to imprison her in any room in his house, is morally defensible? whether it is equitable that a married woman should be incapable of holding property? whether a husband may justly take possession of his wife's earnings against her will, as our law allows him to do?—and so forth. These, and a multitude of similar problems, present themselves for solution. Some principle rooted in the nature of things has to be found, by which they may be scientifically decided—decided, not on grounds of expediency, but in some definite, philosophical way. Does any one holding the doctrine that women's rights are not so great as men's, think be can find such a principle?

If not, there remains no alternative but to take up the third position—that the rights of women are equal with those of men.

2. Whose urges the mental inferiority of women in bar of their claim to equal rights with men, may be met in various ways.

In the first place, the alleged fact may be disputed. A defender of her sex might name many whose achievements in government, in science, in literature, and in art, have obtained no small share of renown. Powerful and sagacious queens the world has seen in plenty, from Zenobia, down to the empresses Catherine and Maria Theresa. In the exact sciences, Mrs. Somerville, Miss Herschel, and Miss Zornlin, have gained applause; in political economy, Miss Martineau; in general philosophy, Madame de Staël; in politics, Madame Roland. Poetry has its Tighes, its Hemanses, its Landons, its Brownings; the drama its Joanna Baillie; and fiction its Austens, Bremers, Gores, Dudevants, &c., without end. In sculpture, fame has been acquired by a princess; a picture like "The Momentous Question" is tolerable proof of female capacity for painting; and on the stage, it is certain that women are on a level with men, if they do not even bear away the palm. Joining to

such facts the important consideration, that women have always been, and are still, placed at a disadvantage in every department of learning, thought, or skill—seeing that they are not admissible to the academies and universities in which men get their training; that the kind of life they have to look forward to, does not present so great a range of ambitions; that they are rarely exposed to that most powerful of all stimuli—necessity; that the education custom dictates for them is one that leaves uncultivated many of the higher faculties; and that the prejudice against blue-stockings, hitherto so prevalent amongst men, has greatly tended to deter women from the pursuit of literary honours;—adding these considerations to the above facts, we shall see good reason for thinking that the alleged inferiority of the feminine mind, is by no means self-evident.

But, waiving this point, let us contend with the proposition on its own premises. Let it be granted that the intellect of woman is less profound than that of man—that she is more uniformly ruled by feeling, more impulsive, and less reflective, than man is—let all this be granted; and let us now see what basis such an admision affords to the doctrine, that the rights of women are not coextensive with those of men.

1. If rights are to be meted out to the two sexes in the ratio of their respective amounts of intelligence, then must the same system be acted upon in the apportionment of rights between man and man. Whence must proceed all those multiplied perplexities already pointed out.

2. In like manner, it will follow, that as there are here and there women of unquestionably greater ability than the average of men, some women ought to have greater rights than some men.

3. Wherefore, instead of a certain fixed allotment of rights to all males and

another to all females, the hypothesis itself involves an infinite gradation of rights, irrespective of sex entirely and sends us once more in search of those unattainable desiderata—a standard by which to measure capacity, and another by which to measure rights.

Not only, however, does the theory thus fall to pieces under the mere process of inspection; it is absurd on the very face of it. . . .

4. That a people's condition may be judged by the treatment which women receive under it, is a remark that has become almost trite. The facts, of which this remark is a generalization, are abundant enough. Look where we will, we find that just as far as the law of the strongest regulates the relationships between man and man, does it regulate the relationships between man and woman. To the same extent that the triumph of might over right is seen in a nation's political institutions, it is seen in its domestic ones. Despotism in the state is necessarily associated with despotism in the family. The two being alike moral in their origin, cannot fail to coexist. . . .

Yet, strangely enough, almost all of us who let fall this observation, overlook its application to ourselves. Here we sit over our tea-tables, and pass criticisms upon national character, or philosophize upon the development of civilized institutions, quietly taking it for granted that we *are* civilized—that the state of things we live under is the right one, or thereabouts. Although the people of every past age have thought the like and have been uniformly mistaken, there are still many to whom it never occurs that we may be mistaken too. Amidst their strictures upon the ill-treatment of women in the East, and the unhealthy social arrangements implied by it, most persons do not see that the same connection between political and domestic oppression exists in this England of ours at the present hour, and that in as far as our laws and customs violate the rights of humanity by giving the richer classes power over the poorer, in so far do they similarly violate those rights by giving the stronger sex power over the weaker. Yet, looking at the matter apart from prejudice, and considering all institutions to be, as they are, products of the popular character, we cannot avoid confessing that such *must* be the case. To the same extent that the old leaven of tyranny shows itself in the transactions of the senate, it will creep out in the doings of the household. If injustice sways men's public acts, it will inevitably away their private ones also. . . .

5. The desire to command is essentially a barbarous desire. . . . Command cannot be otherwise than savage, for it implies an appeal to force, should force be needful. Behind its "You shall," there lies the scarcely hidden, "If you won't, I'll make you." Command is the growl of coercion crouching in ambush. Or we might aptly term it—violence in a latent state. All its accessories—its frown, its voice, its gestures, prove it akin to the ferocity of the uncivilized man. Command is the foe of peace, for it breeds war of words and feelings—sometimes of deeds. It is inconsistent with the first law of morality. It is radically wrong.

All the barbarisms of the past have their types in the present. All the barbarisms of the past grew out of certain dispositions: those dispositions may be weakened, but they are not extinct; and so long as they exist there must be manifestations of them. What we commonly understand by command and obedience, are the modern forms of bygone despotism and slavery. . . . If every man has freedom to exercise his faculties within specified limits; and if . . . slavery is wrong because it transgresses that freedom, and makes one man use his powers, to satisfy not his own wants, but the wants of another; then, whatsoever involves command, or whatsoever implies obedience, is wrong also; seeing that it, too, necessitates the subserviency of one man's actions to the gratifications of another. "You must not do as you will, but as I will," is the basis of every mandate . . . by a husband to his wife. . . . It matters not, in point of principle, whether such domination is entire or partial. To whatever extent the will of the one is overborne by the will of the other, to that extent the parties are tyrant and slave.

There are, without doubt, many who will rebel against this doctrine. There are many who hold that the obedience of one human being to another is proper, virtuous, praiseworthy. There are many to whose moral sense command is not repugnant. There are many who think the subjection of the weaker sex to the stronger legitimate and beneficial. Let them not be deceived. Let them remember that a nation's institutions and beliefs are determined by its character. Let them remember that men's perceptions are warped by their passions. Let them remember that our social state proves our superior feelings to be very imperfectly developed. And let them remember that, as many customs deemed right by our ancestors, appear detestable to us, so, many customs which we think proper, our more civilized descendants may regard with aversion—even as we loathe those barbarian manners which forbid a woman to sit at table with her lord and master, so may mankind one day loathe that subserviency of wife to husband, which existing laws enjoin. . . .

6. A future belief that subordination of sex is inequitable, is clearly prophesied by the change civilization is working in men's sentiments. The arbitrary rule of one human being over another, no matter in what form it may appear, is fast getting recognized as essentially rude and brutal. . . .

In the conduct of the modern gentleman to his friend, we have additional signs of this growing respect for another's dignity. Every one must have observed the carefulness with which those who are on terms of affectionate intimacy, shun any thing in the form of supremacy on either side, or endeavour to banish from remembrance, by their behaviour to each other, whatever of supremacy there may exist. . . .

A further increase of this same refinement will show men that there is a fatal incongruity between the matrimonial servitude which our law recognizes, and the relationship that *ought* to exist between husband and wife. Surely if he who possesses any generosity of nature dislikes speaking to a hired domestic in a tone of authority—if he cannot bear assuming toward his friend the behaviour of a superior—how utterly repugnant to him should it be, to make himself ruler over one on whose behalf all his kindly sentiments are specially enlisted; one to whom he is bound by the strongest attachment that his nature is capable of; and for whose rights and dignity he ought to have the most active sympathy!

7. Command is a blight to the affections. Whatsoever of refinement—whatsoever of beauty—whatsoever of poetry, there is in the passion that unites the sexes, withers up and dies in the cold atmosphere of authority. Native as they are to such widely-separated regions of our nature, Love and Coercion cannot possibly flourish together. The one grows out of our best feelings: the other has its root in our worst. Love is sympathetic: Coercion is callous. Love is gentle: Coercion is harsh. Love is self-sacrificing: Coercion is selfish. How then can they coexist? It is the property of the first to attract; whilst it is that of the last to repel: and, conflicting as they thus do, it is the constant tendency of each to destroy the other. Let whoever thinks the two compatible imagine himself acting the master over his betrothed. Does he believe that he could do this without any injury to the subsisting relationship? Does he not know rather that a bad effect would be produced upon the feelings of both parties by the assumption of such an attitude? . . .

Of all the causes which conspire to produce the disappointment of those glowing hopes with which married life is usually entered upon, none is so potent as this supremacy of sex—this degradation of what should be a free and equal relationship into one of ruler and subject—this supplanting of the sway of affection by the sway of authority. Only as that condition of slavery to which women are condemned amongst barbarous nations is ameliorated, does ideal love become possible; and only when that condition of slavery shall have been *wholly* abolished, will ideal love attain fulness and permanence. The facts around us plainly indicate this. Wherever any thing worth calling connubial happiness at present exists, we shall find that the subjugation of wife to husband is not enforced; though perhaps still held in theory, it is practically repudiated.

8. There are many who think that authority, and its ally compulsion, are the sole agencies by which human beings can be controlled. Anarchy or government are, with them, the only conceivable alternatives. Believing in nothing but what they see, they cannot realize the possibility of a condition of things in which peace and order shall be maintained without force, or the fear of force. By such as these, the doctrine that the reign of man over woman is wrong, will no doubt be combated on the ground that the domestic relationship can only exist by the help of such supremacy. The impracticability of an equality of rights between the sexes will be urged by them in disproof of its rectitude. It will be argued, that were they put upon a level husband and wife would be forever in antagonism—that as, when their wishes clashed, each would possess a like claim to have his or her way, the matrimonial bond would daily be endangered by the jar of opposing wills, and that, involving as it would a perpetual conflict, such an arrangement of married life must necessarily be an erroneous one.

A very superficial conclusion this. It has been already pointed out that there *must* be an inconsistency between the perfect law and an imperfect state. The worse the condition of society, the more visionary must a true code of morality appear. The fact that any proposed principle of conduct is at once fully practicable—requires no reformation of human nature for its complete realization—is not a proof of its truth: is proof rather of its error. And, conversely, a certain degree of incongruity between such a principle and humanity as we know it, though no proof of the correctness of that principle, is at any rate a fact in its favour. Hence the allegation that mankind are not good enough to admit of the sexes living together harmoniously under the law of equal freedom, in no way militates against the validity or sacredness of that law.

But the never-ceasing process of adaptation will gradually remove this obstacle to domestic rectitude. Recognition of the moral law, and an impulse to act up to it, going hand in hand, equality of rights in the married state will become possible as fast as there arises a perception of its justness. That selfish conflict of claims which, according to the foregoing objection, would reduce a union, founded on the law of equal freedom, to a condition of anarchy, presupposes a deficiency in those feelings with which a belief in the law of equal freedom originates, and would decrease with the growth of those feelings. As elsewhere shown, the same sentiment which leads us to maintain our own rights, leads us, by its sympathetic excitement, to respect the rights of our neighbours. Other things equal, the sense of justice to ourselves, and the sense of justice to our fellow-creatures, bear a constant ratio to each other. A state in which every one is jealous of his natural claims, is not therefore a litigious state, because it is one in which there is of necessity a diminished tendency to aggression. Experience proves this. For, as it cannot be denied that there is now a greater disposition amongst men toward the assertion of individual liberty than existed during the feudal ages, so neither can it be denied that there is now a less disposition amongst men to trespass against each other than was then exhibited. The two changes are co-ordinate, and must continue to be so. Hence, whenever society shall have become civilized enough to recognize the equality of rights between the sexes—when women shall have attained to a clear perception of what is due to them, and men to a nobility of feeling which shall make them concede to women the freedom which they themselves claim—humanity will have undergone such a modification as to render an equality of rights practicable.

Married life under this ultimate state of things will not be characterized by perpetual squabbles, but by mutual concessions. Instead of a desire on the part of the husband to assert his claims to the uttermost, regardless of those of his wife, or on the part of the wife to do the like, there will be a watchful desire on both sides not to transgress. Neither will have to stand on the defensive because each will be solicitous for the rights of the other. Not encroachment, but self-sacrifice, will be the ruling principle. The struggle will not be which shall gain the mastery, but which shall give way. Committing a trespass will be the thing feared, and not the being trespassed against. And thus, instead of domestic discord, will come a higher harmony than any we yet know.

There is nothing Utopian in this. We may already trace the beginnings of it. An attitude like that described is not uncommonly maintained in the dealings of honourable men with each other; and if so, why should it not exist between the sexes? Here and there, indeed, may be found, even now, a wedded pair, who preserve such a relationship. And what is at present the exception may one day be the rule.

9. The extension of the law of equal freedom to both sexes will doubtless be objected to, on the ground that the political privileges exercised by men must thereby be ceded to women also. Of course they must; and why not? Is it that women are ignorant of state affairs? Why then their opinions would be those of their husbands and brothers; and the practical effect would be merely that of giving each male elector two votes instead of one. Is it that they might by-and-by become better informed, and might then begin to act independently? Why, in such case, they would be pretty much as competent to use their power with intelligence as the members of our present constituencies.

We are told, however, that "woman's mission" is a domestic one—that her character and position do not admit of her taking a part in the decision of public questions—that politics are beyond her sphere. But this raises the question—Who shall say what her sphere is? . . .

In slave-countries it is within woman's sphere to work side by side with men, under the lash of the taskmaster. Clerkships, cashierships, and other responsible business situations, are comprised in her sphere in modern France. Whilst, on the other hand, the sphere of a Turkish or Egyptian lady extends scarcely an inch beyond the walls of the harem. Who now will tell us what woman's sphere really is? As the usages of mankind vary so much, let us hear how it is to be shown that the sphere *we* assign her is the true one—that the limits *we* have set to female activity are just the proper limits. Let us hear why on this one point of our social polity we are exactly right, whilst we are wrong on so many others.

It is indeed said, that the exercise of political power by women is repugnant to our sense of propriety—conflicts with our ideas of the feminine character—is altogether condemned by our feelings. Granted; but what then? The same plea has been urged in defence of a thousand absurdities, and if valid in one case is equally so in all others. Should a traveller in the East inquire of a Turk why women in his country conceal their faces, he would be told that for them to go unveiled would be considered indecent; would offend the *feelings* of the spectators. In Russia female voices are never heard in church: women not being thought worthy "to sing the praises of God in the presence of men;" and the disregard of this regulation would be censured as an outrage upon public *feeling*. . . .

In China cramped feet are essential to female refinement; and so strong is the *feeling* in this matter, that a Chinese will not believe that an Englishwoman who walks naturally, can be one of a superior class. It was once held unfeminine for a lady to write a book; and no doubt those who thought it so, would have quoted *feelings* in support of their opinion. Yet, with facts like these on every hand, people assume that the enfranchisement of women cannot be right, because it is repugnant to their feelings!

We have some feelings that are necessary and eternal; we have others that, being the results of custom, are changeable and evanescent. And there is no way of distinguishing those feelings which are natural from those which are conventional, except by an appeal to first principles. If a sentiment responds to some necessity of our condition, its dictates must be respected. If otherwise—if opposed to a necessity, instead of in harmony with one, we must regard that sentiment as the product of circumstances, of education, or habit, and consequently without weight. However much, therefore, the giving of political power to women may disagree with our notions of propriety, we must conclude that, being required by that first prerequisite to greatest happiness—the law of equal freedom such a concession is unquestionably right and good.

10. Thus it has been shown that the rights of women must stand or fall with those of men; derived as they are from the same authority; involved in the same axiom; demonstrated by the same argument. That the law of equal freedom applies alike to both sexes, has been further proved by the fact that any other hypothesis involves us in inextricable difficulties.

The Status of Women

What connexion is there between the *status* of women and the type of social organization?

A partial answer was reached when we concluded that there are natural associations between militancy and polygyny and between industrialism and monogamy. For as polygyny implies a low position of women, while monogamy is a pre-requisite to a high position; it follows that decrease of militancy and increase of industrialism, are general concomitants of a rise in their position.

This conclusion appears also to be congruous with the fact just observed. The truth that among peoples otherwise inferior, the position of women is relatively good where their occupations are nearly the same as those of men, seems allied to the wider truth that their position becomes good in proportion as warlike activities are replaced by industrial activities; since, when the men fight while the women work, the difference of occupation is greater than when both are engaged in productive labours, however unlike such labours may be in kind. From general reasons for alleging this connexion, let us now pass to special reasons. . . .

The connexions which we have seen exist between militancy and polygyny and between industrialism and monogamy, exhibit the same truth under another aspect; since polygyny necessarily implies a low *status* of women, and monogamy, if it does not necessarily imply a high *status,* is an essential condition to a high *status.*

Further, that approximate equalization of the sexes in numbers which results from diminishing militancy and increasing industrialism, conduces to the elevation of women; since, in proportion as the supply of males available for carrying on social sustentation increases, the labour of social sustentation falls less heavily on the females. And it may be added that the societies in which these available males undertake the harder labours, and so, relieving the females from undue physical tax, enable them to produce more and better offspring, will, other things equal, gain in the struggle for existence with societies in which the women are not thus relieved. Whence an average tendency to the spread of societies in which the *status* of women is improved.

There is the fact, too, that the despotism distinguishing a community organized for war, is essentially connected with despotism in the household; while, conversely, the freedom which characterizes public life in an industrial community, naturally characterizes also the accompanying private life. In the one case compulsory co-operation prevails in both; in the other case voluntary co-operation prevails in both.

By the moral contrast we are shown another face of the same fact. Habitual antagonism with, and destruction of foes, sears the sympathies; while daily exchange of products and services among citizens, puts no obstacle to increase of fellow-feeling. And the altruism which grows with peaceful co-operation, ameliorates at once the life without the household and the life within the household.

August Bebel (1840–1913) on Women and Socialism

August Bebel was born in Cologne, Germany, the son of a minor officer in the Prussian infantry, and grew up to become a major proponent of socialism and Marxian thought in Germany. His childhood was fraught with tragedy and poverty—by the time August was 4 years old, he had lost both his father and his stepfather to early death. Following these events, his mother moved back to her hometown, where August received a good public education. Unfortunately, in 1853 Bebel's mother died as well, leaving him in the care of his aunt and separating him from his brother, who went to live with another aunt. August worked in his aunt's mill and attended school, graduating in 1854. This period was followed by several years of wandering and the development of a critical political consciousness.

Bebel quickly rose in political influence, winning election to the German Reichstag in 1867, a position he retained for most of his life. Influenced by Wilhelm Liebknecht to become a Marxist, Bebel co-founded (with Liebknecht) the German Social Democratic Party in 1869. Always a controversial figure, in 1872 he was briefly imprisoned for his opposition to the Franco-German War. From 1875 onward he was the acknowledged leader of the German Social Democrats.

In 1879 Bebel published *Woman and Socialism,* an important theoretical work and one of the first serious examinations of woman's place in socialist theory. Bebel's book helped spread Marxist ideas across Germany. He argued that the emancipation of women must be an integral part of any successful socialist revolution against capitalism. The book was a great success, going through at least 50 editions and appearing in numerous languages.

As shown in this work, Bebel was skeptical of the goals of the mainstream women's movement with its focus on "bourgeois" goals of suffrage and legal equality. Such a solution, he thought, would leave in place the vast inequities apparent between worker and capitalist. What was needed, he argued, was a revolution that could lead to equality for all workers, male and female, and could eliminate exploitation of the many by the few in class society. This work is also significant in that Bebel, along with other socialists, points to the different interests of various groups of women, a problem often ignored by writers who treat all women as a unified category.

Major Work

Bebel, August. *Die Frau un der Sozialismus.* London: Modern Press, 1885.

Sources

August Bebel online archive, www.marxists.org/archive/bebel/index.htm. Accessed January 22, 2006.

Bebel, August. 1910. *Reminiscences.* New York: The Socialist Literature Company.

Rossi, Alice S. 1973. *The feminist papers: From Adams to de Beauvoir.* Edited and with introductory essays by Alice S. Rossi. New York: Columbia University Press.

Roth, Gary, and Anne Lopez. 2000. *Men's feminism: August Bebel and the German Socialist Movement.* Amherst, NY: Prometheus Books.

The Selection

August Bebel argues that the woman question is integral to the "whole social question" of how to end inequality and oppression. He opposes those who see women's subordinate family role as natural, but he criticizes as well those who fight for women's equality within the prevailing class-divided and exploitative social structure. He claims that most women's rights movements have aimed primarily at improving the status of upper-class women, not of those from the working classes. Bebel makes a strong plea for a "complete solution" that would give economic and material independence as well as legal equality. As he concludes his introduction, "the complete solution of the Women's Question is as unattainable as the solution of the Labour Question under the existing social and political institutions."

Bebel then discusses the situation of women in various fields of labor, pointing out some of the ways in which employers use sex competition in order to keep wages depressed for both women and men. He presents a fascinating discussion of the protest of male scholars who oppose the entry of women into the "higher" or "liberal" professions such as higher education, science, administration, and medicine. Here he counters some of the scholarship of the time, making a strong case for the role of social conditions in determining women's intellectual and other accomplishments, ending with a plea to improve those conditions. Overall, Bebel proposes promoting a socialist society in which people of all classes have access to the conditions and material bases for the development of their human talents.

From August Bebel, "Introduction" and "In the Present," in *Woman in the Past, Present, and Future,* Trans. H. B. Adams Walther (London: Modern Press, 1885: rep., New York: AMS Press, 1976).

THE WOMAN QUESTION IN SOCIALISM

During the last decades of our social development a certain excitement and perturbation of mind has been making itself more and more apparent throughout all classes of the community. Many questions have arisen, for and against which we are contending. One of the most important of these is indisputably the so-called women's question.

The question as to what position in our social organism will enable woman to become a useful member of the community, will put her in possession of the same rights as its others members enjoy, and ensure the full development of her powers and faculties in every direction, coincides with the question as to the form and organisation which the entire community must receive, if oppression, exploitation, want and misery in a hundred shapes are to be replaced by a free humanity, by a society which is physically and organically sound. The so-called women's question is therefore only one side of the whole social question, which is at the present hour agitating all minds; only in connection with each other can the two questions reach their final solution.

The fact that those whom the women's question chiefly concerns—the women themselves—represent, at any rate in Europe—the larger half of society, is in itself sufficient justification for a special treatment of the subject. It is one well worth "the sweat of the noble."

In the women's question, just as in the general social question, there are naturally various parties, who deal with it from their own particular social and political standpoint, from which they pass their verdict upon it, and propose measures for its settlement.

Some maintain, as in the social question, in which the working classes play the principal part, that there really is no women's question at all, inasmuch as the position which woman occupies in the present and will occupy in the future is circumscribed by her "natural calling," which destines her to become a wife and mother and restricts her to the family circle. What goes on outside her four walls or does not stand in the closest and most visible relation to her housewifely duties does not concern her at all.

The adherents of this view have, as we see, a recipe ready to hand and imagine that they have therewith settled the question. These wise men are not troubled by the consideration that millions of women are unable to fulfil their "natural calling" of housewives and child-bearers, for reasons that will be given in detail further on, and that other millions have in great measure missed this calling, because the marriage tie means subjection and slavery to them, or because they have to support an existence of misery and want. The wise men close eyes and ears to these unwelcome facts, as energetically as to the needs of the people, conforting themselves and others with the reflection that "it has always been so and will always remain so." They absolutely refuse to listen to the argument that woman has a right to share in the results of civilisation, to make use of these results for the alleviation and improvement of her position, and to develop and apply her mental and physical faculties to her own advantage in the same degree as man. If we go still further and claim pecuniary independence for woman, as the only means of ensuring her physical and mental independence and freeing her from subjection to the "goodwill" and "grace" of the opposite sex, they lose patience altogether, their temper is roused, and a volley of angry accusations and invectives against the "madness of the times," and the "arrant folly of women's rights" closes the scene. . . .

Then there are others again, less successful in closing eyes and ears to patent facts; they acknowledge that at no other period of history has the position of women in comparison with the general advance of civilization been so bad as at present, and that it is therefore necessary to enquire what can be done to help them, and what they must do to help themselves. For those who have reached the haven of marriage the question is supposed to be already solved.

Accordingly they demand that all fields of labour for which the strength and faculties of woman qualify her shall be thrown open, and that nothing shall stand in the way of her free competition with man. The more advanced among them condemn the restriction of this competition to the lower employments and trades, and demand its extension to the higher professions, to art and science. They demand the admission of women to all higher training schools and academies, and especially to the Universities, which have hitherto been closed. They direct their attention principally to the various branches of instruction, to the medical profession, and to appointments in the Civil Service (Post Office, Telegraph, Railway), which they consider especially suitable to women, chiefly on account of the practical results obtained in the United States by the employment of women in these branches. A small minority among them go so far as to demand political rights for women. A woman, they say, is just as much a human being and a citizen of the State as a man; the exclusive male legislation which has been practised hitherto proves that men, while keeping women in a state of tutelage, have made use of their privileges only to their own advantage.

It is characteristic of all the suggestions which we have here cursorily summed up, that they do not exceed the limits of the present framework of society. No one asks whether these propositions, if realised, would suffice to essentially ameliorate the position of women. No one recognises that the goal, at least with regard to the admission of women to the various branches of trade and industry, is already practically reached; although under existing social conditions, this admission only results in a competitive struggle between the workers, fiercer than any that ever raged before, and the consequent inevitable lowering of the wages and salaries earned by both sexes in all posts open to their competition.

This want of thoroughness and clearness as to the aims to be attained is explained by the fact that the women's question has so far been almost exclusively taken in hand by women of the upper classes, whose attention was engrossed by the limited circle in which they lived, and for whose benefit their claims were chiefly made. But the position of women in general will remain entirely unaltered, whether or not some hundred or some thousand women of the needy middle classes force their way into the ranks of schoolmasters, doctors, or officials, and there secure more or less lucrative posts. The subjection of the sex under men, the pecuniary dependence of the enormous majority and the consequent sexual slavery which finds its expression in modern marriage and in prostitution, will still remain untouched. Moreover, a fragmentary solution such as this will fail to rouse any enthusiasm among the majority of women; small aims cannot warm or stir the mass. And still less will such a solution appeal to that influential class of men who regard the encroachment of women on well remunerated and honourable posts only as a highly undesirable form of competition for themselves and their sons. They will oppose this encroachment by every means in their power, and, as experience has shown, their opposition will not always respect the limits of either fairness or decency. It is true that these same influential men have not the slightest objection to make when women inundate every department of so-called inferior employment; on the contrary, they consider it perfectly justifiable and encourage it, on the ground that it cheapens labour. But women must not intrude on man's higher social and official domain; the attempt to do so is viewed in a very different light.

Neither is it probable that the modern State, to judge by recent experience, will in the future show itself disposed to appoint women to posts in the Civil Service, and least of all to higher posts, however well qualified the women may be to fill them.

The State and the upper classes have broken down every barrier to competition in trade and among the working classes, but with regard to the higher callings they are endeavouring to raise up fresh barriers. It makes a singular impression on the impartial spectator, to observe the energy with which scholars and higher officials, doctors and lawyers "defend their rights," when an outsider ventures to overstep the traditional limits. And in these circles women are regarded as outsiders *par excellence;* these professional persons are of opinion that they have been specially favoured by God, inasmuch as the powers of comprehension with which they imagine themselves endowed, are, according to them, altogether very exceptional, and quite beyond the reach of ordinary mortals, more particularly of women.

It is clear that if this book had no other object than to prove the necessity of placing men and women on a footing of equality in society as it is, it would better have remained unwritten. The attempt would be more patchwork, and would fail to point the way to any complete solution of the question. By a complete solution I understand not only the equality of men and women before the law, but their economic freedom and material independence, and, so far as possible, equality in mental development. *This complete solution of the Women's Question is as unattainable as the solution of the Labour Question under the existing social and political institutions. . . .*

Consequently we must endeavour to found a society in which all the means of production are the property of the community, a society which recognizes the full equality of all *without distinction of sex,* which provides for the application of every kind of technical and scientific improvement or discovery, which enrolls as workers all those who are at present unproductive or whose activity assumes an injurious shape, the idlers and the drones, and which, while it minimizes the period of labour necessary for its support, raises the mental and physical condition of all its members to the highest attainable pitch. Only thus can woman become as productively useful as man, only thus can she become possessed of the same rights, only thus can she fully develop her bodily and mental capacities, fulfil her sexual duties and enjoy her sexual rights. Such a position of freedom and equality as this will place her for the first time beyond the reach of every degrading demand. . . .

In the Present

[O]ne daily hears the same idle talk about the natural vocation of women being comprised by the home and the family. And this phrase is heard loudest when women make an attempt to force their way into the so-called liberal callings, *i.e.*, into the fields of higher instruction, of natural science, of the administration, of the medical and legal professions. The most untenable and ridiculous objections are brought forward and defended under the cloak of "scholarship." The same thing frequently applies to this appeal to scholarship and science as to the appeal to "order and morality." Probably no one ever represented disorder and immorality as a desirable condition, with the exception, perhaps of those individuals who made use of them to get power in their own hands, and even in this case they always endeavoured to make their actions appear necessary for the maintenance of order, morality, and religion. Nevertheless these injurious catchwords are invariably employed against those who seek to establish true morality and order, by the introduction of conditions more consistent with human dignity than the present ones. Similarly the reference to scholarship and science is made to do service in defending what is most absurd and reactionary. Its advocates argue, for instance, that nature and the physical peculiarities of women point her to the home and family life, within which she has to fulfil her purpose in creation. We have already seen how far this is possible now-a-days. And the highest trump is the assertion that woman is inferior to man in mental capacity, and that it is therefore ridiculous to suppose that she can achieve anything worth mentioning on intellectual ground.

These objections raised by scholars harmonise so completely with the general prejudice of men with regard to the proper sphere and faculties of women, that he who expresses them can reckon on the approval of his own sex, and for the present at least, on that of the majority of women. But the fact that the decision in such matters rests with the majority, and that nothing can be carried through against its will and pleasure, does not prove that its decision is always a reasonable one. New ideas must inevitably meet with stubborn opposition as long as education and intelligence are at their present low level, and as long as social institutions involve the necessity of encroaching on vested interests in the realization of ideas. It is easy for the representatives of these vested interests to turn popular prejudices to their own account, and therefore new ideas when first broached will never convince more than

a small minority; they are ridiculed and defamed and persecuted. But if these ideas are good and reasonable, and the necessary product of circumstances, they will spread; the minority will in time become a majority. This has been the fate of all new ideas in the course of the world's history, and the Socialistic idea, which is so intimately connected with the true and complete emancipation of woman, presents the same spectacle. . . .

Among the German scholars who advocate the entire, or almost entire exclusion of women from advanced studies, we may name Prof. L. Bischof in München, Dr. Ludwig Hirt in Breslau, Prof. A. Sybel, L. von Bärenbach, Dr. E. Reich, and very many others. Bärenbach founds his refusal to admit women to scientific pursuits and his disclaimer of their capacity for such pursuits, on the assertion that the sex has never yet produced a genius, and that women are obviously unfit to study philosophy. It seems to me that the world has had quite enough male philosophers and can afford to dispense with their feminine counter-parts. And the objection that women have brought forth no genius appears to be equally inadequate and inconclusive. Geniuses do not fall from heaven, they must have opportunities to form and mature, and not only have such opportunities been hitherto almost entirely denied to women, as the foregoing historical sketch of their mental development has abundantly shown, but men have kept them for thousands of years in a state of the deepest subjection. It is just as mistaken to say that a woman can never become a genius, because people can discover no spark of genius among the tolerably large number of intellectual women that exist, as to affirm that no more geniuses have been possible among men than the few who have been recognized as such, thanks to the opportunities that were offered them of development. The simplest village schoolmaster knows how much faculty among his scholars remains uncultivated, because there is no possibility of bringing it to maturity. The amount of talent and genius in male humanity is certainly a thousand times greater than that which has hitherto been able to reveal itself: social conditions have crushed it, just as they have crushed the capacities of the female sex, which has for centuries been oppressed, fettered and crippled to a much higher degree. We have at present absolutely no scale by which to measure the amount of mental power and capacity which will develop itself in men and women, when they are enabled to mature under natural conditions of existence.

It is real or wilful blindness to deny that improved social, *i.e.,* improved physical and mental, conditions of training could raise our women to a degree of perfection of which we have no idea to-day. The achievements of solitary women make this appear unquestionable, for these women are at least as superior to the mass of their sex, as male geniuses to the mass of their fellow men. In the government of States women have on an average given proof of even more talent than men, considering their number and measuring their actions by the standard usually applied to princes. We may allude, for example, to Isabella and Blanche of Castille, to Elizabeth of Hungary, Elizabeth of England, Catherine of Russia, Maria Theresa, &c. For the rest, many a great man in history would shrivel up till but little remained, if people always knew what he owed to himself and what to others. For instance a German author, Herr von Sybel, describes Count Mirabeau as the most brilliant orator, and one of the greatest geniuses of the French Revolution. And, now research has shown that this mighty genius was indebted for the manuscript of almost all his speeches, and of the most important without exception, to the ready help and support of some few scholars who worked in retirement and whom he was clever enough to turn to his own account. On the other hand, unusual

phenomena among women, such as Madame Roland, Madame de Staël, and George Sand, beside whom many a masculine star grows pale, are worthy of the greatest attention. The influence exercised by women as the mothers of remarkable men is also well known. Taking all into consideration, the intellect of women has achieved everything that it was possible to achieve, and this justifies the best hopes for further mental development. . . .

A woman inherits from Nature the same rights as a man; the chance of birth cannot alter this fact. It is as senseless and unjust to cut a woman off from the enjoyment of the common rights of humanity because she happens to have been born as a woman instead of as a man,—an accident of which both are equally innocent,—as it would be to make the exercise of these rights depend on religion or politics, or for men to regard each other as enemies, because they happened to belong to different races or nationalities. These notions and restrictions are unworthy of a free being, and the progress of humanity demands their removal at the earliest possible date. *The only dissimilarity which has a right to permanence is that established by Nature for the fulfilment of a natural purpose, which is externally unlike but in substance the same.* Neither sex can overstep natural boundaries, as it would destroy its proper purpose in doing so; upon this we may confidently rely. Neither sex is justified in erecting barriers for the other, any more than one class for another. . . .

Darwin is perfectly right in saying that a list of the most distinguished women in poetry, painting, sculpture, music, science, and philosophy, will bear no comparison with a similar list of the most distinguished men. But surely this need not surprise us. It would be surprising if it were not so. Dr. Dodel-Port answers to the point, when he maintains that the relative achievements would be very different, after men and women had received the same education and the same training in art and science during a certain number of generations. Women are also on an average physically weaker than men, which is not the case in many savage tribes, indeed we may sometimes observe the reverse. The results of practice and training from childhood on the bodily development can be seen in female acrobats and circus riders, who could compete with any man, in courage, daring, dexterity, and strength, and whose performances are frequently astonishing.

As all these things depend on education and on the conditions of life, or, in the plain language of natural science, are a question of "breeding," and as natural laws have already been applied in the case of domestic animals with startling results, there can be no doubt, that by the application of these same laws to the physical and mental development of mankind, even more unforseen results will be attained, in as much as man, the object of training, being conscious of the aim in view, takes an active part in the endeavour.

We see from all this, how close and intimate is the connection between modern natural science and our entire social life and growth, and that scientific laws, applied to human society, can explain conditions, which without them would remain obscure. In the light thrown by these laws on the development of the human organism, we discover the motor forces and perceive that relationships of supremacy, character and bodily pecularities of individuals as well as of whole classes and nations depend primarily on the *physical conditions of existence, in other words, on the social and economic distribution of power*. This again is influenced by the nature of the land, the fertility of the soil, and by the climate. Marx, Darwin, Buckle have all three, each in his own way, been of the greatest significance for modern development, and the future form and growth of human society will to an extreme degree be shaped and guided by their teaching and discoveries.

If then we recognize that bad and unfitting conditions of existence, *i.e.,* deficiencies in social arrangements, are the cause of perverse and incomplete individual development, it necessarily follows that an improvement in these conditions of existence would effect a corresponding improvement in the individual.

Émile Durkheim (1858–1917) on the Division of Labor and Interests in Marriage

Émile Durkheim is a well-known founder of modern sociology whose famous study of suicide set a strong standard for empirical analysis from a sociological (as opposed to a psychological) perspective. His work emphasized the reality of social forces, over and above individual motivations and actions. He especially focused on issues such as solidarity and the collective conscience.

Durkheim was the son of a rabbi in a long line of rabbis, a tradition he intended to follow. His youthful agnosticism led him to other pursuits, however, and his interest in a scientific approach to society developed at an early stage. An outstanding student, he studied at the *École Normale Supérieure* in Paris and afterward taught philosophy in the same city. In 1885 he obtained a scholarship to study in Germany, where he was influenced by the psychologist Wilhelm Wundt's ideas on the reality of moral forces in society—forces that should be treated as "facts." Durkheim returned from his year in Germany to accept employment at the University of Bordeaux, where he offered the first social science

course and, in 1896, became the first professor of social science in France.

During his tenure at Bordeaux, Durkheim wrote his most famous books and published an important sociological journal which he also edited, *L'Année Sociologique*. He spent much of his career at Bordeaux and later at the Sorbonne in Paris (1902–1917), developing sociology as an academic field and defending its legitimacy against criticisms by those who thought a true social science impossible and wrong-headed. His claim that "social facts" were a reality in themselves ("sui generis") was highly influential, and his works continue to be important in the education of sociologists even today. The death of his son André was a blow from which Durkheim never recovered, and he followed his son into death two years later at age fifty-nine.

Durkheim's thoughts on women and gender appear primarily in his study of suicide and in *The Division of Labor in Society*, within discussions of marriage and the roles of husbands and wives. He believed that social evolution had led to the exaggeration of sex differences in personality and abilities, and that social arrangements must be consistent with these differences by establishing role differentiation and functional interdependence. A conservative in these matters, Durkheim at times acknowledged that marriage was more favorable for men than for women, yet he believed that women must sacrifice some of their own needs for the good of society. Women and men fulfill different functions in society, with women specializing in the family and domestic life and men in public life, which goes along with their basic physiology and psychology. Thus, attempts to equalize the roles of men and women were unwise and doomed to fail.

Major Works

Durkheim, Émile. *The Rules of Sociological Method*. Edited by George G. Catlin. Translated by Sarah A. Solovay and John H. Mueller. New York: Free Press, 1938 (Orig. pub. 1895).

———. *Suicide: A Study in Sociology*. Edited by George Simpson. Translated by John A. Spaulding and George Simpson. Glencoe, IL: Free Press, 1951.

———. *The Division of Labour in Society*. Translated by George Simpson. London: Macmillan, 1933 (Orig. pub. 1893).

———. *The Elementary Forms of Religious Life*. Translated by Joseph Ward Swain, New York: Collier Books, 1961 (Orig. pub. 1913).

Sources

Adams, Bert N., and R. A. Sydie. 2001. *Sociological theory*, 90–118. Thousand Oaks, CA: Pine Forge.

Coser, Lewis A. 1977. *Masters of sociological thought*. New York: Harcourt, Brace, Jovanovich.

The Selections

In the first selection, Émile Durkheim discusses the increasing division of labor in society with its specialization of roles and growing interdependence among different roles. He applies this to "conjugal society" or marriage, arguing that the separation of sex roles has led to more solidarity within the marital union. As societies have evolved, men's and women's roles have become increasingly distinct, leading to a more stable institution of marriage that includes notions of fidelity, monogamy, and mutual love. This has been associated with changes in both character and physiology, but it has led to a more stable society.

In the second excerpt, Durkheim notes that suicide rates are higher for unmarried men than for married men, but the reverse is true for women. He explains this by arguing that men and women have different interests in marriage—men need marriage more, in order to "discipline" their desires. Women, on the other hand, may find marriage oppressive, and they have little opportunity to modify their situation. Married men benefit more from marriage, even unhappy ones, and they are not as tied to fidelity as are women. Even so, Durkheim opposes divorce because of its negative effects on men.

THE DIVISION OF LABOR AND MARRIAGE

We are thus led to consider the division of labor in a new light. In this instance, the economic services that it can render are picayune compared to the moral effect that it produces, and its true function is to create in two or more persons a feeling of solidarity. In whatever manner the result is obtained, its aim is to cause coherence among friends and to stamp them with its seal.

The history of conjugal society offers us an even more striking example of the same phenomenon.

Without doubt, sexual attraction does not come about except between individuals of the same type, and love generally asks a certain harmony of thought and sentiment. It is not less true that what gives to this relationship its peculiar character, and what causes its particular energy, is not the resemblance, but the difference in the natures which it unites. Precisely because man and woman are different, they seek each other passionately. However, as in the preceding instance, it is not a contrast pure and simple which brings about reciprocal feelings. Only those differences which require each other for their mutual fruition can have this quality. In short, man and woman isolated from each other are only different parts of the same concrete universal which they reform when they unite. In other words, the sexual division of labor is the source of conjugal solidarity, and that is why psychologists have very justly seen in the separation of the sexes an event of tremendous importance in the evolution of emotions. It has made possible perhaps the strongest of all unselfish inclinations.

Moreover, there may be greater or less division of labor; it can either affect only sexual organs and some secondary activities, or else also extend to all organic and social functions. Thus, we can see in history that it has developed concomitant with conjugal solidarity.

The further we look into the past, the smaller becomes this difference between man and woman. The woman of past days was not at all the weak creature that she has become with the progress of morality. Prehistoric bones show that the difference between the strength of man and of woman was relatively much smaller than it is today. Even now, during infancy and until puberty, the development of the two sexes does not differ in any appreciable way: the characteristics are quite feminine. If one admits that the development of the individual reproduces in its course that of the species, one may conjecture that the same homogeneity was found at the beginning of human evolution, and see in the female form the aboriginal image of what was the one and only type from which the masculine variety slowly detached itself. Travelers report, moreover, that in certain tribes of South America, man and woman, in structure and general appearance, present a similarity which is far greater than is seen elsewhere. Finally, Dr. Lebon has been able to establish directly and with mathematical precision this original resemblance of the two sexes in regard to the preeminent organ of physical and psychic life, the brain. By comparing a large number of crania chosen from different races and different societies, he has come to the following conclusion: "The volume of the crania of man and woman, even when we compare subjects of equal age, of equal height and equal weight, show considerable differences in favor of the man, and this inequality grows proportionally with civilization, so that from the point of view of the mass of the brain, and correspondingly of intelligence, woman tends more and more to be differentiated from the male sex. The difference which exists, for example, between the average cranium of Parisian men of the present day and that of Parisian women is almost double that observed between male and female of ancient Egypt." A German anthropologist, Bischoff, has arrived at the same result on this point.

These anatomical resemblances are accompanied by functional resemblances. In the same societies, female functions are not very clearly distinguished from male. Rather, the two sexes lead almost the same existence. There is even now a very great number of savage people where the woman mingles in political life. That has been observed especially in the Indian tribes of America, such as the Iroquois, the Natchez; in Hawaii she participates in myriad ways in the men's lives, as she does in New Zealand and in Samoa. Moreover, we very often observe women accompanying men to war, urging them on to battle and even taking a very active part. In Cuba, in Dahomey, they are as war-like as the men and battle at their side. One of the distinctive contemporary qualities of woman, gentility, does not appear to pertain to her in primitive society. In certain animal species, indeed, the female prides herself on the contrary characteristic.

Thus, among the same peoples, marriage is in a completely rudimentary state. It is quite probable, if not absolutely demonstrated, that there was an epoch in the history of the family when there was no such thing as marriage. Sexual relations were entered into and broken at will without any juridical obligations linking the union. In any case, we see a family type which is relatively near ours where marriage is still only in a very indistinct, germinal state. This is the matriarchal family. The relations of the mother to her children are very definite, but those of the two married people are very loose. The relation can be terminated at the will of the parties involved, or they can even contract to sustain the relation for a limited time. Conjugal fidelity is not even required. Marriage, or what is so called, consists solely in obligations of restricted scope and often of short duration, which link the husband to the parents of the woman. It is thus reduced to a small thing. Thus, in a given society, the totality of juridical rules which constitute marriage only symbolize the state of conjugal solidarity. If this is very strong, the ties which bind the married people are numerous and complex, and, consequently, the matrimonial set of rules whose object is to define these ties is itself very highly developed. If, on the contrary, conjugal society lacks cohesion, if the relations between man and woman are unstable and intermittent, they cannot take a very determinate form, and, consequently, marriage is reduced to a small number of rules without rigor or precision. The state of marriage in societies where the two sexes are only weakly differentiated thus evinces conjugal solidarity which is itself very weak.

On the contrary, as we advance to modern times, we see marriage developing. The circle of ties which it creates extends further and further; the obligations that it sanctions multiply. The conditions under which it can be contracted, those under which it can be dissolved, are limited with a precision growing as the effects of such dissolution grow. The duty of fidelity gains order; first imposed on the woman only, it later becomes reciprocal. When the dowry appears, very complex rules fix the respective rights of each person according to his or her appropriate fortune and that of the other. It suffices to take a bird's-eye view of our Codes to see what an important place marriage occupies. The union of two people has ceased to be ephemeral; it is no longer an external contact, temporary and partial, but an intimate association, lasting, often even indissoluble during the whole lifetime of the two parties.

It is certain that at the same time sexual labor is more and more divided. Limited first only to sexual functions, it slowly becomes extended to others. Long ago, woman retired from warfare and public affairs, and consecrated her entire life to her family. Since then, her role has become even more specialized. Today, among cultivated people, the woman leads a completely different existence from that of the man. One might say that the two great functions of the psychic life are thus dissociated, that one of the sexes takes care of the affective functions and the other of intellectual functions. In view of the fact that in certain classes women participate in artistic and literary life just as men, we might be led to believe, to be sure, that the occupations of the two sexes are becoming homogeneous. But, even in this sphere of action, woman carries out her own nature, and her role is very specialized, very different from that of man. Further, if art and letters begin to become feminine tasks, the other sex seems to permit it in order to give itself more specially to the pursuit of science. It might, then, be very well contended that this apparent return to primitive homogeneity is nothing else than the beginning of a new differentiation. Moreover, the functional differences are rendered materially visible by the morphological differences that they have determined. Not only are the height, weight, and the general form very dissimilar in men and women, but Dr. Lebon has shown, as we have seen, that with the progress of civilization the brain of the two sexes differentiates itself more and more. According to this observer, this progressive chart would be due both to the considerable development of masculine crania and to a stationary or even regressive state of female crania. "Thus," he says, "though the average cranium of Parisian men ranks among the greatest known crania, the average of Parisian women ranks among the smallest observed, even below the crania of the Chinese, and hardly above those of the women of New Caledonia."

In all these examples, the most remarkable effect of the division of labor is not that it increases the output of functions divided, but that it renders them solidary. Its role in all these cases is not simply to embellish or ameliorate existing societies, but to render societies possible which, without it, would not exist. Permit the sexual division of labor to recede below a certain level and conjugal society would eventually subsist in sexual relations preeminently ephemeral. If the sexes were not separated at all, an entire category of social life would be absent. It is possible that the economic utility of the division of labor may have a hand in this, but, in any case, it passes far beyond purely economic interests, for it consists in the establishment of a social and moral order *sui generis*. Through it, individuals are linked to one another. Without it, they would be independent. Instead of developing separately, they pool their efforts. They are solidary, but it is a solidarity which is not merely a question of the short time in which services are exchanged, but one which extends much further. Conjugal solidarity, for example, such as today exists among the most cultivated people, makes its action felt at each moment and in all the details of life. Moreover, societies created by the division of labor cannot fail to bear its mark. Since they have this special origin, they cannot resemble those determined by the attraction of like for like; they must be constituted in a different fashion, rest upon other foundations, appeal to other sentiments.

The social relations to which the division of labor gives birth have often been considered only in terms of exchange, but this misinterprets what such exchange implies and what results from it. It suggests two beings mutually dependent because they are each incomplete, and translates this mutual dependence outwardly. It is, then, only the superficial expression of an internal and very deep state. Precisely because this state is constant, it calls up a whole mechanism of images which function with a continuity that exchange does not possess. The image of the one who completes us becomes inseparable from ours, not only because it is frequently associated with ours, but particularly because it is the natural complement of it. It thus becomes an integral and permanent part of our conscience, to such a point that we can no longer separate ourselves from it and seek to increase its force. That is why we enjoy the society of the one it represents, since the presence of the object that it expresses, by making us actually perceive it, sets it off more. On the other hand, we will suffer from all circumstances which, like absence or death, may have as effect the barring of its return or the diminishing of its vivacity.

Conflicting Interests between Men and Women in Marriage

Accordingly, the following law may be regarded as beyond dispute: *From the standpoint of suicide, marriage is more favorable to the wife the more widely practiced divorce is; and vice versa.*

From this proposition, two consequences flow.

First, only husbands contribute to the rise in the suicide rate observable in societies where divorces are frequent, wives on the contrary committing suicide more rarely than elsewhere. If, then, divorce can only develop with the improvement of woman's moral situation, it cannot be connected with an unfavorable state of domestic society calculated to aggravate the tendency to suicide; for such an aggravation should occur in the case of the wife, as well as of the husband. A lowering of family morale cannot have such opposite effects on the two sexes: it cannot both favor the mother and seriously afflict the father. Consequently, the cause of the phenomenon which we are studying is found in the state of marriage and not in the constitution of the family. And indeed, marriage may very possibly act in an opposite way on husband and wife. For though they have the same object as parents, as partners their interests are different and often hostile.

In certain societies therefore, some peculiarity of the matrimonial institution may very well benefit one and harm the other. All of the above tends to show that this is precisely the case with divorce.

Secondly, for the same reason we have to reject the hypothesis that this unfortunate state of marriage, with which divorces and suicides are closely connected, is simply caused by more frequent domestic disputes; for no such cause could increase the woman's immunity, any more than could the loosening of the family tie. If, where divorce is common, the number of suicides really depends on the number of conjugal disputes, the wife should suffer from them as much as the husband. There is nothing in this situation to afford her exceptional immunity. The hypothesis is the less tenable since divorce is usually asked for by the wife from the husband (in France, 60 per cent of divorces and 83 per cent of separations). Accordingly, domestic troubles are most often attributable to the man. Then, however, it would not be clear why, in countries of frequent divorce, the husband kills himself with greater frequency because he causes his wife more suffering, and the wife kills herself less often because her husband makes her suffer more.

Nor is it proven that the number of conjugal dissensions increases in the same measure with divorce.

If we discard this hypothesis, only one other remains possible. The institution of divorce must itself cause suicide through its effect on marriage.

After all, what is marriage? A regulation of sexual relations, including not merely the physical instincts which this intercourse involves but the feelings of every sort gradually engrafted by civilization on the foundation of physical desire. For among us love is a far more mental than organic fact. A man looks to a woman, not merely to the satisfaction of the sexual impulse. Though this natural proclivity has been the germ of all sexual evolution, it has become increasingly complicated with aesthetic and moral feelings, numerous and varied, and today it is only the smallest element of the total complex process to which it has given birth. Under the influence of these intellectual elements it has itself been partially freed from its physical nature and assumed something like an intellectual one. Moral reasons as well as physical needs impel love. Hence, it no longer has the regular, automatic periodicity which it displays in animals. A psychological impulse may awaken it at any time: it is not seasonal. But just because these various inclinations, thus changed, do not directly depend upon organic necessities, social regulation becomes necessary. They must be restrained by society since the organism has no means of restraining them. This is the function of marriage. It completely regulates the life of passion, and monogamic marriage more strictly than any other. For by forcing a man to attach himself forever to the same woman it assigns a strictly definite object to the need for love, and closes the horizon.

This determination is what forms the state of moral equilibrium from which the husband benefits. Being unable to seek other satisfactions than those permitted, without transgressing his duty, he restricts his desires to them. The salutary discipline to which he is subjected makes it his duty to find his happiness in his lot, and by doing so supplies him with the means. Besides, if his passion is forbidden to stray, its fixed object is forbidden to fail him; the obligation is reciprocal. Though his enjoyment is restricted, it is assured and this certainty forms his mental foundation. The lot of the unmarried man is different. As he has the right to form attachment wherever inclination leads him, he aspires to everything and is satisfied with nothing. This morbid desire for the infinite which everywhere accompanies anomy may as readily assail this as any other part of our consciousness; it very often assumes a sexual form which was described by Musset. When one is no longer checked, one becomes unable to check one's self. Beyond experienced pleasures one senses and desires others; if one happens almost to have exhausted the range of what is possible, one dreams of the impossible; one thirsts for the non-existent. How can the feelings not be exacerbated by such unending pursuit? For them to reach that state, one need not even have infinitely multiplied the experiences of love and lived the life of a Don Juan. The humdrum existence of the ordinary bachelor suffices. New hopes constantly awake, only to be deceived, leaving a trail of weariness and disillusionment behind them. How can desire, then, become fixed, being uncertain that it can retain what it attracts; for the anomy is twofold. Just as the person makes no definitive gift of himself, he has definitive title to nothing. The uncertainty of the future plus his own indeterminateness therefore condemns him to constant change. The result of it all is a state of disturbance, agitation and discontent which inevitably increases the possibilities of suicide.

Now divorce implies a weakening of matrimonial regulation. Where it exists, and especially where law and custom permit its excessive practice, marriage is nothing but a weakened simulacrum of itself; it is an inferior form of marriage. It cannot produce its useful effects to the same degree. Its restraint upon desire is weakened; since it is more easily disturbed and superceded, it controls passion less and passion tends to rebel. It consents less readily to its assigned limit. The moral calmness and tranquillity which were the husband's strength are less; they are replaced to some extent by an uneasiness which keeps a man from being satisfied with what he has. Besides, he is the less inclined to become attached to his present state as his enjoyment of it is not completely sure: the future is less certain. One cannot be strongly restrained by a chain which may be broken on one side or the other at any moment. One cannot help looking beyond one's own position when the ground underfoot does not feel secure. Hence, in the countries where marriage is strongly tempered by divorce, the immunity of the married man is inevitably less. As he resembles the unmarried under this regime, he inevitably loses some of his own advantages. Consequently, the total number of suicides rises.

But this consequence of divorce is peculiar to the man and does not affect the wife. Woman's sexual needs have less of a mental character because, generally speaking, her mental life is less developed. These needs are more closely related to the needs of the organism, following rather than leading them, and consequently find in them an efficient restraint. Being a more instinctive creature than man, woman has only to follow her instincts to find calmness and peace. She thus does not require so strict a social regulation as marriage, and particularly as monogamic marriage. Even when useful, such a discipline has its inconveniences. By fixing the conjugal state permanently, it prevents all retreat, regardless of consequences. By limiting the horizon, it closes all egress and

forbids even legitimate hope. Man himself doubtless suffers from this immutability; but for him the evil is largely compensated by the advantages he gains in other respects. Custom, moreover, grants him certain privileges which allow him in some measure to lessen the strictness of the regime. There is no compensation or relief for the woman. Monogamy is strictly obligatory for her, with no qualification of any sort, and, on the other hand, marriage is not in the same degree useful to her for limiting her desires, which are naturally limited, and for teaching her to be contented with her lot; but it prevents her from changing it if it becomes intolerable. The regulation therefore is a restraint to her without any great advantages. Consequently, everything that makes it more flexible and lighter can only better the wife's situation. So divorce protects her and she has frequent recourse to it. . . .

We saw that marriage in France, by itself and irrespective of family, gives man a coefficient of preservation of 1.5. We know now to what this coefficient corresponds. It represents the advantages obtained by a man from the regulative influence exerted upon him by marriage, from the moderation it imposes on his inclinations and from his consequent moral well-being. But at the same time we noted that in the same country the condition of a married woman was, on the contrary, made worse with respect to suicide unless the advent of children corrects the ill effects of marriage for her. We have just stated the reason. Not that man is naturally a wicked and egoistic being whose role in a household is to make his companion suffer. But in France where, until recently, marriage was not weakened by divorce, the inflexible rule it imposed on women was a very heavy, profitless yoke for them. Speaking generallly, we now have the cause of that antagonism of the sexes which prevents marriage favoring them equally: their interests are contrary; one needs restraint and the other liberty.

Furthermore, it does seem that at a certain time of life man is affected by marriage in the same way as woman, though for different reasons. If, as we have shown, very young husbands kill themselves much more often than unmarried men of the same age, it is doubtless because their passions are too vehement at that period and too self-confident to be subjected to so severe a rule. Accordingly, this rule seems to them an unendurable obstacle against which their desire dashes and is broken. This is probably why marriage produces all its beneficent effects only when age, supervening, tempers man somewhat and makes him feel the need of discipline.

Finally, . . . we saw that where marriage favors the wife rather than the husband, the difference between the sexes is always less than when the reverse is true. This proves that, even in those societies where the status of matrimony is wholly in the woman's favor, it does her less service than it does man where it is he that profits more by it.

Woman can suffer more from marriage if it is unfavorable to her than she can benefit by it if it conforms to her interest. This is because she has less need of it. This is the assumption of the theory just set forth. The results obtained previously and those arising from the present chapter therefore combine and check each other mutually.

Thus we reach a conclusion quite different from the current idea of marriage and its role. It is supposed to have been originated for the wife, to protect her weakness against masculine caprice. Monogamy, especially, is often represented as a sacrifice made by man of his polygamous instincts, to raise and improve woman's condition in marriage. Actually, whatever historical causes may have made him accept this restriction, he benefits more by it. The liberty he thus renounces could only be a source of torment to him. Woman did not have the same reasons to abandon it and, in this sense, we may say that by submitting to the same rule, it was she who made a sacrifice.

Lester Frank Ward (1841–1913) on the Condition of Women

Lester Frank Ward was an important founder of American sociology, highly respected and influential in his time. He published many articles, lectured widely, and produced several very influential books, including *Dynamic Sociology* (1883), *Pure Sociology* (1903), and *Applied Sociology* (1906). His reputation in the United States can be gauged by the fact that in 1906 he was elected the first president of the American Sociological Society. Moreover, his books were translated into multiple languages, and he corresponded with some of the leading sociologists in Europe. In addition, he was elected president of the Institut International de Sociologie in Paris for 1905, partly on the basis of his major contributions to the 1900 Paris Exhibition on World Progress.

Born in Joliet, Illinois, in 1841, Ward's family barely eked out a living through hard physical labor. According to one chronicler, his early poverty and difficult frontier life "instilled in Ward an outrage at society's injustice and inequalities" (Abell, 2001). Most of Ward's career was spent as a paleo-botanist working for federal agencies in Washington, DC. His interest in sociology developed independently, and only in his last years he obtained a position teaching sociology at Brown University, his only academic post. Yet his influence on the origins of sociology in this country can hardly be exaggerated.

Ward's writings came to be neglected by later sociologists, perhaps because of his strongly progressive and critical leanings, including his pro-feminist stance. He devoted a large portion of his major work to the question of sex inequality, but this was not popular with the sociologists who dominated the field in the 1920s to the 1950s. Ward's evolutionary assumptions also became outmoded by that time, but the scholars who created the canon of sociological origins remembered and preserved the more extreme and laissez-faire evolutionism of Herbert Spencer and William Graham Sumner, while discounting the work of Ward, which in fact is closer in many ways to that of contemporary thinkers. When Ward is remembered today, it is mainly for his notion that social progress should be guided by research and planning, not allowed to "evolve" with no human intervention, as Spencer and Sumner had claimed. However, his work on class, race, and gender is perhaps just as significant, especially given the climate in which he wrote. Ward saw himself as a "man of science," but he believed strongly that scientific knowledge should be put to use in the effort to guide society toward more humane and progressive goals. These goals included improving the condition of women, a condition that he strongly criticized in several of his books.

MAJOR WORKS

Ward, Lester Frank. *Dynamic Sociology*. 2 Vols. New York: Appleton, 1883/1897.
————. *The Psychic Factors of Civilization*. New York: Ginn, 1899.
————. *Pure Sociology: A Treatise on the Origin and Spontaneous Development of Society*. London: Macmillan, 1903.
————. *Applied Sociology*. New York: Ginn, 1906.

SOURCES

Abell, Guy. Lester Frank Ward: Bradford County's Aristotle. *Towanda Daily Review,* June 10, 2001. http://www.rootsweb.com/~srgp/histmark/wardmark.htm (accessed February 14, 2005).
Barnes, Harry Elmer. 1948. Lester Frank Ward: The reconstruction of society by social science. *An Introduction to the History of Sociology,* ed. in Harry Elmer Barnes, 173–90. Chicago: Univ. Chicago Press.
Bierstedt, Robert. 1981. Lester Frank Ward. In *American Sociological Theory: A Critical History,* 45–87. New York: Academic Press.
Finlay, Barbara. 1999. Lester Frank Ward as a sociologist of gender: A new look at his sociological work. *Gender & Society* 13 (2): 251–65.

THE SELECTION

This excerpt is from Lester Frank Ward's first major publication, *Dynamic Sociology*—the first major sociological work published in the United States by an American author. The book's reception was at first disappointing to Ward, but over the years it gained an international reputation, even being banned (and burned) by the Tsarist government of Russia for being too radical. In the reading, Ward describes some of the problems of inequality women have faced, and he turns his attention to thinking about the possibility of sex equality. His analysis includes attention to inequalities in various realms: dress, duties, education, and rights. He draws on Darwinian theory to explain the origins of these differences, but he does not see them as inevitable or just. In a fascinating section Ward imagines what a society would look like "if women were recognized social equals of men." Among other things, he argues that "women would share all the varied occupations and professions" that men hold, and there would be no differences in the education of the sexes.

From Lester Frank Ward, *Dynamic Sociology* (New York: Appleton, 1883), 1:641–63.

In the final section, Ward takes "scientific men" to task for their failure to support progressive change in the area of sexual inequality, and especially for their specious reasoning in supporting the status quo. In the concluding section, one can clearly see Ward's difference from Spencer and other laissez-faire authors, in his claim that "all true social progress is artificial," not the result of natural processes. The aim of science, in Ward's view, should be to improve on the wasteful and amoral processes of nature and to guide social development in progressive and humane directions.

THE CONDITION OF WOMEN
Sociological Effects

If we take a general view of our sexuo-social system, we find men and women living together under special and peculiar rules of conduct, occupying separate spheres of activity, and subjected to separate and distinct social conditions. In a word, we find that society has erected a high barrier between the sexes, so that, although they live together, meet each other constantly, and appear to be companions, they are in fact dwelling in separate elements and on different planes.

SEXUO-SOCIAL INEQUALITIES

It is this general inequality which exists in the social position of the two sexes which especially interests us at present. It is too striking to be overlooked in an inquiry into the conditions of social progress, and, although a portion of it may be regarded as but the natural correlate to their physical inequality, the greater part must be accounted for in some other way. The inequalities which society has established between the sexes may be variously classified. The principal ones may be approximately ranged under the following heads: 1, inequality of dress; 2, inequality of duties; 3, inequality of education; and, 4, inequality of rights. Let us glance at each of these inequalities separately.

Inequality of Dress

In all civilized countries the men dress differently from the women. There seems to be a tendency in society to separate the sexes by some distinguishing mark which enables people to determine the sex of one another at sight. Nature has done the same thing, it is true, through selection. The plumage of birds and the fur of animals are usually different in the males from what they are in the females. Mr. Darwin offers a very ingenious explanation of all this. So the physical appearance of the sexes in the human species differs in many important respects, only a few of which are explainable by their different habits. The absence of the beard in woman and the difference between the male and the female voice are among the best marked of these physical inequalities. Difference of stature, complexion, physical strength, and intellectual vigor may all be more or less satisfactorily accounted for by the difference in their respective social conditions and life, either as imposed by nature or by custom. And man has sought to imitate nature in this respect by clothing the sexes differently.

It is not probable, however, that the custom of dressing one sex differently from the other grew out of any attempt to copy from nature, and the process was certainly wholly unlike the selective processes of nature. If we will examine the matter closely, we shall discover that the dress of women resembles in its general design that of uncivilized races far more than does that of men. It is more as both sexes originally dressed, before the art had been improved upon and adapted to practical wants. Modifications and refinements in the dress of women took the direction of embellishment, while those of men tended toward utility. And thus, while the demands of active life have worked out for man a comparatively convenient and at the same time comely habit, the conditions which surrounded woman, while they have made clothing a means of loading her with ornaments, have left her in the same or in many respects in a worse condition, as regards her adaptation to active usefulness, than in the beginning. Nor has it been altogether because she has been inactive and useless to the industrial world that her mode of dress has not been improved, for she is generally compelled to perform her full share of the labor, especially of the lowest and most purely physical forms of it. It is due rather to her dependent and subordinate place in society which rendered her incapable of making innovations in behalf of her own sex.

The inactive state of the women of the middle and upper classes, however, is doubtless in great part produced by the inconvenient and unmanageable character of their dress; and the refinements which the rich, and some not so rich, have learned to load themselves down with, are the cause of an enormous amount of disease and suffering, and threaten to work a permanent physical deterioration of the race. The dress of men is not in all respects what it should be, but that of women is certainly the disgrace of civilization.

Inequality of Duties

Next with regard to the inequality of duties. Independently of the duties of maternity, the sphere of woman's activity is wholly different from that of man's. If we grant that there is a certain natural connection between the bearing of offspring and the care of the household, which is probably true, there remains a chasm to be filled in order to equalize the duties of the two sexes. Among savages it is usually the women who perform all the real work of their societies. This they do in addition to their maternal and domestic duties. Among the lower classes of so-called civilized society, the case is almost the same. In Germany, women till the soil and tend the flocks, as of yore. Nearly all the menial service in Europe is performed by women. In our large cities thousands of women toil to support families, including often their indolent and inebriate husbands. Go into the great factories and see what proportion of the operatives are women. Consider the thousands of women who make their living, and a very scanty one, by their needle. Yet the most of these have their domestic duties to perform in addition to this labor. We see, then, how false is the assertion that men perform the labor of support, while women confine themselves to maternal and domestic duties. Women who profess to confine themselves to these duties usually seek in every way to escape them, and render themselves unfit to perform them by their devotion to fashion. This is because society has established two arbitrary sets of duties, and insists that woman can not perform the one and that man should not perform the other. This fact alone is a proof of the inferiority which society ascribes to woman, since it assigns her duties which it confesses are beneath the dignity of male labor. At the same time every attempt made by the more courageous of the female sex to encroach upon the domain of man, and seek to perform the duties which he has assigned to himself, is met by the chivalric remonstrance that men's duties are too severe for the delicate constitutions of the mothers of the race! Now, all this is excessively transparent and false, and indicates that it is not nature at all, but society, that has assigned to woman her duties.

If the delicacy of the female constitution is an objection to the admission of women to the harvest-field and the machine-shop, it is equally an objection to her admission to the laundry and the factory. If maternal and domestic duties are all that women can attend to in England, why can they attend to agricultural duties in Germany, pastoral duties in Switzerland, and mercantile duties in France? It will not be said that in these countries the men perform all the household duties.

But it is claimed that woman should by nature preside over the in-door interests and man over the out-door ones. This is probably the most fatal dogma to the health of woman and to the physical condition of the race which can be found in the whole social creed. It is in effect to assert that nature has designed woman to breathe carbonic acid and man oxygen; that sunlight is poisonous to woman, but exhilarating to all other animate beings; and that physical exercise, which is so necessary to the health of every other living thing, is fatal to the female portion of the human species. It is to make woman, in regard to her place and her duties, as she is made in regard to her dress, an entire exception to all the rules of hygiene. If this vicious dogma that woman's place is in the house is persisted in for a few more centuries, there can be no escape from a general physical and intellectual degeneracy of the whole human race.

Inequality of Education

The third and not less important inequality between the sexes is that of education. Not content with shutting woman out of all opportunities for gaining knowledge by experience, society has seen fit to debar her also from the knowledge acquired by instruction. She has been pronounced incapable of coping with man in intellectual contests, and it has not, therefore, been thought worth while to provide her mind with any considerable amount of information. It seems to have been regarded as fitting to have woman's fund of knowledge correspond in quantity to the variety of her duties and be characterized by the same limitation. Her knowledge from instruction has, therefore, only kept pace with her knowledge from experience. Ignoring the important truth that all instruction is profitable to society, ignoring the fact that most of the knowledge imparted to men by educational processes is wholly within the capacity of women to acquire also, society has established schools and school systems for the education of the former, leaving the latter in their natural state of ignorance. Deprived, therefore, for ages of all facilities either of experience or instruction, woman presents herself to the wisdom of this age as a dwarfed and inferior being, destitute of both intellectual energy and intellectual aspiration. For it is in these two respects that her inferiority is chiefly manifest. It is these that produce originality and independence in intellectual labor, and it is originality and independence which distinguish masculine from feminine thought. Granting, as we probably must, with Herbert Spencer, that the gestative process and that of supplying nourishment to infants are at the expense, to some extent, of the intellectual as they certainly are of the physical strength of women, it is certain that, in view of the social condition of woman in the present and in the past, the difference now, however fairly shown to exist, between the intellects of the sexes, can by no means be taken as a criterion of their true relative merits. The fact that, wherever the youth of both sexes are permitted to vie with each other under equal circumstances, no marked average inferiority is observed in the females, is one of vital importance, and proves far more than the other fact that the males are more likely to distinguish themselves in after-life, since in women the spirit has been crushed and the opportunity denied.

Inequality of Rights

Lastly, we find an inequality of rights. And here, as every-where else, this inequality exists to the advantage of the males and to the disadvantage of the females. In all civilized countries the laws have been framed so as to discriminate severely against the personal and proprietary rights of women. Both in civil and political affairs they are usually without redress and without voice, and in the legislature they have always been without representation except by men, while in countries where representatives are chosen by suffrage, this simplest but most valuable of all rights has been persistently withheld. It is as a citizen that woman's position has reached its lowest and most dependent state, she being literally ignored in all matters relating to law or government.

We see therefore, generally, that, whether it be in matters of dress, of labor, of education, or of right, it is the female sex which has had to suffer from the discrimination. The clothing of the male sex is better, more convenient, more comfortable, more healthful. The duties of men are more agreeable, more dignified, more varied, and more interesting. Man's education is more general, more thorough, more profound. The rights of men are comparatively ample, liberal, and manifold. These are facts which, though they may bring the blush to the cheek of a truly chivalrous man, possess the highest interest for the thoughtful and philosophic student of society.

Genesis of Sexuo-social Inequalities

But it was not to deplore them that we have brought them forward in this place. It was rather for the purpose of inquiring into their causes, and establishing if possible a genesis of their existence in society. The first step in any investigation is the discovery and recognition of the facts which bear upon the subject of it. In social matters these facts often stand out in full view without being recognized. The power of custom and the bias of conservatism make us all blind to their existence. The tendency to convert custom into right often makes those facts appear just and equitable which are unjust and despicable. The fear of losing what is good blinds us to what is bad, and men often cling to the very system which makes them its victims. It is thus that society, which includes both sexes, remains incapable of recognizing the patent fact that one sex is in a condition of inequality with the other, that woman is dependent upon man, and that the female sex is in a state of subjection to the male sex. Voltaire's Jovian visitor[1] would be sure at once to observe with astonishment that the inhabitants of this planet were divided into two great castes, dependent on a physical condition which they could not control, and those who had the misfortune to be born females were doomed to perpetual tutelage or servitude to the higher caste of males. And the inferior position of woman, maintained through so many ages, has actually resulted in rendering her both physically and mentally inferior to man.

THE SUBJECTION OF WOMEN

I have classed the inequalities between the sexes under the first great division of the social results of the reproductive forces, as being chiefly due to the operations of the

---

[1]"Philosophic," vol. 1. ("Œuvres complètes," tome xxxii), p. 15.

love-passion—to feeling—and not to those of reproductive processes—to function. The first step toward the subjugation of the female sex was the conquest by the males of her prerogative of selection. This was the surrender of her *virtue* in the primary sense of the term—of her *power* over men, over society, over her own interests. But this crisis was brought on wholly by the force of male passion. It was a victory for male indulgence. Won by the aid of strategy and of superior mental power, it not only secured the result aimed at, but it led to the dominion of man over woman. It is one of the few instances where nature seems to have overshot its mark. The very excess of passion with which man (along with the males of all other species) is endowed, and which was apparently designed to prevent the possibility of the failure of reproduction, became, when coupled with this increased mind-force incident to a certain stage of intellectual development, the means of effecting the most extensive and systematic violations of natural laws, and of imposing serious barriers to reproduction itself. Nothing but its very gradual introduction and the slow habituation of woman to the change could have saved the whole race from extinction before the dawn of civilization. Again, the sexual passion in man was one cause of a more rapid intellectual development in him than in woman. Superior cunning, *i.e.,* sharper wits, may be regarded as a secondary sexual character as much as the tusks of the boar or the spurs of the cock.[2] Whatever was necessary to insure success in courtship was sure to be developed, and, when cunning became a safe weapon, it rapidly increased in the males until they outstripped the females in vigor of intellect.

It is undoubtedly true that the weaker physical condition of women during the period of gestation and parturition did much to give the advantage to the males. Although we do not perceive any special disposition on the part of other female animals at these times to make themselves dependent upon the males, we can readily understand how, with a higher development of the intellect, and especially of the sensibilities, they might learn to do so. In so far as this has been the case, the present dependent state of women upon men is to be referred to the second great class of results of the operations of the social forces.

But, to follow out the first line of development, we find that woman has already made her first great surrender, and permitted man to become the chooser in the matter of sexual unions instead of herself. He could not stop here. We have seen how the various systems of marriage grew up out of this fundamental fact. Woman at once becomes property, since any thing that affords its possessor gratification is property. Woman was capable of affording man the highest of gratifications, and therefore became property of the highest value. Marriage, under the prevailing form, became the symbol of transfer of ownership, in the same manner as the formal seizing of lands. The passage from sexual service to manual service on the part of women was perfectly natural. If woman was man's property for sexual purposes he would certainly claim that she was so also for all other purposes, and thus we find that the women of most savage tribes perform the manual and servile labor of the camp.

In the earliest ages, when nations were devoted to continual warfare, the duties of men were defined, and, while the women were left behind to care for the children and perform the baser services, the men went forth to war, or took upon them the affairs of the state. This distribution of the labor of

---

[2]Darwin, "Descent of Man," vol. 1, p. 246.

the sexes has always been preserved, as nearly as the state of society would permit. No moral or intellectual progress has been sufficient to shake it. The broad recognition of the social equality of the sexes has never been distinctly and practically made. All pretensions to it have been contradicted by the treatment of women, by their exclusion from the most honorable forms of labor, and by withholding from them social, civil, and political rights. To affirm that women are the recognized social equals of men is to betray the prevalent incapacity to see the plainest facts in a rational or abstract light, the inability to see them in any but a conventional light.

If women were the recognized social equals of men, we should see a very different state of society from that which now exists. We should, in the first place, see men and women wearing nearly or quite the same kind of dress. The slight modifications necessary to adapt the dress of each sex to its peculiar physical constitution would not be sufficient to make the difference noticeable, and would not, as now, make the form of dress a badge of sex. For it can not be urged that the present dress of woman is rendered necessary by reason of its adaptation to her physical constitution. The least acquaintance with the comparative physiology of the sexes, on the contrary, is sufficient to show that it is precisely the reverse—that, if either sex can afford to wear heavy skirts hanging from the hips and wrenching the loins, it is the male; that, if either sex needs the lower extremities and parts of the body thoroughly protected from exposure to currents of cold air, it is the female; that the practice of lacing the waist would be far less fatal to man than to woman, with her delicate uterine system so liable to displacement. And, even if nothing but the mere question of modesty were considered, it would be more proper for woman than for man to wear clothing to fit the body.

If the social equality of the sexes were recognized, we should see men and women performing substantially the same duties. In uncivilized races the drudgery and the honorable activities would be equally distributed between them. In civilized countries women would share all the varied occupations and professions with their husbands and brothers. There would be found very few avenues to wealth or happiness which women would be incapacitated to enter from purely physical reasons. There are, indeed, very few of them that women have not in some rare cases actually entered and successfully labored in. But, if their true equality were recognized, it would not be left for the few who dared to defy the rules of propriety to step forth into fields of usefulness to labor by the side of man. Not only would the duties, labors, and occupations of men be shared by women, but their pastimes, recreations, and pleasures as well. We should not see man amusing himself alone and in his own way, or in the society of men only, nor should we see women striving to become happy in the society of their own sex, and to derive pleasure from sources peculiarly their own, to which men are entire strangers. We should see a community of enjoyments, not differing materially, perhaps, from the present, but in which both sexes would join, adding to the animation which they otherwise afford the lively relish of sexual companionship. The present system, both of labor and of recreation, is calculated to bring out the worst side of sexuality. The separate duties and spheres in which the two sexes labor and move tend to render the desire for association a prurient one. The varied restraints of propriety and modesty have the effect of fanning human passions into a flame, and a consequence of this is that both sexes are liable to be whelmed in a vortex of crime, and their character and usefulness ruined. Equality in all respects would prove a certain antidote to all these social evils. It would do far more. It would transfer to the list of productive laborers the legion of women who now deem themselves wholly justified in occupying a position of dependency upon man, and consuming the fruits of his labor without adding the value of a loaf of bread to the wealth of the world. For this non-producing condition of civilized women is an anomaly in the animal world, and even among human races. Among the lower animals the labor of procuring subsistence is performed for the most part by each individual for itself, the males and females doing an equal share of the labor of life. This, also, seems to be substantially the case among the very lowest human beings; but, very early in the progress of the race, this becomes changed, so that most savages have a system in which the greater part of the industrial pursuits are carried on by the women, the men devoting themselves only to war and the chase; though of course both these, and particularly the latter, furnish the means of subsistence to some extent. This stage extends down into semi-civilized peoples and warlike races of all kinds. It is, however, succeeded by a stage in which every thing is reversed in these respects, and, theoretically at least, all industrial operations, war, and the chase devolve upon men alone, women being restricted to the reproductive function, and to that of being ornamental. In theory, this is the present system in civilized communities, but the manifest impossibility of carrying out the theory greatly heightens the evils of woman's condition.

The true progress of society must eventually complete the cycle of changes thus begun, and again make both sexes producers, as in the animal and pre-social stages.

If the equality of the sexes were recognized, we should see both sexes educated alike. We should see women admitted along with men, not merely to the common schools, but to all the higher institutions of learning, to the professions and to the technical departments. We should see the principle applied that it is mind which needs instruction, not male mind. Men and women would then stand on an equal intellectual footing, and intellectual superiority, without regard to which sex it appeared in, would receive its just recognition. Then, if woman fell below, it would be just to infer a natural deficiency. Had the same opportunities and the same restraints existed for both sexes from the beginning, it would then be possible to judge of their relative merits.

If the equality of the sexes had been frankly recognized, both would have been accorded the same rights. Not only would both sexes have labored together in the great duty, along with others, of framing, interpreting, and executing the laws of society, but both would have enjoyed the same protection and advantages under those laws, and both would have been represented in all the branches of government by the same mode of representation, whatever that might be. Nor is it alone in political affairs that equal rights would have been extended. The social rights withheld from women are, if possible, worse than these. For under the head of rights may be ranged all the sexual inequalities named, and all that may be named. Education, industry, nay, even dress, are all of the nature of rights. To alight woman's education, to degrade and circumscribe her sphere of duty, to dress her with burdensome and unsanitary clothes—all these are deprivations of right of the most grievous nature. For every mind has a right to knowledge, every one has a right to choose his duties, and certainly all have the right so to clothe themselves as best to promote their comfort and successful activity.

But there are still higher rights, there is a still greater liberty which society withholds from one half its members. It is the right to themselves, the liberty of controlling their own persons, the possession of their own bodies. What a commentary upon professed civilization is the claim that the inactivity of the female sex is necessary to protect them from exposure to personal violence; that they can not pursue the free and honorable duties of men because thereby they would be exposed to insult! Or, if this be not feared, how shallow is the other plea that, if engaged in other duties than those to which society has restricted her, woman's modesty might be shocked by contact with the vulgar world! To so fine a point has this artificial sentiment been reduced! And this would be the place to show that it is this sentiment, more than any thing else, which has worked the degradation, the subjection, and the social enslavement of woman. To protect her from the rude advances of others, to preserve her in all purity for the use of her owner—these are the prime factors in the accomplishment of woman's present dependent condition.

I can not enter into a thorough discussion of the precise links which connect this whole train of social phenomena. I have outlined the genesis of modesty, and gone back to the origin of all the sexual inequalities. I leave it to the reader to fill in the web of circumstances and conditions which must have attended the slow evolution of these social conditions. I will only say, in concluding this theme, that the result of all these tendencies has been to separate and socially alienate the sexes; that, while the conditions of reproduction, not less than the power of the sexual appetite, naturally draw them toward each other, and must, under any and all circumstances, always keep them bound together indissolubly by bonds of sentiment, affection, passion, and interest, still the vast and ever-widening inequalities which have grown up between them tend to draw them asunder, and make their association and cohabitation more and more those of mere instinct and less and less those of genuine companionship. Incapable, on account of dress, of modesty, and of social custom, of sharing each other's labors or amusements, but compelled by such conditions to plod the path of life alone, each grows less and less necessary to the other, until all congeniality disappears, and marriage itself becomes a conventional formality. Incapable, in consequence of unequal education, of enjoying any intellectual communion, each seems tame to the other, and nothing is left of the conjugal relation but the mere animal gratifications. While the bodies of the two sexes will doubtless always continue to cling together, their souls are drifting apart, and the very elixir of human existence is being wasted upon the most unsubstantial frivolities and conventionalities. The great need of society is to be aroused to these facts, to be awakened to a new sense of the true and the genuine in life, and of the vanity and worthlessness of all forms and fashions not based on the severest rationality, and capable of withstanding the most critical analysis. The one thing which would confer a greater blessing than any other upon society, would be to open its eyes to the exact position which it has reached in its march, and to inspire it with a realizing sense of the wide departure it has made from the normal condition.

It is in the sexual department of social phenomena that the most glaring inconsistencies exist, and that the worst evils have been allowed to develop. It is to show this, and, as far as possible, to account for it, that I have entered into the consideration of the reproductive forces and their effects upon the human race. I realize both the importance and the delicacy of the subject, and hope I have not wholly failed in its elucidation.

The Male Sex Not Responsible

In what has been said respecting the dependent and almost servile social condition of the female sex, I should be sorry to be misunderstood upon one point where I fear I may have left room for an unjust inference. Although I have been careful to avoid all allusion to the question of who is responsible for this condition of things, I am aware that the human mind is prone to infer that where matters are bad some one must be to blame, and to assume that, where a state of things is so organized as to discriminate against one class and in favor of another, the class which derives the benefit must somehow be responsible; and I have feared that for these reasons some of my readers might class me in the list of those who see in the male sex only a confederacy of usurpers and tyrants, who do nothing but seek for further means of humiliating and subjugating the female sex for their own gratification and emolument. If any have been inclined to accuse me of this species of *misandry,* they need simply to be reminded that I have been only seeking to study the condition of society, not to criticise the conduct of its members. If there is any responsibility in a sociological phenomenon, it must rest upon society as a whole. If there is one social fact which has received the sanction and approval of all classes of society, it is the existing relations of the sexes. If there is an evil in the world for which nobody is to blame, it is the inequality of the sexes. If there is an illustration of the victims of an injurious system countenancing and upholding that system, it exists in the case of women and the system which holds them down. The mere handful of enlightened protesters, who have become aroused within the past few years to a vague sense of their true condition, is but the very embryo of the movement which would be required to accomplish the emancipation of woman. And it is not so much experience as philosophy which is agitating the question. The victims of the system are usually silent, or, if they speak, it is but the bitter language of discontent unsupported by the philosophic

analysis of the subject which can alone give weight to their utterances. The greatest champions of social reform are, and will always be, those who possess the capacity to grasp great social truths and an insight into human nature and the causes of social phenomena deep enough to kindle a genuine sympathy, and a sound, rational philanthropy. This phenomenon, like all others, is the result of causes operating through innumerable ages, and for which there is no more responsibility than there is for the physical transformations which species undergo from the operations of similar causes during still more immense periods. And, although the results may be bad and entail evil upon society, though they be irrational, absurd, and pernicious, they are none the less due to causes sufficient in their time to produce them, and their genesis, or true explanation, though perhaps too obscure for man ever to unfold, would still be traceable to their earliest origin if all the circumstances could be known. A state of society, if it be bad for one class, is bad for all. Woman is scarcely a greater sufferer from her condition than man is, and there is, therefore, nothing either improper or inexplicable in man's espousing the cause of woman's emancipation. The freedom of woman will be the ennoblement of man. The equality of the sexes will be the regeneration of humanity. Civilization demands this revolution. It stands in the greatest need of the help which the female sex alone can vouchsafe. Woman is half of mankind. Civilization and progress have hitherto been carried forward by the male half alone. Labor and production are now also suffering from the same cause. It is high time that all the forces of society were brought into action, and it is especially necessary that those vast complementary forces which woman alone can wield be given free rein, and the whole machinery of society be set into full and harmonious operation.

ATTITUDE OF SCIENCE TOWARD THE EQUALIZATION OF WOMAN'S CONDITION

The general movement recently set on foot by the most advanced societies, for the elevation and amelioration of the condition of women, is obviously and confessedly crude. It is still in that stage, common to all progressive movements, in which only irresponsible persons will venture to espouse it, through fear of obloquy; one of the necessary results of which is that among its votaries there are numbered many fanatics on the one hand and charlatans on the other. It has as yet scarcely emerged from the stage of ridicule into that of sober argument. It is still almost completely under the influence of feeling, and is little subject to the control of reason.

In this condition it greatly needs aid from science, and it should be the aim of scientific men, particularly of those who regard the phenomena of society as legitimate scientific data, to furnish so truly progressive a movement with a basis of facts and fundamental principles, thus lending it a tone of serious import and respectability, while at the same time turning it from its manifest errors and directing it into rational and practical channels.

The few true philosophers who have sought to accomplish this object, however, have been disappointed to find that scientific men in general do not rise to their standpoint, while many true advocates of social progress in other things do not think that the relations of the sexes can be rendered more perfect than they are.

It is especially unfortunate to find that the present *status* in this respect is actually defended by arguments from sciences more simple than sociology. Certain facts in biology are cited, and these are assumed to prove that the existing condition of things is a *natural* one, and in all respects analogous to that which exists in the animal world below man.

It is argued that in most mammals the female is in many respects inferior to the male, and performs different functions; that in birds and many other lower creatures the males are more beautiful, larger, more sagacious, and are exempt from the more unpleasant labors incident to the rearing and protection of the offspring. It is claimed that facts of this kind serve to point out the *purposes of Nature,* and it is assumed that whatever can be shown to be *natural* must be the best possible condition.

Arguments of this kind, coming from high scientific sources, have great weight, especially as those to whom they are chiefly addressed are incompetent, as a rule, to judge of the adequacy of the premises, and accept them as resting upon authority.

If it were worth while, it would be easy to deduce from natural history a large number of facts of precisely the opposite class, from which it might with equal force be argued that the purpose of Nature was to favor the females and slight the males. Indeed, it is a fundamental biological truth that, so far as the mere "purposes of Nature" are concerned, the fertile sex is of by far the greater importance, and this increased importance is abundantly shown throughout all the lower forms of life where these purposes are predominant. . . . In the animal world there are many equally forcible examples of Nature's favoritism of the female sex. . . .

But it must also be denied that the condition of the sexes among those animals in which the male is superior is at all analogous to that of men and women whether in their savage or civilized state. Just as the sexual differences in the former are derivative and anomalous, and due to the rise of the cerebral power, so those of the latter are as much more unnatural as that power is more pronounced in man than in animals. Especially is this true with regard to the respective duties of the sexes. In no animal do we find any such differences of function between the sexes as is presented by men, either savage or civilized. The males and females of all animals equally pursue the natural impulses which prompt them to activity, and in no case is it left for the females to perform all the labor necessary to maintain the physical life of both sexes, as is often the case with savages; nor does it ever occur that the female devotes her whole time to the rearing of offspring, while the male procures the subsistence for himself and her and brings her portion to her, which is the theory of the most civilized societies.

While, therefore, there is really no parallel and no analogy—and while, if there were, it would not indicate in the least what the purposes of Nature are in this respect (even if Nature had any purposes), but rather, so far as the paramount object of reproduction is concerned, would prove that, in proportion as female superiority is diminished, this object is defeated—I have nevertheless thought best, before considering the assumptions of this specious argument, so called, from science, to show that the facts themselves are wholly at fault.

Independently, however, of its false facts and false premises, this pretended scientific defense of the undue inequality of the sexes in man is fundamentally unsound in resting upon a thoroughly false assumption, which is only the more pernicious because widely prevalent. It assumes that whatever exists in nature must be the best possible state.

This sort of *scientific optimism* is, if possible, worse than theological optimism. There may be a certain sense in which "whatever is is right," but there is no ground whatever for asserting that whatever is natural is best. All true social progress is *artificial,* and this is just as true of laws and institutions as it is of machinery. All social as well as material progress must aim to alter and improve the old status, or it is no progress at all. Those nations which always point to their ancestors as types of all that is perfect are proverbially stagnant and effete. But what shall we say of scientific men—men who believe in a humble animal origin for the human race—when they point back to that animal world from which they sprang, for examples by which to justify some of the worst features of our still imperfect social relations!

The truth is, that, if they *could* find a parallel in biology or any other science for such a state of inequality, this would be no bar whatever to the attempt to ameliorate that state. The only practical use to which we put science is to *improve upon nature,* to control all classes of forces, social forces included, to the end of bettering the conditions under which we inhabit the earth. This is true civilization, and all of it. It is rather a disgrace to civilization—which has thus redeemed almost every thing else from the rude, wasteful, and heartless dominion of Nature—that it has left the relations of the sexes untouched, or has even aggravated in the human race those existing in the brute. But it is positively shameful, in such a state of things, for scientific men, Bourbon-like, to go back to the brute creation for standards of human excellence and models of social institutions.

We should congratulate ourselves that we are neither lions nor spiders nor yet cave-dwellers, but civilized men, and should seek so to shape the social policy that honor, justice, and equity should prevail, rather than the instincts of brutes or the caprices of savages.

Anna Julia Cooper (1858–1964) on the Voices of Women

Anna Julia Cooper was born into slavery in Raleigh, North Carolina—the daughter of a slave mother and her white "owner." In spite of her humble origins, her life and accomplishments show a remarkable persistence despite multiple social barriers and repeated obstacles. After emancipation Cooper received a teacher's education at the St. Augustine Normal School and Collegiate for Free Blacks, but she abandoned her dream of teaching in 1877 when she married George Cooper. Widowed within two years of marriage, she again took up her studies and teaching. In 1884 she received a bachelor's degree from Oberlin College in Ohio, followed by a master's degree four years later. She taught math and Latin for some years in an all-black school (M-Street High) in Washington, DC, serving at one point as the principal.

Sometimes referred to as a foremother of black feminism, Cooper published a major book on race and gender issues, *A Voice from the South*, in 1892. From this and other work, Cooper became internationally known as a spokesperson on social and racial issues.

Ever interested in her own educational advancement, from 1911 to 1913 she studied French history at the Guilde Internationale in Paris, and in 1914 she entered Columbia University for doctoral studies (at age fifty-six), while still teaching at M-Street High. The following year her studies were interrupted again by the necessity of adopting her half-brother's orphaned children. She was not able to return to her studies until a decade later, when, in 1924, she entered a year of residency at the Sorbonne. At that prestigious university, Cooper completed her doctorate in 1925 at the age of sixty-five, thus becoming the fourth African American woman to obtain a PhD.

Major Works

Cooper, Anna Julia. *A Voice from the South*. With an introduction by Mary Helen Washington. New York: Oxford University Press, 1988 (Orig. pub. 1892).

———. *Slavery and the French Revolutionists (1788–1805)*. Translated by Francis Richardson Keller. New York: Mellen, 1988 (Orig. pub. 1925).

SOURCES

Baker-Fletcher, Karen. 1994. *A singing something: Womanist reflections on Anna Julia Cooper.* New York: Crossroad.

Gable, Leona C. 1982. *From slavery to the Sorbonne and beyond: The life and writings of Anna J. Cooper.* Northampton, MA: Smith College Press.

Johnson, Karen A. 2000. *Uplifting the women and the race: The educational philosophies and social activism of Anna Julia Cooper and Nannie Helen Burroughs.* New York: Garland.

Lemert, Charles, and Esme Bhan, eds. 1998. *The voice of Anna Julia Cooper.* Lanham, MD: Rowman & Littlefield.

THE SELECTION

This essay, "The Status of Woman in America," is from *A Voice from the South,* by Anna Julia Cooper. Written during the fourth centenary of the Columbian discovery of America, Cooper first notes some of the important but often neglected contributions of women to the nation's culture and history. Assuming that women and men have somewhat different values, she highlights the reformist and altruistic nature of women's influence on the nation, seeing it as a necessary counterweight to the materialistic and calculating attitude of many leaders of the "wealth-producing" era just past. She looks forward to a new era when women's values will become more dominant, now that the potential of a comfortable economic situation for all citizens has been reached. As an example of women's best activities and ideas, she mentions the Women's Christian Temperance Union (WCTU).

Cooper then brings up the unique position of women of color, whose needs are not always acknowledged either in white women's or black men's activism. She makes a strong argument for the inclusion of the voices of women of color in both of these movements, pointing to the achievements of many women of color in American history. This essay, like others in *A Voice from the South,* has elements of "standpoint theory" as developed by feminist sociologists in the 1970s and later, including Patricia Hill Collins, Dorothy Smith, and Nancy Hartsock. The fact that Cooper recognizes the need to include the voices of women of color because their experience and knowledge is different from that of white women and black men seems remarkable for her time.

THE STATUS OF WOMAN IN AMERICA

Just four hundred years ago an obscure dreamer and castle builder, prosaically poor and ridiculously insistent on the reality of his dreams, was enabled through the devotion of a noble woman to give to civilization a magnificent continent.

From Anna Julia Cooper, *A Voice from the South.* Xenia, OH: The Aldine Printing House, 1892. (pp. 127–45)

What the lofty purpose of Spain's pure-minded queen had brought to the birth, the untiring devotion of pioneer women nourished and developed. The dangers of wild beasts and of wilder men, the mysteries of unknown wastes and unexplored forests, the horrors of pestilence and famine, of exposure and loneliness, during all those years of discovery and settlement, were braved without a murmur by women who had been most delicately constituted and most tenderly nurtured.

And when the times of physical hardship and danger were past, when the work of clearing and opening up was over and the struggle for accumulation began, again woman's inspiration and help were needed and still was she loyally at hand. A Mary Lyon,[1] demanding and making possible equal advantages of education for women as for men, and, in the face of discouragement and incredulity, bequeathing to women the opportunities of Holyoke.

A Dorothea Dix,[2] insisting on the humane and rational treatment of the insane and bringing about a reform in the lunatic asylums of the country, making a great step forward in the tender regard for the weak by the strong throughout the world.

A Helen Hunt Jackson,[3] convicting the nation of a century of dishonor in regard to the Indian.

A Lucretia Mott,[4] gentle Quaker spirit, with sweet insistence, preaching the abolition of slavery and the institution, in its stead, of the brotherhood of man; her life and words breathing out in tender melody the injunction

Have love. Not love alone for one
But man as man thy brother call;
And scatter, like the circling sun,
Thy charities *on all*.

And at the most trying time of what we have called the Accumulative Period, when internecine war, originated through man's love of gain and his determination to subordinate national interests and black men's rights alike to considerations of personal profit and loss, was drenching our country with its own best blood, who shall recount the name and fame of the women on both sides of the senseless strife,—those uncomplaining souls with a great heart ache of their own, rigid features and pallid cheek their ever effective flag of truce, on the battle field, in the camp, in the hospital, binding up wounds, recording dying whispers for absent loved ones, with tearful eyes pointing to man's last refuge, giving the last earthly hand clasp and performing the last friendly office for strangers whom a great common sorrow had made kin, while they knew that somewhere—somewhere a husband, a brother, a father, a son, was being tended by stranger hands—or mayhap those familiar eyes were even then being closed forever by just such another ministering angel of mercy and love.

But why mention names? Time would fail to tell of the noble army of women who shine like beacon lights in the otherwise sordid wilderness of this accumulative period—prison reformers and tenement cleansers, quiet unnoted workers in hospitals and homes, among imbeciles, among outcasts—

---

[1]Mary Lyon (1797–1849): New England educator, founder of Mount Holyoke College.
[2]Dorothea Dix (1802–1887): reformer and nurse who investigated conditions in asylums, prisons, and poorhouses.
[3]Helen Hunt Jackson (1830–1885): campaigner for Native American rights.
[4]Lucretia Mott (1793–1880): feminist and abolitionist, probably the author of the short poem "Have love . . ." quoted in this paragraph.

the sweetening, purifying antidotes for the poisons of man's acquisitiveness,—mollifying and soothing with the tenderness of compassion and love the wounds and bruises caused by his overreaching and avarice.

The desire for quick returns and large profits tempts capital ofttimes into unsanitary, well nigh inhuman investments,—tenement tinder boxes, stifling, stunting, sickening alleys and pestiferous slums; regular rents, no waiting, large percentages,—rich coffers coined out of the life-blood of human bodies and souls. Men and women herded together like cattle, breathing in malaria and typhus from an atmosphere seething with moral as well as physical impurity, revelling in vice as their native habitat and then, to drown the whisperings of their higher consciousness and effectually to hush the yearnings and accusations within, flying to narcotics and opiates—rum, tobacco, opium, binding hand and foot, body and soul, till the proper image of God is transformed into a fit associate for demons,—a besotted, enervated, idiotic wreck, or else a monster of wickedness terrible and destructive.

These are some of the legitimate products of the unmitigated tendencies of the wealth-producing period. But, thank Heaven, side by side with the cold, mathematical, selfishly calculating, so-called practical and unsentimental instinct of the business man, there comes the sympathetic warmth and sunshine of good women, like the sweet and sweetening breezes of spring, cleansing, purifying, soothing, inspiring, lifting the drunkard from the gutter, the outcast from the pit. Who can estimate the influence of these "daughters of the king," these lend-a-hand forces, in counteracting the selfishness of an acquisitive age?

To-day America counts her millionaires by the thousand; questions of tariff and questions of currency are the most vital ones agitating the public mind. In this period, when material prosperity and well earned ease and luxury are assured facts from a national standpoint, woman's work and woman's influence are needed as never before; needed to bring a heart power into this money getting, dollar-worshipping civilization; needed to bring a moral force into the utilitarian motives and interests of the time; needed to stand for God and Home and Native Land *versus gain and greed and grasping selfishness*.

There can be no doubt that this fourth centenary of America's discovery which we celebrate at Chicago, strikes the keynote of another important transition in the history of this nation; and the prominence of woman in the management of its celebration is a fitting tribute to the part she is destined to play among the forces of the future. This is the first congressional recognition of woman in this country, and this Board of Lady Managers constitute the first women legally appointed by any government to act in a national capacity. This of itself marks the dawn of a new day.

Now the periods of discovery, of settlement, of developing resources and accumulating wealth have passed in rapid succession. Wealth in the nation as in the individual brings leisure, repose, reflection. The struggle with nature is over, the struggle with ideas begins. We stand then, it seems to me, in this last decade of the nineteenth century, just in the portals of a new and untried movement on a higher plain and in a grander strain than any the past has called forth. It does not require a prophet's eye to divine its trend and image its possibilities from the forces we see already at work around us; nor is it hard to guess what must be the status of woman's work under the new regime.

In the pioneer days her role was that of a camp-follower, an additional something to fight for and be burdened with, only repaying the anxiety and labor she called forth by her own incomparable gifts of sympathy and appreciative love; unable herself ordinarily to contend with the bear and the Indian, or to take active part in clearing the wilderness and constructing the home.

In the second or wealth producing period her work is abreast of man's, complementing and supplementing, counteracting excessive tendencies, and mollifying over rigorous proclivities.

In the era now about to dawn, her sentiments must strike the keynote and give the dominant tone. And this because of the nature of her contribution to the world.

Her kingdom is not over physical forces. Not by might, nor by power can she prevail. Her position must ever be inferior where strength of muscle creates leadership. If she follows the instincts of her nature, however, she must always stand for the conservation of those deeper moral forces which make for the happiness of homes and the righteousness of the country. In a reign of moral ideas she is easily queen.

There is to my mind no grander and surer prophecy of the new era and of woman's place in it, than the work already begun in the waning years of the nineteenth century by the W. C. T. U.[5] in America, an organization which has even now reached not only national but international importance, and seems destined to permeate and purify the whole civilized world. It is the living embodiment of woman's activities and woman's ideas, and its extent and strength rightly prefigure her increasing power as a moral factor.

The colored woman of to-day occupies, one may say, a unique position in this country. In a period of itself transitional and unsettled, her status seems one of the least ascertainable and definitive of all the forces which make for our civilization. She is confronted by both a woman question and a race problem, and is as yet an unknown or an unacknowledged factor in both. While the women of the white race can with calm assurance enter upon the work they feel by nature appointed to do, while their men give loyal support and appreciative countenance to their efforts, recognizing in most avenues of usefulness the propriety and the need of woman's distinctive co-operation, the colored woman too often finds herself hampered and shamed by a less liberal sentiment and a more conservative attitude on the part of those for whose opinion she cares most. That this is not universally true I am glad to admit. There are to be found both intensely conservative white men and exceedingly liberal colored men. But as far as my experience goes the average man of our race is less frequently ready to admit the actual need among the sturdier forces of the world for woman's help or influence. That great social and economic questions await her interference, that she could throw any light on problems of national import, that her intermeddling could improve the management of school systems, or elevate the tone of public institutions, or humanize and sanctify the far reaching influence of prisons and reformatories and improve the treatment of lunatics and imbeciles,—that she has a word worth hearing on mooted questions in political economy, that she could contribute a suggestion on the relations of labor and capital, or offer a thought on honest money and honorable trade, I fear the majority of "Americans of the colored variety" are not yet prepared to concede. It may be that they do not yet see these questions in their right perspective, being absorbed in the immediate needs of their own political complications. A good deal depends on where we put the emphasis in this world; and our men are not perhaps to blame if they see everything colored by the light of those agitations in the midst of which they live and move and have their

---

[5]W.C.T.U.: Women's Christian Temperance Union, an organization of women that crusaded against saloons and the drinking of alcohol.

being. The part they have had to play in American history during the last twenty-five or thirty years has tended rather to exaggerate the importance of mere political advantage, as well as to set a fictitious valuation on those able to secure such advantage. It is the astute politician, the manager who can gain preferment for himself and his favorites, the demagogue known to stand in with the powers at the White House and consulted on the bestowal of government plums, whom we set in high places and denominate great. It is they who receive the hosannas of the multitude and are regarded as leaders of the people. The thinker and the doer, the man who solves the problem by enriching his country with an invention worth thousands or by a thought inestimable and precious is given neither bread nor a stone. He is too often left to die in obscurity and neglect even if spared in his life the bitterness of fanatical jealousies and detraction.

And yet politics, and surely American politics, is hardly a school for great minds. Sharpening rather than deepening, it develops the faculty of taking advantage of present emergencies rather than the insight to distinguish between the true and the false, the lasting and the ephemeral advantage. Highly cultivated selfishness rather than consecrated benevolence is its passport to success. Its votaries are never seers. At best they are but manipulators—often only jugglers. It is conducive neither to profound statesmanship nor to the higher type of manhood. Altruism is its *mauvais succès* and naturally enough it is indifferent to any factor which cannot be worked into its own immediate aims and purposes. As woman's influence as a political element is as yet nil in most of the commonwealths of our republic, it is not surprising that with those who place the emphasis on mere political capital she may yet seem almost a nonentity so far as it concerns the solution of great national or even racial perplexities.

There are those, however, who value the calm elevation of the thoughtful spectator who stands aloof from the heated scramble; and, above the turmoil and din of corruption and selfishness, can listen to the teachings of eternal truth and righteousness. There are even those who feel that the black man's unjust and unlawful exclusion temporarily from participation in the elective franchise in certain states is after all but a lesson "in the desert" fitted to develop in him insight and discrimination against the day of his own appointed time. One needs occasionally to stand aside from the hum and rush of human interests and passions to hear the voices of God. And it not unfrequently happens that the All-loving gives a great push to certain souls to thrust them out, as it were, from the distracting current for awhile to promote their discipline and growth, or to enrich them by communion and reflection. And similarly it may be woman's privilege from her peculiar coigne of vantage as a quiet observer, to whisper just the needed suggestion or the almost forgotten truth. The colored woman, then, should not be ignored because her bark is resting in the silent waters of the sheltered cove. She is watching the movements of the contestants none the less and is all the better qualified, perhaps, to weigh and judge and advise because not herself in the excitement of the race. Her voice, too, has always been heard in clear, unfaltering tones, ringing the changes on those deeper interests which make for permanent good. She is always sound and orthodox on questions affecting the well-being of her race. You do not find the colored woman selling her birthright for a mess of pottage. Nay, even after reason has retired from the contest, she has been known to cling blindly with the instinct of a turtle dove to those principles and policies which to her mind promise hope and safety for children yet unborn. It is notorious that ignorant black women in the South have actually left their husbands' homes and re-pudiated their support for what was under-stood by the wife to be race disloyalty, or "voting away," as she expresses it, the privi-leges of herself and little ones.

It is largely our women in the South to-day who keep the black men solid in the Re-publican party. The latter as they increase in intelligence and power of discrimination would be more apt to divide on local issues at any rate. They begin to see that the Grand Old Party regards the Negro's cause as an outgrown issue, and on Southern soil at least finds a too intimate acquaintanceship with him a somewhat unsavory recommendation. Then, too, their political wits have been sharpened to appreciate the fact that it is good policy to cultivate one's neighbors and not depend too much on a distant friend to fight one's home battles. But the black woman can never forget—however lukewarm the party may to-day appear—that it was a Republican president who struck the mana-cles from her own wrists and gave the possi-bilities of manhood to her helpless little ones; and to her mind a Democratic Negro is a traitor and a time-server. Talk as much as you like of venality and manipulation in the South, there are not many men, I can tell you, who would dare face a wife quivering in every fiber with the consciousness that her husband is a coward who could be paid to desert her deepest and dearest interests.

Not unfelt, then, if unproclaimed has been the work and influence of the colored women of America.[6] Our list of chieftains in the service, though not long, is not inferior in strength and excellence, I dare believe, to any similar list which this country can produce.

Among the pioneers, Frances Watkins Harper could sing with prophetic exaltation in the darkest days, when as yet there was not a rift in the clouds overhanging her people:

Yes, Ethiopia shall stretch
Her bleeding hands abroad;
Her cry of agony shall reach the burning
throne of God.
Redeemed from dust and freed from
chains
Her sons shall lift their eyes,
From cloud-capt hills and verdant plains
Shall shouts of triumph rise.

Among preachers of righteousness, an unanswerable silencer of cavilers and objec-tors, was Sojourner Truth, that unique and rugged genius who seemed carved out with-out hand or chisel from the solid mountain mass; and in pleasing contrast, Amanda Smith, sweetest of natural singers and pleaders in dulcet tones for the things of God and of His Christ.

Sarah Woodson Early and Martha Briggs, planting and watering in the school room, and giving off from their matchless and irresistible personality an impetus and inspiration which can never die so long as there lives and breathes a remote descendant of their disciples and friends.

---

[6]In the paragraphs following, Cooper discusses the nineteenth century's most influential "col-ored women of America": Frances Watkins Harper (1825–1911), writer, lecturer and poet, au-thor of the quoted "Yes, Ethiopia . . ."; Sojourner Truth (1797–1883), evangelist, abolitionist, and feminist; Amanda Smith (1837–1915), evangelist and reformer; Sarah Woodson Early (1825–1907), pioneer black feminist-nationalist; Martha Briggs (1838–1889), faculty member and public school administrator, Charlotte Forten Grimké (1837–1914), antislavery poet, educator, and minister's wife; Hallie Quinn Brown (1845–1949), educator and social re-former, a founder of the National Association of Colored Women; and Fanny Jackson Coppin (1837–1913), educator and missionary.

Charlotte Forten Grimké, the gentle spirit whose verses and life link her so beautifully with America's great Quaker poet and loving reformer.

Hallie Quinn Brown, charming reader, earnest, effective lecturer and devoted worker of unflagging zeal and unquestioned power.

Fanny Jackson Coppin, the teacher and organizer, pre-eminent among women of whatever country or race in constructive and executive force.

These women represent all shades of belief and as many departments of activity; but they have one thing in common—their sympathy with the oppressed race in America and the consecration of their several talents in whatever line to the work of its deliverance and development.

Fifty years ago woman's activity according to orthodox definitions was on a pretty clearly cut "sphere," including primarily the kitchen and the nursery, and rescued from the barrenness of prison bars by the womanly mania for adorning every discoverable bit of china or canvass with forlorn looking cranes balanced idiotically on one foot. The woman of to-day finds herself in the presence of responsibilities which ramify through the profoundest and most varied interests of her country and race. Not one of the issues of this plodding, toiling, sinning, repenting, falling, aspiring humanity can afford to shut her out, or can deny the reality of her influence. No plan for renovating society, no scheme for purifying politics, no reform in church or in state, no moral, social, or economic question, no movement upward or downward in the human plane is lost on her. A man once said when told his house was afire: "Go tell my wife; I never meddle with household affairs." But no woman can possibly put herself or her sex outside any of the interests that affect humanity. All departments in the new era are to be hers, in the sense that her interests are in all and through

all; and it is incumbent on her to keep intelligently and sympathetically *en rapport* with all the great movements of her time, that she may know on which side to throw the weight of her influence. She stands now at the gateway of this new era of American civilization. In her hands must be moulded the strength, the wit, the statesmanship, the morality, all the psychic force, the social and economic intercourse of that era. To be alive at such an epoch is a privilege, to be a woman then is sublime.

In this last decade of our century, changes of such moment are in progress, such new and alluring vistas are opening out before us, such original and radical suggestions for the adjustment of labor and capital, of government and the governed, of the family, the church and the state, that to be a possible factor though an infinitesimal in such a movement is pregnant with hope and weighty with responsibility. To be a woman in such an age carries with it a privilege and an opportunity never implied before. But to be a woman of the Negro race in America, and to be able to grasp the deep significance of the possibilities of the crisis, is to have a heritage, it seems to me, unique in the ages. In the first place, the race is young and full of the elasticity and hopefulness of youth. All its achievements are before it. It does not look on the masterly triumphs of nineteenth century civilization with that *blasé* world-weary look which characterized the old washed out and worn out races which have already, so to speak, seen their best days.

Said a European writer recently: "Except the Slavonic, the Negro is the only original and distinctive genius which has yet to come to growth—and the feeling is to cherish and develop it."

Everything to this race is new and strange and inspiring. There is a quickening of its pulses and a glowing of its self-consciousness. Aha, I can rival that! I can aspire to that! I can honor my name and vindicate my race! Something like this, it strikes me, is the enthusiasm which stirs the genius of young Africa in America; and the memory of past oppression and the fact of present attempted repression only serve to gather momentum for its irrepressible powers. Then again, a race in such a stage of growth is peculiarly sensitive to impressions. Not the photographer's sensitized plate is more delicately impressionable to outer influences than is this high strung people here on the threshold of a career.

What a responsibility then to have the sole management of the primal lights and shadows! Such is the colored woman's office. She must stamp weal or woe on the coming history of this people. May she see her opportunity and vindicate her high prerogative.

Thorstein Veblen (1857–1929) on Dress as Pecuniary Culture

Born into a Norwegian immigrant family on a midwestern American farm in Wisconsin, Thorstein Veblen's early life was characterized by poverty, hard work, and hard luck. He developed a distrust and cynicism about business and finance. A very bright but uncooperative student, Veblen spent six years at Carleton College studying for the ministry and graduated in 1880. Not content with the restricted curriculum at Carleton, he read independently to supplement his education. After Carlton, Veblen entered the philosophy graduate program at Johns Hopkins, later transferring to Yale, where he received a doctorate in philosophy in 1884. In spite of his degree, Veblen had to spend several years on the family farm, unable to find an academic position. He entered Cornell's economics program in 1890 and moved the following year to the University of Chicago, where he edited the *Journal of Political Economy* and lectured in economics. He became an assistant professor of economics at the University of Chicago at age forty-three.

Veblen's unorthodox life led to his dismissal from the University of Chicago. He moved to Stanford in 1906 but was asked to resign from there as well in 1909. He went through a number of other positions and spent his last years in isolation in a mountain cabin in California, dying in 1929. During his lifetime, Veblen's work had an occasional following, but he died feeling forgotten, according to Coser (1977). The Depression years saw a renewal of interest in some of his work, especially the highly regarded *Theory of the Leisure Class* (1911). Veblen's work followed the evolutionary pattern of most of his peers, but he also was a keen observer of American foibles. As a marginalized observer, he was deeply critical of many aspects of American culture, often focusing on the irrational aspects of the economic culture. Veblen's work pays attention to the status of women, both in its evolution through various stages of society, and in his analysis of the role of women in his contemporary world.

MAJOR WORKS

Veblen, Thorstein. *The Theory of the Leisure Class: An Economic Study of Institutions.* New York: Macmillan, 1899.

———. "The Barbarian Status of Women." *American Journal of Sociology* 4 (January 1899): 503–514.

———. *Theory of the Business Enterprise.* New York: Scribner's, 1904.

———. *The Instinct of Workmanship, and the State of Industrial Arts.* New York: Macmillan, 1914.

———. *An Inquiry into the Nature of the Peace and the Terms of Its Perpetuation.* New York: Huebsch, 1918.

———. *The Higher Learning in America.* New York: Huebsch, 1918.

SOURCES

Adams, Bert N., and R. A. Sydie. 2001. *Sociological theory.* Thousand Oaks, CA: Pine Forge.

Coser, Lewis A. 1977. *Masters of sociological thought.* New York: Harcourt, Brace, Jovanovich.

THE SELECTION

Thorstein Veblen's discussion of dress and fashion is presented as an illustration of his key concept of "pecuniary culture," the culture that pervades modern capitalistic societies. Pecuniary culture involves a derivation of status from wealth—not the *possession* of wealth but its *display*—and one's ability to avoid work and to live a life of leisure. Veblen introduced such concepts as conspicuous waste, conspicuous leisure, and conspicuous consumption to describe the characteristics of the "successful" classes in the modern world. For this somewhat cynical analyst, people are motivated by status concerns, and wealth becomes a means by which a person can establish standing in the eyes of others—through the purchase and consumption before others of things that have no apparent utility. These are characteristics of the new upper classes in industrial societies— those who do not actually do productive work themselves, but who extract the wealth that is produced by the actual workers in lower classes. These workers, in turn, instead of rebelling against the "superior" classes, learn to emulate them in order to strive for enhanced status themselves.

In the selection presented here, Veblen discusses dress as an example of conspicuous waste and status display. He especially views the dress of *women* as illustrating these characteristics. Women's dress, in its most elegant and prized forms, not only is not worn for its utility, but it is especially designed to show that its wearer cannot do manual labor. High heels, flimsy fabrics, restrictive corsets—these and other traits all attract Veblen's critical eye. In addition, Veblen argues that women's dress becomes the means by which *men* can gain status, by showing other men that "their" wives and daughters need not work, are objects of beauty, and are expensively and fashionably dressed. This is tied to women's continued dependence on men for their economic well-being. Although Veblen does not use the term, the contemporary concept of "trophy wife" seems relevant here.

From Thorstein Veblen, "Dress as an Expression of the Pecuniary Culture," Chap. 7 in *The Theory of the Leisure Class: An Economic study of Institutions* (New York: Macmillan: 1899/1911) 167–87.

DRESS AS AN EXPRESSION OF THE PECUNIARY CULTURE

It will be in place, by way of illustration, to show in some detail how the economic principles so far set forth apply to everyday facts in some one direction of the life process. For this purpose no line of consumption affords a more apt illustration than expenditure on dress. It is especially the rule of the conspicuous waste of goods that finds expression in dress, although the other, related principles of pecuniary repute are also exemplified in the same contrivances. Other methods of putting one's pecuniary standing in evidence serve their end effectually, and other methods are in vogue always and everywhere; but expenditure on dress has this advantage over most other methods, that our apparel is always in evidence and affords an indication of our pecuniary standing to all observers at the first glance. It is also true that admitted expenditure for display is more obviously present, and is, perhaps, more universally practised in the matter of dress than in any other line of consumption. No one finds difficulty in assenting to the commonplace that the greater part of the expenditure incurred by all classes for apparel is incurred for the sake of a respectable appearance rather than for the protection of the person. And probably at no other point is the sense of shabbiness so keenly felt as it is if we fall short of the standard set by social usage in this matter of dress. It is true of dress in even a higher degree than of most other items of consumption, that people will undergo a very considerable degree of privation in the comforts or the necessaries of life in order to afford what is considered a decent amount of wasteful consumption. . . . And the commercial value of the goods used for clothing in any modern community is made up to a much larger extent of the fashion-ableness, the reputability of the goods than of the mechanical service which they render in clothing the person of the wearer. . . . A detailed examination of what passes in popular apprehension for elegant apparel will show that it is contrived at every point to convey the impression that the wearer does not habitually put forth any useful effort. It goes without saying that no apparel can be considered elegant, or even decent, if it shows the effect of manual labour on the part of the wearer, in the way of soil or wear. The pleasing effect of neat and spotless garments is chiefly, if not altogether, due to their carrying, the suggestion of leisure—exemption from personal contact with industrial processes of any kind. Much of the charm that invests the patent-leather shoe, the stainless linen, the lustrous cylindrical hat, and the walking-stick, which so greatly enhance the native dignity of a gentleman, comes of their pointedly suggesting that the wearer cannot when so attired bear a hand in any employment that is directly and immediately of any human use. Elegant dress serves its purpose of elegance not only in that it is expensive, but also because it is the insignia of leisure. It not only shows that the wearer is able to consume a relatively large value, but it argues at the same time that he consumes without producing.

The dress of women goes even farther than that of men in the way of demonstrating the wearer's abstinence from productive employment. It needs no argument to enforce the generalisation that the more elegant styles of feminine bonnets go even farther towards making work impossible than does the man's high hat. The woman's shoe adds the so-called French heel to the evidence of enforced leisure afforded by its polish; because this high heel obviously makes any, even the simplest and most necessary manual work extremely difficult. The like is true even in a higher degree of the skirt and the rest of the drapery which characterises woman's dress. The substantial reason for our tenacious attachment to the skirt is just this: it is expensive and it hampers the wearer at every turn and incapacitates her for all useful exertion. The like is true of the feminine custom of wearing the hair excessively long.

But the woman's apparel not only goes beyond that of the modern man in the degree in which it argues exemption from labour; it also adds a peculiar and highly characteristic feature which differs in kind from anything habitually practised by the men. This feature is the class of contrivances of which the corset is the typical example. The corset is, in economic theory, substantially a mutilation, undergone for the purpose of lowering the subject's vitality and rendering her permanently and obviously unfit for work. It is true, the corset impairs the personal attractions of the wearer, but the loss suffered on that score is offset by the gain in reputability which comes of her visibly increased expensiveness and infirmity. It may broadly be set down that the womanliness of woman's apparel resolves itself, in point of substantial fact, into the more effective hindrance to useful exertion offered by the garments peculiar to women. . . .

There remains at least one point in this theory of dress yet to be discussed. Most of what has been said applies to men's attire as well as to that of women; although in modern times it applies at nearly all points with greater force to that of women. But at one point the dress of women differs substantially from that of men. In woman's dress there is an obviously greater insistence on such features as testify to the wearer's exemption from or incapacity for all vulgarly productive employment. This characteristic of woman's apparel is of interest, not only as completing the theory of dress, but also as confirming what has already been said of the economic status of women, both in the past and in the present.

It has in the course of economic development become the office of the woman to consume vicariously for the head of the household; and her apparel is contrived with this object in view. It has come about that obviously productive labour is in a peculiar degree derogatory to respectable women, and therefore special pains should be taken in the construction of women's dress, to impress upon the beholder the fact (often indeed a fiction) that the wearer does not and can not habitually engage in useful work. Propriety requires respectable women to abstain more consistently from useful effort and to make more of a show of leisure than the men of the same social classes. It grates painfully on our nerves to contemplate the necessity of any well-bred woman's earning a livelihood by useful work. It is not "woman's sphere." Her sphere is within the household, which she should "beautify," and of which she should be the "chief ornament." The male head of the household is not currently spoken of as its ornament. This feature taken in conjunction with the other fact that propriety requires more unremitting attention to expensive display in the dress and other paraphernalia of women, goes to enforce the view already implied in what has gone before. By virtue of its descent from a patriarchal past, our social system makes it the woman's function in an especial degree to put in evidence her household's ability to pay. According to the modern civilised scheme of life, the good name of the household to which she belongs should be the special care of the woman; and the system of honorific expenditure and conspicuous leisure by which this good name is chiefly sustained is therefore the woman's sphere. In the ideal scheme, as it tends to realise itself in the life of the higher pecuniary classes, this attention to conspicuous waste of substance and effort should normally be the sole economic function of the woman.

At the stage of economic development at which the women were still in the full sense the property of the men, the performance of conspicuous leisure and consumption came to be part of the services required of them. The women being not their own masters, obvious expenditure and leisure on their part would redound to the credit of their master rather than to their own credit; and therefore the more expensive and the more obviously unproductive the women of the household are, the more creditable and more effective for the purpose of the reputability of the household or its head will their life be. So much so that the women have been required not only to afford evidence of a life of leisure, but even to disable themselves for useful activity.

It is at this point that the dress of men falls short of that of women, and for a sufficient reason. Conspicuous waste and conspicuous leisure are reputable because they are evidence of pecuniary strength; pecuniary strength is reputable or honorific because, in the last analysis, it argues success and superior force; therefore the evidence of waste and leisure put forth by any individual in his own behalf cannot consistently take such a form or be carried to such a pitch as to argue incapacity or marked discomfort on his part; as the exhibition would in that case show not superior force, but inferiority, and so defeat its own purpose. So, then, wherever wasteful expenditure and the show of abstention from effort is normally, or on an average, carried to the extent of showing obvious discomfort or voluntarily induced physical disability, there the immediate inference is that the individual in question does not perform this wasteful expenditure and undergo this disability for her own personal gain in pecuniary repute, but in behalf of some one else to whom she stands in a relation of economic dependence; a relation which in the last analysis must, in economic theory, reduce itself to a relation of servitude.

To apply this generalisation to women's dress, and put the matter in concrete terms: the high heel, the skirt, the impracticable bonnet, the corset, and the general disregard of the wearer's comfort which is an obvious feature of all civilised women's apparel, are so many items of evidence to the effect that in the modern civilised scheme of life the woman is still, in theory, the economic dependent of the man,—that, perhaps in a highly idealised sense, she still is the man's chattel. The homely reason for all this conspicuous leisure and attire on the part of women lies in the fact that they are servants to whom, in the differentiation of economic functions, has been delegated the office of putting in evidence their master's ability to pay.

There is a marked similarity in these respects between the apparel of women and that of domestic servants, especially liveried servants. In both there is a very elaborate show of unnecessary expensiveness, and in both cases there is also a notable disregard of the physical comfort of the wearer. But the attire of the lady goes farther in its elaborate insistence on the idleness, if not on the physical infirmity of the wearer, than does that of the domestic. And this is as it should be; for in theory, according to the ideal scheme of the pecuniary culture, the lady of the house is the chief menial of the household. . . .

The Progressive Era
Early Twentieth-Century Sociology

Georg Simmel (1858–1918) on Conflict between Men and Women

Born to parents of Jewish descent who had converted to Christianity, Simmel's career was nonetheless limited by anti-Semitic prejudice in Germany during his lifetime. He was educated at the University of Berlin, earning his doctorate in 1881, but he was unable for many years to obtain a permanent faculty position. In spite of this, he was a popular lecturer in philosophy and sociology from 1885 on, and his interests were extremely diverse. Simmel and his wife (herself a philosopher and intellectual) maintained a place for lively discussions among Berlin intellectuals in their home.

Simmel's work was varied in topic and cross-disciplinary, often focusing on the significance of cultural items that went completely unnoticed by others. Known for his essays rather than larger, book-length works, he wrote on such topics as "the secret," the influence of group size on interaction, the nature of metropolitan life, "the handle," "the stranger," conflict, and money. His work was very influential on early American sociologists, including Albion Small, who published some of Simmel's work in the *American Journal of Sociology*. Some of Robert Park's work also bears the imprint of Simmel. He is sometimes seen as a forerunner of symbolic interactionist theory, although the diversity of his work makes him difficult to classify.

MAJOR WORKS

Simmel, Georg. *Conflict and the Web of Group-Affiliations.* New York: Free Press, 1955.

———. *Essays on Sociology, Philosophy & Aesthetics.* New York: Harper Torchbooks, Harper & Row, 1965 (Orig. pub. 1959).

———. *On Individuality and Social Forms: Selected Writings.* Edited by Donald N. Levine. Chicago: University of Chicago Press, 1971.

———. *The Philosophy of Money.* Translated by Tom Bottomore and David Frisby. London: Routledge & Kegan Paul, 1978.

———. *Essays on Religion.* Edited and translated by Horst Jurgen Helle, in collaboration with Ludwig Neider. New Haven: Yale University Press, 1997.

SOURCES

Coser, Lewis A. 1977. *Masters of sociological thought*. New York: Harcourt, Brace, Jovanovich.

Rammstedt, O., and M. C. Mila. 2004. Georg Simmel. In *International encyclopedia of the social and behavioral sciences*, 14091–97. New York: Elsevier. Eds N.J. Smelser and P. B. Baltes.

THE SELECTION

Much of Georg Simmel's work is highly abstract, but the short selection here is a good example of his intuitive mind. This is from the essay *"Conflict,"* probably the most widely read of Simmel's works in translation. Here he discusses the problem resulting from men's greater strength and aggressiveness, which leads to vulnerability of women to exploitation both economically and sexually. He argues that cultures must develop customs to protect women from this inherent conflict between men and women.

MEN, WOMEN, AND CUSTOM

Certain sociological attitudes characteristic of women appear to go back to the same motive. Among the extremely complex elements that make up the over-all relation between men and women, there is a typical hostility which derives from two sources. As the physically weaker sex, women are always in danger of economic and personal exploitation and legal powerlessness[1]; and as the objects of the sensuous desire of men, they must always hold themselves on the defensive against the other sex. This fight, which pervades the inner and personal history of mankind, has rarely led to the direct cooperation of women against men. But there is a superpersonal form which serves as a protection against both of those dangers and in which the female sex is therefore interested, so to speak, *in corpore:* custom (*Sitte*). Its sociological nature has been characterized above; it must once more be shown in its application to the point under discussion.

A strong personality knows how to protect itself individually against attacks, or at most needs legal protection. The weak one would be lost even with legal protection if other, more powerful individuals did not somehow forego the exploitation of their superiority. They do this in part because of

[1]I am speaking here of the relationship as it has obtained throughout the overwhelmingly longest period of known history. I do not discuss the question whether the modern development of the rights and powers of women may invalidate this relationship in the future or has in part already done so.

morality (*Sittlichkeit*). Since morality, however, has no other sanction than the individual's conscience, its effect is uncertain enough and needs complementing through custom. Custom, to be sure, does not have the precision and certainty of the legal norm, and yet it is guaranteed by an instinctive shyness and shame and by certain perceptibly disagreeable consequences of its violation. Custom is the essential protection of the weak who without it could not cope with the conflict of unrestricted forces. Its character, therefore, is on the whole prohibitive, restrictive. It effects a certain equality between the weak and the strong which in restraining the purely natural relationship between the two may even go so far as to prefer the weak—as is shown, for instance, in chivalry. The fact that in the creeping conflict between men and women, men are stronger and more aggressive, forces women under the protection of custom and makes them its custodians—they are called to this office, and called to it by their own interest. This of course also commits them to the most rigorous observance of the whole complex of the prescriptions of custom even where they do not directly concern male transgressions: all customary norms are related to one another through solidary interpendence, since the violation of a single one weakens the principle and thus every other. For this reason, women usually hold together in this respect without reservation. An actual unity corresponds to that peculiarly ideal unity in which men lump them together when they simply speak of "the women." The contrast between the sexes fully has the character of a *party* contrast. This sex-linked solidarity which women have in the eyes of men was expressed long ago by Freidank:

Man bears his shame alone,	("*Der Mann trägt seine Schmach allein,*
But let a woman fall,	*Doch kommt ein Weib zu Falle*
The blame rests on them all.	*So schilt man auf sie alle.*")

The solidarity has a real vehicle in its interest in custom as its common means of fight. It is for this reason that we finally come to see here a repetition of the sociological form under discussion. In respect to a particular woman, women as a rule know only complete inclusion or else complete exclusion from the realm of custom. They have the tendency as much as possible not to admit, or to interpret as harmless, a breach of custom by a woman (except where love of scandal and other individual motives counteract this). But if this is no longer possible, they render an irrevocable and unconditionally harsh judgment of exclusion from "good society." If the breach of custom must be admitted, the culprit is radically eliminated from that unit which is held together by its common interest in custom. It occurs, therefore, that women pass the same judgment of condemnation on Gretchen, Marguerite Gautier, Stella, and Messalina without permitting differences, and thus the possibility of mediation, between those within and those outside custom. Women's position on the defensive does not allow the wall of custom to be lowered even at a single point. Their party, in principle, knows no compromise but only absolute acceptance of the individual woman into the ideal totality of "decent women" or her equally absolute exclusion from it. The purely moral justification of this alternative is by no means beyond all doubt; it can only be understood in terms of the unbreachable unity which a party unified by a common opponent must impose on its members.

Anna Garlin Spencer (1851–1932) on the Woman of Genius

Anna Garlin Spencer was born into an established New England family in 1851, the daughter of an activist abolitionist mother. Her father served in the Union navy and was killed during the Civil War. She attended public schools and studied advanced subjects privately, obtaining a position as a journalist for the *Providence* (Rhode Island) *Journal* as a young woman until her marriage to a Unitarian minister, William Spencer. The couple had two children, one of whom died as an infant. Anna worked alongside her husband in his ministry, and, in 1891 became the first woman in Rhode Island to be formally ordained. In addition to her work in the ministry, Anna Garlin Spencer was a noted lecturer on social topics.

In the 1890s, Spencer began participating in sociological conferences and national meetings of civic organizations. She was active—and in many cases held leadership positions—in such organizations as the Society for Ethical Culture, the New England Suffrage Association, the Women's Christian Temperance Union, the Women's Peace Party, and the Women's International League of Peace and Freedom. Her main interests included women's suffrage, peace, women's rights, and social reform in education and family, including sex education. She also was an active member of several professional organizations, including the American Sociological Society and the American Social Hygiene Association, developing a network of colleagues that included many prominent male and female sociologists of the day, such as E. A. Ross, Franklin Giddings, Jane Addams, Emily Greene Balch, and Charles Henderson. In 1913 she was appointed Hackley Professor of Sociology and Ethics at the Theological School, Meadville, Pennsylvania. She also lectured at the University of Chicago, and from 1918 onward she was a lecturer at Teachers College, Columbia University.

Spencer was a cultural feminist who believed that women and men have different values but that women's values were an important ingredient that could balance the overly rational, aggressive nature of male leadership. Deegan (1991:369) writes of Spencer's book on the family that it "reads more like a contemporary feminist book on the family than the very conservative texts that dominated the sociological literature written after Spencer" (1991:369). Somewhat more conservative than feminists such as Charlotte Perkins Gilman, Spencer nonetheless was an important critic of gender arrangements, calling for more gender equality in the household division of labor, in education, and in politics. She published many articles and books and was a widely known and respected sociologist in her day.

Spencer's *Woman's Share in Social Culture* was published in 1912, based on a series of articles in the monthly journal *The Forum*. She dedicated the book to "the memory of Lucretia Mott, who prophesied in life and in work the Womanhood of the Future." The volume presents Spencer's theory of women's contribution to the development of human culture and calls for more freedom for women so they can reach their full potential. Assuming an evolutionary perspective, Spencer argues that women were the originators of human culture, being more settled and stable than men. They were the first to develop habits of steady and useful labor and organized in a cooperative manner with other women and children. Indeed, the first human group, for Spencer, was the mother–child dyad. Only later in human development did men become a stable and integrated part of the social group.

In *Woman's Share,* Spencer includes a fascinating section on the evolution of the "lady" as a social type—a woman who in modern life does not work for money but who is a symbol of the wealth and power of her husband's family. Even so, modern ladies may make important contributions of social value in terms of their patronage of learning and the arts, for example.

In other chapters, Spencer writes of the "spinster," showing the important contributions that single women can make. Her discussion of women's work is very critical of women's secondary status as workers and the discrimination against them in terms of wages, working conditions, and vocational choice. Spencer goes on to discuss problems of women's education, problems of marriage and divorce, special problems of college graduate women, and women's contribution to democratic society.

Major Works

Spencer, Anna Garlin. *The Family and Its Members.* Philadelphia: Lippincott, 1925.

———. *Woman's Share in Social Culture.* New York: Little & Ives, 1912.

Sources

Deegan, Mary Jo. 1991. Anna Garlin Spencer. In *Women in sociology: A bio-bibliographical sourcebook,* ed. Mary Jo Deegan, 366–74. Westport, CT: Greenwood.

THE SELECTION

The following piece is from *Woman's Share in Social Culture,* which Anna Garlin Spencer wrote to challenge Otto Weininger's *Sex and Character*—a book that promoted the idea of women's inferiority. In this chapter, "The Drama of the Woman of Genius,"

From Anna Garlin Spencer, *Woman's Share in Social Culture* (New York: Little & Ives, 1912). 45–50, 55, 58–63, 66–72, 79–81, 83.

she refutes the commonly held notion that no woman could achieve genius and points out that there in fact have been outstanding women in the arts, politics, and science whose work has been overlooked by historians. Women's relative absence from the ranks of genius, moreover, is largely due to their lack of access to education and opportunity and their exclusion from communities of scholars and artists. In addition, women's work is often interrupted by childbearing and the duties of wives, which cut into their time and energy. All of these factors help to explain the relative lack of women of achievement, but they fail to provide evidence of their lack of ability. The presence of so many women of achievement, in spite of the obstacles, is strong evidence to the contrary.

THE DRAMA OF THE WOMAN OF GENIUS

"There can never be a woman of genius," says the author of *Sex and Character,* in whose view women are hardly human, although it is the duty of men to treat them as if they were.

This book, recently translated from the German into English and already in its third edition, is a curious testimony to the effect of prejudice upon the ability to see facts. The author, strangely precocious in his maturity of thought and style and in his wide reach of learning, yet betrays such an exaggerated and even diseased adolescence in his sex-antagonism that we do not wonder that he committed suicide before he was twenty-four years of age. . . .

The failure of women to produce genius of the first rank in most of the supreme forms of human effort has been used to block the way of all women of talent and ambition for intellectual achievement in a manner that would be amusingly absurd were it not so monstrously unjust and socially harmful. A few ambitious girls in the middle of the nineteenth century in Boston, the Athens of America, want to go to High School. The Board of Education answers them, in effect: Produce a Michael Angelo or a Plato and you shall have a chance to learn a bit of mathematics, history and literature. A few women of marked inclination toward the healing art want a chance to study in a medical school and learn facts and methods in a hospital. Go to! the managing officials in substance reply: Where is your great surgeon; what supreme contribution has any woman ever made to our science? A group of earnest students beg admission to college and show good preparation gained by hard struggle with adverse conditions. You can't come in, the trustees respond, until you produce a Shakespeare or a Milton. The demand that women shall show the highest fruit of specialized talent and widest range of learning before they have had the general opportunity for a common-school education is hardly worthy of the sex that prides itself upon its logic. In point of fact no one, neither the man who denies woman a proper human soul nor the woman who claims "superiority" for her sex, can have any actual basis for accurate answer to the question, Can a woman become a genius of the first class? Nobody can know unless women in general shall have equal opportunity with men in education, in vocational choice, and in social welcome of their best intellectual work for a number of generations. So far women have suffered so many disabilities in the circumstances of their lives, in their lack of training in what Buckle calls "that preposterous system called their education," in their segregation from all the higher intellectual comradeship, in the personal and family and social hindrances to their mental growth and expression, that not even women themselves, still less men, can have an adequate idea of their possibilities of achievement. Nothing therefore is more foolish than to try to decide *a priori* the limits of a woman's capacity. What we do know is this, that there have been women of talent, and even of genius reaching near to the upper circles of the elect; and we know also that these women of marked talent have appeared whenever and wherever women have had opportunities of higher education and have been held in esteem by men as intellectual companions as well as wives and manual workers. The connection between these two facts is obvious. . . .

Women, far more than men, it is reasonable to suppose, have suffered hasty eclipse for want of adequate mention in the permanent records. Sappho has been sadly overworked as an instance of feminine genius; yet to be called "the poetess" as Homer was "the poet" in Greece, nearly five hundred years before our era, was not only proof of her own greatness, but also that there must have been many smaller poetesses to win her that distinction. The ancient world must also have produced numbers of women-philosophers of ability to have made a place for Hypatia at the head of a School; and her powers, which won her a martyrdom for truth equal in dignity to that of Socrates, must have had their rooting in the rich soil of the higher education of women.

[W]e remember Casandre Fidèle who wrote equally well in the languages of Homer, Virgil and Dante and who, it is said, "by her graces embellished even theology." She gave public lessons at Padua, sustained these in public debate, and had also "many agreeable talents such as music." She could

not have stood alone, although probably none of the learned ladies of her town were her equals; and surely to but few women of any age has it been given, as it was to her, to prove that higher education is not inimical to woman's health, by living more than one hundred years. . . .

Victor Hugo says: "The eighteenth century was man's century; the nineteenth is woman's." In that man's century of revolution against class privilege, the lowest level of "female education" seems to have been reached in our Anglo-Saxon civilization. In our own country, in the early days, the vigor of mind as well as of body of both men and women went of necessity into the pioneer building of our mighty States. So much was this the fact that the oft-repeated sneer, "Who reads an American book?" might well have been answered by a showing of Constitutions, Highways, Schools, ordered Settlements, as the front-row volumes in the library of American genius. This practical devotion to doing things that later historians would write about, made the women of colonial and revolutionary and western-pioneering days great persons, but small students. . . .

The provision of "free schools," "schools for the people," etc., left the girls entirely out of the count. Hartford, Connecticut, indeed, in 1771, began to allow girls to learn "reading, spelling, writing" and sometimes "to add"; but not until the close of the eighteenth century did the majority of towns of New England make provision, even in a meagre manner, for the education of girls. . . .

As Abigail Adams wrote in 1817, when over seventy years of age, speaking of the opportunities of women in her day: "The only chance for much intellectual improvement in the female sex, was to be found in the families of the educated class and in occasional intercourse with the learned." To this should be added the partiality of men teachers to some bright girls, which gave an exceptional training to a favored few.

These reminders of the period before the days of the Ladies' Academies for the well-to-do, of which Mrs. Willard's was the most ambitious, and of Mary Lyon's school in which the poorer girls could earn a part of their living by housework, cannot be omitted from consideration of the intellectual output of women in the United States. . . . The establishment of Normal Schools gave the first great democratic opportunity in education to women in America; and, characteristically in the history of women's higher education, this opportunity was given women not for themselves as human beings entitled to intellectual development, but as women who could give the State a larger and cheaper supply of teachers for the free public schools. Even as such it was an innovation bitterly opposed as too radical. . . . In spite of their poverty in education, however, the women of the eighteenth and first half of the nineteenth centuries made some good showing in letters; and their struggles for professional training and opportunity, especially in the field of medicine, show an heroic temper as well as a persistent purpose second to no class of men in a similar effort to obtain rights and chances in the larger life. . . .

"Talent," says Lowell, "is that which is in a man's power; genius is that in whose power a man is." If genius, even in its lesser ranges, be this irresistible pressure toward some unique self-expression, then women cannot be left out of the charmed circle; especially when we remember Helen Hunt with her solitary but wide approach to love and life, and Emily Dickinson, that hermit thrush among poets. Nor can those unique interpreters of art and literature among women whose vital expression has so enhanced the works of genius as to make them seem new creations, be left out of the count. In modern times, the growing company of musicians, some of them composers, and the artists of pen and brush, and the sculptors among women who swell the secondary ranks of genius in numbers and in power, must have increasing recognition.

All this, however, does not reach the deepest considerations involved in taking account of the intellectual contribution of women to art, science, philosophy and affairs. Whatever may be the reasons in nature for the lower level of women along these lines of man's greatest achievement, there are the gravest reasons in circumstance for the comparatively meagre showing. In addition to the handicap of lack of education, a handicap which no exceptional success of the self-made man or woman can offset for the majority of the talented, there is a no less important deprivation which all women have suffered in the past and most women now suffer. This deprivation is that of the informal but highly stimulating training which the good fellowship of their chosen guild of study and of service gives to men, but which is denied for the most part even to professional women. For example, women have been in the medical profession for a considerable time, and have obtained high distinction in it. They have won just recognition from many influential doctors of the other sex. Yet they can hardly be said to have entered the inner circle of their clan. They may stop to dinner at medical conventions, it is true, provided they make no fuss about smoking and do not mind being in the minority; but there are few men, even in that enlightened group, who can so sink sex-consciousness in professional comradeship as either to give or get the full social value that might be gained from a mixed company of like vocation. The women lawyers and members of the clergy are in even smaller minority, and hence suffer still more from that embarrassment of "the exception" which prevents easy and familiar association. In the teaching profession, where the relative numbers of the sexes are reversed, there is often more adequate professional intercourse; but the woman college professor, or college president, is still that one among many whose reception into her special class, even if courteous and friendly, is too formal and occasional for real guild fellowship.

To this negative deprivation must be added the positive opposition of men to the entrance of women into that professional life and work from which the genius arises as the rare flower from a vast field. The whole course of evolution in industry, and in the achievements of higher education and exceptional talent, has shown man's invariable tendency to shut women out when their activities have reached a highly specialized period of growth. . . .

This monopolistic tendency of men is shown most clearly in the history of the learned professions. Women were seldom, if ever, priests but they participated in religious services when religion was a family affair. When a priestly caste arose and became the symbol of peculiar authority, only men entered its ranks. Woman can reënter her natural place as religious leader only through the Theological Schools and Ordination, and these have been forbidden her until very recently and are now seldom open to her in full measure.

A striking illustration of this process of sex-exclusion following the perfecting of standards in training is shown in recent years in the United States in the action of the Methodist Episcopal Church. This religious body, of which Susanna Wesley has been called "the real founder" and Barbara Heck the first and most effective teacher in the United States, had for all its earlier propaganda the services of lay-preachers, later called "licensed exhorters," among whom were many gifted women whose "call" was well attested by the crowds that thronged to hear them. When, however, through an effort to raise all the standards of leadership in the Methodist Church to the plane of an "educated ministry," this lay service was crippled and finally abolished, women were shut out of the Methodist ministry altogether; thus losing to this Church many brilliant and devout preachers.

Again, women developed law and its application to life in the germs of family rule and tribal custom quite as much as did men; but when statutes took the place of tradition, and courts superseded personal judgeship, and when a special class of lawyers was needed to define and administer laws, which grew more difficult to understand with growing complexity of social relationship, men alone entered that profession. Women can now become members of that class only by graduating from law-schools and being "admitted to the bar," and only very recently have they been allowed these privileges. . . .

This process of differentiating and perfecting intellectual labor, the process in which at most acute periods of specialization and advance, women were wholly shut out of their own ancient work, finds its most complete and its most dramatic illustration in the history of the medical profession. Some phases of the healing art have always been connected in primitive society with the priestly office and, hence, in the hands of men. Three great branches, however, were always, in all forms of social organization of which we have knowledge, in the hands exclusively of women, namely, midwifery, the treatment of diseases of women so far as those were cared for at all, and the diseases of children. The growth of Christian missions to foreign countries has been due in large part to the employment of women medical missionaries to enter the secluded homes of women in so-called heathen countries where the primitive taboo still forbids the entrance of a man not her husband into the sickroom of a woman, or into the nursery of her child. That men should attend women in childbirth, or should become to women that most intimate of friends, a "family physician," is still unthinkable to the modesty of the Oriental woman. The result of this sex-segregation in the care of the sick in these important branches has been that women doctors, unschooled but often not unskilled, have served all the past of human experience in childbirth, in child-care, and in the special illnesses of women. This has been true in our own, as well as in older civilizations up to the 18th century. In our own country, in colonial times, only women ushered into a bleak New England the potential citizens of the new world. . . .

Busied with other matters, the Colonies paid little attention to medical science until the war of the American Revolution betrayed the awful results of ignorance in the slaughter of soldiers by preventable disease. When the healing art began to become a true science and took great strides toward better training and facilities of practice for the student, attention was at once drawn to the need for better service in the fields wholly occupied by women. The opening and improvement of the medical schools, however, was a new opportunity for men alone and the new demand for more scientific care of women in childbirth and for higher medical service to childhood and for the women suffering from special diseases, resulted in the greatest of innovations, namely, the assumption by men of the office of midwife and their entrance into the most intimate relationships with women patients. Dr. James Lloyd, after two years' study in England, began to practise "obstetrics" (the new name that disguised in some degree the daring change in medical practice) in Boston, in 1762. Dr. Shippen, similarly trained abroad, took up the same practice in Philadelphia and added lectures upon the subject. Thus began in our own country the elevation of this important branch of the healing art to a professional standard and the consequent exclusion of women from their immortal rights in the sickroom. It was a poor recognition of the debt the race owed to the mother-sex, both as suffering the pangs of

childbirth and as helping to assuage them and in caring for the infants and children of all time. . . .

In addition to these handicaps must be named the well-known but scarcely adequately measured interruptions to both study and self-expression which the women of talent and specialized power have always experienced. Anyone can see that to write *Uncle Tom's Cabin* on the knee in the kitchen, with constant calls to cooking and other details of housework to punctuate the paragraphs, was a more difficult achievement than to write it at leisure in a quiet room. And when her biographer says of an Italian woman poet, "during some years her Muse was intermitted," we do not wonder at the fact when he casually mentions her ten children. No record, however, can even name the women of talent who were so submerged by child-bearing and its duties, and by "general housework," that they had to leave their poems and stories all unwritten. Moreover, the obstacles to intellectual development and achievement which marriage and maternity interpose (and which are so important that they demand a separate study) are not the only ones that must be noted. It is not alone the fact that women have generally had to spend most of their strength in caring for others that has handicapped them in individual effort; but also that they have almost universally had to care wholly for themselves. Women even now have the burden of the care of their belongings, their dress, their home life of whatever sort it may be, and the social duties of the smaller world, even if doing great things in individual work. A successful woman preacher was once asked "what special obstacles have you met as a woman in the ministry?" "Not one," she answered, "except the lack of a minister's wife." When we read of Charles Darwin's wife not only relieving him from financial cares but seeing that he had his breakfast in his room, with "nothing to disturb the freshness of his morning," we do not find the explanation of Darwin's genius, but we do see how he was helped to express it. Men geniuses, even of second grade, have usually had at least one woman to smooth their way, and often several women to make sure that little things, often even self-support itself, did not interfere with the development and expression of their talent. On the other hand, the obligation of all the earlier women writers to prepare a useful cook-book in order to buy their way into literature, is a fitting symbol of the compulsion laid upon women, however gifted, to do all the things that women in general accomplish before entering upon their special task. That brave woman who wanted to study medicine so much that not even the heaviest family burdens could deter her from entering the medical school first opened to her sex, but who "first sewed steadily until her entire family was fitted with clothes to last six months," is a not unusual type.

Added to all this, the woman of talent and of special gifts has had until very lately, and in most countries has still, to go against the massed social pressure of her time in order to devote herself to any particular intellectual task. The expectation of society has long pushed men toward some special work; the expectation of society has until recently been wholly against women's choosing any vocation beside their functional service in the family. . . .

In view of these tremendous obstacles, it is fair to assume that when women in the past have achieved even a second or third place in the ranks of genius they have shown far more native ability than men have needed to reach the same eminence. Not excused from the more general duties that constitute the cement of society, most women of talent have had but one hand free with which to work out their ideal conceptions. Denied, at cost of "respectability" itself, any expression of that obstinate egotism which is nature's protection of the genius in his special task, and in the preparation for it, they have had to make secret and painful experiments in self-expression after spending first strength in the commonplace tasks required of all their sex.

Mary Roberts (Smith) Coolidge (1860–1945) on the Socialization of Girls

Mary Roberts Coolidge (also known as Mary Roberts Smith) was born Mary Elizabeth Burroughs in 1860. Her father, a professor and the dean of agriculture at Cornell University, was a strong supporter of women's achievement and encouraged her keen intellectual interests. From her mother she learned traditional women's skills such as sewing and housekeeping. Mary Burroughs earned her bachelor's and master's degrees at Cornell in 1880 and 1882, respectively, after which she taught school for a few years in Washington, DC, and Chicago. She then obtained a position teaching economics and history at Wellesley College, where she met and married her first husband, Albert W. Smith, changing her name to Mary Roberts Smith. After a few moves, the couple settled for a time at Stanford University in California, where she began graduate work in the new field of sociology. Smith was such an impressive student and scholar that she was appointed assistant professor of sociology at Stanford in 1894 and was promoted to associate professor in 1899. In the meantime, she completed her doctorate in 1896. Thus, Mary Roberts Smith has the distinction of being the first woman to hold a full-time position in an academic sociology department—she taught courses on crime, family, charities, statistics, race, poverty, and other topics. During this period she published articles in such journals as the *American Journal of Sociology* and authored a few books. Among her colleagues were E. A. Ross, George Howard, and H. H. Powers. Smith's later years at Stanford were marked by serious personal and professional turmoil, as the department was embroiled in serious conflicts with the university administration (Ross was fired and several colleagues resigned). Following this academic stress and a divorce, Smith suffered a mental breakdown, resigning from her position for health reasons in 1903.

By 1904 Mary Roberts Smith had recovered but Stanford refused to rehire her. She moved to a San Francisco settlement house as director and later to Berkeley, remarrying a former student, Dane Coolidge, adopting his surname from that time. This marriage was apparently very happy and lasted until his death in 1940.

Coolidge worked as a researcher, city planner, writer, lecturer, and feminist activist and social critic for many years. Among her works was a major study of Chinese immigration (1906), developed for the Carnegie Institute, and her book *Why Women Are So* (1912), which analyzed women's socialization and roles from a feminist perspective. During these years, Coolidge was also active as a leader of the suffrage movement for women.

In 1918 Coolidge again entered academia as a professor at Mills College, a private women's college. There she established a sociology department and became its first chair. She retired from that institution in 1926, receiving an honorary LLD from Mills the following year. After this, she and her husband spent almost two decades studying the Native cultures of the American Southwest and Mexico, publishing a number of works from these efforts. Coolidge died in 1945, about five years following the death of her husband.

Among Coolidge's extensive writings, Deegan identifies several themes: the documentation of women's inferior social position and appeals for reform; an analysis of poverty and its effects, with suggestions for improved services; an understanding of the social construction of gender and the need for greater attention to women in social policy; and a focus on the lives of minority peoples in the United States and Mexico. In Coolidge's *Chinese Immigration* (1909), Deegan writes, the analysis of competition and assimilation "predated the more well-known work of Park and Burgess (1921)" and "is more sophisticated as well." Deegan calls this book "an overlooked gem of scholarship and theoretical power," a comment that could aptly be applied to much of Coolidge's work.

MAJOR WORKS

Smith, Mary Roberts. *Almshouse Women: A Study of Two Hundred and Twenty-Eight Women in the City and County Almshouses of San Francisco*. Vol. 3, *Leland Stanford Junior University Publications: History and Economics*. Stanford, CA: Stanford University, 1896.

Coolidge, Mary Roberts. *Chinese Immigration*. New York: Henry Holt, 1909.

———. *Why Women Are So*. New York: Henry Holt, 1912. (Also see the recent reprint edition with an introduction by Mary Jo Deegan, Vol. 13, *Classics in Women's Studies* (Amherst, NY: Humanity Books, 2004)).

———. *The Rain Makers: Indians of Arizona and New Mexico*. Boston: Houghton Mifflin, 1926.

Coolidge, Dane, and Mary Roberts Coolidge. *The Navajo Indians*. Boston: Houghton Mifflin, 1930.

SOURCES

Deegan, Mary Jo. 1991. Mary E. B. R. S. Coolidge. In *Women in Sociology: A bio-bibliographical sourcebook*, ed. Mary Jo Deegan, 100–109. Westport, CT: Greenwood.

———. 2004. Introd. to *Why women are so*, by Mary Roberts Coolidge. Classics in Women's Studies. Amherst, NY: Humanity Books.

THE SELECTION

Below is the introductory chapter (edited and excerpted) from Mary Roberts Coolidge's book *Why Women Are So* (1912). Her main thesis is that "sex traditions rather than innate sex character have produced what is called 'feminine' as distinguished from

From Mary Roberts Coolidge, *Why Women Are So* (New York: Henry Holt, 1912) 3–18.

womanly behavior" (p. v). In other words, Coolidge was an early proponent of the notion of the social construction of gender as opposed to biological determination. She criticized thinkers who saw mother-hood as the primary purpose of women and argued strongly for expanded opportunities for women. In this selection, she focuses on the problems in socialization of girls.

THE CONVENTIONS OF GIRLHOOD

"Creatures of circumstance who waited to be fallen in love with. . . . We stood and waited—on approval. And then came life itself and tore our mother's theories to tatters."

—CICELY HAMILTON

"The chief element of a good time . . . as these countless rich young women judge it, are a petty eventfulness, laughter, and to feel you are looking well and attracting attention. Shopping is one of its chief joys. . . . My cousins were always getting and giving, my uncle caressed them with parcels and checks. . . . So far as marriage went, the married state seemed at once very attractive and dreadfully serious to them, composed in equal measure of becoming important and becoming old. I don't know what they thought about children. I doubt if they thought about them at all."

—H. G. WELLS

"Fine girls sittin' like shopkeepers behind their goods, waitin' and waitin' and waitin'. . . ."

—OLIVER WINDELL HOLMES

Feminine life in the middle Nineteenth Century, and to a degree now almost inconceivable, was permeated with the current traditions of what good women had been, and by the assumption that these stood for the pattern of what they should still be. From the moment of birth their sex was outwardly marked by the color of their ribbons, which became the embodiment, as it were, of their discreet and pallid characteristics.

Throughout the weeks that followed the mother watched impatiently to see whether the baby's hair would be curly—"for curly hair is so pretty in a girl, you know." By the time the infant could walk and talk, she had learned that there were things taboo for her which were perfectly proper for the little male creatures of her kind: *she* might not yell, nor romp, nor scuffle, nor, in short, "be a tomboy," because it was not nice for a little girl.

While the little boys of her age were gradually emancipated from lingerie garments, she still remained the charming baby-doll of the household. Her clothes continued to be made of light-colored and fragile materials, which she was constantly adjured not to soil. Her complexion, her hair, her tiny hands and feet were discussed in her presence as if they were marketable assets. Almost the first words in her vocabulary were "nice" and "pretty;" the one subtly stimulating sex-consciousness, the other associated with her physical limitations and the good looks which were to be a chief end of her existence. For her alone was coined the phrase: pretty is that pretty does. Boys did not have to be pretty, only good and smart; and, therefore, in the initial rivalry of the sexes she instinctively learned to lay her emphasis on prettiness. As a consequence, while she was still in knee-length dresses, clothing, manners, and appearance became of superlative importance. Her guardians need not have been surprised, when, a few years later, she became a vain and self-conscious creature, already measuring her beauty against that of other girls, and prematurely trying it on the males of her acquaintance.

But alas for her if her hair did not curl—if she turned out plain, or "not so pretty as her mother was"! She heard from grandmothers and other ladies of fading complexions and charms, over their needlework and tea, a chorus of pity. Many a little girl has cried her eyes out in secret because she had straight hair, large ears, or a muddy skin. This constant emphasis upon appearance had the effect, upon one temperament, of concentrating the desire of her whole nature on the attainment of conventional prettiness; upon another more sensitive one to create a morbid embarrassment amounting to tragedy; and sometimes upon stronger natures, to turn their aspirations toward some form of practical efficiency or to intellectual pursuits. However it turned out, before the girl-child was ten years old she had received an indelible impression that beauty, particularly a purely physical and luscious loveliness—such as would have been a disadvantage to a boy—was the most important attainment of a young girl's life.

Very early in this process of inculcating femininity it was necessary to check and pervert her physical impulses. Like the racing-horse, she must be trained while yet a colt never to break her gait. The goal of conventional prettiness permitted no indulgence in dirt or sunburn, therefore she could not run or play freely out-of-doors nor develop her muscles in competitive games that required speed and wind, a quick eye and a sure aim. Being a lively animal, her natural energy would try to find outlet somewhere at first, according to her temperament and coerced by her parents' ideals of woman's sphere. If she had a robust body and a strong-willed, original personality, she would kick over the traces and

break through the corral fence a good many times before the habits of domestication became ingrained. Such a temperament was always a source of trouble until she submitted to the life predestined for her by the traditions of her foremothers. She was, indeed, fortunate if her temper was not embittered, her health undermined, or her life made unhappy by the thwarting of her natural character.

But if she were born not too vigorous, and both docile and pretty, her path was smooth for her from the very beginning. Before she had mastered her letters she learned the horror of dirt, and set out on that approved career of dainty fastidiousness which is the glory of womankind. Instead of developing her muscles in large, free movements, she spent her placid girlhood in dressing girl-dolls that were models of ladylikeness; in giving little girls' tea-parties, where the social game of their elders was imitated in the exhibition of best clothes, the practice of polite, conversational gossip, and the rehearsal of the attractive arts; and in learning to make patchwork and her own clothes, prize cakes and fancy jellies if her mother were of the older school; or, at a later date, in doing monstrous fancy-work and embroidering her undergarments.

While her brothers played baseball and shinny or went swimming, she sat on a piano-stool, with her feet a few inches from the floor, practising the hour or two a day necessary to attain a meager proficiency. For in that day the ideal young lady must play the piano; not at all because she had musical talent worthy of serious cultivation, or because it was a necessary equipment for life—one scarcely knows why, unless to keep her out of mischief, or, perhaps, to make her more alluring to that future husband who might like a little music in the evenings now and then to soothe his nerves.

Nor was her domestic training of a much more thorough sort, although the tradition that the women of the household should be cooks and manufacturers was still widespread. Among middle-class American families the domestic habits of Europe persisted long after manufactured goods were to be had in stores, and even at the beginning of a new century country women are still canning fruit, making bedding, crocheting lace—still clinging to the handicrafts of a bygone industrial period. But the daughters of the latter half of the Nineteenth Century have had, on the one hand, slight respect for these homely accomplishments; and, on the other, scant opportunity for training in the more serious duties of administration of the household.

The feminine training of the Eighteenth Century was purely domestic; that of our generation purely academic; and thus there has been at least sixty years in the interim when girls were brought up almost without education for domestic life, and wholly without practical preparation for any other kind of life. During this period the manufacture of cotton and woolen goods in factories was superseding domestic processes; and even the preparation of food products was being transferred from the home to large collective agencies. As the processes of production were taken out of the house the physically stronger girls and women without male support followed it into the factory, there to become producers again, or into great department stores, to be distributors. But the great body of mothers and daughters left behind in homes still clung instinctively to the convention that domestic life was the economic sphere of women, although the necessary handicrafts which had made it so were all but gone.

The housewife of the Eighteenth Century earned her own living, and often quite half that of the family, by her labor, beside bearing and rearing children; and many women in our time, on the other hand, are rapidly acquiring economic independence; but, in the century between, thousands of women in America scarcely earned their salt. Not because they were lazy or incapable, but because the older ideal did not permit any but a serving-woman to go outside the home to earn money, and the occupations which had formerly made the home both a workshop and a storehouse no longer demanded their service.

So when our docile young girl in her immaculate frock had tired of playing with dolls and giving mannerly parties, she occupied herself in painting on velvet, in embroidery, crochet, or tatting, and in piano practice, in the intervals of a very polite education. In school she learned the common branches and, if she kept on long enough, acquired a superficial knowledge of English and American literature, made a painful reading-acquaintance with classical French, absorbed a little political history of by-gone European states, and, occasionally, a little mathematical astronomy and polite, herbarium botany. In those days, no knowledge of physiology, no discoveries of the laws of life in the biological laboratory, ever disturbed the guarded decency of the mind of any potential mother of the race.

This purely cultural and well-intentioned, but misdirected, education for young girls was one of the early by-products of the theories of democracy. In the Old World men and women had been born to a definite status in society, in which economic opportunities, duties, training, and even costume, were predetermined; but in the newer world, when the pioneers of the Colonial period had established their families with a competence, it became their ambition to lift their descendants into a higher social class. While the father was earning the money to fulfil their ambition, and the mother continued to practise the traditional handicrafts of the household, the daughters went to school and expressed, by their white-handedness and all but useless accomplishments, the rising social status of the family.

As domestic manufactures were superseded by factory-made products, there was less and less for girls to do at home, and there arose a kind of spurious feminine craft in the shape of inartistic and perfectly useless fancy-work. When the patchwork quilt, the hand-woven bed-cover and linen sheet had been replaced by the manufactured comforter and cheap cotton, women began to devise pillow shams, bedspreads of cloth cut into crazy-shaped pieces, or knitted of a thousand tiny shells. When the feather pillow, which once cost the housewife so much labor, came to be made in quantities by machinery, she turned her ambition into baby-pillows, pine-pillows, headrests, throws, tidies, feather and hair flowers, sofa cushions, and rag rugs—in short, into a vast variety of quasi-ornamental, altogether hideous, and generally useless articles. The tradition that the woman should be a manufacturer—a tradition handed down from the dim ages when the female tanned the skins, wove the mats and blankets, and built the tepee—died slowly, and is not yet wholly vanished.

It may seem very strange that girls did not learn at least to cook, that being the oldest and most universal of women's occupations; and all the more as the chief pride of their mothers lay in housewifery, the center of which lay in the kitchen. As other handicrafts became less imperative, the housewife of the earlier period concentrated her whole mind on feeding her men-folks lavishly. Imbued with the colonial-English tradition of good eating, and spurred on by the rivalry of neighbor women equally energetic, she piled cake, pie, doughnuts, preserved fruit, and pancakes, with meat and vegetables, on the creaking table. She would doubtless have insisted on her pretty daughter learning to make all these elaborate dishes as she had learned them from her own mother, but for the arrival of thousands of immigrant Irish and German servants to give her cheap and willing assistance.

Nobody, not even a sturdy pioneer woman, continues to do hard manual labor when it is no longer either compulsory or admirable. The highly-skilled house-mother, remembering the hot stove, the aching feet, and the never-ending "woman's work," wanted her daughters to have an easier life than she had had, and was glad to accept the help of clumsy peasant hands in order to release them from such hardship. Moreover, the plain American fathers and mothers still associated gentle-hood with freedom from manual labor of an obligatory kind, and would not permit their soft-handed daughters to compete with foreign servant girls.

During the years of adolescence girls went to school, not because they expected to use the education they were getting in any practical way, but largely to fill up the time in a ladylike manner until they should be courted and married. If now and then some girl—too plain to join in the beauty contest, or too vital and ambitious to be contented with so tame a program of life—attempted to break through the meshes of the feminine cult into a larger sphere, she found few opportunities for solid education or occupation open to her, and was greeted with general disapproval. If she had a sturdy, fighting temper, and a love of learning or achievement, she sometimes threw away her pack of feminine traditions and took the trail in pursuit of the ideal. It was, indeed, a desert that they traveled—those first, few, strong-minded young women—and, however the adventure turned out, the effect of opposition, of lack of sympathy and opportunity, the starvation of the natural human soul hungering for justice and for the approval of its kind, could only be to pervert character. Some came out of the struggle strong creatures, but masculine imitations rather than fully developed women; others, maddened by injustice or misunderstanding, set their hands against every man; championing wild or premature causes; but the larger number disappeared from history, merely defeated feminine souls carrying too great a handicap.

During all those years when plain and pretty girls alike were growing up, they came somehow to know that their destiny was to be married. Not that any one asked them what they were going to be or do— that would have been quite improper or might have precipitated questions which girls should not ask. Their brothers, even before they left the grammar school, were encouraged to talk of their future occupations, and to make preparation for them. But while girls heard from the pulpit and the rostrum, and read in the harmless romances of Sunday-school books or ladies' magazines, that marriage and motherhood were the inevitable and only admirable career of woman, nothing was ever said to them, except by way of a joke, about either. Indirectly, some conscientious mother might approach it shamefacedly, suggesting that the daughter should learn some household task, "because you may have a home of your own, some day;" but never a serious word was said about wifehood and motherhood. The atmosphere of prudery surrounding marriage and child-bearing, which was all but universal a century ago, is still common enough among ignorant women, who will never discuss before a spinster of any age, not even before a charity visitor, the facts incident to pregnancy. While boys were learning in the farmyard and from other men the facts and processes of reproduction, girls-walked in a mist of secrecy and innuendo. When their mothers were bearing children they were sent away from home on some pretense, lest they should witness the great travail and be afraid; or, perhaps, because their parents were ashamed; or, it may be, solely because the convention was that young girls must be kept "innocent."

But girls are no more fools than boys, and the atmosphere of prudish or vulgar suggestion aroused in the keen-witted ones a determination to know how babies came, and what marriage meant. Many a young girl, not daring to ask what she wanted to know of older women, got a perverted knowledge from vulgar-minded servants, or from the medical dictionaries in the library; or puzzled out the obscene advertisements and tragedies of the half-world covertly described in the newspapers; or pored over the sexual horrors of the ancient scriptures, to satisfy her curiosity.

In the less curious and less original type of girl the conventional silence about her future career created a shrinking disgust from the facts of reproductive life. She became ashamed of her functions without knowing why. She could not help seeing that the figures of women were not beautiful during gestation, and that pregnancy and childbirth were a period of inconvenience, if not of semi-invalidism. While the "glory" of motherhood was constantly preached at her, she heard women criticising the indecency of wives who appeared in public in the later months of pregnancy, and sometimes saw the lascivious smiles, or overheard the comments of men upon them. Nor could she escape knowing that some men were wild beasts, nor the suggestion that men in general were not to be trusted in the dark. Thus everything in her own nature and everything in the social influences about her tended to produce repulsion, if not terror, for the only approved destiny held out before her.

Meanwhile, during the adolescent years of both the inquisitive and the acquiescent young woman, her mind was being colored by the effeminate fiction of the day, whose chief note was love and lovers, with a happy ending in marriage. That the experiences of the heroine did not seem to correspond with the lives of the women she knew, made it all the more alluring. In this dream-world there were no puzzling and inevitable facts of nature—the lover was always pure and brave and considerate; the heroine beautiful and adored. There was no baby even, as in real life, to precipitate difficulties, except on the last page, when he might arrive to fulfil the hope of an heir to some great property.

Somewhere along this road of female destiny the girl received a shock; from the newspapers, perhaps, or more often through some tragedy in her own community, she heard that some unhappy girl had murdered her baby or ended her unwedded romance in *suicide*. Then, suddenly, if she were capable of reasoning at all, she would realize that motherhood was only considered sacred when licensed by the State and by the Church.

At last, when she had filled in a few years following her schooldays with "helping her mother," "going into society," playing the piano, and teaching a Sunday-school class, and in modestly trying out her charms on the young men of her acquaintance, *The Lover* arrived. It is not without reason that the period of courtship has been depicted from time immemorial as the happiest of life. The exhilaration of quickening instinct, the zest of the game of advance and retreat, the grateful mutual flattery, are full of joy to the woman even more than to the man. For while to the man it might become the highest experience of his life if the ending were happy, it seldom had the full allurement of novelty. Very few men, probably, brought to their final courtship an unvulgarized mind, a chaste person, and an entire ignorance of the other sex, such as girls are expected to have. To the woman courtship and marriage were the culmination of a long dream, in which her natural instincts and hunger for life—a real life of her own—overcame her fear of men and her innocent dread of the travail of motherhood. Whether their temperaments were really domestic and maternal or not, passion, romance, and a desire for a career, combined with the tradition that marriage is the highest if not the only destiny to make young women take the path of least resistance.

It used to be said that childhood was the happiest time of life, and girlhood, even more than boyhood, full of joy. Certainly it was so when the parents were wise and sympathetic, and the children born with a harmonious temperament in a normal body. But the unconscious joy usually attributed to childhood has not so often existed in fact. Not even yet are parents wise enough to restrain without arbitrary coercion; to make the path of discipline and duty more alluring than that of self-indulgence; and to provide a wholesome outlet for physical energy. Nor are they sympathetic enough to enter into the fearsome questions of the young soul, and, out of the richness of adult experience, guide it till it attains courage and self-poise. In a girlhood such as I have been describing, happiness was only possible to the girl who submitted to the conventional mold. The more vigorous she was, the more potential character she had, the less easy she would find it to conform to the pattern laid before her. And if she did conform she was likely to arrive at womanhood physically undeveloped, and robbed of a part of her bodily vigor; prudish and ignorant, yet eager to be married; without preparation for domestic and maternal cares, and incapable of earning a fair living wage by any other means; and with an abnormally feminized conscience, which had no conception of men or the moral issues of their lives. The girl of the middle Nineteenth Century was fortunate if, by the grace of God and the accident of heedless parents, she sometimes arrived at the goal of marriage a little less docile, pretty, anemic, conscientious, and incompetent than the ideals of her time would have had her become.

Charlotte Perkins Gilman (1860–1935) on the Economics of Private Housekeeping

Charlotte Perkins Gilman was recognized as a leading American intellectual in the women's rights movement of the late nineteenth and early twentieth centuries. Even though she identified herself as a sociologist and was defined by many others as such (Deegan and Hill, 1997:10–11), her current reputation rests more on her works of fiction, including the widely reprinted short story "The Yellow Wall Paper." In addition to her books on women's place in society and culture, Gilman's sociological work can be found in many scholarly journals, such as the *American Journal of Sociology* and the *Annals of the American Academy of Political and Social Sciences*.

Gilman wrote in a diversity of genres, including poetry, novels, essays, and nonfiction articles and books. She was perhaps best known as a lecturer on women's issues, traveling throughout the United States and Europe to present her ideas on these topics, and as the founder and editor of an important magazine on women's issues, *The Forerunner*. Her most important sociological work was the book *Women and Economics: A Study of the Economic Relation between Men and Women as a Factor in Social Evolution* (1898), in which she emphasized the need for women's independence in marriage and suggested reforms to housework and child care to achieve that aim. A friend and admirer of Lester Frank Ward and his work on women, Gilman popularized many of his ideas on the position of women.

MAJOR WORKS

Gilman, Charlotte Perkins. *Women and Economics: A Study of the Economic Relation between Men and Women as a Factor in Social Evolution.* Boston, MA: Small, Maynard, 1898.

———. *The Home: Its Work and Influence.* New York: McClure, Phillips, 1903.

———. *The Man-Made World: or, Our Androcentric Culture.* New York: Charlton, 1911.

———. *His Religion and Hers: A Study of the Faith of Our Fathers and the Work of Our Mothers.* New York: Century, 1923.

SOURCES

Deegan, Mary J., and Michael R. Hill. 1997. *With her in Ourland: Sequel to Herland.* Westport: Praeger.

Gilman, Charlotte Perkins. 1990. *The living of Charlotte Perkins Gilman: An autobiography.* Madison: University of Wisconsin Press.

Lane, Ann J. 1990. *To Herland and beyond: The life and work of Charlotte Perkins Gilman.* New York: Pantheon Books.

Meyering, Sheryl L., ed. 1989. *Charlotte Perkins Gilman: The woman and her work.* Ann Arbor: UMI Research Press.

THE SELECTION

In this brief article, Charlotte Perkins Gilman criticizes the role of "domestic industry" as a holdover from an earlier stage of economic development, when slaves and often wives were expected to work for their owner-husbands as a duty without monetary compensation. In her contemporary society, woman was expected to do household and mothering work "because she is a woman, without any regard to special fitness or experience." This attitude toward women and domestic work is contrasted with the principles of work in industrial societies, where specialization and division of labor are basic to achieving efficiency. The contemporary organization of household work, Gilman argues, is a legacy from an earlier stage of economic development that inhibits the efficient accomplishment of this necessary labor. The present system that requires each woman to do only domestic work for her own separate household is wasteful in many ways, denying the economy the talents of many women while denying women the opportunity to work according to their interests and talents.

THE WASTE OF PRIVATE HOUSEKEEPING

The principal waste in our "domestic economy" lies in the fact that it is domestic.

Domestic industry is the earliest form of labor. Its original type is mother-service, to which was soon added wife-service and slave-service, often embodied in the same person. This primitive labor type increased in numbers where more than one slave, or wife, or slave-wife was possessed, and was slightly raised in grade as slave labor became serf labor, and that gradually turned to contract labor in a modified form.

The domestic servant is still expected to take part wage in barter, food and shelter being given instead of the full price in money; to live in the house of the employing family, to show the virtues of the earlier status, humility, loyalty, faithfulness, and, as belonging to that earlier status, no high degree of skill is expected.

From Charlotte Perkins Gilman, "The Waste of Private Housekeeping," *Annals of the American Academy of Political and Social Science* 48 (July 1913): 91–5.

Where no servants are employed, which in our country is the case in fifteen families out of sixteen, domestic industry is still at its first stage, mother-service. As such it is not regarded as labor, in any economic sense, but as a sex-function proper to the woman. She is expected to do the work because she is a woman, without any regard to special fitness or experience, this view being frequently expressed in the words "every girl should know how to cook," while no single trade is ever so mentioned as necessary to every boy.

Industrial efficiency grows along lines of specialization, organization and interchange. In the stage of industrial evolution when each man provided for himself by his own unaided exertions we find the maximum of effort with the minimum of product.

Domestic industry is the only survival of that stage in our otherwise highly differentiated economic system. While every woman is expected to follow one trade the grade of efficiency must remain at the lowest possible average.

The servant is but a shade higher in specialization, and this advantage is nullified by two conditions: first, that owing to its status few persons are willing to perform this service except those incompetent for more highly evolved duties; and second, that owing to the natural tendency of women to marry, the grade of domestic service is that of a perpetual apprenticeship.

Neither the labor of the overworked average mother, nor the labor of the perpetual low-grade apprentice, can ever reach high efficiency. This element of waste is inherent in domestic industry and cannot be overcome. No special training can be applied to every girl and produce good results in all; no psychological gymnastics can elevate housework when housework, in economic status, is at the very bottom of industrial evolution.

This is the first element of waste in domestic industry—permanent inefficiency. The second is in the amount of labor required.

While each man, however poor, requires one whole woman to cook for him, we have a condition in which half the people of the world are engaged in house-service.

Today some seven million women in the United States are working at gainful occupations, but several million of these are employed as house-servants, and the general division of labor is that women as a whole, 50 per cent of the world's workers, are in domestic industry.

The waste here is between this proportion and the proportion such work really requires, which is about 10 per cent. For fifty women to spend all their time doing what ten women could do in the same, or even less time, is a waste of 40 per cent of the world's labor.

Estimating the present market value of women's labor at charwoman's wages, $1.50 a day, and assuming that we have 15,000,000 working housewives, their labor is worth, per year, some $7,500,000,000. One-fifth of them could do the work at a cost of $1,500,000,000, making an annual saving of $6,000,000,000, about $300 per family. This element of waste has not been considered because we are not accustomed to consider women's work as having any cash value. Our lack of perception does not however alter the economic facts. While wasting, in house-service, 40 per cent of the productive industry of the woman world, we thus lose not only by the low average of capacity here stated, but all the higher potentiality of many women for the more valuable forms of world-service. In this connection no one should be allowed to claim that house-service is in itself noble, high, supremely valuable, while at the same time willing to leave its performance to the lowest grade of labor in the world.

The third element of waste in domestic industry is in the repetition of plant.

Under this head we will group the building expense involved in attaching a kitchen and laundry to every house (the smaller the house the greater the proportion of space given to this purpose; if but one room it must serve as the workshop), the furnishing of each kitchen with its stove, tubs, boilers, sink, and all the dishes, ironware, and utensils appurtenant, and the further supplying of each kitchen with water, light and fuel; also the amounts due for breakage and depreciation.

No definite figures can be given in estimates based on such widely varying conditions as those here considered, but it is shown from ample experience that one properly constituted kitchen can provide food for five hundred people, equal to one hundred families, and with space, fittings and supplies certainly not exceeding those of ten private kitchens.

A waste of 90 per cent is a conservative estimate here. If this seems too great we should hold in mind not only the reduction in original expense, between building one large kitchen and a hundred small ones, between the one outfit and the hundred in boilers, tubs, sinks, ranges, tables, refrigerators, pantrys, cupboards, etc., and not only the difference in the amount of fuel and other supplies needed, but the difference in the bills for breakage and repairs. Ten skilled experts, working under the proper conditions with proper tools, are not so expensive as a hundred clumsy beginners in a hundred necessarily imperfect average kitchens.

Beyond this comes the fourth great element of waste in domestic industry—that involved in the last and least extreme of retail purchasing.

Our economists should establish for us the difference between the "cost" and the "price" of living; what it really costs to raise and deliver our food, and what we are charged for it.

Here again the field of study is too wide, too varying in conditions, for exact tabulation in figures, but the amount wasted may

be roughly suggested by the difference between apples by the barrel at $3, and apples by the quart at 15 cents, or $12 a barrel—a waste of three-fourths.

In some commodities it is higher than this, in others much lower; but it is more than safe to say that we expend full twice as much as we need to for our food, by our small private purchasing. The poorer the purchaser the higher the price and the lower the value obtained.

We must remember that the high cost of living is not only in what we pay, but in what we buy; we are taxed not merely in the increased price, but in the decreased value. Ten cents a quart for good milk is high price. Ten cents a quart for a medicated, half-cooked, repulsive white fluid that does not sour but reeks instead, is a higher price.

We are striving in many ways, from federal laws to local inspection, to improve the quality of our food supplies, but no one seems to see that the one permanent continuing cause of poor food is the helplessness of the private purchaser.

The working housewife is not only the cook but the purchaser of food. She has little time and less money, and almost no knowledge. She has no machinery for testing the products offered her, no time to search widely, no cash to pay for the better grades. She must buy and buy quickly, close at home—for the baby is heavy to carry or left to uncertain risks.

Even if, by some gross miracle, all these millions of poor women could be taught to know bad food, that would not give them the means to pay for the good.

We have, of course, our Housewives' League, doing excellent work, but remember that the women who keep servants are but one-sixteenth of the whole; fifteen-sixteenths of our families are poor. This condition of ignorance and financial helplessness is what enables the bad food products to be kept on the market.

Now look at the difference in purchasing power when one skilled experienced buyer orders, at wholesale, for hundreds, perhaps thousands, of customers. Such a person would have the special knowledge and wide experience to recognize the best, and the power to demand it. No one condition would more promptly raise the standard of our food supply than this knowledge and power in the purchaser.

It is of no use to urge that "all women should be so trained." You could not make a skilled "tea-taster" of all men, nor a skilled caterer of all women. Specialization is necessary to develop skill. The domestic worker, wife, or servant, is eternally unspecialized.

This study is one of criticism, devoted to pointing out the wastes in our system of living, and to showing that they are inherent in that system. It is not possible at the same time and in the same space to present a convincing revelation as to how we might live otherwise. This much, however, may be stated: that the specialization of those industries now lumped together as "domestic" will no more injure "the privacy of the home," the "sanctity of the family," than has the specialization of the spinning-wheel. Neither maid nor matron may be now assailed with, "Go spin, you jade, go spin!" They do not spin—yet the home and family endure. This trade was once considered so wholly, so essentially a "feminine function" that we still have the term "spinster" to prove it. Similarly we might call a woman "a cookster" long after she had ceased to cook. But the integrity of the family, the happiness and wholesomeness of home life, are no more dependent on the private cook-stove than they were on the private spinning-wheel.

To conclude our list of wastes we ought to indicate a little of the waste of human life involved in this process, the waste of health, of energy, of the growing power of the world.

While the women waste four-fifths of their labor on this department of work, the men must make up by extra earnings. They are saddled with this extravagant and inefficient low-grade private industry, must pay its expenses and suffer from its deficiencies.

Our general food habits, and standard of health in the alimentary processes, are not such as to justify the dragging anachronism of domestic industry. If the world were kept healthy, happy, and well-fed, we might be willing to do it wastefully, but such is by no means the case.

The professionalization of cooking, cleaning and laundry work should be hailed not only by the economist but by the hygienist, the eugenist, and the social psychologist as a long upward step in world progress.

For the specific purposes of this paper it is enough to show that of all waste and extravagance in the cost of living none can equal this universal condition in which we waste four-fifths of the world's labor, more than half of our living expenses, and call it "domestic economy."

Edith Abbott (1876–1957) on Women in Industry

Edith Abbott was born in 1876 on the Nebraska frontier into a family that encouraged her independence and studies. Her mother was "a feminist, abolitionist, republican, and Quaker" who had graduated from Rockford Female Seminary in 1868. Her father was a lawyer and banker and served as the lieutenant governor of Nebraska. At the age of six, Edith met Susan B. Anthony, who, during a campaign for women's suffrage, stayed with the Abbott family.

After high school, Abbott attended the University of Nebraska, graduating in 1901. Two years later she received a fellowship for graduate study at the University of Chicago, earning a doctorate in political economy in 1905. In 1906 she went to London, where she studied research methods with Beatrice Webb, after which she worked in the Department of Economics and Sociology at Wellesley College. Later she returned to Chicago, where she lived at Hull House, continued her research on women, and taught in the Department of Sociology. When the University of Chicago School of Social Service Administration was formed in 1920, Abbott was appointed as associate professor and was later named dean, serving in that capacity from 1924 to 1942. She worked to obtain administrative positions for women and contributed to the formation of public policy relevant to women, children, and labor. She worked closely with Sophonisba Breckinridge, her sister Grace Abbott, Jane Addams, Florence Kelley, Emily Green Balch, and other prominent women social scientists/activists, their work often labeled "radical" because of its progressive quality. In her later years, Abbott was depressed over the rise of conservative McCarthyism, the death of some of her close friends, and the decline of the vitality of Hull House. She spent her last few years back in Nebraska with her brother until her death in 1957. In 1975 Abbott was inducted into the Women of Nebraska Hall of Fame.

MAJOR WORKS

Abbott, Edith. *Women in Industry: A Study of American Economic History*. New York: Appleton, 1910.

———. *Democracy and Social Progress in England.* University of Chicago War Papers 8. Chicago: University of Chicago Press, 1918.

———. *Immigration: Select Document and Case Records.* Chicago: University of Chicago Press, 1924.

———. *Social Welfare and Professional Education.* Chicago: University of Chicago Press, 1931.

———. *Public Assistance.* Chicago: University of Chicago Press, 1941.

SOURCES

Deegan, Mary Jo, and Michael R. Hill. 1991. Edith Abbott. In *Women in sociology: A bio-bibliographical sourcebook,* ed. Mary Jo Deegan, 29–36. Westport, CT: Greenwood.

Costin, Lela B. 1983. *Two sisters for social justice: A biography of Grace and Edith Abbott.* Urbana: University of Illinois Press.

THE SELECTION

In this final chapter of Edith Abbott's study of the history of American women in industry, she summarizes her findings and refutes the common assumption that women's employment outside the home is a recent phenomenon (in 1910) and that women were "doing men's work." She points out that many jobs that once were done by women are now done by men, and vice versa, so there is no absolute standard of what type of job "belongs" to one sex or the other. In the early days of the American colonies, women were expected to be gainfully employed, and as early factories were developed, this took them out of the home. In more recent years, women have attempted to become independent by joining the professions, but working-class women have always had to work to contribute to the family income. Thus, many of the common assumptions about women's role in the workplace are mistaken.

PUBLIC OPINION AND THE WORKINGWOMAN

In a study of our economic development it becomes clear that women have been from the beginning of our history an important factor in American industry. In the early days of the factory system they were an indispensable factor. Any theory, therefore, that women are a new element in our industrial life, or that they are doing "men's work," or that they have "driven out the men," is a theory unsupported by facts.

In order to avoid the vagueness which might come from generalizations dealing with our industrial system as a whole, an attempt has been made to review the history of the employment of women in several different industries. In this way, it has been

---

From Edith Abbott, "Public Opinion and the Workingwoman," in *Women in Industry: A Study in American Economic History* (New York: Appleton, 1910), 317–23.

possible to ascertain what work women were doing before and after the establishment of the factory system, and to show in what occupations and in what proportions women have been substituted for men, or men for women. A study of the five industries which employ to-day the largest numbers of women has furnished some interesting illustrations of the way in which the introduction of machinery and the establishment of the factory system have made necessary a readjustment of the work both of men and of women, and in the long run it has meant the breaking down of old customary lines of delimitation between women's work and men's work.

In the cotton manufacture and in the clothing trades, it was found that occupations such as spinning, weaving, and sewing, which historically had been pretty exclusively women's work in this country, are to-day not only shared with men but are in process of being taken over by men. On the other hand, printing and shoemaking are examples of skilled trades which may be said on the whole to have belonged to men in the colonial period, but which are now employing large numbers of women. Printing required very little physical strength, and women, therefore, became printers long before they entered the shoemaker's trade, which was too heavy to be carried on by women until a system of division of labor made it possible to give them lighter portions of the work. Cigarmaking, although it is an industry which has no history in the seventeenth and eighteenth centuries, has been carried on at different times both by men and by women, and furnishes an interesting example of the way in which work that was done originally by women but later taken over by men, may come to be women's work again.

In the cotton industry and in the clothing trades, therefore, men are doing work which for the most part was once done by women. In the printing trade and in the manufacture of boots and shoes, women are doing the work which would a century ago have been done by men. It should, however, be noted as a point of interest, that to-day the men's share in the two women's industries is much greater than the share of women in the two men's industries. That is, nearly 250,000 men, approximately one half of the total number of persons employed in the cotton and clothing industries, are men, while the number of women in "printing" and "boots and shoes" is, in round numbers, but 70,000 or not quite one third of the total number in those trades. It would appear, therefore, that men have gained more than women by this readjustment of work. But it may be again repeated that in all of these five industries, women have been employed for more than a hundred years, and it is now too late to look upon them as entering a new field of employment in which they have no right. It should be especially emphasized, too, that during all of these years, women not only were industrially employed in large numbers, but that they were liberally encouraged by the public opinion of an earlier day to enter these occupations.

Throughout the colonial period, and for more than half a century after the establishment of our Republic, the attitude not only of the statesman but of the public moralist was that of rigid insistence on the gainful employment of women, either in the home, or as the household industries grew decreasingly profitable, away from it. In the seventeenth and eighteenth centuries court orders directed that the women of the various towns should be kept employed, and Puritan ministers warned them of the dangers of idle living. Spinning schools were founded to assist women in earning their own maintenance; and when the first cotton factories were established, they were welcomed as a means of enriching the country by women's labor. The same confident approval of every means of providing gainful occupations for women, particularly poor women, is to be found in the discussion which centered about the policy of encouraging and protecting our infant industries after the present government had been established.

NUMBER OF PERSONS EMPLOYED IN 1905

	Women	Men
In the cotton mills	128,163	147,283
In the clothing industry	147,710	101,373
Total	275,873	248,656
In "boots and shoes"	49,535	95,257
In printing and publishing	19,975	65,293
Total	69,510	160,550

Looking back at the change in the domestic economy of the household which was being wrought at this time, we see the carding, spinning, weaving, dyeing—the old historic occupations of women in the home, being taken away from them; a great demand for hands to police the new machines; and the women quietly following their work from the home to the factory. This was not only the natural thing for them to do but it was demanded of them by the public opinion of their day, and there was no voice lifted then to remind them that woman's proper place was at home.

It is clear that it was primarily as an economic problem, and in relation to other economic problems that Hamilton, Treneh Coxe, Gallatin, Matthew Carey, Hezekiah Niles, H. C. Carey, and the minor pamphleteers who followed in their wake, concerned themselves with women's work. Here was a fund of labor from which a larger return could be obtained if it were employed in manufacturing industries, and they made precise computations as to just how much that gain would be. More than that, here was also a defensive argument sustaining an important measure of public policy and

suggesting a solution for one of the economic problems of the time. Unfortunately the employment of women was not considered, on its own merits, and how far it would have met condemnation instead of encouragement if it had not fitted into the scheme of a contemporary policy it is impossible to say.

It has become something of a public habit to speak of the women who work in factories to-day as if they were invaders threatening to take over work which belongs to men by custom and prior right of occupation. This mistake is due to the fact that there has been an increase in gainful employment among women, and although attention is frequently called to this fact, it is not pointed out that this increase is not equally distributed in all groups of occupations. Tables from the data furnished by the last census, which have already been given, show that this increase is disproportionate only in the group, trade and transportation, and that in the manufactures group men are increasing more rapidly than women. In this connection, attention may be called once more to the fact that the "woman movement" of the last century belongs most exclusively to educated women. So far as industrial employments are concerned, they were considered especially suited to women at a time when men did not regard such work as profitable enough for themselves. By prior right of occupation, and by the invitation of early philanthropists and statesmen, the workingwoman holds a place of her own in this field. In the days when the earliest factories were calling for operatives the public moralist denounced her for "eating the bread of idleness," if she refused to obey the call. Now that there is some fear lest profuse immigration may give us an oversupply of labor, and that there may not be work enough for the men, it is the public moralist again who finds that her proper place is at home and that the world of industry was created for men. The woman of the working classes was self-supporting and was expected to be self-supporting more than three quarters of a century ago, and even long before that she was reproached for "eating the bread of idleness." The efforts of the professional woman to realize a new ideal of pecuniary independence, which have taken her out of the home and into new and varied occupations, belong to recent, if not contemporary history. But this history, for her, covers a social revolution, and the world she faces is a new one. The woman of the working classes finds it, so far as her measure of opportunity goes, very much as her great grandmother left it.

Leta Stetter Hollingworth (1886–1939) on Compelling Women to Bear Children

Nebraska native Leta Stetter Hollingworth was a major contributor to the growing field of psychology, researching and publishing work in the psychology of women, education, and sex differences. Her early life was fraught with difficulties. At age 3, her mother died and her care was taken over by her maternal grandparents, with whom she developed a close relationship. When she was 13, she and her younger sisters were taken away from that home by her father, whose new wife refused to allow the girls to have any contact with their beloved grandparents or any members of their mother's family. The three sisters were forced to live in the strict and abusive household of the stepmother and father, and Leta became the surrogate mother to her younger sisters. At age 15, after graduation from high school, she was able to escape the oppressive household by entering the University of Nebraska at Lincoln, where she excelled in her studies and discovered the field of psychology. It was in one of her psychology classes that she met her husband-to-be, Harry Levi Hollingworth, whom she married in 1908. He completed a doctorate and was appointed to the faculty at Barnard College in New York.

For a few years, Leta taught high school while attempting to write short stories for magazines, but her writing hopes were frustrated by rejections of her work. By 1911 the couple had saved enough to allow Leta to attend Columbia's Teachers College, where she entered the educational psychology program. She earned a PhD in 1916 with a dissertation that examined the then-popular hypothesis that women's "periodicity" affected their mental ability. Afterward, she was offered a position on the Educational Psychology faculty of Teachers College, Columbia, where she spent her entire career, achieving the rank of Full Professor in 1929.

Hollingworth's career as a psychologist was associated with a number of key studies that successfully called into question commonly held stereotypes about women and their abilities. She took a strongly empiricist stance, demonstrating successfully that data from careful research did not support the prejudicial attitudes that characterized much of social and psychological thinking about women.

According to one account, "Leta Hollingworth's work was among the first scientifically to challenge the assertions of the biological inferiority of women" (Benjamin and Shields, 1990:179). Her work appeared in several sociological journals, such as the *American Journal of Sociology* and the *Journal of Educational Psychology*. She was recognized as the "scientific pillar" of the women's movement because of her work on women; her research on gifted children also was influential. Hollingworth was one of only fourteen women included in Robert Watson's *Eminent Contributors to Psychology* (1974, 1976), an indication of her importance in the field. Her life was cut short by abdominal cancer in 1939 at age 53.

Major Works

Hollingworth, L. S. "Variability as Related to Sex Differences in Achievement: A Critique." *American Journal of Sociology* 19 (1914): 510–30.

———. "Social Devices for Impelling Women to Bear and Rear Children." *American Journal of Sociology* 22 (1916):19–29.

———. "Comparison of the Sexes in Mental Traits." *Psychological Bulletin* 15 (1918): 427–32.

———. *Gifted Children.* New York: Macmillan, 1926.

Sources

Benjamin, Ludy T., Jr., and Stephanie A. Shields. 1990. Leta Stetter Hollingworth (1886–1939). In *Women in psychology: A biographical sourcebook,* ed. Agnes N. O'Connell and Nancy Felipe Russo, 173–83. Westport, CT: Greenwood.

Watson, Robert I. 1974/1976. *Eminent contributors to psychology.* 2 vols. New York: Springer.

The Selection

This 1916 *American Journal of Sociology* article applies E. A. Ross's categories of social control to illuminate the ways societies "impel" women to have children. Leta Stetter Hollingworth points out that pregnancy and childbearing involve serious sacrifices and dangers for women, similar to those for soldiers, and she asks why women continue to accept this burden. Her analysis reveals a very thoughtful and creative scholar whose article even today is fascinating and worthy of consideration.

Social Devices for Impelling Women to Bear and Rear Children

"Again, the breeding function of the family would be better discharged if public opinion and religion conspired, as they have until recently, to crush the aspirations of woman for a life of her own. But the gain would not be worth the price."

—E. A. Ross, *Social Control* (1904).

From Leta S. Hollingworth, "Social Devices for Impelling Women to Bear and Rear Children," *American Journal of Sociology* 22, no. 1 (1916):19–29.

In this quotation from Ross we have suggested to us an exceedingly important and interesting phase of social control, namely, the control by those in social power over those individuals who alone can bring forth the human young, and thus perpetuate society. It is necessary that at the very outset of this discussion we should consent to clear our minds of the sentimental conception of motherhood and to look at facts. Sumner[1] states these facts as well as they have ever been stated, in his consideration of the natural burdens of society. He says:

> Children add to the weight of the struggle for existence of their parents. The relation of parent to child is one of sacrifice. The interests of parents and children are antagonistic. The fact that there are or may be compensations does not affect the primary relation between the two. It may well be believed that, if procreation had not been put under the dominion of a great passion, it would have been caused to cease by the burdens it entails.

This is especially true in the case of the mothers.

The fact is that child-bearing is in many respects analogous to the work of soldiers: it is necessary for tribal or national existence; it means great sacrifice of personal advantage; it involves danger and suffering, and, in a certain percentage of cases, the actual loss of life. Thus we should expect that there would be a continuous social effort to insure the group-interest in respect to population, just as there is a continuous social effort to insure the defense of the nation in time of war. It is clear, indeed that the social devices employed to get children born, and to get soldiers slain, are in many respects similar.

But once the young are brought into the world they still must be reared, if society's ends are to be served, and here again the need for and exercise of social control may be seen. Since the period of helpless infancy is very prolonged in the human species, and since the care of infants is an onerous and exacting labor, it would be natural for all persons not biologically attached to infants to use all possible devices for fastening the whole burden of infant-tending upon those who are so attached. We should expect this to happen, and we shall see, in fact, that there has been consistent social effort to establish as a norm the woman whose vocational proclivities are completely and "naturally" satisfied by child-bearing and child-rearing, with the related domestic activities.

There is, to be sure, a strong and fervid insistence on the "maternal instinct," which is popularly supposed to characterize all women equally, and to furnish them with an all-consuming desire for parenthood, regardless of the personal pain, sacrifice, and disadvantage involved. In the absence of all verifiable data, however, it is only common-sense to guard against accepting as a fact of human nature a doctrine which we might well expect to find in use as a means of social control. Since we possess no scientific data at all on this phase of human psychology, the most reasonable assumption is that if it were possible to obtain a quantitative measurement of maternal instinct, we should find this trait distributed among women, just as we have found all other traits distributed which have yielded to quantitative measurement. It is most reasonable to assume that we should obtain a curve of distribution, varying from an extreme where individuals have a zero or negative interest in caring for infants, through a mode where there is a moderate amount of impulse to such duties, to an extreme where the only vocational or personal interest lies in maternal activities.

The facts, shorn of sentiment, then, are: (1) The bearing and rearing of children is necessary for tribal or national existence and

---

[1] W. G. Sumner, *Folkways*, 1906.

aggrandizement. (2) The bearing and rearing of children is painful, dangerous to life, and involves long years of exacting labor and self-sacrifice. (3) There is no verifiable evidence to show that a maternal instinct exists in women of such all-consuming strength and fervor as to impel them voluntarily to seek the pain, danger, and exacting labor involved in maintaining a high birth rate.

We should expect, therefore, that those in control of society would invent and employ devices for impelling women to maintain a birth rate sufficient to insure enough increase in the population to offset the wastage of war and disease. It is the purpose of this paper to cite specific illustrations to show just how the various social institutions have been brought to bear on women to this end. Ross has classified the means which society takes and has taken to secure order, and insure that individuals will act in such a way as to promote the interests of the group, *as those interests are conceived by those who form "the radiant points of social control."* These means, according to the analysis of Ross, are public opinion, law, belief, social suggestion, education, custom, social religion, personal ideals (the type), art, personality, enlightenment, illusion, and social valuation. Let us see how some of these means have been applied in the control of women.

Personal Ideals (the Type)

The first means of control to which I wish to call attention in the present connection is that which Ross calls "personal ideals." It is pointed out that "a developed society presents itself as a system of unlike individuals, strenuously pursuing their personal ends." Now, for each person there is a "certain zone of requirement," and since "altruism is quite incompetent to hold each unswerv-

ingly to the particular activities and forbearances belonging to his place in the social system," the development of such allegiance must be—

> effected by means of types or patterns, which society induces its members to adopt as their guiding ideals. . . . To this end are elaborated various patterns of conduct and of character, which may be termed social types. These types may become in the course of time personal ideals, each for that category of persons for which it is intended.

For women, obviously enough, the first and most primitive "zone of requirement" is and has been to produce and rear families large enough to admit of national warfare being carried on, and of colonization.

Thus has been evolved the social type of the "womanly woman," "the normal woman," the chief criterion of normality being a willingness to engage enthusiastically in maternal and allied activities. All those classes and professions which form "the radiant points of social control" unite upon this criterion. Men of science announce it with calm assurance (though failing to say on what kind or amount of scientific data they base their remarks). For instance, McDougall[2] writes:

> The highest stage is reached by those species in which each female produces at birth but one or two young, and protects them so efficiently that most of the young born reach maturity; the maintenance of the species thus becomes in the main the work of the parental instinct. In such species the protection and cherishing of the young is the constant and all-absorbing occupation of the mother, to which she devotes all her energies, and in the course of which she will at any time undergo privation, pain, and death. The instinct (maternal instinct) becomes

---

[2]W. McDougall, *Social Psychology,* 1908.

more powerful than any other, and can override any other, even fear itself.

Professor Jastrow[3] writes:

. . . . *charm* is the technique of the maiden, and *sacrifice* the passion of the mother. One set of feminine interests expresses more distinctly the issues of courtship and attraction; the other of qualities of motherhood and devotion.

The medical profession insistently proclaims desire for numerous children as the criterion of normality for women, scornfully branding those so ill-advised as to deny such desires as "abnormal." As one example among thousands of such attempts at social control let me quote the following, which appeared in a New York newspaper on November 29, 1915:

Only abnormal women want no babies. Trenchant criticism of modern life was made by Dr. Max G. Schlapp, internationally known as a neurologist. Dr. Schlapp addressed his remarks to the congregation of the Park Avenue M.E. Church. He said, "The birth rate is falling off. Rich people are the ones who have no children, and the poor have the greatest number of offspring. Any woman who does not desire offspring is abnormal. We have a large number, particularly among the women, who do not want children. Our social society is becoming intensely unstable."

And this from the *New York Times,* September 5, 1915:

Normally woman lives through her children; man lives through his work.

Scores of such implicit attempts to determine and present the type or norm meet us on every hand. This norm has the sanction of authority, being announced by men of greatest prestige in the community. No one wishes to

be regarded by her fellow-creatures as "abnormal" or "decayed." The stream of suggestions playing from all points inevitably has its influence, so that it is or was, until recently, well-nigh impossible to find a married woman who would admit any conflicting interests equal or paramount to the interest of caring for children. There is a universal refusal to admit that the maternal instinct, like every other trait of human nature, might be distributed according to the probability curve.

PUBLIC OPINION

Let us turn next to public opinion as a means of control over women in relation to the birth rate. In speaking of public opinion Ross says:

Haman is at the mercy of Mordecai. Rarely can one regard his deed as fair when others find it foul, or count himself a hero when the world deems him a wretch. . . . For the mass of men the blame and the praise of the community are the very lords of life.

If we inquire now what are the organs or media of expression of public opinion we shall see how it is brought to bear on women. The newspapers are perhaps the chief agents, in modern times, in the formation of public opinion, and their columns abound in interviews with the eminent, deploring the decay of the population. Magazines print articles based on statistics of depopulation, appealing to the patriotism of women. In the year just passed fifty-five articles on the birth rate have chanced to come to the notice of the present writer. Fifty-four were written by men, including editors, statesmen, educators, ex-presidents, etc. Only one was written by a woman. The following quotation is illustrative of the trend of all of them:

M. Emil Reymond has made this melancholy announcement in the Senate: "We are living in

---

[3]J. Jastrow, *Character and Temperament,* 1915.

an age when women have pronounced upon themselves a judgment that is dangerous in the highest degree to the development of the population. . . . We have the right to do what we will with the life that is in us, say they."

Thus the desire for the development of interests and aptitudes other than the maternal is stigmatized as "dangerous," "melancholy," "degrading," "abnormal," "indicative of decay." On the other hand, excessive maternity receives many cheap but effective rewards. For example, the Jesuit priests hold special meetings to laud maternity. The German Kaiser announces that he will now be godfather to seventh, eighth, and ninth sons, even if daughters intervene. The ex-President has written a letter of congratulation to the mother of nine.

LAW

Since its beginning as a human institution law has been a powerful instrument for the control of women. The subjection of women was originally an irrational consequence of sex differences in reproductive function. It was not *intended* by either men or women, but simply resulted from the natural physiological handicaps of women, and the attempts of humanity to adapt itself to physiological nature through the crude methods of trial and error. When law was formulated, this subjection was defined, and thus furthered. It would take too long to cite all the legal provisions that contribute, indirectly, to keep women from developing individualistic interests and capacities. Among the most important indirect forces in law which affect women to keep them child-bearers and child-rearers only are those provisions that tend to restrain them from possessing and controlling property. Such provisions have made of women a comparatively possessionless class, and have thus deprived them of the fundamentals of power. While affirming the essential nature of woman to be satisfied with maternity and

with maternal duties only, society has always taken every precaution to close the avenues to ways of escape therefrom.

Two legal provisions which bear directly on women to compel them to keep up the birth rate may be mentioned here. The first of these is the provision whereby sterility in the wife may be made a cause of divorce. This would be a powerful inducement to women who loved their husbands to bear children if they could. The second provision is that which forbids the communication of the data of science in the matter of the means of birth control. The American laws are very drastic on this point. Recently in New York City a man was sentenced to prison for violating this law. The more advanced democratic nations have ceased to practice military conscription. They no longer conscript their men to bear arms, depending on the volunteer army. But they conscript their women to bear children by legally prohibiting the publication or communication of the knowledge which would make child-bearing voluntary.

Child-rearing is also legally insured by those provisions which forbid and punish abortion, infanticide, and infant desertion. There could be no better proof of the insufficiency of maternal instinct as a guaranty of population than the drastic laws which we have against birth control, abortion, infanticide, and infant desertion.

BELIEF

Belief, "which controls the hidden portions of life," has been used powerfully in the interests of population. Orthodox women, for example, regard family limitation as a sin, punishable in the hereafter. Few explicit exhortations concerning the birth rate are discoverable in the various "Words" of God. The belief that family limitation will be punished in the hereafter seems to have been evolved mainly by priests out of the slender materials of a few quotations from Holy Writ, such as "God said unto them, 'Multiply and replenish the earth,'" and from the scriptural allusion to children as the gifts of God. Being gifts from God, it follows that they may not be refused except at the peril of incurring God's displeasure.

EDUCATION

The education of women has always, until the end of the nineteenth century, been limited to such matters as would become a creature who could and should have no aspirations for a life of her own. We find the proper education for girls outlined in the writings of such educators as Rousseau, Fénelon, St. Jerome, and in Godey's *Lady's Book*. Not only have the "social guardians" used education as a negative means of control, by failing to provide any real enlightenment for women, but education has been made a positive instrument for control. This was accomplished by drilling into the young and unformed mind, while yet it was too immature to reason independently, such facts and notions as would give the girl a conception of herself only as future wife and mother. Rousseau, for instance, demanded freedom and individual liberty of development for everybody except Sophia, who was to be deliberately trained up as a means to an end. In the latter half of the nineteenth century when the hard battle for the real enlightenment of women was being fought, one of the most frequently recurring objections to admitting women to knowledge was that "the population would suffer," "the essential nature of woman would be changed," "the family would decay," and "the birth rate would fall." Those in control of society yielded up the old prescribed education of women only after a stubborn struggle, realizing that with the passing of the old training an important means of social control was slipping out of their hands.

ART

A very long paper might be written to describe the various uses to which art has been put in holding up the ideal of motherhood. The mother, with children at her breast, is the favorite theme of artists. The galleries of Europe are hung full of Madonnas of every age and degree. Poetry abounds in allusions to the sacredness and charm of motherhood, depicting the yearning of the adult for his mother's knee. Fiction is replete with happy and adoring mothers. Thousands of songs are written and sung concerning the ideal relation which exists between mother and child. In pursuing the mother-child theme through art one would not be led to suspect that society finds it necessary to make laws against contraconception, infanticide, abortion, and infant desertion. Art holds up to view only the compensations of motherhood, leaving the other half of the theme in obscurity, and thus acting as a subtle ally of population.

ILLUSION

This is the last of Ross's categories to which I wish to refer. Ross says:

> In the taming of men there must be provided coil after coil to entangle the unruly one. Mankind must use snares as well as leading-strings, will-o-the-wisps as well as lanterns. The truth by all means, if it will promote obedience, but in any case obedience! We shall examine not creeds now, but the films, veils, hidden minors, and half lights by which men are duped as to that which lies nearest them, their own experience. This time we shall see men led captive, not by dogmas concerning a world beyond experience, but by artfully fostered misconceptions of the pains, satisfactions, and values lying under their very noses.

One of the most effective ways of creating the desired illusion about any matter is by concealing and tabooing the mention of all the painful and disagreeable circumstances connected with it. Thus there is a very stern social taboo on conversation about the processes of birth. The utmost care is taken to conceal the agonies and risks of child-birth from the young. Announcement is rarely made of the true cause of deaths from child-birth. The statistics of maternal mortality have been neglected by departments of health, and the few compilations which have been made have not achieved any wide publicity or popular discussion. Says Katharine Anthony, in her recent book on *Feminism in Germany and Scandinavia* (1915):

> There is no evidence that the death rate of women from child-birth has caused the governing classes many sleepless nights.

Anthony gives some statistics from Prussia (where the figures have been calculated), showing that

> between 1891 and 1900 11 per cent of the deaths of all women between the ages of twenty-five and forty years occurred in child-birth. . . . During forty years of peace Germany lost 400,000 mothers' lives, that is, ten times what she lost in soldiers' lives in the campaign of 1870 and 1871.

Such facts would be of wide public interest, especially to women, yet there is no tendency at all to spread them broadcast or to make propaganda of them. Public attention is constantly being called to the statistics of infant mortality, but the statistics of maternal mortality are neglected and suppressed.

The pains, the dangers, and risks of child-bearing are tabooed as subjects of conversation. The drudgery, the monotonous labor, and other disagreeable features of child-rearing are minimized by "the social guardians." On the other hand, the joys and compensations of motherhood are magnified and presented to consciousness on every hand. Thus the tendency is to create an illusion whereby motherhood will appear to consist of compensations only, and thus come to be desired by those for whom the illusion is intended.

There is one further class of devices for controlling women that does not seem to fit any of the categories mentioned by Ross. I refer to threats of evil consequence to those who refrain from child-bearing. This class of social devices I shall call "bugaboos." Medical men have done much, to help population (and at the same time to increase obstetrical practice!) by inventing bugaboos. For example, it is frequently stated by medical men, and is quite generally believed by women, that if first child-birth is delayed until the age of thirty years the pains and dangers of the process will be very gravely increased, and that therefore women will find it advantageous to begin bearing children early in life. It is added that the younger the woman begins to bear the less suffering will be experienced. One looks in vain, however, for any objective evidence that such is the case. The statements appear to be founded on no array of facts whatever, and until they are so founded they lie under the suspicion of being merely devices for social control.

One also reads that women who bear children live longer on the average than those who do not, which is taken to mean that child-bearing has a favorable influence on longevity. It may well be that women who bear many children live longer than those who do not, but the only implication probably is that those women who could not endure the strain of repeated births died young, and thus naturally did not have many children. The facts may indeed be as above stated, and yet child-bearing may be distinctly prejudicial to longevity.

A third bugaboo is that if a child is reared alone, without brothers and sisters, he will grow up selfish, egoistic, and an undesirable citizen. Figures are, however, so far lacking to show the disastrous consequences of being an only child.

From these brief instances it seems very clear that "the social guardians" have not really believed that maternal instinct is alone a sufficient guaranty of population. They have made use of all possible social devices to insure not only child-bearing, but child-rearing. Belief, law, public opinion, illusion, education, art, and bugaboos have all been used to re-enforce maternal instinct. We shall never know just how much maternal instinct alone will do for population until all the forces and influences exemplified above have become inoperative. As soon as women become fully conscious of the fact that they have been and are controlled by these devices the latter will become useless, and we shall get a truer measure of maternal feeling.

> One who learns why society is urging him into the straight and narrow way will resist its pressure. One who sees clearly how he is controlled will thenceforth be emancipated. To betray the secrets of ascendancy is to forearm the individual in his struggle with society.

The time is coming, and is indeed almost at hand, when all the most intelligent women of the community, who are the most desirable child-bearers, will become conscious of the methods of social control. The type of normality will be questioned; the laws will be repealed and changed; enlightenment will prevail; belief will be seen to rest upon dogmas; illusion will fade away and give place to clearness of view; the bugaboos will lose their power to frighten. How will "the social guardians" induce women to bear a surplus population when all these cheap, effective methods no longer work?

The natural desire for children may, and probably will, always guarantee a stationary population, even if child-bearing should become a voluntary matter. But if a surplus population is desired for national aggrandizement, it would seem that there will remain but one effective social device whereby this can be secured, namely, *adequate compensation,* either in money or in fame. If it were possible to become rich or famous by bearing numerous fine children, many a woman would no doubt be eager to bring up eight or ten, though if acting at the dictation of maternal instinct only, she would have brought up but one or two. When the cheap devices no longer work, we shall expect expensive devices to replace them, if the same result is still desired by the governors of society.

If these matters could be clearly raised to consciousness, so that this aspect of human life could be managed rationally, instead of irrationally as at present, the social gain would be enormous—assuming always that the increased happiness and usefulness of women would, in general, be regarded as social gain.

Alexandra Kollontai (1873–1952) on Women and Class

Alexandra Kollontai was born in Russia in 1873 to a solidly bourgeois family: her father was a tsarist general and her mother came from a family of wealthy merchants. Her childhood was spent in the privileged atmosphere of this class, although in her autobiography she comments that she often felt guilty at the unearned benefits of her class. At age 20 she married a distant cousin, V. L. Kollontai, against her parents' wishes. Between 1896 and 1898 she began to engage in political work on behalf of political prisoners, teaching in schools for workers and attending the formative conference of the Russian Social Democratic Party. In March 1898 she left Russia to avoid arrest, arriving in Zurich, where she studied political economy.

During the next decades, Kollontai rose to leadership positions in the emerging European socialist movement; she frequently communicated with such notables as Clara Zetkin, Rosa Luxemburg, and Karl Kautsky. From around 1905 she began to pay attention to the problems of women, a central concern throughout her career. She traveled widely and lectured all over Europe and across the Atlantic. After the October Revolution of 1917 Kollontai was named Commissar of Social Welfare, a position she resigned from after a few months. Following this, she served on the Central Executive Committee under Lenin and later as ambassador to Norway and head of the Mexican legation. She was a constant supporter of reform for women's issues, promoting birth control, abortion rights, and other rights for women. With the accession of Stalin, many of the progressive reforms introduced earlier were reversed, women's departments were closed, and in 1936 abortion was made illegal. Despite her personal misgivings about Stalin, Kollontai remained an active member of the government, twice receiving the Red Banner of Labor for outstanding service to the state. She died March 9, 1952, just about a year before the death of Stalin.

According to Alix Holt (1977), Kollontai is usually remembered (if at all) for her free-love sexual ideas, especially her comment that "sex should be as easy and uncomplicated as drinking a glass of water" (Kollontai, Holt, 1997:13). Although she was usually considered an extremist by Western scholars and historians, her reputation as a feminist thinker was rescued during the heyday of the women's movement in the 1970s. In Kollontai's important works, it is evident that she critically analyzed women's social situation and made suggestions for reform and radical revision. Her outspoken work was courageous, sometimes leading to her arrest or to the necessity to flee Russia to escape prosecution. The extent of sexism in the culture she opposed is illustrated by the response to a women's conference in which she participated in 1908. A St. Petersburg newspaper described the event as "a gathering of old and ugly ladies," and opined that "women in Russia should be concerned about the extension of only one right—the right to be a wife and mother and housekeeper. There were no normal women at the congress" (Holt, 1977:16). Kollontai believed that women were oppressed, but she followed the Marxian notion that the real basis of all oppression was class oppression. Liberation of women could only come through the establishment of a socialist society in which all groups—male and female—would be freed from domination. Nevertheless, in her political work she fought against sexism among her socialist peers and worked to persuade them of the importance of "the woman question." Her major criticisms, however, were for the "bourgeois feminists," who fought for equal rights for women of their own class only and ignored class divisions. The right to vote and to own and control property, for example,

were relevant mainly to middle-class or privileged women, and these were the goals of most feminist movements. Kollontai always identified with women of the working classes, whose needs were not sufficiently recognized by more privileged feminists—the need for child care, for birth control, for equal wages, shorter working hours, and for the same rights that male workers sought. She was one of the first feminist writers to discuss the problem of personal relationships as corrupted by power, and she did argue in favor of women's sexual rights as opposed to the double standard. Her work was opposed not only by conservatives, but often by other socialists of her time, who considered women's issues a marginal concern.

MAJOR WORKS

Kollontai, Alexandra. *The Social Basis of the Woman Question,* 1909. First published as a pamphlet, Sotsial'nye Osnovy Zhenskogo Voprosa.
———. *Communism and the Family.* New York: Contemporary Publishing, 1920.
Kollontai's major works available in English can be found in *Alexandra Kollontai, Writings.* Translated by Alix Holt. London: Allison & Busby, 1977.

SOURCES

Holt, Alix. 1977. Introduction. In *Alexandra Kollontai, writings.* London: Allison & Busby.
Deegan, Mary Jo. 1991. Alexandra Kollontai. In *Women in sociology: A bio-bibliographical sourcebook,* ed. Mary Jo Deegan, 231–38. Westport, CT: Greenwood.

THE SELECTION

"The Social Basis of the Woman Question" was first published in 1909 as a pamphlet, presenting Alexandra Kollontai's basic criticism of bourgeois feminism as not

being sufficiently attentive to the class question. Feminists in the West, she argued, sought to undo male privilege, but were unconcerned with the class domination resulting from capitalism. They wanted to share in the privileges of the men of their class, while allowing working-class women and men to continue to suffer exploitation. In this she agrees with August Bebel. This insight has grown in importance in feminist scholarship, especially since the mid-1980s, as the need to examine the intersections of class, race, and gender became more apparent in the sociology of gender. Kollontai's analysis, in spite of its simplistic "socialism as the solution" stance, is an important early statement of this issue. In addition, she does point out a number of common interests of women of all classes—interests that she hopes will draw feminists of different ranks into joint action. Of importance is her assumption that women of different classes have different interests and perspectives, according to their social location and experience. This has become a very important point for contemporary standpoint theorists such as Dorothy Smith and Patricia Hill Collins. The main shortcoming of this essay (and much of her other work) is its failure to criticize other socialist thinkers for their sexism and lack of attention to women's issues: an overly rosy view of socialist organization as a panacea to all inequalities.

THE SOCIAL BASIS OF THE WOMAN QUESTION

Leaving it to the bourgeois scholars to absorb themselves in discussion of the question of the superiority of one sex over the other, or in the weighing of brains and the comparing of the psychological structure of men and women, the followers of historical materialism fully accept the natural specificities of each sex and demand only that each person, whether man or woman, has a real opportunity for the fullest and freest self-determination, and the widest scope for the development and application of all natural inclinations. The followers of historical materialism reject the existence of a special woman question separate from the general social question of our day. Specific economic factors were behind the subordination of women; natural qualities have been a secondary factor in this process. Only the complete disappearance of these factors, only the evolution of those forces which at some point in the past gave rise to the subjection of women, is able in a fundamental way to influence and change their social position. In other words, women can become truly free and equal only in a world organised along new social and productive lines.

This, however, does not mean that the partial improvement of woman's life within the framework of the modern system is impossible. The radical solution of the workers' question is possible only with the complete reconstruction of modern productive relations; but must this prevent us from working for reforms which would serve to satisfy the most urgent interests of the proletariat? On the contrary, each new gain of the working class represents a step leading mankind towards the kingdom of freedom and social equality: each right that woman wins brings her nearer the defined goal of full emancipation. . . .

From Alexandra Kollontai, "The Social Basis of the Woman Question," in *Alexandra Kollontai, Writings*, translated with an introduction and commentaries by Alix Holt (London: Allison & Busby, 1977), 58–73. First published as a pamphlet in 1909.

Social democracy was the first to include in its programme the demand for the equalisation of the rights of women with those of men; in speeches and in print the party demands always and everywhere the withdrawal of limitations affecting women; it is the party's influence alone that has forced other parties and governments to carry out reforms in favour of women. And in Russia this party is not only the defender of women in terms of its theoretical positions but always and everywhere adheres to the principle of women's equality.

What, in this case, hinders our "equal righters" from accepting the support of this strong and experienced party? The fact is that however "radical" the equal righters may be, they are still loyal to their own bourgeois class. Political freedom is at the moment an essential prerequisite for the growth and power of the Russian bourgeoisie; without it, all the economic welfare of the latter will turn out to have been built upon sand. The demand for political equality is for women a necessity that stems from life itself.

The slogan of "access to the professions" has ceased to suffice; only direct participation in the government of the country promises to assist in raising women's economic situation. Hence the passionate desire of women of the middle bourgeoisie to gain the franchise, and hence their hostility to the modern bureaucratic system.

However, in their demands for political equality our feminists are like their foreign sisters; the wide horizons opened by social democratic learning remain alien and incomprehensible to them. The feminists seek equality in the framework of the existing class society; in no way do they attack the basis of this society. They fight for prerogatives for themselves, without challenging the existing prerogatives and privileges. We do not accuse the representatives of the bourgeois women's movement of failure to understand the matter; their view

of things flows inevitably from their class position. . . .

THE STRUGGLE FOR ECONOMIC INDEPENDENCE

First of all we must ask ourselves whether a single united women's movement is possible in a society based on class contradictions. The fact that the women who take part in the liberation movement do not represent one homogeneous mass is clear to every unbiased observer.

The women's world is divided, just as is the world of men, into two camps; the interests and aspirations of one group of women bring it close to the bourgeois class, while the other group has close connections with the proletariat, and its claims for liberation encompass a full solution to the woman question. Thus although both camps follow the general slogan of the "liberation of women", their aims and interests are different. Each of the groups unconsciously takes its starting point from the interests of its own class, which gives a specific class colouring to the targets and tasks it sets itself. . . .

However apparently radical the demands of the feminists, one must not lose sight of the fact that the feminists cannot, on account of their class position, fight for that fundamental transformation of the contemporary economic and social structure of society without which the liberation of women cannot be complete.

If in certain circumstances the short-term tasks of women of all classes coincide, the final aims of the two camps, which in the long term determine the direction of the movement and the tactics to be used, differ sharply. While for the feminists the achievement of equal rights with men in the framework of the contemporary capitalist world represents a sufficiently concrete end in itself, equal rights at the present time are, for the proletarian women, only a means of advancing the struggle against the economic slavery of the working class. The feminists see men as the main enemy, for men have unjustly seized all rights and privileges for themselves, leaving women only chains and duties. For them a victory is won when a prerogative previously enjoyed exclusively by the male sex is conceded to the "fair sex". Proletarian women have a different attitude. They do not see men as the enemy and the oppressor; on the contrary, they think of men as their comrades, who share with them the drudgery of the daily round and fight with them for a better future. The woman and her male comrade are enslaved by the same social conditions; the same hated chains of capitalism oppress their will and deprive them of the joys and charms of life. It is true that several specific aspects of the contemporary system lie with double weight upon women, as it is also true that the conditions of hired labour sometimes turn working women into competitors and rivals to men. But in these unfavourable situations, the working class knows who is guilty. . . .

The woman worker, no less than her brother in misfortune, hates that insatiable monster with its gilded maw which, concerned only to drain all the sap from its victims and to grow at the expense of millions of human lives, throws itself with equal greed at man, woman and child. Thousands of threads bring the working man close. The aspirations of the bourgeois woman, on the other hand, seem strange and incomprehensible. They are not warming to the proletarian heart; they do not promise the proletarian woman that bright future towards which the eyes of all exploited humanity are turned. . . .

The proletarian women's final aim does not, of course, prevent them from desiring to improve their status even within the framework of the current bourgeois system, but the realisation of these desires is constantly hindered by obstacles that derive from the very nature of capitalism. A woman can possess equal rights and be truly free only in a world of socialised labour, of harmony and justice. The feminists are unwilling and incapable of understanding this; it seems to them that when equality is formally accepted by the letter of the law they will be able to win a comfortable place for themselves in the old world of oppression, enslavement and bondage, of tears and hardship. And this is true up to a certain point. For the majority of women of the proletariat, equal rights with men would mean only an equal share in inequality, but for the "chosen few", for the bourgeois women, it would indeed open doors to new and unprecedented rights and privileges that until now have been enjoyed by men of the bourgeois class alone. But each new concession won by the bourgeois woman would give her yet another weapon for the exploitation of her younger sister and would go on increasing the division between the women of the two opposite social camps. Their interests would be more sharply in conflict, their aspirations more obviously in contradiction.

Where, then, is that general "woman question"? Where is that unity of tasks and aspirations about which the feminists have so much to say? A sober glance at reality shows that such unity does not and cannot exist. In vain title feminists try to assure themselves that the "woman question" has nothing to do with that of the political party and that "its solution is possible only with the participation of all parties and all women"; as one of the radical German feminists has said, the logic of facts forces us to reject this comforting delusion of the feminists. . . .

The conditions and forms of production have subjugated women throughout, human history, and have gradually relegated them to the position of oppression and dependence in which most of them existed until now.

A colossal upheaval of the entire social and economic structure was required before women could begin to retrieve the significance and independence they had lost. Problems which at one time seemed too difficult for the most talented thinkers have now been solved by the inanimate but all-powerful conditions of production. The same forces which for thousands of years enslaved women now, at a further stage of development, are leading them along the path to freedom and independence. . . .

In face of the growing social difficulties, the sincere fighter for the cause must stop in sad bewilderment. She cannot but see how little the general women's movement has done for proletarian women, how incapable it is of improving the working and living conditions of the working class. The future of humanity must seem grey, drab and uncertain to those women who are fighting for equality but who have not adopted the proletarian world outlook or developed a firm faith in the coming of a more perfect social system. While the contemporary capitalist world remains unchanged, liberation must seem to them incomplete and impartial. What despair must grip the more thoughtful and sensitive of these women. Only the working class is capable of maintaining morale in the modern world with its distorted social relations. With firm and measured step it advances steadily towards its aim. It draws the working women to its ranks. The proletarian woman bravely starts out on the thorny path of labour. Her legs sag; her body is torn. There are dangerous precipices along the way, and cruel beasts of prey are close at hand.

But only by taking this path is the woman able to achieve that distant but alluring aim—her true liberation in a new world of labour. During this difficult march to the bright future the proletarian woman, until recently a humiliated, downtrodden slave with no rights, learns to discard the slave mentality that has clung to her; step by step she transforms herself into an independent worker, an independent personality, free in love. It is she, fighting in the ranks of the proletariat, who wins for women the right to work; it is she, the "younger sister", who prepares the ground for the "free" and "equal" woman of the future.

For what reason, then, should the woman worker seek a union with the bourgeois feminists? Who, in actual fact, would stand to gain in the event of such an alliance? Certainly not the woman worker. She is her own saviour; her future is in her own hands. The working woman guards her class interests and is not deceived by great speeches about the "world all women share". The working woman must not and does not forget that while the aim of bourgeois women is to secure their own welfare in the framework of a society antagonistic to us, our aim is to build, in the place of the old, outdated world, a bright temple of universal labour, comradely solidarity and joyful freedom.

The 1920s and 1930s
Institutionalizing the Discipline, Defining the Canon

W. E. B. Du Bois (1868–1963) on the "Damnation of Women"

W. E. B. (William Edward Burghardt) Du Bois was born in Great Barrington, Massachusetts, on February 23, 1868, into a long-established family of the area. Raised by his mother, who was a domestic worker, Du Bois exhibited outstanding abilities from an early age, graduating as valedictorian from his high school in 1884. He received a bachelor's degree from Fisk University in Nashville in 1888, after which he entered Harvard University, from which he earned a second bachelor's degree, *cum laude*, in 1890. Du Bois continued at Harvard for graduate work in history, receiving a master's in 1891 and a doctorate in 1895—the first African American to be granted a PhD by Harvard. During the years 1892–1894, he studied at the University of Berlin, where he attended lectures by Max Weber (who later visited Du Bois in Atlanta on a trip to the United States).

Du Bois taught classical languages for a few years at Wilberforce University and then was invited to carry out a research project in the "Negro Seventh Ward" of Philadelphia by the University of Pennsylvania. He was there for one year (1896–1897) as an Assistant Instructor in the sociology department. He later wrote of the uncordial reception he had there:

> I was given no real academic standing, no office at the University, no official recognition of any kind; my name was even eventually omitted from the catalogue; I had no contact with students, and very little with members of the faculty, even in my department. (Quoted in Baltzell, 1967: xix)

In spite of the discrimination and prejudice, Du Bois carried out a brilliant community study published as *The Philadelphia Negro* (1899), one of the first such studies in American sociology. He then moved to Atlanta to spend several years at Atlanta University, building a sociology program and carrying out important empirical research in the African American communities of that city. Eventually Du Bois grew frustrated with academia and left to do more activist work and writing. He was a founding member of the Niagra Movement and the National Association for the Advancement of Colored People (editing its monthly magazine, *Crisis,* for two decades). He also founded the social science journal *Phylon* in 1940.

Du Bois was an activist-scholar who stood for antiracism, women's rights, labor, peace, and social justice. He published over 100 articles and essays and more than 20 books. In 1961, Du Bois, discouraged by the conservative racial and economic politics of the United States, moved to Ghana, where he spent the final two years of his life, dying in August of 1963.

MAJOR WORKS

Du Bois, W. E. B. *The Philadelphia Negro.* Philadelphia: University of Pennsylvania Press, 1899.
———. *The Souls of Black Folk.* Chicago: McClurg, 1903.
———. *The Negro American Family.* Atlanta: Atlanta University Press, 1909.
———. *Darkwater: Voices from within the Veil.* New York: Harcourt, Brace & Howe, 1920.

SOURCES

Baltzell, E. Digby. 1967. Introd. to *The Philadelphia Negro: A social study,* by W. E. B. Du Bois, ix–xliv. New York: Schocken Books.

Feagin, Joe R. 2003. Introd. to *Darkwater,* ed. W. E. B. Du Bois, 9–24. New York: Humanity Books.

Lewis, David Levering. 1993. *W. E. B. Du Bois: Biography of a race, 1868–1919.* New York: Henry Holt.

Marable, Manning. 2005. *W. E. B. Du Bois: Black radical democrat.* Boulder, CO: Paradigm.

THE SELECTION

In 1920, W. E. B. Du Bois published a collection of essays, *Darkwater: Voices from Within the Veil.* In that book, he presents ten chapters with insights "unrivaled in perceptiveness for their time" (Feagin, 2003:9). The seventh chapter of *Darkwater* has the provocative title "The Damnation of Women," and it is the source of the following excerpt. The "veil" Du Bois refers to is a metaphor he developed in his *Souls of Black Folk* (1903), to represent the division between the world of whites and that of blacks. Blacks, he argued, could see and understand both sides of the veil, while the dominant whites were usually completely unaware of the world of meanings and experience behind the veil. This idea is carried further in this essay to examine the experiences of black women.

He notes the accomplishments of Black women—women who were forced by circumstance to be independent and to work outside the home. Compared with white women, who were restricted in their roles and expected to be beautiful ornaments, black women have always had to be more independent. This, combined with the wage and job discrimination against black men, led to a higher divorce/separation rate. However, the false chivalry that white men granted to white women was, for Du Bois, a poor substitute for true respect and equality. Du Bois asserts that "the uplift of women" is one of the most important of the modern causes, and black women have the double burden of race and sex discrimination. He is strongly critical of the common moralistic condemnation of black single mothers, who worked hard to

From W. E. B. Du Bois, *Darkwater: Voices from Within the Veil* (New York: Harcourt, Brace & Howe, 1920), chap. 7, 103–8.

support their families, and of the shallow use of the white beauty standard to judge the worth of women. This hard-hitting critical view was rare among American sociologists of the day, no doubt explaining why Du Bois grew tired of the academic life.

THE DAMNATION OF WOMEN

As I look about me today in this veiled world of mine, despite the noisier and more spectacular advance of my brothers, I instinctively feel and know that it is the five million women of my race who really count. Black women (and women whose grandmothers were black) are today furnishing our teachers; they are the main pillars of those social settlements which we call churches; and they have with small doubt raised three-fourths of our church property. If we have today, as seems likely, over a billion dollars of accumulated goods, who shall say how much of it has been wrung from the hearts of servant girls and washerwomen and women toilers in the fields? As makers of two million homes these women are today seeking in marvelous ways to show forth our strength and beauty and our conception of the truth.

In the United States in 1910 there were 4,931,882 women of Negro descent; over twelve hundred thousand of these were children, another million were girls and young women under twenty, and two and a half-million were adults. As a mass these women were unlettered,—a fourth of those from fifteen to twenty-five years of age were unable to write. These women are passing through, not only a moral, but an economic revolution. Their grandmothers married at twelve and fifteen, but twenty-seven percent of these women today who have passed fifteen are still single.

Yet these black women toil and toil hard. There were in 1910 two and a half million Negro homes in the United States. Out of these homes walked daily to work two million women and girls over ten years of age,—over half of the colored female population as against a fifth in the case of white women. These, then, are a group of workers, fighting for their daily bread like men; independent and approaching economic freedom! They furnished a million farm laborers, 80,000 farmers, 22,000 teachers, 600,000 servants and washerwomen, and 50,000 in trades and merchandizing.

The family group, however, which is the ideal of the culture with which these folk have been born, is not based on the idea of an economically independent working mother. Rather its ideal harks back to the sheltered harem with the mother emerging at first as nurse and homemaker, while the man remains the sole breadwinner. What is the inevitable result of the clash of such ideals and such facts in the colored group? Broken families.

Among native white women one in ten is separated from her husband by death, divorce, or desertion. Among Negroes the ratio is one in seven. Is the cause racial? No, it is economic, because there is the same high ratio among the white foreign-born. The breaking up of the present family is the result of modern working and sex conditions and it hits the laborers with terrible force. The Negroes are put in a peculiarly difficult position, because the wage of the male breadwinner is below the standard, while the openings for colored, women in certain lines of domestic work, and now in industries, are many. Thus while toil holds the father and brother in country and town at low wages, the sisters and mothers are called to the city. As a result the Negro women outnumber the men nine or ten to eight in many cities, making what Charlotte Gilman bluntly calls "cheap women."

What shall we say to this new economic equality in a great laboring class? Some people within and without the race deplore it. "Back to the homes with the women," they cry, "and higher wage for the men." But how impossible this is has been shown by war conditions. Cessation of foreign migration has raised Negro men's wages, to be sure—but it has not only raised Negro women's wages, it has opened to them a score of new avenues of earning a living. Indeed, here, in microcosm and with differences emphasizing sex equality, is the industrial history of labor in the 19th and 20th centuries. We cannot abolish the new economic freedom of women. We cannot imprison women again in a home or require them all on pain of death to be nurses and housekeepers.

What is today the message of these black women to America and to the world? The uplift of women is, next to the problem of the color line and the peace movement, our greatest modern cause. When, now, two of these movements—woman and color—combine in one, the combination has deep meaning.

In other years women's way was clear: to be beautiful, to be petted, to bear children. Such has been their theoretic destiny and if perchance they have been ugly, hurt, and barren, that has been forgotten with studied silence. In partial compensation for this narrowed destiny the white world has lavished its politeness on its womankind,—its chivalry and bows, its uncoverings and courtesies—all the accumulated homage disused for courts and kings and craving exercise. The revolt of white women against this preordained destiny has in these latter days reached splendid proportions, but it is the revolt of an aristocracy of brains and ability,—the middle class and rank and file still plod on in the appointed path, paid by the homage, the almost mocking homage, of men.

From black women of America, however, (and from some others, too, but chiefly from black women and their daughters' daughters) this gauze has been withheld and without semblance of such apology they have been frankly trodden under the feet of men. They are and have been objected to, apparently for reasons peculiarly exasperating to reasoning human beings. When in this world a man comes forward with a thought, a deed, a vision, we ask not, how does he look,—but what is his message? It is of but passing interest whether or not the messenger is beautiful or ugly,—the message is the thing. This, which is axiomatic among men, has been in past ages but partially true if the messenger was a woman. The world still wants to ask that a woman primarily be pretty and if she is not, the mob pouts and asks querulously, "What else are women for?" Beauty "is its own excuse for being," but there are other excuses, as most men know, and when the white world objects to black women because it does not consider them beautiful, the black world of right asks two questions: "What is beauty?" and, "Suppose you think them ugly, what then? If ugliness and unconventionality and eccentricity of face and deed do not hinder men from doing the world's work and reaping the world's reward, why should it hinder women?"

Other things being equal, all of us, black and white, would prefer to be beautiful in face and form and suitably clothed; but most of us are not so, and one of the mightiest revolts of the century is against the devilish decree that no woman is a woman who is not by present standards a beautiful woman. This decree the black women of America have in large measure escaped from the first. Not being expected to be merely ornamental, they have girded themselves for work, instead of adorning their bodies only for play. Their sturdier minds have concluded that if a woman be clean, healthy, and educated, she is as pleasing as God wills and far more useful than most of her sisters. If in addition to this she is pink and white and straight-haired, and some of her fellow-men prefer this, well and good; but if she is black or brown and crowned in curled mists (and this to us is the most beautiful thing on earth), this is surely the flimsiest excuse for spiritual incarceration or banishment.

The very attempt to do this in the case of Negro Americans has strangely over-reached itself. By so much as the defective eyesight of the white world rejects black women as beauties, by so much the more it needs them as human beings,—an enviable alternative, as many a white woman knows. Consequently, for black women alone, as a group, "handsome is that handsome does" and they are asked to be no more beautiful than God made them, but they are asked to be efficient, to be strong, fertile, muscled, and able to work. If they marry, they must as independent workers be able to help support their children, for their men are paid on a scale which makes sole support of the family often impossible.

On the whole, colored working women are paid as well as white working women for similar work, save in some higher grades, while colored men get from one-fourth to three-fourths less than white men. The result is curious and three-fold: the economic independence of black women is increased, the breaking up of Negro families must be more frequent, and the number of illegitimate children is decreased more slowly among them than other evidences of culture are increased, just as was once true in Scotland and Bavaria.

What does this mean? It forecasts a mighty dilemma which the whole world of civilization, despite its will, must one time frankly face: the unhusbanded mother or the childless wife. God send us a world with woman's freedom and married motherhood inextricably wed, but until He sends it, I see more of future promise in the betrayed girl-mothers of the black belt than in the childless wives of the white North, and I have more respect for the colored servant who yields to her frank longing for motherhood than for her white sister who offers up children for clothes. Out of a sex freedom that today makes us shudder will come in time a day when we will no longer pay men for work they do not do, for the sake of their harem; we will pay women what they earn and insist on their working and earning it; we will allow those persons to vote who know enough to vote, whether they be black or female, white or male; and we will ward race suicide, not by further burdening the over-burdened, but by honoring motherhood, even when the sneaking father shirks his duty.

"Wait till the lady passes," said a Nashville white boy.

"She's no lady; she's a nigger," answered another.

So some few women are born free, and some amid insult and scarlet letters achieve freedom; but our women in black had freedom thrust contemptuously upon them. With that freedom they are buying an untrammeled independence and dear as is the price they pay for it, it will in the end be worth every taunt and groan. Today the dreams of the mothers are coming true. We have still our poverty and degradation, our lewdness and our cruel toil; but we have, too, a vast group of women of Negro blood who for strength of character, cleanness of soul, and unselfish devotion of purpose, is today easily the peer of any group of women in the civilized world. And more than that, in the great rank and file of our five million women we have the up-working of new revolutionary ideals, which must in time have vast influence on the thought and action of this land.

For this, their promise, and for their hard past, I honor the women of my race. Their beauty,—their dark and mysterious beauty of midnight eyes, crumpled hair, and soft, full-featured faces—is perhaps more to me than to you, because I was born to its warm and subtle spell; but their worth is yours as well as mine. No other women on earth could have emerged from the hell of force and temptation which once engulfed and still surrounds black women in America with half the modesty and womanliness that they retain. I have always felt like bowing myself before them in all abasement, searching to bring some tribute to these long-suffering victims, these burdened sisters of mine, whom the world, the wise, white world, loves to affront and ridicule and wantonly to insult. I have known the women of many lands and nations,—I have known and seen and lived beside them, but none have I known more sweetly feminine, more unswervingly loyal, more desperately earnest, and more instinctively pure in body and in soul than the daughters of my black mothers. This, then,—a little thing—to their memory and inspiration.

Edward Alsworth Ross (1866–1951) on Masculinism

Edward Alsworth Ross, sociologist and economist, was one of the most important founders of American sociology. After completing his PhD at Johns Hopkins University in 1891, he taught economics at Stanford University from 1893 to 1900, leaving after being fired for his political views that displeased the Stanford family. The greater part of his career was spent at the University of Wisconsin (1906–1937), where he served on the sociology faculty, chairing the Department of Sociology and Anthropology from its formation in 1929 to his retirement in 1937. Ross was a pioneer in the field, known especially for his contributions on social control, collective behavior, and early social psychology. He published many articles and books in these areas. A scholar of broad interests, he also published a number of studies of other countries (Russia, China, Panama, Mexico, Portuguese Africa) and was active as an early demographer.

An early "conflict" sociologist, Ross differed from many of his contemporaries in his emphasis on the pervasiveness of conflicts within society and the role of *interests* and *exploitation* as well as culture and biology in human social life. Ross was never a single-factor theorist, instead arguing from an early age for multiple causation and influences on social processes and outcomes. He was also a strong proponent of civil liberties, becoming involved in many progressive political issues. According to Hertzler (1951:608), Ross "strongly believed that sociology, like all science for that matter, is for the advancement of human welfare, not 'science for its own sake.'" In this attitude, he followed his first wife's uncle and his own mentor, Lester Frank Ward. Among the issues he considered important were academic freedom, birth control, and war and militarism. He was highly critical of American involvement in World War I and wrote of the negative impacts of war and militarism for democratic institutions. In terms of women's issues, E. A. Ross was a strong supporter of women's rights and included discussions of gender issues in a number of his books and writings over the years.

MAJOR WORKS

Ross, E. A. *Social Control: A Survey of the Foundations of Order.* New York: Macmillan, 1901.
———. *The Old World and the New.* New York: Century, 1914.
———. *The Russian Soviet Republic.* New York: Century, 1923.
———. *Principles of Sociology.* New York: Century, 1925.

———. *New Age Sociology.* New York: Appleton-Century, 1940.

SOURCES

Ross, Edward Alsworth. 1936. *Seventy years of it.* New York: Appleton-Century.
Hertzler, J. O. Edward Alsworth Ross: sociological pioneer and interpreter. *American Sociological Review* 16 (October 1951): 597–613.

THE SELECTION

Edward Alsworth Ross, an early conflict theorist, saw relations between the sexes as based on inherent conflict. In his 1920 *Principles of Sociology,* he outlined several causes, including instinctual differences, men's monopoly over institutions of power and culture, and the lack of accepted social roles for unmarried women. Ross includes the following brief discussion of what he termed *masculinism,* perhaps one of the first uses of this term among mainstream sociologists. In the excerpt, Ross discusses the need for balance between extremes in social life. Reminiscent of Comte, he presents his essentialist argument that women's social influence is absolutely necessary to a healthy society in order to temper men's more dangerous and destructive tendencies.

> Many wars have no other cause [than the male fighting instinct], and if the policies of states obeyed the wills of men and women rather than of men only, the world would enjoy more peace.

Ross is strongly critical of the masculinist tendencies of the majority of governments that lead them to value the soldier and policeman over the teacher, factory worker, or health officer. Representatives of these governments usually oppose allowing women to vote precisely because they fear that women will bring a different (that is, more peaceful and cooperative) set of values into government. These values would include greater concern, for example, for the quality of foods and water, for protection of children, and for worker safety. For the committed masculinist, these "soft" ideas are viewed as an unhealthy interference in business. Ross also notes, like some recent feminists, that most of the alcoholism, violent crime, and other social ills are committed by men—another reason he gives to enhance the influence of women in society.

Ross's analysis is quite essentialist, assuming certain inherent differences between men and women; he is feminist in his call for the inclusion of feminine influence in social institutions. His term *masculinist* is consistent with much later feminist usage, but few of us would recognize that this early male sociological pioneer used the term in his analyses.

"Sex Conflict" (Chapter 15) in *New Age Sociology* by Edward Alsworth Ross. 1940 New York: Appleton Century Croft.

MASCULINISM

While women, owing to their being largely occupied with bearing and rearing children, have developed fewer specialists than men, they ought to be conceded a large social influence in order to counteract certain bad masculine tendencies. The fighting instinct of the male sex seriously unfits it to take sole charge of society. Many wars have no other cause, and if the policies of states obeyed the wills of *men and women* rather than of *men* only, the world would enjoy more peace. Male pugnacity conceives government as mere keeper of the lists rather than a machinery for serving certain common needs. The gradual transformation of government from coercion into service reflects in part the growing influence of women. Those with rank male proclivities, the ultra-he-men, scoff at votes for women on the ground that the essence of government is force and women citizens have little of that to contribute. To such men soldier and policeman appear as fit symbols of the state, whereas the teacher, the school nurse, the factory inspector, the health officer, the rural organizer and the agricultural adviser are but bastard and ambiguous representatives of the state's purposes.

By "business" a rational being understands the social system of making and distributing economic goods. That the claims of business should take precedence over life and limb, over health and family, is monstrous. Yet the fighting instinct leads thoughtless men generally to look upon it as a prize ring, with the implication of course, that somebody is bound to get hurt. This is why good men long justified child labor, the wrecking of the health of working girls, the night work of women, preventable work accidents. Even yet many disinterested men feel that stopping the sale of diseased meat or "doctored" canned goods is unfair interference, like depriving prize fighters of their best blows and ruses. Women, on the contrary, insist, in their simplicity of mind, that the palming off of putridity and poison, under the guise of food, upon mothers buying nourishment for the children they have risked their lives to bring into the world is not in any sense *business,* but *villainy.*

Male irrationality comes out again in the needless taking of chances. Human reason labors continually to eliminate hazard, and all insurance rests on the reasonable desire to substitute certainty for risk. Yet men who sweat for their money will gamble away their week's wage in an evening. No one, however, has ever seen working women regularly risk their wages on a card. Women have an instinct for security and strive to lessen risk, while men fatuously create it. In gold-mining camps recklessness is habitual, and to save himself a little trouble in handling explosives and timbering shafts the miner endangers the life he is toiling to enrich. After the arrival of wives men gain a rational view and learn to shun needless dangers.

Men nearly monopolize the consumption of alcohol and narcotics, even though many are well aware of the harm these do. Women, on the other hand, shrink from self-poisoning. In the slums the spread of heavy drinking among women is a sure sign of demoralization born of despair. In China the women never generally took to opium smoking till the district was hopeless. Doubtless woman's gain in social influence will make for a firmer dealing with race poisons. Again, women, with their better psychological insight, would hardly have been guilty of the follies men have committed in the penal field. One cannot imagine them treating juvenile offenders as if they were adult, expecting to make bad men good by solitary confinement, shutting up people who cannot pay for their debts, imprisoning persons without any provision for feeding them, or settling cases by judicial combat. Only men are foolish enough to persist in applying pain to offenders without self-control, who manifestly can never be improved by punishment.

The state of women under masculine ascendancy may be seen in China. Man-made throughout, Chinese culture is full of male contempt for women. Thus, double the ideograph for "woman" and you have "to wrangle"; triple it and the meaning is "intrigue"! In Chinese thought the world is divided between good and evil, Yang and Yin. Darkness is "Yin," cold is "Yin," earth spirits are "Yin," *and woman is "Yin."* Although necessary, she is inferior and should be held under a firm control. The ancient sages stressed the danger of letting women become educated and go about freely, for thus might they gain the upper hand and wreck society.

A girl who remains for life unwed, her betrothed having died before their marriage, is deemed worthy of a memorial portal or *pailow;* but no *pailow* is raised to the youth who remains true to the memory of his lost sweetheart, for such constancy would be ridiculed. From the male point of view it is fitting that woman be sacrificed to the man, but not that man, the superior being, be sacrificed to the woman. This is why some centuries ago the Chinese held that a widow ought to kill herself at her husband's funeral, whereas the notion that a widower ought to do the same at his wife's funeral never entered the Celestial mind. The unfaithful wife is stoned or drowned; but the worst that can happen to the unfaithful husband is a tongue lashing, which he is expected to bear patiently.

The boy's upbringing is not shaped to please the other sex, but everything in the upbringing of the girl—her foot binding, "tottering lily" gait, hairdressing, skill in embroidery, innocence, ignorance, obedience—is obviously a catering to the male. Again, the women of the classes for the most part pass their lives within four walls, . . . and rarely go out save in a closed cart or a covered chair. They have few acquaintances save relatives, and take no part in picnics, excursions, and feasts. Social diversion is organized for men, not for women. Toilet, opium smoking, gossiping with the servants, visits from a few friends—no wonder the doctors find their worst cases of nervous exhaustion among these repressed creatures!

How does the female sex fare under this masculine tutelage? Since the married daughter belongs completely to her husband's family and cannot be looked to by her parents in their old age, it is female infants that are done away with as superfluous, never male infants. The estimate of Chinese observers in 1910 was that from 5 to 10 per cent of girl babies were exposed.

Foot binding was a disability imposed by men, for until recently it was a rare father who would marry his son to a girl with natural feet. Mothers subjected their little daughters to the torturing bandages because, without the "golden lilies," they stood no chance whatever of marriage.

Chinese ladies are excessively small and frail in comparison with their men folk, owing no doubt to the foot binding and the confinement imposed by male opinion. They suffer much from neurasthenia and heart lesion, owing to the strain of their lot, and their faces are stamped with pain, patience, and gentle resignation rather than happiness.

In the West suicide is from three to five times as frequent among men as among women, whereas among the Chinese the women kill themselves from five to ten times as often as men. The slavery to mother-in-law, which drives many brides to suicide, and the ideas of wifely propriety that impel young widows to make away with themselves originated with men and have never been molded in the least by the sex they affect. Thus masculinism conserved the happiness of women!

Anna Garlin Spencer on Husbands and Wives

Here we have a second selection by Anna Garlin Spencer, whose biography can be seen earlier in this volume. The reading below is taken from her 1923 book, *The Family and Its Members*. The book was written to help prepare students for marriage in the "modern" world, incorporating the ideal of democracy in personal as well as societal relationships. Spencer argues in her introduction that the family is key to the establishment of the character necessary for full development of personality and democratic society. She hopes to show how families can become even more supportive of the full development of all members of the family, including women, who in the past have often had to devote such time to the care of others that they did not cultivate their own talents.

THE SELECTION

The chapter reprinted here gives advice to couples contemplating marriage, outlining a series of questions that should be addressed before marriage. They cover a broad range, including whether the woman should work outside the home, whether to have children, and whether she should keep her own surname. Anna Garlin Spencer's questions reveal a more modern approach than we might assume, given the fact that this was written in the early 1920s.

From Anna Garlin Spencer, *The Family and Its Members* (Philadelphia: Lippincott, 1923), 142–62.

HUSBANDS AND WIVES

NOT FANCIED BUT GENUINE HAPPINESS IN MARRIAGE NOW DEMANDED

The fairy tales ended with the wedding and "they lived happily forever after." The dramas and novels of to-day are often devoted to telling how they did not live happily ever after and what or who caused the unhappiness. Although no one need be alarmed that some people get divorced when marital unhappiness becomes acute, every right-minded person wishes that every marriage should turn out happily. We now, however, demand that it shall be genuine, not make-believe happiness, and that places a heavier strain upon all concerned. We have grown wise enough to see that holding people together who should never have been brought into close relationship does not really conduce to high family morality or social well-being. That, however, only makes it seem the more important that we should somehow learn how to prevent the marriage of those who cannot make their union a success. . . .

SHALL THE WIFE TAKE THE HUSBAND'S NAME?

In the first place, the matter of the name for the married couple must be now considered. Shall it be one or two? Shall the new sense of personal dignity, so common to the modern woman, increase the already spreading fashion of retention of the maiden name, her inherited family name, as permanently her own, untouched by the fact of marriage union? No one can be cognizant of the conviction and practice of many feminists without understanding that this is a real problem to be settled surely before the marriage cere-

mony. There is already in the field a "Lucy Stone League" to give the support of the practice of a great and beloved woman to the fashion of keeping one's own name. The question of the desirability of having children bear the same name as both parents is left for the most part in abeyance by those who thus advocate two names for the married couple. It may be that each child is expected to bear as a second name his mother's and as a last name his father's family name, as, for example, John Jones Jackson, Jones being the mother's and Jackson the father's personal signature; but when the child marries, by what name shall the family line be carried on?

To most of us who see in the family name adopted by both husband and wife at marriage a sign of family unity not to be lost without serious embarrassment to offspring, and some danger of easy drifting apart without the knowledge of others, the name seems not to be of vital importance. Why, then, it is asked, should the woman always give up her family connection as indicated by inherited name, and the man retain his? The fact that the custom has grown up by reason of the legal absorption of the wife's life in that of the husband is obvious, and gives much color to the claim that now, when a woman is a recognized personality in the law whether married or single, she should keep the name by which her personality has become known. That is easily seen to be advantageous in the case of professional women of wide influence. The great singer, the great writer, any creative genius or artist, continues, as a rule, to be known by the name under which greatness has been achieved. In such cases, however, women often bear two names, the professional name either of family inheritance or a chosen *nom de plume,* and the social name, which is their husband's and engraved on calling cards. The tendency now is increasing to keep the one designation to which one is born and make no concessions to conventional nomenclature. It must be remembered that in such cases it is the father's name by which the married daughter is called and the mother's maiden name is lost with all the rest of the silent majority of her sex. The fact that men have given the wedded name for ages, and that men are most often senior partners in the marriage firm, and the fact that any other suggested plan gives two names for one family instead of one seems to make that a part of the old inheritance that may not cause great uneasiness if one accepts it without revolt. There is a compromise method which long has been a custom among Friends and is growing even more rapidly than that of holding permanently to the full maiden name. That is the plan of keeping the father's name, or the "maiden name," as a middle one, and adding the husband's name; so that Miss Mary Jane Wood shall, on marrying John Hartley Stone, become, not Mrs. John Hartley Stone, but Mrs. Mary Wood Stone. That keeps in memory her family designation and yet gives her children a chance to call themselves by the one name which is a sign of the family unity. However the settlement may be made, the point is that such a vital question, entering into the legal signature for business purposes as well as into all social relationship, shall reach conclusion before the two enter upon the marriage bond.

SHALL THE WIFE TAKE THE HUSBAND'S NATIONALITY?

In the second place, there is now a question of nationality to be settled, a most important one in all its political and legal bearings. The old law made a wife the subject of her husband's national law and took her automatically away from her own country if her husband was born and was citizen of another country. The national allegiance of her birth and her family was thus automatically transferred to that of the man she had married. The suffering of many a woman in the late war when her husband's national allegiance made her legally an "enemy alien" to her own beloved land has sharpened the claim that now, when women have the franchise, they should have complete choice of the body politic to which they owe allegiance. If they wish to marry men of another country they shall have the determination of whether or not they shall become naturalized by his government or whether they shall keep political relation with their own native country. The League of Women Voters is now hard at work to make the national allegiance of women, as of men, a personal matter whether women are married or single. The Federal Bill that is called for by this body would make it incumbent upon all women of foreign birth desiring to use the franchise in the United States to become naturalized, and would protect any woman on marrying from the loss of her own national allegiance, whatever her husband's might be. Surely such a protection of individual citizenship is best for both men and women, whatever their marital state. It is, however, a matter that often comes up for adjustment in international marriages. It is matter of importance that women of foreign birth as well as men coming to this country from other lands should personally seek for full citizenship and not have it handed to them with a marriage certificate. It is equally of importance that no person should lose allegiance to the country of his or her birth and affection simply by reason of marriage. This question of what country shall one continue to belong to after marriage is one for settlement on high grounds of patriotism and civic duty before the marriage is consummated.

WHO SHALL CHOOSE THE DOMICILE?

In the third place, the matter of chosen domicile is now up for discussion or may be in the near future. The law from time immemorial has given the choice of residence of the family, wife as well as children, into the complete control of the husband and father. A woman may be "posted" in the public press as "leaving her husband's bed and board," and thereby the husband may be released from any responsibility for her debts or support. The inference is that married women have no rights in marriage that can survive independent choice on her part of a residence apart from the husband. Now we have a movement that if successful would place the law behind an equal choice by married men and married women, of domicile, and of all that goes with that possible separation of residence. There are those who declare that separate residence for husbands and wives might keep the flame of romantic love burning longer and more ardently, since "familiarity often breeds contempt" and the absence of the loved one often kindles desire. This is not, however, the general feeling, and the demand for independent choice of domicile has many side-issues not at present fully met, if at all understood, by those who make the demand noted above. The legal right of choice of domicile goes consistently with the legal obligation to "support." The law still makes it incumbent upon a husband to give financial support to his wife commensurate with his earnings or income and still more demands of the father the full support of minor children. Naturally, if he has these obligations to meet, a man must go where he can earn sufficient to meet them. He may be unwise or mistaken in his choice, but, having the responsibility, he must try to meet it as best he can, and among the necessary elements in that trial are free movement to the place or places in which he can find work.

If, therefore, the family are all to be kept in one residence, father, mother and children, this economic aspect of the father's responsibility must be considered. If the father and mother each "gang their ain gait," and decide for business reasons or from personal preference to live in separate places, perhaps far apart from each other, then which one is to have the child or children? The old idea that men should have the power to hold women in wholly unsuitable surroundings, and that no matter what home was offered her a wife must submit and accept, is long outgrown in all the States of this Union. The wife has now the right to help choose domicile, and in point of fact, at least among the older Americans, has often more than an equal share in such determination; but to pass a "blanket law" that at once gave the suggestion of two choices for the family domicile without any qualifying statement of release of men from "support" clauses in the family legislation as those clauses relate to wives might be neither just nor wise. The one in the family upon whom is placed the heavier economic burden for support of children must have much freedom of choice of residence. To restrict that freedom might be to add to present family difficulties without really giving women better chances in marriage. Now, any woman who feels herself oppressed in the matter of domicile has the remedy in her own hands. She can make complaint to a court or she can leave her husband and no one can prevent her, and she can establish a separate establishment if she has the means and make herself eligible thereby to a practical if not a legal divorce. But if the twain stay together, and mean to do so, there are mutual considerations that require an adjustment, and there is now little danger of women having to submit to injustice in the matter of choice of domicile, except in cases where no home together would seem desirable to either or to both.

The matter of choice of domicile is now in the United States so much a mutual question and to be decided upon economic grounds, that it is one of the things that it is well to discuss from the bottom up if two people wish to marry, provided there are any reasons why the relative merits of two or more places of residence are involved in the issue. The reasonableness and generosity of the average American man quite equals the like qualities in the average American woman; hence the domicile question may well be left in abeyance in any struggle for "equality of rights between the sexes" and confined to personal debate and decision; but in that personal debate and decision it should have recognized place.

SHALL THE MARRIED WOMAN EARN OUTSIDE THE HOME?

The fourth question, now sometimes a burning one, and one most intimately related to that of choice of domicile, is that concerning the continuance of professional or business connection by the woman after marriage. Shall I keep on with my work or not? This is the problem that besets many a woman when the question of marriage with the chosen one is imminent. For the woman who is a teacher, and already established in the educational field in the city or town where both the man and the woman concerned find it easy to choose to live after marriage, there is a probability that she can continue her work after marriage with comparative ease. The laws that used to penalize the woman teacher who married are rapidly ceasing to operate, and although the common legal requirement for a two years' vacation from public school employment when a child is to be born may exert a strong influence upon the birth-rate (either for or against) the fact that marriage does not disqualify for teaching and that teaching is so near the home interest may lead to much continuance of that type of professional work after marriage. The question, however, is not one for the woman alone to solve. Many women find that the ideal of "taking care of his wife," which long ages of law and custom have ingrained in man's nature, may stand in the way of her earning outside the home after marriage. To be settled right this question must be settled by full consent of both parties and that consent may be hard to get from the man who fears that he will be considered incapable if he "lets his wife earn." What is to be done in such a case? That must be determined by the possibility of compromise on both sides.

If the woman has attained a high position in some profession, law, or medicine, as preacher, teacher, or nurse, as business manager or welfare worker, the chances are that she feels she can best help in the family life by hiring things done in the household, which she has little skill, perhaps, to do herself, and keeping on with the vocation for which she has been trained and in which she has already gained a place. But she may have attained her vocational opportunity and to keep it must continue to live in a locality remote from the man's home and work. What then? To be near each other and to live together is the chief desire of genuine lovers. That would be no home which had two centres of vocational activity miles apart. Circumstances may compel such separation for economic reasons long after marriage has bound two lives together so closely that distance even cannot really separate them. But at the outset, if two people are to belong to each other, they must be able to combine their home life if that is to be a help and not a hindrance to the joint affection that alone makes the two one. The question of domicile, bound up with that of whether or not the woman shall continue her vocational connection after marriage, sometimes becomes acute in this manner—the woman earns more than the man and her place of earning is in a far-away location from his and the transplanting of his life has no promise of economic readjustment. Shall she give up her larger salary and go with him to a place in which she is less likely than if single to gain a professional foothold and they both make the smaller income do? Or shall she insist, if he is willing, that the economic advantage of the married firm requires his removal to the seat of her labors at any risk of his getting another hold upon vocational opportunity?

Those who ask such a question should remember that the facts of life, social and economic, all make the upsetting of the man in his work seldom a safe or a happy solution. In the first place, the position of a man who even temporarily depends upon his wife's vocational success and relinquishes his own economic position, is far more difficult than that of a woman who sacrifices her own professional standing to go with her husband to a new centre. Any woman asks more of a man in the way of sacrifice, both of his standing as a man and his chances as a worker, if she demands that he take her income as the basic economic element in the joint family treasury (when such demand entails a change of residence and a giving up of assured income on his part) than any man asks of a woman when the conditions proposed are the reverse. No woman loses "caste" who depends upon her husband in an economic sense. Perhaps the time will come when it will cost a woman the loss of social prestige and of the best chance for work outside the home (as it now does a man) when the choice is made to follow the larger income from one locality to another. Now, however, it means that a woman can adjust herself to such change far better than a man, and hence that equal right to demand sacrifice and equal duty to mutually help each other demand that where such acute problems arise the woman shall give the man's relation to his work right of way. Moreover, even those

who, like Doctor Patten, believe that women should continue vocational work after marriage place the chief economic burden of the family permanently upon the husband and father. The wife may earn outside the home if both agree and the opportunity offers in the place where the man's work already is; but the maintenance of the economic standing and the improvement of social condition remain, as of old, with the man. And for the obvious reason that if the woman has children they may take a large portion of her interest and of her strength and energy and, in any case, the married woman, if she really makes a home, must mix her vocational work with a more or less extended devotion to that home-making. Also, although a woman at marriage may be in receipt of a larger income from vocational service than is the man she wishes to marry, he will be more likely, if worth-while, to gain steadily toward a much larger compensation. The positions which women fill are for the most part self-limited. They are fast developing high qualities for routine work in the professions, like school doctor and hospital clinician and workers for legal aid and other like salaried employments. These are not highly paid, but have manifest advantages for women in that they give a fixed income, if small, and in that they allow for regulation of hours of service that may easily be made half-time work in case of divided effort. Hence, although at a given point in earlier life (when the usual greater precocity of women give some women the advantage in salary and position), a woman may have a higher salary at marriage, a far greater rise in both income and leadership may be on the husband's side as the years go on.

ECONOMIC CONSIDERATIONS INVOLVED

At any rate, the question of whether or not the woman shall earn outside the home after her marriage must wait upon the deeper question, shall she do anything which will disturb or render more difficult the man's economic adjustment? There are exceptions, a growing number of exceptions, but as a general thing the question of domicile and the question of which one shall give way when there is difficulty of both being well situated in individual work in one place, must be settled on the basis of the man's longer, larger, and more continuous responsibility for the economic standing of the family.

The exceptions make their own excuse and shape their own defense. The average married woman carries on two vocations if she keeps on with her own work, one inside and one outside the home. The one in which she earns outside the home must in the long run and the large way be subordinated to the joint partnership of the household in which she bears a larger share of the internal management and he the heavier burden of the outside support.

Any thorough-going discussion of the questions involved in the wage-earning of married women and mothers outside the home must include study of actual expense of alternate plans. The fundamental question may be one concerning the social value of the woman's vocational work. The next must certainly be what would the family treasury gain or lose by the housemother's continued vocational service outside the home. In the suggestive and encouraging book by Mrs. Mary Hinman Abel, entitled *Successful Family Life on the Moderate Income,* this economic aspect of the problem is treated with definiteness. In addition to the general conclusion reached by many that a family income of from $2,500 to $3,000 must be reached before continual hired help can be economically justified, Mrs. Abel shows by tables at pre-war prices that unless a married woman has a high-grade profession with a good independent income the duties performed by the average housemother within the home cannot be hired without a distinct economic loss to the family treasury. For example, reckoning conservatively the cost of the full-time hired girl or working housekeeper at $600 to $1,000 per year, and estimating the economic value of the woman who does all her own housework except washing and heavy cleaning at only fifteen cents an hour, the saving by the average married woman who is competent and well and does all her own work is a large one. There are the best of reasons, therefore, why, for the woman who is in ordinary circumstances and not so averse to household care and work as to insure her failure in it, the answer to the question, Shall I keep on with my outside earning after marriage?—should be in the negative. The old notion that all women were domestic and would enjoy housework if only they could do it in their own homes is indeed exploded. The natural differences among women are now allowed. The advantages, social, economic, and in matters of health and control of work-time and of leisure, which the average housemother enjoys over the average woman who works at manual labor under the factory system of industry, were, however, never better known or more justly evaluated. . . .

It is a sign, among other things, of desired and needed flexibility in domestic arrangements that there were listed in 1910 as married twenty-five per cent, of the women at work in "gainful occupations." Not all the conditions indicated by this count were socially helpful; since in the textile industries, in which many married women are employed, there are fewer children born and more die before the end of the second year than in the average population. It does, however, indicate that among those of higher opportunity in life there is a growing disposition to treat the question of women's continuance in vocational service outside the home after marriage as a real problem and one to be settled in freedom, and with social approval of that freedom, by the two persons most deeply concerned. Only, it must be insisted, that all a married woman gains in salary or wages cannot be reckoned as increase of the family income. The economic value of the average housemother's contribution is now definitely computed and must be reckoned hereafter as so much actually contributed to the family income. And so far, if a woman is physically able, temperamentally adjustable, and adequately trained for household tasks, she can in the vast majority of cases serve her day and generation in no better fashion than by assuming and carrying the multiple duties of the private home.

Hence, although freedom means new choice, prudence and affection alike oftenest point to the old paths of family service for the average woman. As Mrs. Abel well says of the competent housemother who chooses full and personal service to the home and the family, "At her best she represents individual effort fully utilized. She fits her tasks together; she utilizes bits of time; she invents short cuts in her work." Of such it may be truly declared, in the new time as in the old, that she translates every dollar of the family income into many dollars' worth of comfort, of health, and of happiness.

IS IT BAD FORM TO EARN AFTER MARRIAGE?

One more consideration, quite new in its full significance, should be given place in any discussion of the wife's relation to work outside the home. That consideration is concerned with the use of her time not needed in household tasks. The modern aids to those tasks, of which mention has been made, give many women who assume full responsibility for the housemother's work a considerable amount of strength and time which may be used in some chosen way outside the strictly family service. The general

idea is that such time should be given in gratuitous "social welfare work" or in some form of activity divorced from regular vocations. An able President of the Federation of Women's Clubs, the body most distinctly representing the interest and service of women in volunteer social service in this country, has said, in addressing her large constituency, "Sport is work we do without pay—we are all sports." The sentiment was applauded and with evident sense of superiority to the "paid worker." The feeling, so general in many circles of society, that women lose "caste" if they work for wages or salary, reaches its maximum of prejudice in the case of married women. It is thought highly honorable to sell things in a "Fair" for a good cause and come in contact with a crowd of strangers in the process among people who would consider "keeping a shop," unless from dire necessity, a very questionable proceeding. It is thought most virtuous and wifely for a woman married to a minister of the church to give her time and strength gratuitously in multitudinous religious helps to the organization which usually counts on getting the service of two first-class people for a second- or third-class salary for one. But for the wife of such a minister, realizing that the income is generally insufficient for proper living, to work out-side her home, even for a few hours each day, for pay, is to lay herself and her husband also open to harsh criticism; even if her house is kept well and her children properly cared for. It is also thought by many people that the only really justifiable use of time that can be spared from household duties is in furthering the husband's work, if he is struggling up; or, if he has "arrived," in these miscellaneous gratuitous social services in which the club-women so abound.

There is great need that this judgment be revised. Not only is this true in the interest of women whose devotion to a chosen vocation has right of way in justice when the debate is on as to the use of any left-over time she may save from domestic duties. It is also true that we can not have the democratic feeling and influence from women of social position which our political life so sadly needs unless it is understood that it is as honorable for a woman, married or unmarried, to earn money for her work as it is for a man with or without an inherited fortune. The class feeling that makes all married women range themselves with those of their sex who have inherited fortunes, and leads them to place those who serve the community in salaried positions as less unselfish and less honorable social workers than themselves, is one to outgrow. An interest divorced from professional standards or professional compensation is not necessarily nobler or more useful. This fact makes the choice of women before marriage as to the use of time that may justly be spared, even when the home makes its heaviest demands upon them, a choice of social as well as of personal significance.

Every year social effort once strictly of private provision and support becomes a public service, with organized supervision and standardized compensation. When such volunteer social effort becomes a public service it is highly desirable that the trained women it demands for its staff should (some of them, at least) be married women. Otherwise, the same loss of efficiency that the rapid turnover of the women teaching staff of our schools occasions will be discovered in our social work as it changes its centre of gravity from the private to the public organization.

There is a far greater need from this point of view for reorganization of hours and details of work so as to give more half-time or quarter-time employment to women of proved ability, than for any wholesale condemnation of the woman who works outside her home for pay, even when her husband is able and willing to "take care of her." It is for society to say, indeed, that women marrying and having children owe first duty to the home. It is for women themselves to say whether they shall use any time at their disposal after that duty is met in continuing such relation to their vocation as is now possible, or in being "sports."

The fact that men are trying to see both sides of this vexed question and that women, as a rule, are trying to make adjustment that will hold an equitable and happy balance between the personal and the family well-being means that this problem will work itself to a democratic result without social loss.

SHALL PARENTHOOD BE CHOSEN?

The fifth question that should come up for serious discussion and some measure of agreement in advance of the wedding ceremony is that of children. Shall there be any? If so, how many, if we can afford them? If so, how soon shall we try to call about us the new life? If not, why not, and how shall we live together without hope of offspring? These are vital questions. For want of agreement, or at least of understanding of disagreement before marriage, many unions are shipwrecked.

In the old days there were no questions of this nature. Every woman must have as many children as nature allowed, and when she could bear no more must give way to a new wife and a step-mother to carry on the family life; and if there were more children in a family than the father and family friends could support, they had to be cared for by the community. The modern condition is the same in the case of those below a certain grade of intelligence and self-control. But as human beings become more rational in other respects, they apply reason, common sense, and prudence to the great function of parenthood. Indeed, so much is this the case that the social danger of breeding only from below the higher levels is felt to be an increasing one. There are not wanting those who believe that rationalism in parenthood is wrong and should be prevented, if possible, but those are the people who decry the use of reason in all other matters, except it may be in the strictly economic field. The fact is that whatever may be said on the side of ancient religious sanction and inherited sentiment, the tendency on all sides is irresistibly toward the personal choice in parenthood as in marriage.

SOME PEOPLE HAVE A RIGHT TO MARRY AND REMAIN CHILDLESS

There are many, however, who believe that no one should marry unless wishing and expecting to have children. That is a belief which will doubtless be more and more outgrown. There are young people, children of dependent parents and near relatives, who see no way of starting a family of their own, who yet should not be denied the comfort and help of married life. The tragedies of sons and daughters made to drag out a lonely existence and either condemning the one they love to like denial or else giving up the hope of union and seeing their chosen one wedded to another—the sort of tragedy that forms the subject of many novels—is a tragedy to be outgrown. It may be that social burdens in behalf of parents or other dependents can not be lifted to the extent of making a completed family life possible to some young people. All the more, two people who truly love each other and are bound to one great sacrifice, namely, that of children of their own, should be able to escape another, that of denial of marriage.

There are other cases in which marriage is right and child-bearing may be wrong. There are tendencies to disease, in which, although there may be a long and useful life for the one bearing a family taint, it may be socially wrong to risk carrying on that taint. If all who need to know are agreed, and there is a chance of living many years of real

union together, no law should step in to prevent, and no inherited view of the limitation of marriage to those seeking parental relation should refuse assent to the union. There are many conceivable limitations to parental functioning, even for those who are keenly aware of the social significance of parenthood, which do not apply to marriage of those truly mated in thought and purpose. It is, however, the height of irrationality, and will more and more be seen to be such, for men and women to enter a relation the natural result of which, in the vast majority of cases, is the bearing of children, with no idea on either side as to what is the ideal and the wish and the purpose of the other party in the marriage union.

The question, again, for those who are agreed that they want to start a family as well as begin a mating is definitely to be considered, namely, that of the right time to begin the family they wish to have. It may be, as many believe, that too hasty adding of the strenuous discipline of parenthood to the often difficult task of adjustment of two mature and forceful natures, such as marriage so often brings together, is likely to give an unnecessarily hard start in the new life. Two people who have just got used to themselves, perhaps, have at marriage to get used to each other. It may be that they could succeed better in this great task if they had not so often to adjust themselves during the first year to the needs and masterful claims of a baby. There is no form of tyranny equal to that of the infant, who, assured of his right to unlimited service from all in sight, makes his demands at all times and in all ways. He pays for his subjection of parents and grandparents and they are all usually willing slaves. But it is often a great advantage if the parents, at least, have had a chance to make full acquaintance with each other's pet weaknesses and each other's best qualities before "the baldheaded tyrant from No

Man's Land" makes his appearance. It is, therefore, clearly a matter of frank and full discussion and settlement before marriage not only as to the fundamental question of whether or not there shall be children, but also if, as is the case in the overwhelming majority of cases, the young people hope for offspring, when they shall begin to call them to the home.

The thing of all others to be avoided is the outgrown idea that heavenly magic attends completely to these matters. It is earthly wisdom and unselfishness and good intent that are needed in this as in all the great decisions of life. Hence, there can be nothing more absurdly out of drawing with a rationalized civilization than any law which forbids the serious discussion of this most vital of social questions or one that forbids the full dissemination of scientific knowledge needed by those who would do the right thing in the parental as in all other relations of life.

WHAT IS THE JUST FINANCIAL BASIS OF THE HOUSEHOLD?

The sixth question that has right of debate before the marriage ceremony is that of the financial support of the household and of the distribution of the joint income. The use of the words joint income prejudges the case on this point. The old idea was of one purse, of right that of the "head of the family," and whatever it held was his to disburse. He it was who determined how the wife should be fed and clothed and sheltered. If he were generous and kind she fared well; if the opposite she fared ill. Her legal right was only the same as that of her minor child. Now the case is wholly different. In spite of some inconsistent left-over laws that can make a showing of belated tyranny when culled from old statute books, the financial right of the wife in the household is generally recognized. It is, however, still true that no logical system of financial sharing has been worked out so clearly as to be accepted by the common mind. We still have talk of a wife being "supported" when, as housemother, she works harder and more hours than her husband. We still have listing of those housemothers, who are the majority of the women of every country, as "without occupation." It is possible for men to speak of "giving" their wives what they think is needed for the household and without reference to any personal preference of the wives in expenditure, as if it were an act of charity and not a debt owed the family life.

On the other hand, some women, having achieved partial or entire financial independence of the husband and earning handsome sums in work outside the home, look upon all that the man earns as "belonging to the family," and all that they earn as wholly belonging to themselves. "What's John's belongs to us all; what is mine belongs to me," said one wife, without any idea of the absurd injustice of taking all the advantage that new conditions had made possible for women and at the same time hanging on to all that old-time privilege gave to wives. There is need of the strictest and most balanced thinking along the line of the economics of the household.

If, as seems in the vast majority of cases the best plan, the husband and father can be and is depended upon for the entire financial support of the family in the matter of earning and the housemother gives an actual service of great economic value in saving and service (as the competent housewife assuredly does give), then what is earned and what is produced by housework and management makes in justice one family treasury. If to that is added some special earning outside the home which the housemother is able to mix in with her family service, then that also is a part of the family treasury. After the marriage there should be a real partnership. There may be a separate account on either side of the gifts of inheritance or savings preceding the marriage, but after the twain are one in home-building they may justly be one in a common treasury. Two bank-books they may have, it is true, and perhaps better so, although many find one in the name of both husband and wife sufficiently convenient. The main thing is to get firmly in mind on both sides before any actual adjustments are necessary what, on the financial side, is the right attitude and plan of married life. The best way seems to be, for some people, at least, the division of the family treasury into three distinct parts. The first, and alas, in most families the much larger share, to be dedicated to common household expenses. The excellent work of specialists in family budgets shows us how this fund should be distributed in details of rent or dwelling, cost of food, clothing, reading, church, recreation, etc. Any one can now make up with prudence and wisdom such an estimate in proportion to the known income and the ascertained cost of living in any given locality. After this common expense is provided for, with due regard for the duty of saving for future needs, the remaining portion, be it much or little, should be equally divided as the personal fund of the husband and the wife. Some of those who have written on the family budget think that the contribution of the housewife in work, for which wages would have to be paid if she did not give this personal labor in the home, should be estimated in wages value, and should go into her part of a separate fund, after the common household expenses are deducted. That, it seems, would not be fair, for if the man puts in his labor value the woman should put in hers for the first and indispensable expense of the common life together. What is to be made right is the old custom of reckoning the savings and common property acquired after marriage as "his" estate. It is the estate of both, and should be so considered, even if he has earned outside and she saved and earned and helped him earn from within the household only.

WHAT SHALL BE THE ACCEPTED STANDARD OF LIVING?

The final question that must be considered by the two who are to marry and set up housekeeping is the scale of living they shall aim to attain. It has been well said that "the standard of living is what we desire; the scale of living what we can achieve." What is desired often, and what seems to the young only reasonable for all to have, is the scale of living the parents' households have attained after a life of hard work. It is a matter for profound ethical thinking to decide what measure of increase in expense of home upkeep should follow upon increase of income where there are children to be affected by changes. It may sometime be seen to be a social duty to keep much farther within bounds the natural desire to expand expense as income increases; both for the reason that income may decrease with advancing years for the parents and retrenchment be necessary when it is hardest, and also for the more important reason that children naturally make standards at the height of parental expenditure and may find it thereby the more difficult to "begin at the bottom" when they marry. At any rate, the young couple starting out must keep within their means or suffer from the worst of fortunes, the dread of arriving bills and the shame of inability to pay them. That means some agreement before housekeeping begins as to what is involved in that adventure.

A witty woman said, "I love to travel with my friend Mary, for her economies and mine are the same." Some uniformity of temperamental reaction both to regular economies and to occasional extravagances is, if not an essential, a valuable basis for happy marriage. That means that the engaged couple might well start a game of "Must Haves" and "Would Like to

Haves" in the moments that can be spared from other pursuits, a game in which without the other's knowledge each should write the secret wishes and requirements to be later compared for mutual enlightenment. The woman who would gladly go with two meals a day for a fortnight in order to get a ticket for the opera or symphony, and the man who would sacrifice a needed new suit of clothes with pleasure for a fishing trip, may be able to compromise on essentials, but will find it difficult in the matter of extras unless warned beforehand. Affection bridges many chasms, and sensible people learn that even in the best regulated families father, mother, and the children may all get some of their best times apart. A basis of mutual understanding is, however, essential. The necessity to get at a common plan for the economic standards of the household is a vital one. How many men have run in debt for what they believed essential to the wife's happiness because she had such things in her father's house, without letting the wife know that economy was necessary, only to find out that if full confidence had been given a mutual effort would have secured better results. How many women have gone without things they might have had for want of knowledge of their husband's income and suffered fears that need not have been in the mind. How many also, alas, both of men and women, have lived beyond their means from selfish demand one upon the other, a demand which might have been chastened, at least, if full knowledge of economic resources had been attained before the scale of living was fixed.

All these items of suggested conference and decision given above are counsels of prudence and wisdom. Many, perhaps most, however, of the young couples starting out in life "go it blind" in all or some of these particulars. The wonder is that these who stand on the most serious of compacts and the one leading to the greatest extremes of both happiness and unhappiness with so little knowledge of each other's condition, capacity, or deepest wishes, get along, on the whole, so well. We see them on every side starting on the sea of married life with gaiety of heart because the chosen one is obtained for company and with no conception of the difficulties that may make the voyage tempestuous. But they often make safe harbor of comfortable comradeship for middle life and old age, and if they have had a harder time than they need have had at least prove that "love is the greatest thing in the world."

THE NEED FOR FULL AND MUTUAL UNDERSTANDING BEFORE MARRIAGE

The rising tide of divorce, however, gives point to the plea of this chapter for a more careful charting of the sailing course in advance. The fact that so many get their discipline of knowledge and direction as they go along and do not make shipwreck even if matrimonial storms grow frequent or heavy, is a very good testimony to the native goodness of men and women and to their ability to make good their mistakes and work out success even from failure provided the indispensable north star of unselfish affection leads them on. It would be well, however, to lessen the failures if that can be done. When men and women show what marriage can become for the wise, the idealistic, and the loving, it gives a picture of satisfaction and mutual service that makes most other human associations seem trivial and short-lived. Only parenthood is equal or superior to marriage in its possibilities of moral discipline and personal development. To make it successful is worth striving for.

Literature, science, and art have many great marriages to their credit—men and women brought together by identical tastes and similar capacities, working together in high pursuits through a long life of achievement. They illumine the way of life with a peculiar glow. Elizabeth Barrett Browning sang:

"Unlike are we, unlike, O princely Heart!
    Our ministering two angels look surprise
    On one another as they strike athwart
    Their wings in passing."

but her union with Robert Browning showed that they were nearer alike than in her sad humility she had fancied. Jonas Lie, the Norwegian novelist, and his gifted wife, it is said, "knew the felicity of a perfect union," and he himself has testified, "If I have ever written anything of merit, my wife has as great a share in it as myself, and her name should appear on the title-page as collaborator." The joint discoveries of the Curies are well known, linking husband and wife together in a great gift to humanity. In humble circles of the gifted and the talented the married couples as becoming more numerous each decade whose work as well as whose affection binds them together.

THE SUPREME SATISFACTIONS OF SUCCESSFUL MARRIAGE

Take it all in all, although no particular marriage may be "made in heaven," the sort of union that monogamic marriage has worked out at its highest reaches is without a rival in depth of feeling in satisfaction of association, in wealth of comradeship, and in social value as a foundation for family life and for initial training toward social serviceableness. No wise person can do aught to lessen its opportunity for ethical drill, or for that due mingling of attraction and duty which make all the vital associations of human beings helps toward the higher life. No wise person will continue in the ancient error of mistaking show for substance in these weighty matters.

All who believe that the family is an institution whose gift to the social order is not yet outgrown and whose possibilities of social value are not yet fully developed, must work to make the right marriages easier to secure, and the wrong ones less easy to be consummated, and to purge the ideals of home of selfishness and of superficiality by constant portrayal of the best in the married life.

The stage and the moving picture should more often portray the world's marriage successes rather than perpetual reproductions of the marriage failures. The novel should more often show how many people save, so as by fire, the dreams of youth in rescue of their married life from threatening ills. Such portrayal would not be against a realistic ideal of art, but a more perfect and balanced use of realism. The rise of people on "stepping-stone of their dead selves to higher things" is quite as dramatic as the succession of falls that land them in the pit of despair. The struggles that succeed are quite as capable of exciting emotional response as are those that fail.

Real life shows a larger measure of successful achievement than of bitter failure, else would life not go on. Marriage at its highest is yet to be used in any adequate measure as the theme of the artist and the stimulant of response to art.

The day will come when "Main Street" will reveal its best and not its worst; its richest, and not its poorest products, for the satisfaction of universal sentiment.

Robert E. Park (1864–1944) and Ernest W. Burgess (1886–1966) on Sex Differences

Robert Ezra Park grew up the son of a prosperous businessman in Red Wing, Minnesota, on the banks of the Mississippi River. He attended the University of Minnesota for a year and then transferred to the University of Michigan, where he pursued a bachelor's degree in philology and philosophy. After graduation, Park worked for a few years as a journalist for various daily newspapers, later entering Harvard University to study philosophy and psychology. After acquiring his master's degree in 1899, he left for Germany for further graduate work, taking a course with Georg Simmel at the University of Berlin and earning a doctorate at Heidelberg in 1903. Except for the course with Simmel, Park never had any formal education in sociology—most of his formal training being in history, philosophy, and political economy.

Park taught at Harvard for a short time but left to get back to the "real world" and out of academia. His interest in racial issues was sparked by his acquaintance with Booker T. Washington, for whom Park worked for several years at Tuskegee Institute in Al-

abama. In 1914, at age 50, Park returned to academic life at the invitation of W. I. Thomas, who asked him to offer a course at the University of Chicago on "The Negro in America." Park was soon invited to join the department and continued teaching there until 1936. After Small retired and Thomas was asked to resign, Park became the leading member of the department.

Never a prolific writer, Park nevertheless mentored many students and demanded much from them. Unfortunately, he was not friendly to the women who had been part of the University of Chicago sociology department, and he looked with disdain upon "do-gooders" who wanted to use social research to reform society. Under Park, women sociologists were moved into a new "social work" department—a new field with less prestige. Feagin and Vera (2001:77) write that Park was "opposed to the more activist and emancipatory sociology of the early white women and black sociologists" and that Park himself had a major role "in shifting emphasis from a sociology concerned with studying and eradicating serious social problems to an 'objective science.'" Thus, it is no surprise that he paid little attention to gender issues and included a conservative analysis of sex differences in his major textbook.

Park led the University of Chicago to a dominant position in the field and many of his students went on to become well known academies. He was elected President of the American Sociological Society in 1925 and was a member of many learned societies. After his retirement, he taught and oversaw student research at Fisk University in Nashville until his death in 1944, still focused on racial issues. Thus, although something of a pioneer in the field of race relations, Park was nevertheless conservative on issues of gender, and he promoted and helped institutionalize a "value-free" sociology that dominated the field for some decades.

Ernest W. Burgess was a younger colleague of Park's at the University of Chicago, also a strong proponent of "scientific" sociology that had predictive value. He was born in Ontario, the son of a Congregational minister. He earned his doctorate in sociology from the University of Chicago in 1913 and after three years at other universities, he joined the faculty at Chicago as an assistant professor. Burgess did research in a number of areas, and he and Park together edited the influential textbook *Introduction to the Science of Sociology* in 1921. He later served as departmental chair and carried out empirical research on various topics, including divorce, crime, aging, and marital prediction. He disliked abstract theory and preferred empirical research aimed at achieving predictability of

social phenomena. According to Deegan (1986), Burgess's attitude toward women was mixed, with more negative attitudes in his earlier years—the years during which he and Park edited their textbook. Burgess mellowed over time, serving as the first president of the Society for the Study of Social Problems. He had a long career at Chicago and died in 1966, just short of his eightieth birthday.

Major Works

Park, Robert E., and Ernest W. Burgess. *Introduction to the Science of Sociology*. Chicago: University of Chicago Press, 1921.

Park, Robert E. *The Immigrant Press and Its Control*. New York: Harper & Row, 1922.

Park's most important papers were collected and published as Robert E. Park, *Race and Culture* (New York: The Free Press), and Ralph H. Turner, ed., *Robert Park on Social Control and Collective Behavior* (Chicago: University of Chicago Press, 1967).

Sources

American Sociological Association, "Ernest W. Burgess." July 1, 2005. name=Ernest+W.+Burgess & section=President. Accessed 23 January 2006.

Coser, Lewis A. 1977. *Masters of sociological thought*. New York: Harcourt, Brace, Jovanovich.

Deegan, Mary Jo. 1986. *Jane Addams and the men of the Chicago school*, 211–13. New Brunswick, NJ: Transaction Books.

Feagin, Joe R., and Hernan Vera. 2001. *Liberation sociology*. Boulder, CO: Westview.

THE SELECTION

While Robert Ezra Park wrote very little about women, he and Burgess included a small entry on sex differences in their influential textbook *Introduction to the Science of Sociology* that argues for the permanence and inherent nature of sex differences, with women being less active and less likely to excel where intelligence is needed—but also less likely to commit crimes. This textbook was used by generations of American sociology students in the 1920s and 1930s. Although its articles and chapters were written by other authors, because Park and Burgess were the editors we can assume that they agree with the conclusions of the pieces they selected. The "Sex Differences" chapter included here appeared in at least the first two editions of the book, in the section "Human Nature." The entry is by Albert Moll, originally published in *Sexual Life of the Child* in 1902.

Moll views the sexes as essentially different by nature in abilities, temperament, and behavior. Early childhood differences emerge that reflect the future roles of boys and girls, with boys being more active, rough, and less inclined to nurturance. Girls love doll-play, kitchen occupations, needlework, and adornment, while boys prefer the outdoors and noisy, rough games. The author goes on to state emphatically that, while some people believe these differences are due to "education," he believes the evidence points to "direct inheritance" as the cause, proponents of women's rights notwithstanding. Although education can alter some tendencies, sex differences appear to be too deeply ingrained and strong to be overcome. Moll also used crime data to support his idea that sex differences are inborn. The strong and emphatic support of biologically based sex differences must have influenced many to believe that sex equality was a futile goal.

SEX DIFFERENCES

As children become physically differentiated in respect of sex, so also does a mental differentiation ensue. Differences are observed in the matter of occupation, of games, of movements, and numerous other details. Since man is to play the active part in life, boys rejoice especially in rough outdoor games. Girls, on the other hand, prefer such games as correspond to their future occupations. Hence their inclination to mother smaller children, and to play with dolls. Watch how a little girl takes care of her doll, washes it, dresses and undresses it. When only six or seven years of age she is often an excellent nurse. Her need to occupy herself in such activities is often so great that she pretends that her doll is ill.

In all kinds of ways, we see the little girl occupying herself in the activities and inclinations of her future existence. She practices house work; she has a little kitchen, in which she cooks for herself and her doll. She is fond of needlework. The care of her own person, and more especially its adornment, is not forgotten. I remember seeing a girl of three who kept on interrupting her elders' conversation by crying out, "New clothes!" and would not keep quiet until these latter had been duly admired. The love of self-adornment is almost peculiar to female children; boys, on the other hand, prefer rough outdoor games, in

From Albert Moll, "Sex Differences," pp. 85–9: In *Introduction to the Science of Sociology,* ed. Robert E. Park and Ernest W. Burgess (Chicago: University of Chicago Press, 1921).

which their muscles are actively employed, robber-games, soldier-games, and the like. And whereas, in early childhood, both sexes are fond of very noisy games, the fondness for these disappears earlier in girls than in boys.

Differences between the sexes have been established also by means of experimental psychology, based upon the examination of a very large number of instances. Berthold Hartmann has studied the childish circle of thought, by means of a series of experiments. Schoolboys to the number of 660 and schoolgirls to the number of 652, at ages between five and three-fourths and six and three-fourths years, were subjected to examination. It was very remarkable to see how, in respect to certain ideas, such as those of the triangle, cube, and circle, the girls greatly excelled the boys; whereas in respect of animals, minerals, and social ideas, the boys were better informed than the girls. Characteristic of the differences between the sexes, according to Meumann, from whom I take these details and some of those that follow, is the fact that the idea of "marriage" was known to only 70 boys as compared to 227 girls; whilst the idea of "infant baptism" was known to 180 boys as compared to 220 girls. The idea of "pleasure" was also much better understood by girls than by boys. Examination of the memory has also established the existence of differences between the sexes in childhood. In boys the memory for objects appears to be at first the best developed; to this succeeds the memory for words with a visual content; in the case of girls, the reverse of this was observed. In respect of numerous details, however, the authorities conflict. Very striking is the fact, one upon which a very large number of investigators are agreed, that girls have a superior knowledge of colors.

There are additional psychological data relating to the differences between the sexes in childhood. I may recall Stern's investigations concerning the psychology of evidence, which showed that girls were much more inaccurate than boys.

It has been widely assumed that these psychical differences between the sexes result from education, and are not inborn. Others, however, assume that the psychical characteristics by which the sexes are differentiated result solely from individual differences in education. Stern believes that in the case of one differential character, at least, he can prove that for many centuries there has been no difference between the sexes in the matter of education; this character is the capacity for drawing. Kerschensteiner has studied the development of this gift, and considers that his results have established beyond dispute that girls are greatly inferior in this respect to boys of like age. Stern points out that there can be no question here of cultivation leading to a sexual differentiation of faculty, since there is no attempt at a general and systematic teaching of draughtsmanship to the members of one sex to the exclusion of members of the other.

I believe that we are justified in asserting that at the present time the sexual differentiation manifested in respect of quite a number of psychical qualities is the result of direct inheritance. It would be quite wrong to assume that all these differences arise in each individual in consequence of education. It does, indeed, appear to me to be true that inherited tendencies may be increased or diminished by individual education; and further, that when the inherited tendency is not a very powerful one, it may in this way even be suppressed.

We must not forget the frequent intimate association between structure and function. Rough outdoor games and wrestling thus correspond to the physical constitution of the boy. So, also, it is by no means improbable that the little girl, whose pelvis and hips have already begun to indicate by their development their adaption for the supreme functions of the sexually mature woman, should experience obscurely a certain impulsion toward her predestined maternal occupation, and that her inclinations and amusements should in this way be determined. Many, indeed, and above all the extreme advocates of women's rights, prefer to maintain that such sexually differentiated inclinations result solely from differences in individual education: if the boy has no enduring taste for dolls and cooking, this is because his mother and others have told him, perhaps with mockery, that such amusements are unsuited to a boy; whilst in a similar way the girl is dissuaded from the rough sports of boyhood. Such an assumption is the expression of that general psychological and educational tendency, which ascribes to the activity of the will an overwhelmingly powerful influence upon the development of the organs subserving the intellect, and secondarily also upon that of the other organs of the body. We cannot dispute the fact that in such a way the activity of the will may, within certain limits, be effective, especially in cases in which the inherited tendency thus counteracted is comparatively weak; but only within certain limits. Thus we can understand how it is that in some cases, by means of education, a child is impressed with characteristics normally foreign to its sex; qualities and tendencies are thus developed which ordinarily appear only in a child of the opposite sex. But even though we must admit that the activity of the individual may operate in this way, none the less we are compelled to assume that certain tendencies are inborn. The failure of innumerable attempts to counteract such inborn tendencies by means of education throws a strong light upon the limitations of the activity of the individual will; and the same must be said of a large number of other experiences.

Criminological experiences appear also to confirm the notion of an inherited sexual differentiation, in children as well as in adults. According to various statistics, embracing not only the period of childhood, but including as well the period of youth, we learn that girls constitute one-fifth only of the total number of youthful criminals. A number of different explanations have been offered to account for this disproportion. Thus, for instance, attention has been drawn to the fact that a girl's physical weakness renders her incapable of attempting violent assaults upon the person, and this would suffice to explain why it is that girls so rarely commit such crimes. In the case of offenses for which bodily strength is less requisite, such as fraud, theft, etc., the number of youthful female offenders is proportionately larger, although here also they are less numerous than males of corresponding age charged with the like offenses. It has been asserted that in the law courts girls find more sympathy than boys, and that for this reason the former receive milder sentences than the latter; hence it results that in appearance merely the criminality of girls is less than that of boys. Others, again, refer the differences in respect of criminality between the youthful members of the two sexes to the influences of education and general environment. Morrison, however, maintains that all these influences combined are yet insufficient to account for the great disproportion between the sexes, and insists that there exists in youth as well as in adult life a specific sexual differentiation, based, for the most part, upon biological differences of a mental and physical character.

Such a marked differentiation as there is between the adult man and the adult woman certainly does not exist in childhood. Similarly in respect of many other qualities, alike bodily and mental, in respect of many inclinations and numerous activities, we find that in childhood sexual differentiation is less marked than it is in adult life. None the less, a number of sexual differences can be shown to exist even in childhood; and as regards many other differences, though they are not yet apparent, we are nevertheless compelled to assume that they already exist potentially in the organs of the child.

William Graham Sumner (1840–1910) on Women's Natural Roles

William Graham Sumner, sometimes called the first American sociologist because he developed the first courses in the area, was born in Paterson, New Jersey, October 30, 1840. The son of English immigrant parents, he attended public schools in Hartford, Connecticut, and later received a bachelor's degree with many honors from Yale College. Although he was drafted into military service, he was able to avoid it by buying his way out (by purchasing a substitute). Instead, he left for Europe, where he continued his education in languages and theology in Geneva, Göttingen, and finally Oxford, where he studied with Henry Thomas Buckle, an important historian and social scientist. On his return to the United States, Sumner accepted a position at Yale as a math and Greek tutor, later resigning to become an assistant to the rector at Calvary Church (Episcopal) in New York City, where he served for a year.

Preferring teaching to ministry, Sumner was able to obtain an appointment in 1872 at Yale as professor of political and social science, a position he held through the rest of his career. About this time, he began to read with great appreciation the work of Herbert Spencer, English prophet of laissez-faire government, survival of the fittest, and other concepts of evolutionary sociology. Sumner became widely known as a promoter of these ideas, opposing "sentimentalists" who try to reform society or develop programs to aid the poor or other needy groups. A tireless worker, Sumner published some 300 items, including books and articles in history, economics, politics, public policy, and sociology.

Sumner's major contributions to sociology were the concepts developed in his *Folkways*, a study of the diversity of cultures. The work is more descriptive than theoretical, but it is replete with concepts that have become commonplace in later sociological discussions of culture and society, including *mores, ethnocentrism, in-group* and *out-group* feeling, *institutions*, and *laws*. Among other ideas introduced in the book was the statement that "the mores can make anything right," a notion that is basic to the development of cultural relativism (in place of the common moralism of early sociology). This helped move sociology forward in the direction of examining cultural variation without engaging in Eurocentric bias.

Sumner was one of the leading proponents of Social Darwinism, following Spencer and others who argued for allowing the natural forces of society to work free from the interference of government, charity, or artificial reform. In this, Sumner was in strong opposition to the reformist impulses of Lester Frank Ward, Charlotte Perkins Gilman, and other thinkers of the Progressive Era.

Late in his life, Sumner was elected the second President of the American Sociological Society (following Ward), a decision that shocked Albion Small and others who opposed his radical Social Darwinist philosophy. He died in April of 1910, a few months following a third stroke suffered in December 1909 while he was in New York City to deliver his presidential address. Many of Sumner's writings were edited and coauthored by his Yale colleague, Albert Galloway

Keller, with several being published in the 1920s, including the four-volume opus *The Science of Society* (1927).

MAJOR WORKS

Sumner, William Graham. *Folkways and Mores.* Edited by Edward Sagarin. New York: Schoken Books, 1979 (Orig. pub. 1907).

Sumner, W. G., and Albert G. Keller. *The Science of Society.* 4 vols. New Haven: Yale University Press, 1927.

Sumner, William G. *What Social Classes Owe Each Other.* New York: Harper, 1883.

Sumner, W. G. "Modern Marriage." *Yale Review* 13 (1924): 249–275.

SOURCES

Adams, Bert N., and R. A. Sydie, 2001. *Sociological theory,* 81–88. Thousand Oaks, CA: Pine Forge Press.

Bierstedt, Robert. 1981. William Graham Sumner. In *American Sociological Theory: A Critical History,* 1–43. New York: Academic Press, 1981.

THE SELECTION

The following excerpt from William G. Sumner and Alfred G. Keller's work, *The Science of Society* (1927), represents well Sumner's mature views on the sexes and women's role in society. Since he believed that societies develop according to "natural" laws, he saw the differences between men and women as natural and inevitable. He saw women as adapted to reproduction, and men to enterprise, war, and politics.

Sumner and Keller (who dedicated the book to "the men we have taught") argue that sex differences are "essential contrasts,

representing 'thorough-going, all pervasive, inevitable, and immutable' traits of individuals expressed in social roles" (p. 111). They saw sex role differences as the first specialization in societal evolution, leading to the first cooperative relations in human existence. For Sumner, this fundamental differentiation underlay all human social groups, remaining constant through time and stage of social development.

In the excerpt that follows, the authors discuss sex differences as found in Section 57-64 of the larger work. Here they present

From William Graham Sumner and Alfred G. Keller, *The Science of Society* (New Haven: Yale University Press, 1927) 1:111–26, 140.

their analysis of the essential roles of woman as rooted in biology. The argument can be summarized briefly as follows: since woman experiences pregnancy, childbirth, and lactation, she is rendered weaker than man. Maternity and the maternal instinct are in effect disabilities in the competitive struggle for social existence, although necessary for species survival. While human males are stronger and more aggressive, females are more passive, productive, and stable. The female nervous system, being weaker, is more often affected by such ailments as neurasthenia, hallucinations, and hysteria. Women have greater propensities to dreaming, mental illness, intuition, and feeling than men, and less ability to use logic or inductive reasoning. Women also lack originality and are dependent, docile,

and capricious, according to Sumner. Overall, although women lack the capacity for genius, they are more adaptable and less self-absorbed than men.

Sumner and Keller saw these sex differences as resulting from the long history of natural selection, enhancing the survival of new generations. However, socialization and training also play a role in reinforcing the differences: girls are given less freedom than boys and are rewarded more for showing affection. They are "trained to docility" even when not born to it. Thus, women are socialized for conformity and conservatism, unlike men. Most women, according to Sumner, never even notice their relative lack of rights and freedom, owing to the pervasive cultural assumptions about sex differences.

LABOR: SEX-SPECIALIZATION

SPECIALIZATION BY SEX

Specialization, the factor which leads off in organization, takes place between unlikes; and the greatest opportunity for specialization lies between extremes of unlikeness. The organization for self-maintenance began, as organization is wont to begin, where there was the greatest differentiation between the factors present in the field, that is, between man and woman. For there exists among human beings no other dissimilarity, whether of age, temperament, social position, or anything else, that approaches in scope, constancy, and universality that of sex. The fact that *Homo* is a bi-sexual organism remains, and will ever remain, one of the steadfast and inexorable ultimates of human life, to which, through mores and institutions that take shape about the attending interest, adjust-

ment will be made. Primary and secondary sex-differences constitute, as between man and woman, a series of essential contrasts, thorough-going, all-pervasive, inevitable, and immutable, such as do not exist as between man and man and woman and woman. It follows, of course, that if sex-specialization was the first specialization, then sex-coöperation was the first coöperation. Some peoples are so weak in general coöperation that they resemble boys picking up chestnuts from the ground, with no one to go up the tree and shake for all; but even such peoples have sex-coöperation in some form of sex-union.

Since these differences of sex represent a life-condition of an elemental order, adjustments to which are to be noted in all the divisions of our subject, we shall take up the general case here and now, that it may be before us almost from the outset. In the following general characterization of the sexes, and chiefly of woman, much of the evidence is derived from observations on non-primitive subjects; but we believe the underlying differences to be characteristic of sex and that their general type is of all stages and times.

SEX-DIFFERENCES

No amount of reasoning, complaining, or protesting can alter the fact that woman bears children and man does not, and that the former is rendered periodically weaker than the latter, not only by reason of the accompaniments and sequels of child-birth but also because of more frequently recurrent incapacities incidental to female sex-life. Maternity is a disability in the struggle for existence, and a special peril. Even if woman and man were equal in physical strength and alertness at ordinary times, as seems to be the case among some primitive tribes, women would be periodically the weaker. Such inequality is due to what might be called primary sex-differences; and with these might be classed also the instinct of mother-love, which handicaps the female individual in the interest of the species. Furthermore, among the higher animals, the male is regularly more powerful than the female, and is often endowed with fighting weapons—a superior outfit, to account for which Darwin developed the theory of sexual selection. It is obvious that, within the human race, the male is regularly larger and stronger than the female. . . . It requires no demonstration, except, perhaps, a reference to the records of athletic history, to justify the statement that woman cannot vie with man, even when she is not under her special sexual handicap, in strength, speed, and other qualities which must once have been all-important for liv-

ing. Ellis reports that woman's rate, rapidity, and precision of movement are inferior to man's; that, while she tires less easily at her own level of routine action, she gives way speedily at man's level, which is that of intense concentration for a time, or of intermittent spurts of energy. She lives at a more continuous, lesser tension, is passive rather than aggressive, industrial rather than militant.

The female nervous system is less stable than the male, being more affectable and susceptible to neurasthenia, hallucinations, hypnotic influences, and hysteria. The last of these terms is derived from the Greek *hystera,* meaning "womb." Woman dreams more and is more likely to become abnormal under anæsthesia. Female mediums are commoner than male, and witches figure more prominently in the history of manias and persecutions than do their male counterparts. "Nervous as a witch" is one of those folk-summaries whose import, in proverbs, apothegms, and the like, we do not hold as lightly as we once did. In her mental processes, woman is characterized by intuition and feeling rather than by logic. . . . She is quick to perceive and alert to act; of nimble wit compared with the more massive and deliberate processes of man. She does not think things out as steadily but proceeds by indirection rather than by dogged frontal attack. Deduction comes to her more readily than induction; and she has shown much less mental power in activities demanding the latter. She is imitative rather than original, doing the appointed rather than the self-appointed task; she is therefore, as any teacher knows, more docile, patient, and amenable to discipline. . . .

SEX-MORES

Women are said to be mentally more adaptable. This is shown in their tact, which is regarded as a product of their desire to adapt themselves to the stronger sex, with whose muscular strength they cannot cope. If a woman should resist her husband she would provoke him, and her life would be endangered. Passive and resigned women would survive. 'Here at any rate we have *one* of the reasons why women are more passive and resigned than men.' Their tact is attributed to their quicker perception and to their lack of egoism. 'The man, being more self-absorbed than the woman, is often less alive than she to what is going on around.' The foregoing would point to natural selection as the agency productive of sex-qualities; but this is not by any means the whole story. Girls are in very early childhood accustomed to inhibitions strengthened by affection and imitation; so are boys, but girls are subjected, from the outset, to a greater number. There are many more things that boys may do, and girls not do than *vice versa*. And the girls are more influenced by sentiment and are in more constant intimacy with the mothers who keep up the inhibitions, to say nothing of the precepts, without interruption. Hence the girls are trained to docility, whether or not they are born to it. The notion of doing what is "right," that is, what parents, teachers, pastors, and other authorities, especially if beloved, have always presented as right, becomes part of their being, and the habit of conforming conduct to it comes to be a norm of life. It promotes conservatism. Especially does all this apply to woman's own status, her relations to men, in and out of marriage, and to all that concerns sex-relations. Women acquiesce and submit without reflection or struggle in whatever pain and loss this system of notions, rules, standards, and dogmas brings to them individually, and they do it so unconsciously that they are not aware of pain from it—certainly not of any suffering comparable with the pangs incident to breaking through the bonds of mores and law.

The conservatism of women, to which allusion has been made, has been observed by many commentators on human nature. It is unquestionably a matter of the mores; just how far, however, it is to be referred to a more recondite source in biological differences, is not clear.

There develops, as a fact of observation, a code for each sex, covering behavior all the way from the details of boy and girl life to the "double standard of morality." What is to be especially noted is that the divergence goes back always to the fact of sex, and basically to the physical sex-differences represented at last analysis by the condition that the female carries the ovum and the male the spermatozoön. . . . The female bears the passive, relatively heavy, inert, impregnatable ovum; the male the active, light, impregnating spermatozoön. The female is the sought, the male the aggressive seeker. Other sex-differences of a physical, mental, and social character follow upon this basic diversity. There is no "equality" of the sexes, thus differently endowed from the outset. There is no equality between an etching and a sonata, for there is no measure common to them; and the case is similar as between man and woman. The sexes are complementary one to the other, as we shall see, but "equality is an incongruous predicate" in the case. The sums of the characteristics accordant with sex, when set over against each other, form a sharp contrast representing a cleavage through the whole societal structure. It is futile to try to argue or denounce away such vital differences. The only way to make the sexes equal would be to get back along the course of evolution and interfere at the point where bi-sexuality first appeared. As well attempt to argue away or decry gravitation or capillary attraction.

SEX-CODES

The mores are acquired characteristics and are not inherited but transmitted from generation to generation by imitation and inculcation. Even in babyhood the sex-codes begin to form, and in early and almost sexless childhood their divergence is clearly marked. In the code of boyhood it is contemptible to play with dolls, however much the small urchin shamefacedly longs to do so; while the girl enacts the mother from the beginning. Then comes puberty, with all its subtle awakenings, and the codes draw farther apart. The young man must be manly, though it does not do, despite recent exhibitions of "emancipation," for the young woman to be altogether mannish; while the latter must be feminine, the former may not be effeminate. Objects of imitation and courses of education are diverse for the sexes; they are more nearly alike now than ever before, but the irreducible fact of sex is always implicit. Why must girls be escorted, chaperoned, and otherwise protected? Why is a parent more terrified at the thought of a young daughter rather than a young son wandering into some low part of a big city? The latter may be robbed or assaulted with intent to kill. That is bad enough. But the boy cannot be so abused that the consequence is lifelong shame and impairment of career and destiny. Why is there a "double standard"? Because only one of the sexes has borne across the ages the unconcealable physical consequences of transgression of chastity, and so has been exposed to the punishment for it which the mores have demanded. This is not "fair"; but then it is not fair either that women alone should suffer the childbirth pangs. Nature cares nothing about our ideas of fairness and equality; it is our business to realize them as we can. A genuine standard of sex-morality is lived up to by some men now, where once it was not within the mental horizon of anybody; the code of the enlightened and chivalrous gentleman, his sense of personal honor and of that due his future wife and the mother of

his children, demands it of him. He will not use his superiority in physical strength to beat a woman, nor yet his exemption from consequences in order to impose upon her in much more coarse and cowardly ways.

Notions of conduct befitting sex, though of inexhaustible number and variety, all go back with different degree of directness to the primal sex-distinctions.

Drinking, swearing, expectorating, slouchiness of person and dress, and other such habits seem worse in a woman than in a man. The dowdy woman is seldom condoned, even if she is exhibiting simply the eccentricities of genius. Women are coming to smoke, but they confine themselves, as yet, to dainty cigarettes. The feelings revolt at the idea of a female butcher or pugilist. Many occupations of this order are regarded as distinctly unfeminine; and while the traditional prejudice against woman in the professions is declining, there is still a feeling that she is more in place as a nurse than as a doctor. To some extent she must drop femininity when she enters the lists with men; she must not, says one lawyer, use any of the traditionally feminine arts to soften the judge or jury. Coming into direct competition with men, she must, in a sense, surrender much of the chivalrous consideration long accorded her in the mores; for every privilege attained carries with it the renunciation of immunities incident to exclusion from it. Despite the change of ideas, however, as to what women may do—and it must be remembered that they have penetrated, long ere this, into activities, such as play-acting, that had been strenuously and traditionally denied them—for the great bulk of mankind there will always be, while sex exists, standards of conduct based upon sex, just as there are standards based upon the lesser diversities of age, occupation, social position, and the rest.

SEX-DESTINY

In view of the foregoing it is clear that women are the destined mothers and home-makers. Love and marriage are said to be incidental to man's career, while they are to woman, the very career itself: "Man's love is of man's life a thing apart, 'Tis woman's whole existence." If one is inclined, in the light of recent events, to differ with this view, he must yet recall that it correctly represents the sentiment of long ages of recorded and unrecorded time, as well as the axiom revealed in usage by the masses of present-day mankind. Why have women never occupied the eminent positions in societal life: in the state and church, in science and art, in the professions, in the industrial organization, and elsewhere? Partly, doubtless, because of lack of the physical and mental powers called for; partly, too, because of the absence of a measure of opportunity open to men; but also, in largest degree, because they have been otherwise interested and occupied. Many a modern woman has gladly sacrificed a public career for a domestic destiny, and that in an age when the mores have not proscribed the former and prescribed the latter. . . .

We take it to be self-evident that women have seldom or never vied with men in most branches of what might be called the reputation-producing activities of life. Where are the female counter-parts of the eminent inventors, merchants, captains of industry, explorers, scientists, historians, poets, musical composers, statesmen—to mention at random a list of careers in each of which men have gained world-wide renown? The names of women fit to rank even with the second-rate and third-rate men are almost as conspicuous by their rarity as would be those of women who might enter the singles of a championship tennis tournament in serious competition with men. The female counterpart of Napoleon or Columbus is not forthcoming, for very obvious reasons, it may be said: women have not been fitted for war or the hardships of discovery; as a sex they have been unsuited. Furthermore it cannot be believed that women have been so systematically deprived of opportunity through the ages as not to have developed cases of eminence in other lines, had they not been inhibited, not by man, but by their sex and its concomitants. Under conditions of great oppression, men of talent have emerged. All who have attained eminence have not had freedom, education, and privileges. And in some lines, certainly, women have had all the opportunity that men have enjoyed—in music, for instance. Yet where is the woman who ranks, not with Beethoven, but with much lesser masters? It is incredible to us that, with all the actual and alleged subjection of women, they would not have shown more instances of eminence if they had had it in them, or had they not been under a constant stress in another direction that distracted their minds as from a minor interest to a major. And we take this major interest to have been the attraction of marriage and the family, something which goes straight back to sex. In this field the most decisive successes remain unrecorded; but we dare affirm that if superiority in woman's particular sphere conferred such public renown as is gained by eminence in the outer activities, man would be outranked in the domestic range as much as woman appears to be in the world of recorded eminence. "The hand that rocks the cradle rules the world." The fact is that each sex is superior in its own domain.

WOMAN AND MARRIAGE

A famous artist who refused, at length, to take any more young women as students, gave as his reason that his promising female pupils were too likely to marry and re-nounce a career. The relatively low wages of women, the economists tell us, have been due to the fact that most girls in business or industry regard such employment as tempo-rary; they often engage in it, in fact, solely for the sake of the pin-money or the social life to be derived from employment. It is not serious business leading to promotion and a career; it is a sort of stage between school and marriage. In the past this state of mind has been unfavorable to union organization.

The Sexes Are Complementary

The fact is that sex, instead of being a com-paratively unimportant and superficial dif-ference between man and woman, is a deep-seated structural diversity, affecting probably every organ, every tissue, and every cell of the entire body. The division of the human race into two sexes is the most important of all anthropological facts. It be-comes at least one of the most important of all facts for a science of society, forming as it does a major life-condition to which society must adjust as it adjusts to other equally ba-sic conditions. The outlines of the general case of sex-differentiation being now before us, we turn to the necessary reflection of this differentiation within society's mainte-nance organization. If man is, by nature, ac-tive, aggressive, and not limited, while woman is passive (so much so, we are told, that even in case of suicide, she adopts pas-sive methods), patient, and limited in her sphere of action, there is here a case of di-versely endowed beings capable of advanta-geous coöperation. One sex acts under high pressure, the other under low pressure; one revolts at monotony, the other takes natu-rally to routine; one shows a restless pursuit of the new and untried, the other an "or-ganic conservatism." It is unnecessary to summarize the physical, mental, and social differences involved in sex; but it is clear

enough that the sexes are complementary. That being the case, the peculiar utility of their coöperation may be inferred on general principles. It would appear that, ignoring re-production, the man-woman combination is stronger for success in living than that of man with man or woman with woman. Many soldiers of this generation have ob-served the reluctance of their fellows who were assigned to "kitchen police"; it is for men really a punitive task. Many will recall the bickerings and paltry sophistry over whose turn it might be to attend to the kitchen-functions of a man's camping-party. Those duties, however, are precisely the ones that women in general would by na-ture prefer as against drilling, bayonet-practice, fighting, or even wading all day in trout-streams. "Woman's work" was not thrust upon her wholly by superior force.

Since it is more difficult to see man's ad-vantage than woman's in sex-coöperation, let us reconstruct a situation with his stand-point chiefly in mind. Suppose the back-ground to be the early hunting stage, and the use but not the generation of fire to be un-derstood. Two men are pursuing the struggle for existence together, and they have no women. At best they must take turns doing what they do not want to do or have no special capacity for doing; there will hardly be any specialization, in the absence of en-slavement (for which our stage is too prim-itive), whereby one constitutes himself the ranger and the other the headquarters. Yet the extra weapons and utensils, and espe-cially the fire, must be tended and carried safely, and the person who is doing that cannot be hunting freely. There is no natu-ral and inevitable specialization of function in such masculine association because the associates are too nearly alike. The details of inconvenience, cross-purposes, clashing of will, and so on, can be supplied without difficulty. Suppose now that of the two as-sociates one is a woman, and, to make the case the more conclusive, suppose her encumbered with her young. The differentiation of function carries itself out spontaneously. The woman, even if she is able, does not wish to range far and wide; she is well content to tend the fire and to move slowly, laden with the joint possessions, to the next resting-place, leaving the man relieved of whatever may hinder the full prosecution of activities along his line. She gets in return some production for herself and her young and the remnants or superfluity of his quarry. He comes back to an abiding-place and to the protecting and comforting blaze; there is no uninteresting transportation or routine drudgery for him to do; he may sleep or loll and smoke; and yet the headquarters have been shifted conveniently to his movements.

COERCION OF WOMAN

Reports on primitive peoples sometimes inform us that the men force the women to do the drudgery. Undeniable as such evidence may be, it is incorrect to assume that it includes the whole story or that primitive women feel themselves tyrannously oppressed and wronged by their men. Travellers see the women hoeing incessantly in the field, while the men loaf about the camp; but they have not seen the men on the night-hunt while the women slept in the lodges. It is regarded as good economy that the savage, after the strenuous exertion of hunting, lies about while his wife drudges.

It is possible to get a thoroughgoing insight into sex-specialization only by according proper weight to these considerations. Yet it would be foolish to suppose that man, in those stages where chivalry was not, failed to use his sex-superiorities for what they were worth. He was superior in brute force; and that was not all. As our cases presently to come will show, man special-

ized in hunting and war. This meant that he developed the apparatus corresponding and became the wielder of weapons of offense and defense. Boys were early trained in the use of these, while girls, besides being unfitted physically for the use of a number of the weapons, especially those that were thrown, received little or no practice in such exercises; they were trained to the domestic tasks. Even if man had been physically the weaker, his weapons would have occured him dominance over woman, as they did over the beasts that were so much more powerful than he. . . .

In view of these facts, and of the combination of contempt and fear which often represented man's attitude toward woman, it is to be expected that he would have coerced and oppressed her; and the facts prove that he did. It is a mistake to believe that she was at any time utterly defenseless; the savage man is frequently sadly henpecked; but in general, whether or not she would have chosen the sort of tasks with which she is found to be busied, she had to perform them anyhow or else suffer for her omissions or reluctance. In fact, she fell in contentedly with the current mores, than which she knew nothing different, and did not resent the loss of "rights" of which she had not dreamed. . . .

In short, all of these items and notions get into the mores, show or do not show survival-value under selection, and are transmitted or not transmitted from generation to generation as the traditional code. Had it not been for the fact of sex and the complementary abilities and disabilities connected with it, no such mores and codes could have appeared. The domination of man was inevitable; under it the coöperation of the sexes developed as we find it, and the human race moved on toward what it has become. If there is any fault to be found with the process, in the matter of its unfairness or its oppressiveness, the complaint must be carried back and lodged against whatever power produced bi-sexuality in *Homo;* for, given that condition, the consequences are inevitable. It is a great error to charge woman's present position to man's base behavior in the past. That behavior, however detestable from the standpoint of our later code, could not have been otherwise. It was not deliberately planned out, but lived into automatically. And it is a still greater error to wish to ignore the basic and derived sex-differences, in the mutual adjustment to which were laid down the fundamentals of a sex-code that has been tested by the ages.

Sophonisba P. Breckinridge (1866–1948) on Women as Workers and Citizens

Sophonisba P. Breckinridge was born in 1866 to a prominent Kentucky family, just after the end of the Civil War. Her father, who took on many customarily feminine roles in the family because of the illness of his wife, took a keen interest in his daughter and strongly supported her broad education. Owing to his intervention, she was admitted to college in Lexington, Kentucky, and soon thereafter she transferred to Wellesley, where she graduated at the head of her class in 1888. After graduation she taught math and privately studied law, becoming the first woman to be admitted to the Kentucky bar in 1892. Her law career was disappointing because of the lack of trust clients had in women lawyers. Finally, she discovered the graduate program in political science at the University of Chicago, a university that had recruited and welcomed a number of strong women students in the 1890s. Breckinridge earned a master's degree in 1897 and a doctorate magna cum laude in 1901. In spite of her outstanding performance as a graduate student, she was unable to obtain an academic position in political science or economics similar to those of her male classmates.

Breckinridge was active in the work of Hull House, where she lived from 1907 to 1920. She began teaching in 1907 with the Chicago School of Civics, a social work training school. Her determination to forge a career in progressive empirical research and activism in the social sciences eventually paid off, although in a field that was "reserved" for women—social work. Breckinridge eventually helped found the School of Social Service Administration at the University of Chicago in 1920, where she had a long and distinguished career as a researcher, teacher, and mentor—becoming a full professor in 1925. Breckinridge helped to develop and promote the idea of government-funded public welfare—an idea influential in the New Deal. As an activist in the progressive Chicago community, she was a founding member of the Women's Peace Party, the Women's International League of Peace and Freedom, and other volunteer progressive organizations. Breckinridge died in 1948.

MAJOR WORKS

Breckinridge, Sophonisba P., and Edith Abbott. *The Delinquent Child and the Home*. Baltimore: Russell Sage Foundation, 1912.

Breckinridge, Sophonisba P., and Marion Talbot. *The Modern Household*. Boston: Whitcomb & Barrows, 1919.

Breckinridge, Sophonisba P. *New Homes for Old*. New York: Harper, 1921.

Breckinridge, Sophonisba P. *Marriage and the Civic Rights of Women*. Chicago: University of Chicago Press, 1931.

———. *Women in the Twentieth Century: A Study of Their Political, Social, and Economic Activities*. New York: McGraw-Hill, 1933.

———. *The Family and the State*. University of Chicago Press, 1934.

SOURCES

Deegan, Mary Jo. 1991. *Women in sociology: A bio-bibliographical sourcebook*. Westport, CT: Greenwood.

Fitzpatrick, Ellen. 1990. *Endless crusade: Women social scientists and progressive reform*. New York: Oxford University Press.

James, Edward T., Janet W. James, and Paul S. Boyer, eds. 1974. *Notable American women 1607–1950: A biographical dictionary*. 3 vols. Cambridge, MA: Harvard University Press, Belknap.

Lengermann, P. M., and J. Niebrugge-Brantley 1998. *The women founders: Sociology and social theory 1830–1930*. Boston, MA: McGraw-Hill.

THE SELECTION

These chapters are taken from Sophonisba P. Breckinridge's 1993 book, a major study of American women of the twentieth century. At the time she was professor of public welfare administration in the School of Social Service Administration at the University of Chicago. The study covers women's voluntary associations, their political involvements, and their economic activities, and is based on a wide variety of documentary and other sources. These were the fields in which American women at the time were making gains in education and professional employment, although Breckinridge documents disappointing resistance to the hopes that had come with the gaining of the vote. In comments that sound as if they could have been written recently, she describes increases in women's gainful employment and concerns by some over the

associated effects on family and men's employment. Breckinridge argues that the changes in women's work brought about by the industrial revolution effectively reduced their income-producing capacity in the home. This encouraged women's labor participation outside the home as an important support ensuring the well-being of families. Breckinridge also notes that women were poor wage bargainers, which she attributes to discrimination and lack of legal support for fair wages. She argues that women's supposed incapacities for craftwork had been disproved when, during the war, women had learned and performed these jobs successfully. Women's war experiences also showed that the long apprenticeship system for men had not been necessary and had only served to keep the labor supply scarce. Breckinridge also refutes the preju-

From Sophonisba P. Breckinridge, "Women as Workers" and "Conclusion," in *Women in the Twentieth Century: A Study of Their Political, Social, and Economic Activities* (New York: McGraw-Hill, 1933), 99–107, 343–46.

dice against women's supposed intellectual capacities that kept them out of most professions. Finally, she mentions some of the problems introduced into the competitive system when the rapid inclusion of women increased the labor supply.

In the second selection, the concluding chapter to the book, Breckinridge reiterates her earlier findings. As the home offers less opportunity for women to contribute to family well-being, and as it fails in educating girls for modern adult roles, women have responded by demanding more active roles in society. They have done this through the organization of a wide variety of clubs and organizations with reform and social welfare goals, through increasing their participation in higher education, and through increasing entry into employment and demands to be allowed to work after marriage. They have especially made gains in professional occupations and in universities. Colleges and universities were leading the way in research on ways to "adjust" individual family and work roles with the needs of children and society. Breckinridge points to the increase in women serving as juvenile court judges, probation officers, police officers, and in prominent government positions as a positive trend. This was a time when women's educational and professional achievements were at a high point in American history, soon to fall off again and not to recover until the 1970s. Breckinridge documented both women's gains and the continuing obstacles to their attempts to enter the worlds of politics and the economy. This is an important book: as Deegan (1991:84) writes, "Any student and scholar of women's role in society from 1890 to 1933 will find *Women in the Twentieth Century* (1933) mandatory reading."

I. WOMEN AS WORKERS

The Census of 1900 attracted the attention of students to the steady increase in the number of women who were gainfully employed, and raised the question whether or not great changes were taking place in the amount and character of the work of women, so that they were both invading men's fields of employment and affecting the home disastrously. There was wide discussion in the press, and the period was also characterized by scientific discussions in which it was shown that in the major industrial occupations women were not displacing men, and were as a whole probably doing no more work than they had always done. They were, however, in many cases offering their labor outside the home and collecting their own earnings, where, before, either they had rendered unpaid services in the home or their husbands or fathers had owned and collected their earnings.

It was even then clear that the occupations of women in connection with family life had been of fundamental importance in the production of the commodities or services available and likewise in the determination of the ways in which those commodities and services should be enjoyed. There were, to be sure, always women for whom the home did not make satisfactory provision, and, it is interesting to note that, except in the matter of inheritance under the law of primogeniture, the common law made no distinction between the unmarried adult woman and the man. For the married woman, on the other hand, the difference in legal capacity was very great. So far as her activities were concerned, however, her occupations were largely connected with the domestic organization, as wife, mother, daughter, or sister, or as hired assistant in the performances of tasks of a domestic character. When, however, the factory system developed and products hitherto produced in the home were manufactured elsewhere, women and children were employed under the new conditions. This process of women following, not the flag, but the job, is still continuing, with resulting changes of attitude on the part of both men and women, and confusion on the part of both as to what effects of the change on important social institutions are to be anticipated.

Interest in these questions led, during that early decade of this century, to the investigation by the United States Bureau of Labor to which reference has been made, which brought out the facts with reference to the dependence of great numbers of families on the wage-paid labor of women and girls as well as of men and boys, which destroyed the myth of the pin-money girl, emphasized the bargaining disadvantage as compared with the employer under which women and girls sought employment, and made obvious the relative inequality between men and women as wage bargainers. From that time, the inequality of women as compared to men with respect to occupational opportunity has been recognized as one of the chief disadvantages under which they have suffered, and has resulted in an effort to widen the range of their employment and to mitigate the results of their relative weakness. Especially it has been recognized that these features of their employment retard and impede effective organization among them.

The results of this bargaining weakness manifested themselves in excessively long hours, in frequent employment at night which rendered enormously difficult the maintenance of home standards or of sound family life, in lack of Saturday half holidays or Sunday rest, in conditions of work less than decent or morally safe, and in wage scales inferior to those of men workers even where skill or professional equipment might characterize their work.

From the recognition of these features of women's employment developed efforts, some educational, like trade education and vocational guidance, to remove the pressure of competition at the lowest level; some social, like the mothers' pensions, to remove the non-industrial person from the working group; some legislative, apparently protective in character but really an item in the program of emancipation, taking the form of efforts (1) to secure legislative regulation of conditions of work; (2) to secure a statutory minimum wage for women since trade unionism seemed unable to accomplish this in the case of women; (3) and to formulate standards by which employment might be judged. This last effort was restricted largely to public employment.

This new occupational and domestic position, together with the granting of suffrage, has been giving women a wider share in the life of the community. It is not the purpose of this study to discuss that share in its entirety. The participation of women in family relationship and family life is not presented here; but, in the following pages, an attempt is made to discover and to discuss some of the activities of women outside the home and the direction taken by those activities. The selection of material is not simple, nor is the order in which the data should be presented perfectly obvious. It has seemed best to review the recent figures with reference to women's employment. . . .

With reference to their employment, a few preliminary remarks will make clearer the later discussion.

Although it is not intended here to devote any considerable space to the changes that have been brought about in the law of the family group, which by 1900 had been substantially revolutionized with reference to reciprocal rights and duties both of husband and wife and of parent and child, there are several aspects of the subject, in its relation to the employment of women, on which it is worth while to comment. Under the older family organization, the services of both the wife and the daughter or their wages if they were gainfully employed, belonged to the husband and father. Whether work was done within or outside the home, the goods, services or earnings accrued to the composite family income, to which much attention has been given during these recent years by students of family life, of the labor problem, and of the problem of poverty. Services rendered in the home by the wife or minor children were unpaid, without other compensation than provision of support, which, being a poorly enforced obligation, gave excuse for characterizing marriage as a sweated trade. . . .

While no evidence is given, to the effect that women are capable of doing the various tasks which they have chosen, notice may be taken of the theory of different physiological structure, . . . which at an earlier date seemed to justify the exclusion of women from higher academic opportunities. It was generally thought that nature, in making special provision for child bearing, caused women to breath costically while men breathed abdominally, and that this [structural difference] rendered it forever impossible for men and women to be treated alike in the things of the mind. From the point of view of those who would exclude, the sequence proceeded from the incapacity of childhood, to the incapacity of adolescence, to the incapacity of child bearing and child caring, and through the incapacity of the menopause to the incapacity of senility. It was complete. But that theory was abandoned before the beginning of the century and it may be assumed that such evidence would now be superfluous.

However, it may perhaps be profitable to recall the fact that for much of the work for which a long period of training was formerly necessary—craftsmanship—the machine or the altered organization has reduced the period of preparation. During the war, for example, women would learn, in a few weeks, processes, which would enable them to replace the men called to the front, for which the period of training previously required by the trade union was longer than the whole period of the war. In other words, the requirements for apprenticeship and other previous preparation had often for their purpose not only the maintenance of high standards of work but also the limitation of the supply of workers, the reduction of the competitive pressure, and often the exclusion of a less dignified or less respected group of workers—women, Negroes, aliens, and other . . . groups.

In some cases, the exclusion was secured by developing ideas of superiority. The "legal mind," for example, was a masculine mind of peculiar quality and the exclusion of women was based on mere economy and on consideration for the feelings of women to prevent their inevitable humiliation and embarrassment. It is also true that the duties of various public offices, *e.g.,* jailor, sheriff, member of the House of Representatives, governor, United States senator, were characterized by features of public honor, and were supposed to require certain characteristics of personal vigor, courage, ability to command respect. It has, however, been found appropriate to fill positions in each of these categories by persons whose qualifications have consisted in having been married to a person holding such an office and being widowed. More than once in most of the offices named, the widow has replaced the deceased husband, and has successfully continued to hold the prisoners in safe-keeping, to direct the protective or law-enforcing agencies of the county, to take her place among the representatives in Congress or to direct the governmental activities of a sovereign commonwealth. In fact, the artificial glamour by which many occupations have been surrounded has not infrequently been competitive, and those seeking the "opportunity," as in the clever verse of Charlotte Perkins Stetson, are learning to walk "right through the obstacle as though it were not there." It should be easy to understand these developments. To the feminists perhaps it seems a survival of the attitude so satisfying to the author of *Paradise Lost*.

> . . . "Though both
> Not equal, as their sex not equal seemed;
> For contemplation he and valour formed,
> For softness she and sweet attractive grace;
> He for God only, she for God in him."
>
> (*Paradise Lost,* Book IV, lines 295–99)

> "To whom thus Eve, with perfect beauty adorned:
> 'My author and disposer, what thou bidd'st
> Unargued I obey; so God ordains:
> God is thy law, thou mine: to know no more
> Is woman's happiest knowledge, and her praise.'"
>
> (*Ibid.,* Book IV, lines 634–38)

On further examination, it is a manifestation of the rough common sense of the English guildsmen, as over against the logic of the French craftsmen, that let widows of deceased guildsmen "carry on," although wives and daughters were excluded from the opportunity to qualify. . . .

It should be noted that the entrance of women into the world of gainful occupation causes an increase in the supply of labor, and clearly in connection with any addition to the labor supply many questions arise. The interests of those already in the working group cannot be ignored. With the growing number of women offering their labor power, there are in fact two main questions. First: Is the pressure of poverty, the disorganized state of industry, the low scale of men's industrial or agricultural earnings, forcing women, mothers of small children, to remain breadwinners when the technical resources of industry and commerce could provide conditions under which they could more successfully perform their marital and maternal duties? A second question is whether or not in a world in which the productive forces are so developed as to make possible a shorter day, a shorter week, and a fuller life, the access of women to the satisfactions of life must either require celibacy or continue to be vicarious, or indirect through a husband, or whether the contact of a woman, married or single, may be immediate and her participation in productive life and in domestic life be individual and direct.

II. CONCLUSION

In the preceding pages an attempt has been made to set out the developments that have taken place during these three decades of the twentieth century in the relation of women under three sets of conditions: (1) those characteristic of their incalculably varied organization on a voluntary basis for the accomplishment of innumerable purposes; (2) those characteristic of their relationship as employed or employer; and (3) those determining their success or failure in their relation to government. The three phases of their activity have seemed to call for different methods of treatment and discussion.

In the case of the clubs or organizations, an attempt was made by a chronological account to suggest the response of women in their leisure time to the great numbers of stimuli to which they were subjected. By 1900, the separate clubs had federated, national affiliations were being developed, women associated themselves with other women for the accomplishment of innumerable common purposes. It is hoped that something of the variety has been suggested, and that with the increasing freedom from occupational, pecuniary, political and domestic restraints, the possibly increasing emphasis on individual satisfactions may have emerged.

It likewise seems clear that as the home offers less opportunity for girls both to be educated for adult life and to contribute by services to the well-being of the family life and as the standard of educational requirements are raised, young persons between ten and twenty are going in larger numbers to school and into the labor market.

It also appears that as the home offers fewer opportunities for the wife and mother to render services that make a definite contribution to the family income, more adult women, and among them more married women, are entering the labor market. This subject needs, however, more complete information, since the mothers' pension movement should remove from the market those whose presence there is due largely to the inadequate income of the husband and father or to the lack, through his incapacity, of any income from that source. There should also be further analysis to determine the counterbalancing influence of the professional woman's demand for opportunity to continue in the wage-earning group and the influence of migration or of changed economic status on the attitude of men who under the earlier situation felt compelled to acquiesce in their wives' remaining wage earners and who now find their own prestige affected by so doing.

With reference to the choice of employment, the range is still restricted although it is not possible at the moment to say whether or not it is more or less so than at the beginning of the century. The demand for women's labor, as for men's, has been so affected by the reorganizations that have taken place, that for the time the old avenues of employment in manufacturing and in certain forms of domestic or personal service and agriculture are less wide. What the implications of these changes are can only be definitely stated when certain terms such as "operatives" and "laborers" have been more fully discussed and expounded by the census; on the other hand, new chances are found in the distributive services and in the adjustments among and between administrative divisions of activity. A great variety of situations and relationships and activities are concealed under the term "clerical." In the levels of employment calling for more extended training or for professional education, there are still natural resistances on the part of men, who see not only the readjustment necessary if the marginal level is raised but the threat of cheapness which has been the weapon of all groups handicapped by non-occupational prejudices, the Negro, the alien, as well as the woman.

In the strata of higher business, of the professions, and of the academic world, there are evidences of the same resistances, but likewise of a steady wearing away of the oppositions. In university faculties a few more women are admitted to higher rank and pay; in the world of research, of athletics and sport, they likewise widen the sphere and make possible an objective testing of achievement.

As to unemployment, the relative cheapness of women may keep them in where it has got them in, and may get them in where they have not been before. On the other hand, many of the newer occupations in which they have found opportunity are greatly affected, and the evidence as to their occupational opportunity shows how accidental and precarious all employment is—being determined as between men and women or between older and younger or between more skilled and less skilled by the profitable use of the invention. That subject, too, is discussed elsewhere.

With reference to their public activity, the moment seems an unhappy one at which to attempt to take account of stock. Great effort had been necessary to secure the ballot, and much was expected from its possession. Women thought that they could by the ballot more easily rectify the mistakes that had been made in the governmental field, and men expected that within a brief period evil or anti-social situations would be constructively dealt with. Disappointment and disillusionment are therefore expressed by both men and women. Yet it seems clear that women are increasingly learning to use the governmental agencies that had been developed and they will be increasingly clear as to whether the older forms of organization should or should not be discarded. In the meantime, in the organization of clubs and the provision of club houses, through the demand to be allowed to continue in gainful employment after marriage, in discarding the older social restraints, they are widening the spiritual bounds within which both men and women must find their fullest satisfaction. It is in the college and university gymnasiums that preparation is being made for full participation by women in the activities requiring continuity and stability. It is in the laboratories and libraries of colleges and universities that scientific bases for emancipation are being assembled. In building upon those bases, women are experimenting in the adjustment of their needs as individuals to their requirements as members of families, whether as wife, mother, daughter or sister, and as members of the larger group. It is of interest that of the amendments to the proposed platforms suggested by various delegates to the Democratic convention the only one accepted by the convention was one pledging protection to childhood, offered by a woman who had been for years active in the so-called woman's movement.

It seems incomplete and fragmentary to close any discussion of women's place in the community organization without renewed reference to their earlier responsibility for the distribution of goods, and without discussion of their important services in the protection of the adolescent and the safe conduct of young persons from the simpler conditions of childhood through the confusions of the years between childhood and adult life. Those topics belong to other sections of the inquiry, however, and here reference to them is made only that frank acknowledgment may again be expressed of the fragmentary character of this presentation. In that connection the reader may be reminded of the development, meager but observable, in the use of women as juvenile court judges, as policewomen, as probation officers and as members of staffs of correctional institutions where girls and women are under custody. The presence of an able woman as head of the Labor Department of the most populous and industrialized state, of a woman in the cabinet of the commissioner of police in the greatest city, of a woman at the head of the department of public welfare in each of three great states, and of a woman chief of the Federal Bureau steadfastly demanding that the needs of the children and young persons of the whole country be recognized and dealt with after the principle of adequate care, suggests a recognition on the wider platform of national development of those same services as essential to the community well-being.

Margaret Mead (1901–1978) on the Cultural Basis of Sex Difference

Born December 16, 1901, in Philadephia, to well-educated parents who had met as graduate students at the University of Chicago, Margaret Mead grew up around academia and progressive social activism. She was also influenced strongly by the independent thinking of her paternal grandmother, who lived with the family until her death in 1927.

Mead initially studied sociology and economics at Barnard. She soon discovered a love of anthropology, and under the influence and tutelage of Franz Boas, eventually earned a doctorate under his supervision at Columbia. During her successful career, she taught at various prestigious universities, including Columbia, New York University, Fordham, Yale, and the New School for Social Research. An eminent scholar, she served as elected president of a number of professional organizations, including the American Anthropological Association, the Anthropological Film Institute, and the Society for Applied Anthropology. Mead was also the first elected president of the American Association for the Advancement of Science. In

her long and active lifetime, she received many other honors and was very widely known.

In the early 1920s, Mead traveled to Samoa for fieldwork on adolescence, focusing especially on girls. Her first book, *Coming of Age in Samoa,* was based on that experience. In 1931 she did fieldwork in New Guinea, resulting in a book that helped revolutionize thinking about gender. The book, *Sex and Temperament in Three Primitive Societies,* argued that the expectations associated with being male and female vary by culture and are not biologically determined. This was one of the first major statements of what we now refer to as the social construction of gender, based on her studies of the diverse sex roles found in different tribes.

Mead lived an active and productive life, writing in both scholarly and popular outlets and lecturing widely on topics such as child rearing, sex differences, cooperation, and social psychology in a cross-cultural perspective. Her work often took a comparative perspective, looking at the implications of anthropological findings in other cultures for understanding American society. Mead died in 1978, leaving behind a lasting and wide-ranging legacy of work and influence.

MAJOR WORKS

Mead, Margaret. *Coming of Age in Samoa: A Psychological Study of Primitive Youth for Western Civilization*. New York: Morrow, 1928.

———. *Growing Up in New Guinea: A Comparative Study of Primitive Education*. New York: Morrow, 1930.

———. *The Changing Culture of an Indian Tribe*. New York: Columbia University Press, 1932.

———. *Male and Female: A Study of the Sexes in a Changing World*. New York: Morrow, 1949.

———. *New Lives for Old: Cultural Transformations—Manus, 1928–1953*. New York: Morrow, 1956.

———. *American Women: The Report of the President's Commission on the Status of Women*. Edited by Margaret Mead and Frances Balgley Kaplan, with an Introduction by Margaret Mead. New York: Scribner's, 1965.

———. *Culture and Commitment: A Study of the Generation Gap*. Garden City, NY: American Museum of Natural History, Natural History Press, 1970.

———. *Blackberry Winter: My Earlier Years*. New York: Morrow, 1972.

SOURCES

Flaherty, Tarraugh. Margaret Mead, 1901–1978. In *Women's intellectual contributions to the study of mind and society*. http://www.webster.edu/~woolflm/margaretmead.html, accessed 23 January 23, 2006.

Howard, Jane. 1984. *Margaret Mead: A life*. New York: Simon and Schuster.

Kottak, Conrad Phillip. 1997. *Anthropology: The exploration of human diversity*. New York: McGraw-Hill.

Mead, Margaret. 1972. *Blackberry winter: My earlier years*. New York: Morrow.

Rossi, Alice. 1988. Cultural Stretch: Margaret Mead (b. 1901). In *The feminist papers*, 652–78. Boston: Northeastern University Press. (Orig. pub. 1973.)

THE SELECTION

The following reading is from Margaret Mead's highly influential study *Sex and Temperament in Three Primitive Societies*. Included are brief excerpts from the chapters "The Standardization of Sex Differences," "The Deviant," and "Conclusion." Mead introduced her study by explaining how it differed from those of most researchers of sex differences: she was not looking for universal differences, nor wondering whether men or women are more variable in abilities. Instead, she aimed to give an account of "how three primitive societies have grouped their social attitudes towards temperament" in relation to sex difference (p. viii). She is perhaps the first to use the term *social construct* in relation to sex and gender differences, stating that comparing the three primitive societies' views and expectations of male and female temperament and behavior can give us "a greater insight into what elements are social constructs" not related to "biological facts of sex-gender" (p. ix). She also points out that our society has had diverse expectations historically—further reinforcing the notion that gender differences are not biologically given.

From Margaret Mead, *Sex and Temperament in Three Primitive Societies* (New York: Morrow, 1935), 279–81, 286–87, 297–99, 308–9, 311–14, 321–22. Reprinted by permission of HarperCollins Publishers.

In the excerpt below, Mead presents the major findings and implications of her study of three simple societies in New Guinea—the peaceful Arapesh, the aggressive Mountain Mundugumor, and the Tchambuli. In this third society, the expectations for men and women were the opposite of what Westerners have come to accept as normal sex differences, while in the first two, no real sex differences in temperament were recognized.

Mead concludes that there is much more individual variation than we usually recognize, and that social conditioning and definitions attempt to mold individuals into their "appropriate" sex roles. However, the fact that not everyone fits these molds represents a loss to our culture of their actual talents. Her conclusion calls for a more open society in which individual diversity is appreciated and socially constructed role categories are de-emphasized.

SEX AND TEMPERAMENT IN THREE PRIMITIVE SOCIETIES

We have now considered in detail the approved personalities of each sex among three primitive peoples. We found the Arapesh—both men and women—displaying a personality that, out of our historically limited preoccupations, we would call maternal in its parental aspects, and feminine in its sexual aspects. We found men, as well as women, trained to be cooperative, unaggressive, responsive to the needs and demands of others. We found no idea that sex was a powerful driving force either for men or for women. In marked contrast to these attitudes, we found among the Mundugumor that both men and women developed as ruthless, aggressive, positively sexed individuals, with the maternal cherishing aspects of personality at a minimum. Both men and women approximated to a personality type that we in our culture would find only in an undisciplined and very violent male. Neither the Arapesh nor the Mundugumor profit by a contrast between the sexes; the Arapesh ideal is the mild, responsive man married to the mild, responsive woman; the Mundugumor ideal is the violent aggressive man married to the violent aggressive woman. In the third tribe, the Tchambuli, we found a genuine reversal of the sex-attitudes of our own culture, with the woman the dominant, impersonal, managing partner, the man the less responsible and the emotionally dependent person. These three situations suggest, then, a very definite conclusion. If those temperamental attitudes which we have traditionally regarded as feminine—such as passivity, responsiveness, and a willingness to cherish children—can so easily be set up as the masculine pattern in one tribe, and in another be outlawed for the majority of women as well as for the majority of men, we no longer have any basis for regarding such aspects of behaviour as sex-linked. And this conclusion becomes even stronger when we consider the actual reversal in Tchambuli of the position of dominance of the two sexes, in spite of the existence of formal patrilineal institutions.

The material suggests that we may say that many, if not all, of the personality traits which we have called masculine or feminine are as lightly linked to sex as are the clothing, the manners, and the form of head-dress that a society at a given period assigns to either sex. When we consider the behaviour of the typical Arapesh man or woman as contrasted with the behaviour of the typical

Mundugumor man or woman, the evidence is overwhelmingly in favour of the strength of social conditioning. In no other way can we account for the almost complete uniformity with which Arapesh children develop into contented, passive, secure persons, while Mundugumor children develop as characteristically into violent, aggressive, insecure persons. Only to the impact of the whole of the integrated culture upon the growing child can we lay the formation of the contrasting types. There is no other explanation of race, or diet, or selection that can be adduced to explain them. We are forced to conclude that human nature is almost unbelievably malleable, responding accurately and contrastingly to contrasting cultural conditions. The differences between individuals who are members of different cultures, like the differences between individuals within a culture, are almost entirely to be laid to differences in conditioning, especially during early childhood, and the form of this conditioning is culturally determined. Standardized personality differences between the sexes are of this order, cultural creations to which each generation, male and female, is trained to conform. There remains, however, the problem of the origin of these socially standardized differences.

While the basic importance of social conditioning is still imperfectly recognized—not only in lay thought, but even by the scientist specifically concerned with such matters—to go beyond it and consider the possible influence of variations in hereditary equipment is a hazardous matter. The following pages will read very differently to one who has made a part of his thinking a recognition of the whole amazing mechanism of cultural conditioning—who has really accepted the fact that the same infant could be developed into a full participant in any one of these three cultures—than they will read to one who still believes that the minutiae of cultural behaviour are carried in the individual germ-plasm. If it is said, therefore, that when we have grasped the full significance of the malleability of the human organism and the preponderant importance of cultural conditioning, there are still further problems to solve, it must be remembered that these problems come *after* such a comprehension of the force of conditioning; they cannot precede it. The forces that make children born among the Arapesh grow up into typical Arapesh personalities are entirely social, and any discussion of the variations which do occur must be looked at against this social background.

With this warning firmly in mind, we can ask a further question. Granting the malleability of human nature, whence arise the differences between the standardized personalities that different culture decree for all of their members, or which one culture decrees for the members of one sex as contrasted with the members of the opposite sex? . . .

The traits that occur in some members of each sex are specially assigned to one sex, and disallowed in the other. The history of the social definition of sex-differences is filled with such arbitrary arrangements in the intellectual and artistic field, but because of the assumed congruence between physiological sex and emotional endowment we have been less able to recognize that a similar arbitrary slection is being made among emotional traits also. We have assumed that because it is convenient for a mother to wish to care for her child, this is a trait with which women have been more generously endowed by a carefully teleological process of evolution. We have assumed that because men have hunted, an activity requiring enterprise, bravery, and initiative, they have been endowed with these useful attitudes as part of their sex-temperament.

Societies have made these assumptions both overtly and implicitly. If a society insists that warfare is the major occupation for the male sex, it is therefore insisting that all male children display bravery and pugnacity. Even if the insistence upon the differential bravery of men and women is not made articulate, the difference in occupation makes this point implicitly. When, however, a society goes further and defines men as brave and women as timorous, when men are forbidden to show fear and women are indulged in the most flagrant display of fear, a more explicit element enters in. Bravery, hatred of any weakness, of flinching before pain or danger—this attitude which is so strong a component of *some human* temperaments has been selected as the key to masculine behaviour. The easy unashamed display of fear or suffering that is congenial to a different temperament has been made the key to feminine behaviour.

Originally two variations of human temperament, a hatred of fear or willingness to display fear, they have been socially translated into inalienable aspects of the personalities of the two sexes. And to that defined sex-personality every child will be educated, if a boy, to suppress fear, if a girl, to show it. If there has been no social selection in regard to this trait, the proud temperament that is repelled by any betrayal of feeling will display itself, regardless of sex, by keeping a stiff upper lip. Without an express prohibition of such behaviour the expressive unashamed man or woman will weep, or comment upon fear or suffering. Such attitudes, strongly marked in certain temperaments, may by social selection be standardized for everyone, or outlawed for everyone, or ignored by society, or made the exclusive and approved behaviour of one sex only. . . .

Consider . . . the way in which children in our culture are pressed into conformity: "Don't act like a girl." "Little girls don't do that." The threat of failing to behave like a member of one's own sex is used to enforce a thousand details of nursery routine and cleanliness, ways of sitting or relaxing, ideas of sportsmanship and fair play, patterns of expressing emotions, and a multitude of other points in which we recognize socially defined sex-differences, such as limits of personal vanity, interest in clothes, or interest in current events. Back and forth weaves the shuttle of comment: "Girls don't do that." "Don't you want to grow up to be a real man like Daddy?"—tangling the child's emotions in a confusion that, if the child is unfortunate enough to possess even in some slight degree the temperament approved for the opposite sex, may well prevent the establishment of any adequate adjustment to its world. Every time the point of sex-conformity is made, every time the child's sex is invoked as the reason why it should prefer trousers to petticoats, baseball-bats to dolls, fisticuffs to tears, there is planted in the child's mind a fear that indeed, in spite of anatomical evidence to the contrary, it may not really belong to its own sex at all.

How little weight the anatomical evidence of own sex has, as over against the social conditioning, was vividly dramatized recently in a case in a Middle Western city, where a boy was found who had lived twelve years as a girl, under the name of Maggie, doing a girl's tasks and wearing a girl's clothes. He had discovered several years before that his anatomy was that of a boy, but that did not suggest to him the possibility of being classified as a boy socially. Yet when social workers discovered the case and effected the change of his classification, he did not show any traits of inversion; he was merely a boy who had been mistakenly classified as a girl, and whose parents, for some reasons that were not discovered, refused to recognize and rectify their error. This bizarre case reveals the strength of social classification as over against merely anatomical membership in a sex, and it is this social classification which makes it possible for society to plant in children's minds doubts and confusions about their sex-position.

Such social pressure exerts itself in a number of ways. There is first the threat of sex-disenfranchisement against the child who shows aberrant tendencies, the boy who dislikes rough-and-tumble play or weeps when he is rebuked, the girl who is only interested in adventures, or prefers battering her playmates to dissolving in tears. Second, there is the attribution of the emotions defined as feminine to the boy who shows the mildest preference for one of the superficial sex-limited occupations or avocations. A small boy's interest in knitting may arise from a delight in his own ability to manipulate a needle; his interest in cooking may derive from a type of interest that might later make him a first-class chemist; his interest in dolls may spring from no tender cherishing feelings but from a desire to dramatize some incident. Similarly, a girl's overwhelming interest in horse-back-riding may come from a delight in her own physical co-ordination on horseback, her interest in her brother's wireless set may come from pride in her proficiency in handling the Morse code. Some physical or intellectual or artistic potentiality may accidentally express itself in an activity deemed appropriate to the opposite sex. This has two results: The child is reproached for his choice and accused of having the emotions of the opposite sex, and also, because the occupational choice or hobby throws him more with the opposite sex, he may come in time to take on much of the socially sex-limited behaviour of that opposite sex. . . .

A third way in which our dichotomy of social personality by sex affects the growing child is the basis it provides for a cross-sex identification with the parents. The invocation of a boy's identification with his mother to explain his subsequent assumption of a passive rôle towards members of his own sex is familiar enough in modern psychiatric theory. It is assumed that through a distortion of the normal course of personality development the boy fails to identify with his father and so loses the clue to normal "masculine" behaviour. Now there is no doubt that the developing child searching for clues to his social rôle in life usually finds his most important models in those who stand in a parental relationship to him during his early years. But I would suggest that we have still to explain why these identifications occur, and that the cause lies not in any basic femininity in the small boy's temperament, but in the existence of a dichotomy between the standardized behaviour of the sexes. We have to discover why a given child identifies with a parent of opposite sex rather than with the parent of its own sex. The most conspicuous social categories in our society—in most societies—are the two sexes. Clothes, occupation, vocabulary, all serve to concentrate the child's attention upon its similarity with the parent of the same sex. Nevertheless some children, in defiance of all this pressure, choose the parents of opposite sex, not to love best, but as the persons with whose motives and purposes they feel most at one, whose choices they feel they can make their own when they are grown.

Before considering this question further, let me restate my hypothesis. I have suggested that certain human traits have been socially specialized as the appropriate attitudes and behaviour of only one sex, while other human traits have been specialized for the opposite sex. This social specialization is then rationalized into a theory that the socially decreed behavior is natural for one sex and unnatural for the other. . . .

Modern cultures that are in the throes of adjusting to women's changing economic position present comparable difficulties. Men find that one of the props of their dominance, a prop which they have often come to think of as synonymous with that dominance itself—the ability to be the sole support of their families—has been pulled from beneath them. Women trained to believe that the possession of earned income gave the right to dictate, a doctrine which worked well enough as long as women had no incomes, find themselves more and more often in a confused state between their real position in the household and the one to which they have been trained. Men who have been trained to believe that their sex is always a little in question and who believe that their earning power is a proof of their manhood are plunged into a double uncertainty by unemployment; and this is further complicated by the fact that their wives have been able to secure employment.

All such conditions are aggravated in America also by the large number of different patterns of decreed behaviour for each sex that obtain in different national and regional groups, and by the supreme importance of the pattern of intersex behaviour that children encounter within the closed four walls of their homes. Each small part of our complex and stratified culture has its own set of rules by which the power and complementary balance between the sexes is maintained. But these rules differ, and are sometimes even contradictory, as between different national groups or economic classes. So, because there is no tradition which insists that individuals should marry in the group within which they were reared, men and women are continually marrying whose pictures of the interrelationships between the sexes are entirely different. Their confusions are in turn transmitted to their children. The result is a society in which hardly anyone doubts the existence of a different "natural" behaviour for the sexes, but no one is very sure what that "natural" behaviour is. Within the conflicting definitions of appropriate behaviour for each sex, almost every

type of individual is left room to doubt the completeness of his or her possession of a really masculine or a really feminine nature. We have kept the emphasis, the sense of the importance of the adjustment, and at the same time we have lost the ability to enforce the adjustment.

There are at least three courses open to a society that has realized the extent to which male and female personality are socially produced. Two of these courses have been tried before, over and over again, at different times in the long, irregular, repetitious history of the race. The first is to standardize the personality of men and women as clearly contrasting, complementary, and antithetical, and to make every institution in the society congruent with this standardization. If the society declared that woman's sole function was motherhood and the teaching and care of young children, it could so arrange matters that every woman who was not physiologically debarred should become a mother and be supported in the exercise of this function. It could abolish the discrepancy between the doctrine that women's place is the home and the number of homes that were offered to them. It could abolish the discrepancy between training women for marriage and then forcing them to become the spinster supports of their parents.

Such a system would be wasteful of the gifts of many women who could exercise other functions far better than their ability to bear children in an already overpopulated world. It would be wasteful of the gifts of many men who could exercise their special personality gifts far better in the home than in the market-place. It would be wasteful, but it would be clear. It could attempt to guarantee to each individual the rôle for which society insisted upon training him or her, and such a system would penalize only those individuals who, in spite of all the training, did not display the approved personalities. There are millions of persons who would gladly return to such a standardized method of treating the relationship between the sexes, and we must bear in mind the possibility that the greater opportunities open in the twentieth century to women may be quite withdrawn, and that we may return to a strict regimentation of women.

The waste, if this occurs, will be not only of many women, but also of as many men, because regimentation of one sex carries with it, to greater or less degree, the regimentation of the other also. Every parental behest that defines a way of sitting, a response to a rebuke or a threat, a game, or an attempt to draw or sing or dance or paint, as feminine, is moulding the personality of each little girl's brother as well as moulding the personality of the sister. There can be no society which insists that women follow one special personality-pattern, defined as feminine, which does not do violence also to the individuality of many men.

Alternatively, society can take the course that has become especially associated with the plans of most radical groups: admit that men and women are capable of being moulded to a single pattern as easily as to a diverse one, and cease to make any distinction in the approved personality of both sexes. Girls can be trained exactly as boys are trained, taught the same code, the same forms of expression, the same occupations. This course might seem to be the logic which follows from the conviction that the potentialities which different societies label as either masculine or feminine are really potentialities of some members of each sex, and not sex-linked at all. If this is accepted, is it not reasonable to abandon the kind of artificial standardizations of sex-differences that have been so long characteristic of European society, and admit that they are social fictions for which we have no longer any use? In the world today, contraceptives make it possible

for women not to bear children against their will. The most conspicuous actual difference between the sexes, the difference in strength, is progressively less significant. Just as the difference in height between males is no longer a realistic issue, now that lawsuits have been substituted for hand-to-hand encounters, so the difference in strength between men and women is no longer worth elaboration in cultural institutions.

In evaluating such a programme as this, however, it is necessary to keep in mind the nature of the gains that society has achieved in its most complex forms. A sacrifice of distinctions in sex-personality may mean a sacrifice in complexity. The Arapesh recognize a minimum of distinction in personality between old and young, between men and women, and they lack categories of rank or status. We have seen that such a society at the best condemns to personal frustration, and at the worst to maladjustment, all of those men and women who do not conform to its simple emphases. . . .

However, the only solution of the problem does not lie between an acceptance of standardization of sex-differences with the resulting cost in individual happiness and adjustment, and the abolition of these differences with the consequent loss in social values. A civilization might take its cues not from such categories as age or sex, race or hereditary position in a family line, but instead of specializing personality along such simple lines recognize, train, and make a place for many and divergent temperamental endowments. It might build upon the different potentialities that it now attempts to extirpate artificially in some children and create artificially in others.

Historically the lessening of rigidity in the classification of the sexes has come about at different times, either by the creation of a new artificial category, or by the recognition of real individual differences. Sometimes the idea of social position has transcended sex-categories. In a society that recognizes gradations in wealth or rank, women of rank or women of wealth have been permitted an arrogance which was denied to both sexes among the lowly or the poor. Such a shift as this has been, it is true, a step towards the emancipation of women, but it has never been a step towards the greater freedom of the individual. A few women have shared the upper-class personality, but to balance this a great many men as well as women have been condemned to a personality characterized by subservience and fear. Such shifts as these mean only the substitution of one arbitrary standard for another. A society is equally unrealistic whether it insists that only men can be brave, or that only individuals of rank can be brave.

To break down one line of division, that between the sexes, and substitute another, that between classes, is no real advance. It merely shifts the irrelevancy to a different point. And meanwhile, individuals born in the upper classes are shaped inexorably to one type of personality, to an arrogance that is again uncongenial to at least some of them, while the arrogant among the poor fret and fume beneath their training for submissiveness. . . .

The second way in which categories of sex-differences have become less rigid is through a recognition of genuine individual gifts as they occurred in either sex. Here a real distinction has been substituted for an artificial one, and the gains are tremendous for society and for the individual. Where writing is accepted as a profession that may be pursued by either sex with perfect suitability, individuals who have the ability to write need not be debarred from it by their sex, nor need they, if they do write, doubt their essential masculinity or femininity. An occupation that has no basis in sex-determined gifts can now recruit its ranks from twice as many potential artists. And it is here

that we can find a ground-plan for building a society that would substitute real differences for arbitrary ones. We must recognize that beneath the superficial classifications of sex and race the same potentialities exist, recurring generation after generation, only to perish because society has no place for them. Just as society now permits the practice of an art to members of either sex, so it might also permit the development of many contrasting temperamental gifts in each sex. It might abandon its various attempts to make boys fight and to make girls remain passive, or to make all children fight, and instead shape our educational institutions to develop to the full the boy who shows a capacity for maternal behaviour, the girl who shows an opposite capacity that is stimulated by fighting against obstacles. No skill, no special aptitude, no vividness of imagination or precision of thinking would go unrecognized because the child who possessed it was of one sex rather than the other. No child would be relentlessly shaped to one pattern of behaviour, but instead there should be many patterns, in a world that had learned to allow to each individual the pattern which was most congenial to his gifts.

Such a civilization would not sacrifice the gains of thousands of years during which society has built up standards of diversity. The social gains would be conserved, and each child would be encouraged on the basis of his actual temperament. Where we now have patterns of behaviour for women and patterns of behaviour for men, we would then have patterns of behaviour that expressed the interests of individuals with many kinds of endowment. There would be ethical codes and social symbolisms, an art and a way of life, congenial to each endowment.

Historically our own culture has relied for the creation of rich and contrasting values upon many artificial distinctions, the most striking of which is sex. It will not be by the mere abolition of these distinctions that society will develop patterns in which individual gifts are given place instead of being forced into an ill-fitting mould. If we are to achieve a richer culture, rich in contrasting values, we must recognize the whole gamut of human potentialities, and so weave a less arbitrary social fabric, one in which each diverse human gift will find a fitting place.

Willard Walter Waller (1899–1945) on Rating and Dating

Willard Walter Waller was born in Murphysboro, Illinois, the son of a school superintendent, from whom he perhaps developed his future interest in teaching and education. Waller earned an undergraduate degree in classics from the University of Illinois in 1920, a master's degree in sociology from the University of Chicago in 1925, and a doctorate from the University of Pennsylvania in 1929. He went on to make significant contributions to the sociology of education and family. During his doctoral work, he served as an instructor in sociology at the University of Pennsylvania, leaving for an assistant professor position at the University of Nebraska. From 1931 to 1937 he was on the faculty at Penn State College, after which he moved to his last position as associate professor of sociology at Columbia's Barnard College. He served there until his untimely death in 1945. Waller's contributions were often original and controversial. His most famous article is the one reprinted here about "rating and dating."

Major Works

Waller, Willard Walter. *The Old Love and the New: Divorce and Readjustment.* New York: Liveright, 1930.

———. *The Sociology of Teaching.* New York: Russell, 1932.

———. "The Rating and Dating Complex." *American Sociological Review* 2, no. 5 (1937): 727–34.

———. *The Family: A Dynamic Interpretation.* New York: Dryden, 1938.

———. *The Veteran Comes Back.* New York: Dryden, 1944.

Source

Hill, Reuben L. 1968. Waller, Willard W. In *International encyclopedia of the social sciences,* Vol. 16, ed. David Sills, 443–45. New York: Macmillan.

THE SELECTION

This selection is an edited version of Waller's well-known article on "rating and dating" on a college campus. Waller describes what he sees as a new pattern of interaction between young men and women—the relatively new phenomenon of dating. Dating arose as a popular activity after young people were able to leave their parental homes to attend college, a middle-class pattern with origins primarily in the 1920s and 1930s. Unobserved by parents and community, young adults suddenly had freedom to interact in ways not possible before. Replacing the more controlled and marriage-oriented pattern of courtship, dating was less serious and was seen as a form of "amusement," not primarily as a prelude to marriage. In this situation, Waller points out, the possibility of exploitation arises, which finds expression in gendered ways.

Waller describes the characteristics of dating on a small prestigious college campus. He notes that there is a hierarchy of status on the campus: for men, status characteristics include membership in the best fraternities, participation in campus activities, having cash to spend, having "smooth" manners and dress, having a "good line," being a good dancer, and possession of a car. For women, corresponding traits include being well dressed, having a "smooth line," being a good dancer, and being a popular date. Waller describes coeds as being obsessed with popularity, especially being in the position of having others see one as being popular. The "games" they play include never appearing too eager to date a young man, being seen at the best places, and being seen with "Class A" men. The entire complex of activities and norms seems very artificial, but in discussing this with women who remember those days, it seems that this was the expectation for many of them. And even younger generations often recognize some of these types of behavior and expectations.

THE RATING AND DATING COMPLEX

Courtship may be defined as the set of processes of association among the unmarried from which, in time, permanent matings usually emerge. This definition excludes those associations which cannot normally eventuate in marriage—as between Negro and white—but allows for a period of dalliance and experimentation. In the present paper we propose to discuss the customs of courtship which prevail among college students.

Courtship practices vary from one culture group to another. In many cultures marriage eventuates from a period of sexual experimentation and trial unions; in others the innocence of the unmarried is carefully

From Willard W. Waller, "The rating and dating complex," *American Sociological Review* 2, no. 5 (1937): 727–34.

guarded until their wedding day. In some cultures the bride must be virginal at marriage; in others this is just what she must not be. Sometimes the young are allowed no liberty of choice, and everything is determined for them by their elders. Sometimes persons marry in their own age group, but in other societies older men pre-empt the young women for themselves. Although there are endless variations in courtship customs, they are always functionally related to the total configuration of the culture and the biological needs of the human animal. It is helpful to remember that in a simple, undifferentiated, and stable society a long and complex process of choosing a mate is apparently not so necessary or desirable as in our own complex, differentiated, and rapidly changing society.

The mores of courtship in our society are a strange composite of social heritages from diverse groups and of new usages called into existence by the needs of the time. There is a formal code of courtship which is still nominally in force, although departures from it are very numerous; the younger generation seems to find the superficial usages connected with the code highly amusing, but it is likely that it takes the central ideas quite seriously. The formal code appears to be derived chiefly from the usages of the English middle classes of a generation or so ago, although there are, of course, many other elements in it.

The usual or intended mode of operation of the formal mores of courtship—in a sense their "function"—is to induct young persons into marriage by a series of progressive commitments. In the solidary peasant community, in the frontier community, among the English middle classes of a few decades back, and in many isolated small communities in present-day America, every step in the courtship process has a customary meaning and constitutes a powerful pressure toward taking the next step—is in fact a sort of implied commitment to take the next step. The mores formerly operated to produce a high rate of marriage at the proper age and at the same time protected most individuals from many of the possible traumatic experiences of the courtship period.

The decay of this moral structure has made possible the emergence of thrill-seeking and exploitative relationships. A thrill is merely a physiological stimulation and release of tension, and it seems curious that most of us are inclined to regard thrill-seeking with disapproval. The disapproving attitude toward thrill-seeking becomes intelligible when we recall the purpose of such emotional stirrings in the conventional mores of courtship. Whether we approve or not, courtship practices today allow for a great deal of pure thrill-seeking. Dancing, petting, necking, the automobile, the amusement park, and a whole range of institutions and practices permit or facilitate thrill-seeking behavior. These practices, which are connected with a great range of the institutions of commercialized recreation, make of courtship an amusement and a release of organic tensions. The value judgment which many lay persons and even some trained sociologists pass upon thrill-seeking arises from the organizational mores of the family—from the fact that energy is dissipated in thrills which is supposed to do the work of the world, i.e., to get people safely married.

The emergence of thrill-seeking furthers the development of exploitative relationships. As long as an association is founded on a frank and admitted barter in thrills, nothing that can be called exploitative arises. But the old mores of progressive commitment exist, along with the new customs, and peculiar relationships arise from this confusion of moralities. According to the old morality a kiss means something, a declaration of love means something, a number of Sunday evening dates in succession means something, and these meanings are enforced by the customary law, while under the new morality such things may mean nothing at all—that is, they may imply no commitment of the total personality whatsoever. So it comes about that one of the persons may exploit the other for thrills on the pretense of emotional involvement and its implied commitment. When a woman exploits, it is usually for the sake of presents and expensive amusements—the common pattern of "gold-digging." The male exploiter usually seeks thrills from the body of the woman. The fact that thrills cost money, usually the man's money, often operates to introduce strong elements of suspicion and antagonism into the relationship.

With this general background in mind, let us turn to the courtship practices of college students. A very important characteristic of the college student is his bourgeois pattern of life. For most persons, the dominant motive of college attendance is the desire to rise to a higher social class; behind this we should see the ideology of American life and the projection of parents' ambitions upon children. The attainment of this life goal necessitates the postponement of marriage, since it is understood that a new household must be economically independent; additional complications sometimes arise from the practice of borrowing money for college expenses. And yet persons in this group feel very strongly the cultural imperative to fall in love and marry and live happily in marriage.

For the average college student, and especially for the man, a love affair which led to immediate marriage would be tragic because of the havoc it would create in his scheme of life. Nevertheless, college students feel strongly the attractions of sex and the thrills of sex, and the sexes associate with one another in a peculiar relationship known as "dating." Dating is not true courtship, since it is supposed not to eventuate in marriage; it is a sort of dalliance relationship. In spite of the strength of the

old morality among college students, dating is largely dominated by the quest of the thrill and is regarded as an amusement. The fact that college attendance usually removes the individual from normal courtship association in his home community should be mentioned as a further determinant of the psychological character of dating.

In many colleges, dating takes place under conditions determined by a culture complex which we may call the "rating and dating complex." The following description of this complex on one campus is probably typical of schools of the sort:

X College, a large state-supported school, is located in a small city at a considerable distance from larger urban areas. The school is the only industry of the community. There are few students who live at home, and therefore the interaction of the young is but little influenced by the presence of parents. The students of this college are predominantly taken from the lower half of the middle classes, and constitute a remarkably homogeneous group; numerous censuses of the occupations of fathers and of living expenses seem to establish this fact definitely. Nevertheless, about half of the male students live in fraternities, where the monthly bill is usually forty-five or fifty dollars a month, rarely as high as fifty-five. There is intense competition among the fraternities. The desire for mobility of class, as shown by dozens of inquiries, is almost universal in the group and is the principal verbalized motive for college attendance.

Dating at X College consists of going to college or fraternity dances, the movies, college entertainments, and to fraternity houses for victrola dances and "necking"; coeds are permitted in the fraternity parlors, if more than one is present. The high points of the social season are two house parties and certain formal dances. An atypical feature of this campus is the unbalanced sex ratio, for there are about six boys to every girl; this makes necessary the large use of so-called "imports" for the more important occasions, and brings it about that many boys do not date at all or confine their activities to prowling about in small industrial communities nearby; it also gives every coed a relatively high position in the scale of desirability; it would be difficult to say whether it discourages or encourages the formation of permanent attachments. Dating is almost exclusively the privilege of fraternity men, the use of the fraternity parlor and the prestige of fraternity membership being very important. Freshman men are forbidden by student tradition to have dates with coeds.

Within the universe which we have described, competition for dates among both men and women is extremely keen. Like every other process of competition, this one determines a distributive order. There are certain men who are at the top of the social scramble; they may be placed in a hypothetical Class A. There are also certain coeds who are near the top of the scale of dating desirability, and they also are in Class A. The tendency is for Class A men to date principally Class A women. Beneath this class of men and women are as many other classes as one wishes to create for the purposes of analysis. It should be remembered that students on this campus are extremely conscious of these social distinctions and of their own position in the social hierarchy. In speaking of another student, they say, "He rates," or "He does not rate," and they extend themselves enormously in order that they may rate or seem to rate.

Young men are desirable dates according to their rating on the scale of campus values. In order to have Class A rating they must belong to one of the better fraternities, be prominent in activities, have a copious supply of spending money, be well-dressed, "smooth" in manners and appearance, have a "good line," dance well, and have access to an automobile. Members of leading fraternities are especially desirable dates; those who belong to fraternities with less prestige are correspondingly less desirable. I have been able to validate the qualities mentioned as determinants of campus prestige by reference to large numbers of student judges.

The factors which appear to be important for girls are good clothes, a smooth line, ability to dance well, and popularity as a date. The most important of these factors is the last, for the girl's prestige depends upon dating more than anything else; here as nowhere else nothing succeeds like success. Therefore the clever coed contrives to give the impression of being much sought after even if she is not. It has been reported by many observers that a girl who is called to the telephone in the dormitories will often allow herself to be called several times, in order to give all the other girls ample opportunity to hear her paged. Coeds who wish campus prestige must never be available for last minute dates; they must avoid being seen too often with the same boy, in order that others may not be frightened away or discouraged; they must be seen when they go out, and therefore must go to the popular (and expensive) meeting places; they must have many partners at the dances. If they violate the conventions at all, they must do so with great secrecy and discretion; they do not drink in groups or frequent the beer-parlors. Above all, the coed who wishes to retain Class A standing must consistently date Class A men.

Cressey has pointed out that the taxi-dancer has a descending cycle of desirability. As a new girl in the dance hall, she is at first much sought after by the most eligible young men. Soon they tire of her and desert her for some newer recruit. Similarly the coed has a descending cycle of popularity on the campus which we are describing, although her struggle is not invariably a losing one. The new girl, the freshman coed, starts out with a great wave of popularity; during her fresh-man year she has many dates. Slowly her prestige declines, but in this case only to the point at which she reaches the level which her qualities permanently assure her. Her descent is expedited by such "mistakes," from the viewpoint of campus prestige, as "going steady" with one boy (especially if he is a senior who will not return the following year), by indiscretions, and by too ready availability for dates. Many of the girls insist that after two years of competitive dating they have tired of it and are interested in more permanent associations.

This thrill-dominated, competitive pro-cess involves a number of fundamental antagonisms between the men and the women, and the influence of the one sex group accentuates these. Writes one stu-dent informant, a girl, "Wary is the only word that I can apply to the attitude of men and women students toward each other. The men, who have been warned so repeatedly against coeds, are always afraid the girls are going to 'gold-dig' them. The coeds wonder to what degree they are dis-cussed and are constantly afraid of being placed on the black list of the fraternities. Then too they wonder to what extent they can take any man seriously without being taken for a 'ride'." Status in the one-sex group depends upon avoiding exploitation by the opposite sex. Verbatim records of a number of fraternity "bull sessions" were obtained a few years ago. In these sessions members are repeatedly warned that they are slipping, those who have fallen are teased without mercy, and others are warned not to be soft. And almost all of the partici-pants pretend a ruthlessness toward the op-posite sex which they do not feel.

This competitive dating process often inflicts traumas upon individuals who stand low in the scale of courtship desirability. "While I was at X College," said a thirty year old alumnus, "I had just one date. That was

a blind date, arranged for me by a friend. We went to the dorm, and after a while my girl came down and we were introduced. She said, 'Oh, I'm so sorry. I forgot my coat. I'll have to go get it.' She never came down again. Naturally I thought, 'Well what a hit I made!'" We have already seen that nonfra-ternity men are practically excluded from dating; it remains to note that many girls elect not to date rather than take the dates available to them. One girl writes as follows: "A girl's choice of whom to fall in love with is limited by the censorship of the one-sex group. Every boy that she dates is discussed and criticized by the other members of the group. This rigid control often keeps a girl from dating at all. If a girl is a member of a group in which the other girls are rated higher on the dating scale than she, she is of-ten unable to get dates with boys who are considered desirable by her friends. In that event she has to decide whether to date the boys that she can and choose girl friends who would approve, or she must resign herself to not dating."

Since the class system, or gradient of dating desirability on the campus, is clearly recognized and adjusted to by the students themselves, there are interesting accommo-dations and rationalizations which appear as a result of inferior status. Although mem-bers of Class A may be clearly in the ascen-dant as regards prestige, certain groups of Class B may contest the position with them and may insist upon a measuring stick which will give them a favorable position. Ratio-nalizations which enable Class D men and women to accept one another are probably never completely effective.

The accommodations and rationaliza-tions worked out by one group of girls who were toward the bottom of the scale of cam-pus desirability are typical. Four of these girls were organized in one tightly compact "bunch." All four lived off campus, and worked for their room and board. They had little money to spend for clothes, so there was extensive borrowing of dresses. Members of the group co-operated in getting dates for one another. All of them accepted eleventh hour invitations, and probably realized that some stigma of inferiority was attached to such ready availability but they managed to save their faces by seeming very reluctant to accept such engagements, and at length doing so as a result of the persuasion of another member of the bunch. The men apparently saw through these devices, and put these girls down as last minute dates, so that they rarely received any other invitations. The bunch went through "dating cycles" with several fraternities in the course of a year, starting when one of the girls got a date with one member of the fraternity, and ending, apparently when all the girls had lost their desirability in that fraternity.

Partly as result of the unbalanced sex ratio, the boys of the group which we are discussing have a widespread feeling of antagonism toward the coeds. This antagonism is apparently based upon the fact that most of the male students are unable to date with coeds, at least not on terms acceptable to themselves. As a result of this, boys take great pride in the "imports" whom they bring in for house parties, and it is regarded as slightly disgraceful in some groups to date a coed for one of the major parties. Other men in the dateless group take on the role of misogynists—and read Schopenhauer.

During the winter term the preponderance of men assures to every coed a relatively high bargaining power. Every summer witnesses a surprising reversal of this situation. Hundreds of women school teachers flock to this school for the summer term, and men are very scarce; smooth, unmarried boys of college age are particularly scarce. The school-teachers are older than the boys; they have usually lost some of their earlier attractiveness; they have been living for some months or years within the school-teacher

role. They are man-hungry, and they have a little money. As a result, there is a great proliferation of highly commercialized relations. The women lend their cars to their men friends, but continue to pay for repairs and gasoline; they take the boys out to dinner, treat them to drinks, and buy expensive presents for them. And many who do not go so far are available for sex relations on terms which demand no more than a transitory sort of commitment from the man.

The rating and dating complex varies enormously from one school to another. In one small, coeducational school, the older coeds instruct the younger that it is all right for them to shop around early in the year, but by November they should settle down and date someone steadily. As a result, a boy who dates a girl once is said to "have a fence around her," and the competition which we have described is considerably hampered in its operation. In other schools, where the sex ratio is about equal, and particularly in the smaller institutions, "going steady" is probably a great deal more common than on the campus described. It should be pointed out that the frustrations and traumas imposed upon unsuccessful candidates by the practice of "going steady" (monopolistic competition) are a great deal easier to bear than those which arise from pure competition. In one school the girls are uniformly of a higher class origin than the boys, so that there is relatively little association between them; the girls go with older men not in college, the boys with high school girls and other "townies." In the school which is not coeducational, the dating customs are vastly different, although, for the women at least, dating is still probably a determinant of prestige.

True courtship sometimes emerges from the dating process, in spite of all the forces which are opposed to it. The analysis of the interaction process involved seems to be quite revealing. We may suppose that in our collegiate culture one begins to fall in love with a certain unwillingness, at least with an ambivalent sort of willingness. Both persons become emotionally involved as a result of a summatory process in which each step powerfully influences the next step and the whole process displays a directional trend toward the culmination of marriage; the mores of dating break down and the behavior of the individuals is governed by the older mores of progressive commitment. In the fairly typical case, we may suppose the interaction to be about as follows: The affair begins with the lightest sort of involvement, each individual being interested in the other but assuming no obligations as to the continuation of the affair. There are some tentatives of exploitation at the beginning; "the line" is a conventionalized attempt on the part of the young man to convince the young woman that he has already at this early stage fallen seriously in love with her—a sort of exaggeration, sometimes a burlesque, of coquetry—it may be that each person, by a pretence of great involvement, invites the other to rapid sentiment-formation—each encourages the other to fall in love by pretending that he has already done so. If either rises to the bait, a special type of interaction ensues; it may be that the relation becomes exploitative in some degree and it is likely that the relationship becomes one in which control follows the principle of least interest, i.e., that person controls who is less interested in the continuation of the affair. Or it may be that the complete involvement of the one person constellates the other in the same pattern, but this is less likely to happen in college than in the normal community processes of courtship.

If both persons stand firm at this early juncture, there may ensue a series of periodic crises which successively redefine the relationship on deeper levels of involvement. One form which the interaction process may assume is that of "lover's quarrels," with which the novelists have familiarized us. A and B begin an affair on the level of light involvement. A becomes somewhat involved, but believes that B has not experienced a corresponding growth of feeling, and hides his involvement from B, who is, however, in exactly the same situation. The conventionalized "line" facilitates this sort of "pluralistic ignorance," because it renders meaningless the very words by means of which this state of mind could be disclosed. Tension grows between A and B, and is resolved by a crisis, such as a quarrel, in which the true feelings of the two are revealed. The affair, perhaps, proceeds through a number of such crises until it reaches the culmination of marriage. Naturally, there are other kinds of crises which usher in the new definition of the situation.

Such affairs, in contrast to "dating," have a marked directional trend; they may be arrested on any level, or they may be broken off at any point, but they may not ordinarily be turned back to a lesser degree of involvement; in this sense they are irreversible. As this interaction process goes on, the process of idealization is re-enforced by the interaction of personalities. A idealizes B, and presents to her that side of his personality which is consistent with his idealized conception of her; B idealizes A, and governs her behavior toward him in accordance with her false notions of his nature; the process of idealization is mutually re-enforced in such a way that it must necessarily lead to an increasing divorce from reality. As serious sentimental involvement develops, the individual comes to be increasingly occupied, on the conscious level at least, with the positive aspects of the relationship; increasingly he loses his ability to think objectively about the other person, to safeguard himself or to deal with the relationship in a rational way; we may say, indeed, that one falls in love when he reaches the point where sentiment-formation overcomes objectivity.

The love relationship in its crescendo phase attracts an ever larger proportion of the conative trends of the personality; for a time it may seem to absorb all of the will of the individual and to dominate his imagination completely; the individual seems to become a machine specially designed for just one purpose; in consequence, the persons are almost wholly absorbed in themselves and their affair; they have an *egoisme à deux* which verges upon *folie à deux*. All of these processes within the pair-relationship are accentuated by the changes in the attitude of others, who tend to treat the pair as a social unity, so far as their association is recognized and approved.

The 1940s

Questions about Women's New Roles

Edward Alsworth Ross (1866–1951) on Conflict between the Sexes

Edward Alsworth Ross's biographical data has been presented with an earlier selection. This is from one of his last publications, a book with the forward-looking title *New-Age Sociology* (1940).

THE SELECTION

The following selection is basically an updated and expanded version of a chapter that first appeared in Edward Alsworth Ross's earlier *Principles of Sociology* (1920). Even in the original version, Ross brings his conflict perspective to the issue of the relations between the sexes, which he saw as inherently problematic. Ross outlines several causes of sex conflict. These include certain "instinctual" differences—women's maternal instincts and men's stronger "pugnacious" ones and their stronger desires to dominate others. The remainder of Ross's discussion of women's status highlights social and cultural supports for male dominance, including (1) men's monopoly over institutions of power, a fact that in more recent times has come to be resented by "thinking women"; (2) the fact that men (not women) have established cultural ideals for women in terms of their own (men's) interests; and (3) society's lack of roles for unmarried women, which sets up a conflict between the interests of married and unmarried women and between single women and men.

Ross argues that, as cultural supports for sex differences decline (for example, the decline of religious dogma), women come to

From Edward Alsworth Ross, "Sex Conflict," in *New-Age Sociology* (New York: Appleton-Century, 1940), Chap. 15.

view their status as unfair and begin to demand change. However, because the sexes depend on each other and their lives are intertwined, sex conflict rarely leads to physical combat or open conflict between men and women.

Instead it emerges in struggles to define cultural values, as between the traditional "masculine, woman-depreciating culture" and what he terms a "bi-sexual culture built on science." As long as there remain differences in basic rights, this conflict will occasionally erupt in episodes of cultural agitation (perhaps now we would refer to this as "culture wars").

Ross argued that religious and cultural myths are fundamental to the persistence of women's inferior status; until these are gone, full equality will not be possible. However, he optimistically believed that religious supports for male dominance were rapidly declining under the influence of scientific studies. Other obstacles to women's equality he notes include wars and militarism, the loss of household industries, the rise of consumerism, the cultural glorification of sports, and the weakening of democratic institutions. Positive developments for equality included

the development of "mental testing," which refuted notions of women's intellectual inferiority; family limitation; day care centers and employment for mothers; equal education for both sexes; technological advances making physical strength less relevant for work; and women's access to the vote and public office. Ross saw these as worldwide trends that could not easily be reversed. In the end, however, he falls back to a biologically based argument about women's "duty" to have children and men's "natural" proclivity to be the pursuer in love and the sexual initiator in marriage. While the major portion of this discussion is thoughtful and surprisingly critical and supportive of feminist goals, his final paragraphs seem defensive (perhaps a response to criticism?) and a bit inconsistent with his earlier remarks. However, from his perspective, Ross is moving strongly into dangerous scholarly territory, and his closing comments may well be a sign of his recognition of that fact. His support for the eugenic notions of the time (for example, the need to maintain the birthrate among educated women) is also apparent here. Overall, though, the discussion contains many points worthy of consideration, even today.

SEX CONFLICT

Between individual men and women in the love relation there are, of course, innumerable clashes of personality; but even between the sexes as groups there smolders an antagonism which ever and anon bursts into flame. Among its causes are:

THE SEXES DIFFER IN INSTINCTUAL EQUIPMENT

Woman has at least one instinct all her own, the maternal; while man has the stronger pugnacious impulses. Nor do the sexes share

equally in the will to dominate, to display one's self. . . . That they react so differently in many situations makes each sex seem at times "queer" to the other. In the refined classes the sexes are carefully trained from childhood to conventional attitudes toward each other; but among the "plain folk" each sex views the other with some distrust, dislike, or contempt. Rough old farmers talking freely by themselves conclude that women generally are touchy, unstable, flighty, vain, irresponsible and sly. But their women about a quilting frame agree that for the most part men are coarse, sensual, self-willed, violent, egotistic and unreasonable. Both groups underrate the might of the going culture in determining the traits of men and women.

MAN HAS MONOPOLIZED POWER

As chief trouble maker, and protector of his own from trouble, man has arrogated to himself the shaping of the large events and institutions conditioning the life of family, community, tribe and state. For the ages that his decisions related to little else than war, peace, and security, women consented to their exclusion. Tied down by their babies they left fighting and all that it involves to the men. But since *written law,* instead of *ancestral custom,* has come to fix the rights and duties of spouses, and since the man-managed state has laid its hand on family, children, education, recreation, industry, public health and public morals, thinking women more and more resent exclusive male control of law and state.

MAN HAS SET UP IDEALS FOR WOMEN AS WELL AS FOR MEN

On the whole the ideals for men have been wrought out by men, but the ideals for women have not been wrought out by women. In Japan, for example, the mould into which the daughter's soul is poured is plainly man-made, whereas the mould into which the son's soul is poured is by no means woman-made. The female is to be modest, self-abnegating, gentle, retiring and domestic because the male wants her so. The world over, man imposes his own notions of what women ought to be and do. In gratifying his sex impulses he claims for himself a degree of liberty he is quite unready to concede to woman. The wide divergence in the meanings of "virtue," "honor," "modesty," "liberty," as applied to the two sexes is man's work. How much it irks the human female to be what he requires her to be, how many of her best possibilities she sacrifices, and whether she is happy in the role

he forces on her, are questions which never occur to the self-confident male. For him *That is the way I like 'em* is final and sufficing!

Where the spirit of our Old South reigns, an elaborate upper-class "lady"-worship fails to conceal the naive assumption that God placed women here for the sake of the male sex. As a matter of course, women should find their mission in serving, pleasing, and inspiring man, but no one suggests that the male sex has its end in anything it does for women; *its end is within itself.* The young woman should cultivate a conciliating and caressing manner, and avoid opposing or disagreeing with men. If she has opinions she dissembles them and if she has learning she hides it, lest male irritation blast her with the reproach "unwomanly." To please men she must wear delicate and flimsy clothes no matter what they cost her fingers or her purse, and shun the plain but convenient "tailor-made" garments. Male opinion blames the widow who remarries for putting her own happiness above loyalty to a man's memory; but no one thinks less of the widower who remarries. The divorced man goes everywhere, but the divorced woman is socially ostracized, no matter what her justification. The men hold under constant surveillance the reading, associations, and activities of their women-folk, and expect the woman to subordinate her own notion of what is proper for her to the judgment of her nearest male relative. In a word, her repute and standing concern her menfolk more than they do herself.

The mountain of balderdash literature on "the woman question," stressing impressively the disabilities which Nature has imposed on the female sex and solemnly warning of the terrible risks of making women free, is, to the reflective, a gigantic index of male self-conceit and fatuousness. The parade of learning, logic, and impartiality in thousands of such sermons, articles, pamphlets, and books appears on close inspection to be as empty as a soap bubble!

GENESIS OF SEX CONFLICT

An inter-sex adjustment comes to be imbedded in the culture patterns and unthinkingly we adapt our behavior to it, but when the culture patterns disintegrate hidden injustices show up. Hence, in our day, with the crumbling of venerable religious dogmas, the decay of the principle of authority, the overtaking of the clergy by other learned professions, the adequacy of fewer births, and the opening to women of no end of doors to self-support, the right of one sex to forge the destiny of the other is challenged. Why—it is asked—are men so eager to bar women from the skilled trades, the higher educational walks, the professions, public service, and public office, unless it is that they want to keep the soft berths and the power seats for themselves!

FEATURES OF SEX CONFLICT

Sex conflict does not slump into sheer carnage, as may race conflict or class conflict. The sexes are cross-linked by countless close ties—lovers, spouses, brothers, and sisters, mothers and sons, fathers and daughters—so that they *never* face each other in hostile array. Physical combat between the sexes has not been, will not be. Nor is it a conflict between *all* men and *all* women; rather it is a duel between the old, masculine, woman-depreciating culture and the new bi-sexual culture built on science. Always some women uphold male domination and some men are ired at the spectacle of female repression; as each group tries to win converts from the other. The champions of male rule work artfully upon the feelings of emotional women to make them distrust themselves and accept an assigned status; while the friends of aspiring women appeal to the fair play sense of men to persuade them to let their restive sisters go free.

As agitation thrusts "women's rights" into the focus of attention, sex antagonism flares up a bit; then, as women are conceded instalment after instalment of freedom and opportunity, which blithely they hasten to get and enjoy, the sexes with a sigh of relief settle contentedly into the altered relations and their antagonism speedily dies away. Always, however, there is a residue *owing to differences in the reaction of the sexes to elemental life situations.*

WHAT DETERMINES THE OUTCOME OF SEX CONFLICT?

In some fields, namely, intersex association and manners, status of the wife, of the mother, domestic seclusion, the education of daughters, etc., the outcome of the conflict in the higher social classes practically settles it for the rest, unless society is cleft by deep racial or cultural chasms. On the other hand, upper-class example cannot remove the grievances of woman in respect to her legal status in home, industry, education, the church, and the state; so battle rages about these citadels of masculine power.

Not fists nor weapons settle intersex conflict, not always even argument and debate. Factors from outside the field may decide. Quite in their day's work delvers into biology, psychology, sociology, or church history may explode baleful dogmas which for ages have buttressed male domination: such as, that God is male, that woman was created as an afterthought and solely for man's pleasure and comfort, that the Fall in Eden was due to Eve's tempting Adam, that owing to her menstrual flow woman is "impure," that about conception there is something guilty and shameful, that celibacy is exalted and God-pleasing, that the father is sole author of the child's being, that women have no souls, that woman as the chief ally of the Devil in dragging men down to perdition must be kept cloistered or veiled, that "it is shameful for a woman to speak in a church," that woman's intellectual powers are contemptible, that it is not worth while to educate her, etc., etc. Once those ancient props are dust little is left on which the male sex can base its claim to dominate.

DEVELOPMENTS KEEPING WOMEN UNDER THE YOKE

Although the theological dogmas which buttressed male domination are crumbling, certain current developments tell against sex equality: (a) war and "preparedness" exalt the sex that fights; therefore, if savage struggle for domination is to rule the international scene in the immediate future, the cause of women will lose ground; (b) decay of the household industries shrinks the economic importance of the home-staying wife and makes her depend more on her man; (c) heavy athletic contests emphasize the physical superiority of males to females; (d) the popular connecting of happiness with the owning of things (a by-product of modern salesmanship) is hostile to idealism in the relations of the sexes; (e) abandonment of democracy in favor of single-party rule maintained by ruffian methods (Nazi-ism) tells against the weaker and less pugnacious sex. . . .

DEVELOPMENTS RELEASING WOMEN

(a) Mental testing proves the intellectual parity of Darby and Joan; (b) limiting the size of the family spares wives from being looked upon as mere brood mares; (c) communal nurseries (as in Soviet Russia and among the Jewish settlers of Palestine) allow the mothers to keep on with their jobs; (d) parents give their daughters as good a schooling as they give their sons; (e) admission of women in growing numbers to the higher walks and the learned professions; (f) the power-driven machine enables women physically weak to hold millions of jobs in industry; (g) sex equality in voting, access to public office and participation in public life add to women's power and prestige in society.

WORLD-WIDE SWEEP OF SEX CONFLICT

In the ages to come changes in life conditions or ruling ideas may cause reversions to male dominance, but our time, at least, should witness the swift spread through most of mankind of the freedom, opportunity, and respect attained already by about a fifth of the world's women. Three-fifths of humanity are steeped in Oriental cultures which, in the main, subordinate the female sex to a degree hardly to be matched in any culture of which we have record. The readjustments between the sexes throughout the Asiatic world will make fireworks, we may be sure, for several decades. "In China bobbing the hair is a symbol for which women die martyrs, able and energetic girls, killed in backward villages during some militarist reaction." In Moslem Asia there are villages where women who leave off the veil are bound to a post and stoned. Without growing tension, sex embitterment, female self-assertion and occasional savage reaction women's day cannot dawn in the Orient.

THE OUTLOOK

Should a reaction develop against sex-equalization, the primary cause will be not men's old craving to dominate, but spread of the conviction that "emancipated" women are in a way "falling down" on their race-continuance "job." It will be shown that not a sufficient number of children are being born owing to the wife's dread of pregnancy; that the wives of superior and successful men are not delivering their due quota of heirs; that gifted women achieve rather than marry and bear children inheriting their gifts; that children are not being looked after and cared for as self-sacrificingly as of yore; that mothers are bringing up their daughters to demand too much from life, or to sidestep the duties which fall upon them as women; or mothers are too absorbed in their pursuits or pastimes to acquire over their sons that character-building influence which was often the reward of the old-fashioned home-staying mother.

Upon these functions the leaders of women should center their attention. If too many capable women are frittering away their newly won freedom in pleasure-seeking, beauty culture, the sex chase, struggle for social recognition, pursuit of a career, etc., then will rise a tide of opinion unfriendly to sex-equality.

There are limits beyond which sex-equalization cannot go. The time may come when women collectively will have as much weight in society and state as men; but there is no prospect that in sex relations the man will lose his prerogative to make the advances, to woo, to propose marriage, because it rests on physiology. A marriage may be fulfilled even if the wife does not respond to the amorous advances of her husband, whereas it fails utterly in the case the husband does not respond to the amorous advances of his wife.

Alva Myrdal (1902–1986) on Women as a Social Problem

Alva Reimer Myrdal was born in a rural community in Sweden in 1902 and graduated from Stockholm University in 1924, after struggling to win the right to pursue her education beyond grade school. She married a fellow economics student, the subsequently famous economist Gunnar Myrdal, in the same year. The couple worked together to contribute greatly to the development of progressive social welfare policies in Sweden in the 1930s. Their work included attention to population problems, housing, and education. Alva Myrdal had an outstanding career on her own as a diplomat, political leader, and advocate of disarmament. In the 1940s she was involved in prominent national committees planning for the postwar period. After the war she became more active in international issues. Among other accomplishments, she served as the Swedish ambassador to India, Burma, and Ceylon, and in the 1960s was a member of the parliament. Her outstanding work on disarmament won her world recognition and a Nobel Prize for Peace in 1982. Alva Myrdal died in 1989.

As a sociologist, Alva Myrdal both studied and contributed to policy on issues relating to family and women. Her book *Women's Two Roles,* coauthored with Viola Klein, was an effort to study and propose a solution to the conflicts between work and domestic roles for women—following up on an earlier discussion in her *Nation and Family,* published in 1941. Myrdal was a moderate in her proposed solutions to family–work conflicts for women, seeking solutions that would allow mothers to be at home with young children while still being able to engage in successful careers. She emphasized, among other things, the impact that increasing longevity has on women's career and life possibilities, pointing out that even if women choose to have children, the greater part of their adult lives will be spent without child care responsibilities.

MAJOR WORKS

Alva Myrdal and Viola Klein. *Women's Two Roles.* Rev. ed. London: Routledge & Kegan Paul, 1968.

Alva Myrdal. *The Game of Disarmament: How the United States and Russia Run the Arms Race.* New York: Pantheon, 1982 (Orig. pub. 1976).

———. *War, Weapons and Everyday Violence.* Manchester: University of New Hampshire Press, 1977.

———. *Dynamics of European Nuclear Disarmament.* Nottingham: Spokesman, 1981.

SOURCES

Bok, Sissela. 1991. *Alva Myrdal: A daughter's memoire.* Reading, MA: Addison-Wesley.

Herman, Sondra R. 1993. From international feminism to feminist internationalism: The emergence of Alva Myrdal, 1936–1955. *Peace & Change* 18 (4): 325–46.

THE SELECTION

The following reading is from a chapter on women as a "social problem," in her book, *Nation and Family,* on family and population policy in Sweden in the 1930s and 1940s. Sweden had instituted many legal reforms to make possible women's equality with men in the workplace and society, the topic of Alva Myrdal's book. However, in this chapter she discusses the impacts of these changes in women's employment patterns and the problems of combining marriage and childrearing with employment. In the final part of the chapter (the selection reprinted here), Myrdal discusses the problems that still exist under very liberal legal policies for women. Here is an early discussion of work–family conflicts for married women in the labor force. Many of the problems she defines will sound familiar to readers in contemporary American society, and her proposed reforms are thought-provoking.

ONE SEX A SOCIAL PROBLEM

Although the ideological battle has been fought and won, many practical difficulties remain to be overcome before the dilemma of the working mother is solved. Legally the dilemma is now abolished in Sweden. Also the condemning attitudes are being gradually vanquished. But this does not conjure away the very real troubles of an economic, institutional, and psychological nature standing in the working mother's way. The difficulties here touched upon go deep down to the fundamental problems of modern marriage itself; they concern women's fate as such, the purposiveness of their lives, and the inherent doubt as to how to plan them. It would be futile even to try to specify a practical solution of these basic problems in any truly realistic terms. The only thing that can be attempted is a sort of check list of still open problems.

Has the wage-earning mother found any sensible solution to her home organization

From Alva Myrdal, "One Sex a Social Problem," in *Nation and Family: The Swedish Experiment in Democratic Family and Population Policy* (New York: Harper, 1941), Chap. 22: 418–26 problem? Has she found some satisfactory adjustment to the traditonal demands upon her time by husband and children? Have women on the whole found some means of harmonizing investment in training and vocational ambitions with the incidence of marriage? Does marriage serve as a break in their life plans or are the life plans even of the spinsters arranged mainly with marriage in view, or is a rational balance possible?

The feminine sex is a social problem. Whether a woman is young or old, whether she is married or not, whether a wife works or not, she is likely to be a problem. This problem is largely economic in origin as marriage and family are as yet poorly adjusted to the new economic order. This is of vital importance to the individual and society as the family is the essential societal relationship.

THE ECONOMIC DILEMMA

Looking first upon women as competitors in the labor market, there certainly has been some reason to fear them. By their closer affiliation with the family economy the incomes of both unmarried and married women have often had the character of being supplementary as against the fundamental importance in ordinary cases of men's incomes for support of selves and others. Thus, women have been tempted not to sustain the wage demands of their fellow workers but rather to undercut them. Such competition has helped to depress the wage level. The complaints will probably not stop and can not rightly stop before women take their participation in the labor market in full sincerity. The uncertainty of women, tending as they do to keep up two possible future bases for support, will have to end. Still in this balancing of accounts it should be remembered that the inimical effect on the labor market is not one of women working but rather one of marriage itself as incessantly threatening to

redetermine women's lives. From the family aspect nothing but good in an economic sense could presumably come from the fact that the wife is a wage earner. The few cases where a completely incorrect economic calculation about costs and gains to the household induces her to work outside the home may be disregarded.

A problem of quite different importance is created by the fact that the very existence of income-earning wives puts nonearning wives in a questionable position. It cannot be denied that the economic situation of housewives appears in a most unfavorable light when marriages are divided into two types, those with two supporters and those with only a man supporter. The inherent dilemma of the housewives is derived from the fact that what is even now the customary family type, namely, the average man-supported family, has in reality never been "normal" but is a transitional phenomenon. The family of old could rightly be called the mutually supported family. All family members, without calculation as to exact shares, took part in both production and consumption. The nature and the degree of dependency were relatively similar for all. Only in the transition stage, when the male heads of households had surrendered to industrialism but that process had not yet markedly changed the functions of women, did the special dilemma of wives appear. Their status in the family has declined in comparison with that of the preindustrial period of familial economic organization. The wives have become dependent, i.e., they have no free and interchangeable basis of support. However much they perfect their housework to become truly professional, they do not receive remuneration in direct relation to their activities. They cannot even submit their work to the test of competition. They do not enter into labor contracts. In other words, they fall outside the economic order. Their incomes are never directly related to their toil but only to the level of the husbands' incomes. The most exquisite talent or the most laborious solicitude may be rewarded with starvation wages, while expensive leisure, even demanding attendance of others in the smallest personal affairs, may cost far more than the women enjoying it could ever have earned themselves.

This complete dissolution within the home between work and remuneration, tasks and security, is illuminated by the very presence of income-earning wives. It does not always remain a latent dilemma of housewives but often comes to the surface on the occasion of death or separation. Widowhood occurs less frequently than formerly, divorce much more frequently. And women have a longer average life to plan for. Sweden has attempted to alleviate this particular type of insecurity through the system of pensions to widows' children during their minority and the advance of support to children involved in divorces. Complete security, however, for the married women themselves has been neither achieved nor even attempted. Society has not considered it proper to provide for the discontinuity in women's lives and their risks in marriage by assuming social responsibility for their support. If marriage is no longer an economically profitable status, some fundamental rearrangements in marriage itself and in its connection with work and support have to be demanded. To find any practical solution at all for individuals there seems to be no better advice than that women should try to retain some occupational skill as a final resource if the security slips or the marriage fails.

THE VOCATIONAL DILEMMA

This disharmony in the relation between marriage and gainful employment is at the bottom of many of women's problems. How shall life be planned so as to reconcile these two factors? Knowing that in Sweden only

about three-fourths of the women 40 years of age have married and knowing that at least 10 per cent of those also have gainful employment outside the home, knowing further that the duration of women's marriages does not wholly coincide with their adult lives, and that the tasks of caring for minor children occupy a still smaller period, it seems incredible that the life of a whole sex could long continue to be planned only for motherhood, even supposing that the fate and the security of the mothers were fully satisfactory. Knowing, on the other hand, that so many women really do give up gainful work for their homes, it would be equally irrational to disregard the reasons for such a rupture in the world of work and support for women.

One practical conclusion must concern young women at their first decisive crossroad. Their vocational choice must probably take one of two main directions: either toward occupations which could be given up with all interests directed toward home or toward occupations which mean a more serious devotion for life. Young women ought to be able to decide with a certain degree of firmness whether they mainly desire eventually to desert wage earning for making a home of their own or whether they would rather think in terms of keeping up their vocational activities even after marriage. In our day young girls with their ability to analyze their own inclinations and aptitudes could certainly make this choice consciously. Thereafter the more detailed choice of vocation could fall under these two categories. In the one case, the young woman would choose as any young man chooses and devote all her energy to training and work. In the other case, she would choose work or training which would be of service to the home later to be set up but which would also offer an eventual career so related to housework that opportunities and skills would not be altogether lost even after years of household work. Thus the discontinuity of tasks now marring a woman's life would be applicable only to the woman deliberately choosing it and, even so, would be somewhat neutralized by her preparation for a career auxiliary to the tasks she performs within the family.

This is a plea for rationality. Regardless of whether it is possible of realization or not, it remains the only arrangement that could change what is now the most profound curse on every woman's life, the uncertainty of her life plan. As her life now evolves, on the average, it contains first some vocational preparation, although often shortsighted, and then some years of work, professional or otherwise, with a low independent income. Thereafter one of two things happens. Either that kind of life is prolonged, most often without the training and the zest sufficient for much of a career, with an ever-growing disillusion as the expectation of exchanging the job for a good marriage does not materialize. Or, for some other women, marriages do take place and then there normally follows a score of years occupied with housework, for which training has rarely prepared them. When the busy years are over and the children are grown, there are only empty decades ahead for the mother with neither sufficient work in her home nor much chance to be reinstated in the earlier vocational life. To make it worse, in these middle years the affective and the sexual bases for the marriage are often wavering. In an age far too early for death the feeling of justification of life and of security in economic support won through marriage start to give way even for those who do not experience the loss of the husband through divorce or death.

There are only questions for this problem. What ought to be the proper relation between work and marriage? How should work in the home be defined and how should it be economically provided for so as to fit within the framework of modern economic life? How should the marriage contract be combined with the home labor contract? How should training be chosen so as neither to handicap the married women in the home nor to handicap all women at large?

THE HOME ORGANIZATION DILEMMA

The home organization of the wife who works outside the home also constitutes a problem. It is true that in many cases the woman's own wages enable her to pay a servant to substitute for her in the home. A testimony in that direction is the common experience that the best domestic servants flock to the homes of professional women. So profitable may such division of labor be, utilizing the best fitted for the household tasks, that the net burden of housework under such circumstances becomes much smaller for the married woman than for the unmarried one. In a comprehensive survey of women teachers the Swedish Committee on Women's Work found that the unmarried teachers were far more subjected to household chores than the married ones. While 37 per cent of the unmarried teachers in the higher grades and 69 per cent of those in the primary grades managed their households singlehanded, this was the case in only 11 per cent and 25 per cent of the corresponding married groups. This left the married teachers more time for recreation, for study, or for that extra burden which is children.

To solve working mothers' home problems or any family problems by servants will, however, be possible only for a small group and not at all possible for that majority which takes employment when the husband's income is too low. Also, this solution is becoming increasingly impracticable as servants become more expensive and less accessible, and as, on account of their legitimate demands for regularity in amount of work and of leisure, they become less and less fitted for that flexibility which is considered the very charm of having a household of one's own. The old-fashioned virtue of liberal and irregular hospitality is being just as efficiently drained out of the modern homes which are dependent upon servants as it was once made possible by those very servants. In that respect, unimportant as it is in comparison with the larger issues under discussion, it will become important to gain flexibility by attaching one's own need of services to an enterprise on a larger scale than the small private unit of one family's home.

Pooling of household work would appeal even more to the working woman with regard to her children. She knows that optimum care for her children is much more difficult to buy than expert care for her material needs. She is particularly aware that the person engaged for the one series of these tasks will seldom be the right one also for the other series. But the types of service are only possible in another organizational structure than that of ordinary private households. Translated into the world of reality, this means simply cooperation among many households. Urban housing for those families which contain working wives could easily be transformed into more rational family houses with cooperative service. More differentiation on the housing market is needed for serving that large proportion of families who do not have a full-time person assigned to home duty.

The younger families in Sweden have been looking for some kind of household organization with more cooperation for the work but just as much, or really more, of the family privacy retained. Neither the private servant nor the public day nursery quite fits their needs. Instead of the private servant for the individual family, there is a tendency to organize household work and child supervision cooperatively for several families through some sort of collective or cooperative apartment house with a nursery for the children. Particularly as the whole trend as to occupations for women is to increase the middle-class groups—lighter work in industry, decreased work in agriculture, increased employment in clerical work, social service, and professions—some such intermediary step between private luxury and public charity becomes a crying need.

This new form of housing organization has not only been advocated in Sweden, but it has already been developing. A number of the housing projects belonging to the Cooperative Housing Society have in varying degrees met the needs through cooperative nurseries, through shops for ready-to-serve or half-prepared food, and other services. A privately organized cooperative society built the first collective house in 1934 with one large kitchen serving meals both in a restaurant and through food elevators directly in the private apartments, with floor maids to be engaged by the hour, with a common nursery, and with other cooperative devices. Lately the business and professional women in Stockholm have built a novel family house according to a similar scheme. Because of the joint nursery, the workshop for fathers, and other homelike details, but above all because of the cooperative administration, these houses have a distinctly different character from apartment hotels.

This is arguing from a new angle for the same scheme which has been treated at length in the previous chapter as providing mothers with opportunity for relaxation or time for work and providing the children in small families and restricted environments with educative facilities for enriching their lives. There is no doubt that a functional setup could be established which would be far more adequate for the modern type of family than the present vain attempt at urban imitation of the closed family unit on a country estate.

THE PSYCHOLOGICAL DILEMMA

To rectify the organizational forms of housekeeping to take cognizance of the fact that for some women the tie between marriage and homework is dissolved will take both decades and tremendous courage and open-mindedness. The relations between husband and wife when both are engaged in gainful work will probably take still longer to settle harmoniously. Looking at it practically, however, an improvement in this psychological adjustment could really be effected through reforms in verbalisms concerning the family, in the deeply propagandistic advertisements and comics, and in the teachings of home, school, and church about the natural superiority of men and their duty of being sole supporters. As it now is, few are educated or mentally prepared for the new mode of family living.

Within the homes the change to be expected is a mutually helpful division of the laborious family tasks which cannot be farmed out to paid persons. This is already taking place, although no country in the Old World can yet compete with the New World in the domestic helpfulness of its men. The proposals in Sweden, by both the Population Commission and the Committee on Women's Work, that boys be given courses in home economics and family relations is one important step in that direction. These proposals are being indefatigably pushed by the powerful organizations of housewives, of women teachers, and of professional women. Such instruction will be valuable not only for the practical help in the home but even more for changing popular attitudes concerning sex and marriage and the role of women.

The psychological relation of the working mother to her children, finally, is not necessarily a difficult one. But as a certain tension is observable, it may be that some subtle changes in public opinion are needed, so that real companionship and not only number of hours spent in common shall become most highly valued in the relation between parents and children.

The most disquieting questions as to psychological satisfaction are not those concerning the working mothers. Given time, a practical will to reform less important details in life and some adaptation to the new partnership marriages will probably result in the emergence of a fairly stable organization for family life. What is more puzzling to the young woman considering her future married life is her status if a homemaker. What was called the economic dilemma of the homemaker also has a psychological aspect. When the homemaker chooses the lot of dependence, she chooses dependence on some one individual. How will that dependence work out in terms of mental tensions and satisfactions? How long is a woman going to accept the fact that when young so much of her life is organized just to "catch" a man and become married? Could her life be rearranged so as to give her a more clearly definable status? Could marriage be made to require real "man-sized" tasks of women? How are women to endure the lack of a schematic network of daily work routine, such as characterizes other strata of life? How are they going to stand that time distribution which scatters much of their work when the rest of the world is at leisure and gives them leisure at odd hours when nobody else has it? How are they going to adjust to the fact that they have the hardest job and the least freedom of movement when young and when they are so close to the period when they were freely playing around? How are they going to get help in their job of caring for the children when small? And how are they going to get some tasks to put meaning into their lives when the children are gone? How are they going to avoid aging too early, when their life-chosen tasks of marriage and childbearing so often end in their early forties or fifties? How can security be gained and equality reached if only the man is going to be incorporated in the complex economic world? Can that sort of life still be made truly personal and filled with primary satisfactions or will it have to decline into a life secondary in character, thus breeding secret dissatisfaction?

These problems may seem willfully exaggerated, but they are already at work in the subconscious of wives and of all women. They play an indubitable, even if indefinable, role in attitudes with regard to childbearing among women today. As they have been listed here, they give hints of a complicated pattern of brooding over riddles, never solved and rarely even openly expressed. Introducing a new form of marriage where most of the determinants causing troubles and questions are done away with will by comparison expose the problems of the more old-fashioned family. Reviewing all discussions on the problem, "Should married women work?" this seems to be the fundamental dilemma: that *the very existence of one type of marriage begs the question as to the other type.* This criticism works both ways, making both kinds of wives unduly uncertain of themselves. The irritation noticeable in all the discussion about the working mother may in the last instance be attributable to that very threat which men and women feel against the marriage type so long taken for granted.

That such uncertainty exists with regard to the whole field of married women's status is of tremendous importance for the population problem itself. This was the implication drawn by some women members of the Population Commission who published as a separate appendix an analysis and an accusation called "The Crisis of Women." If it is true, and it seems to be from the wealth of discussion in fiction, magazines, and books on the subject, that mothers are in danger of becoming a mentally malcontent group, no population program can remain indifferent. It might then happen that, despite all income equalization for children, despite all of society's solicitude for mothers and children, the whole population program might fail because women are fundamentally dissatisfied with the status defined for them. There is in the end the danger that it might be one day said of the Swedish Population Commission that it failed to tackle the very problems of marriage itself.

Summarizing what may be expected from these women themselves in regard to the future of Swedish population, it is believed that the reforms called into being in Sweden will help them better to combine motherhood and remunerative work. The practical difficulties are so numerous, however, that there will probably be a long transitional period when women will either have to shun too heavy maternal responsibilities or give up their gainful work. The risk is great that society will proceed so slowly in solving these problems of women's existence that new and even more desperate crises may invade the whole field of women, family, and population.

Talcott Parsons (1902–1979) on Sex in the United States Social Structure

Talcott Parsons was a major twentieth-century sociologist whose theories were very influential in the 1940s and 1950s, after which his work came under increasing criticism. His father was a liberal Congregational minister and professor at Colorado College, and his mother, an activist in feminist and progressive causes. The family later moved to New York City, where Talcott graduated from a high school associated with Columbia University's Teachers College. He entered Amherst College with the intention of majoring in biology, but in his junior year he discovered the social sciences and changed his plans. Following graduation from Amherst in 1924, he attended London School of Economics and later the University of Heidelberg, Germany, for a doctorate.

In 1927 Parsons returned to the United States to accept an instructor position in economics at Harvard. He remained in low-ranked non–tenure-track positions for nine years at Harvard, first in economics and later in sociology. In 1935 his materials were evaluated for appointment to the tenure-track faculty, and he was granted such an appointment (without tenure), over the resistance of Pitirim Sorokin and others. Parsons eventually received tenure and left the sociology department to head a new department of social relations. He remained at Harvard until his death in 1979.

Parsons was a functionalist whose theoretical contributions were highly abstract and often tedious to read. These writings emphasized a notion of society as an interlocking series of "systems" of action, each functioning according to certain system rules. His analyses often focused on the consequences of action for the survival of the system or for parts of the system, and how change in one part of the system stimulates adjustments in other, related system parts. He thought a great deal about these issues in his writings about the development of societies through the gradual process of modernization. For example, his discussions of family functions focused on how the family contributes to the stability of society, and how as the economic system evolved from agricultural to industrial, previous family functions were taken over by other more specialized institutions such as the economy, education, religious institutions, and civic institutions. Among his important themes were the notions of *differentiation* and *specialization:* as societies progress or develop, their institutions tend to become differentiated (more complex in structure) and specialized (each has more narrow and specific functions, but they are performed more efficiently as a result).

Although Parsons is usually remembered for his abstract "grand theories," he wrote a number of essays that were more limited in scope and accessible to broader audiences. A collection of these is published as *Essays in Sociological Theory* (Free Press, 1949, 1954). Two essays in that volume reprinted from *American Sociological Review* articles originally published in 1942 and 1943 deal in part with gender issues: "Age and Sex in the Social Structure of the United States" (1942) and "The Kinship System of the Contemporary United States" (1943). Parsons also coauthored with Robert Bales a book, *Family, Socialization, and Interaction Process* (1954), which contains some of his thinking about gender and the roles of men and women in "the modern family."

Major Works

Parsons, Talcott. *The Structure of Social Action.* Glencoe, IL: Free Press, 1949.

———. *Essays in Sociological Theory.* Glencoe, IL: Free Press, 1949/1954.

Parsons, Talcott, and Edward A. Shils, eds. *Toward a General Theory of Action.* Cambridge: Harvard University Press, 1951.

Parsons, Talcott. *The Social System.* Glencoe, IL: Free Press, 1951.

Parsons, Talcott and Robert F. Bales. *Family, Socialization and Interaction Process.* Glencoe, IL: The Free Press, 1955.

Parsons, Talcott. *Personality and Social Structure.* Glencoe, IL: Free Press, 1964.

———. *The System of Modern Societies.* Upper Saddle River, NJ: Prentice Hall, 1971.

Sources

Adams, Bert N., and R. A. Sydie. 2002. *Contemporary sociological theory.* Thousand Oaks, CA: Pine Forge.

Smelser, Niel J., and Paul B. Baltes, eds. 2001. *International encyclopedia of the social and behavioral sciences.* New York: Elsevier.

The Selection

Parsons elaborates on several themes in the following extracts, painting a rather bleak picture of adult sex roles in middle-class America. First, he argues that most of the differences in the responsibilities and privileges of children in the United States are not based on sex but on age and birth order, with boys and girls treated very similarly. In the modern urban setting, the sexes are becoming more equal, as earlier differences in dress and play activities are diminishing. Such differences as exist are the result of adult sex role differentiation between mothers, who usually remain home with young children, and fathers, who are less available to children owing to their work. This makes it easier for girls to learn the "feminine role" than for boys to learn expectations of masculinity.

From Talcott Parsons, "Age and Sex in the Social Structure of the United States," *American Sociological Review* 7 (October 1942): 604–14. © 1942. Reprinted by permission of The American Sociological Association.

Parsons points out that most educational experiences are very similar for boys and girls, except for education that has vocational relevance. However, sex differentiation begins to emerge during early adolescence and is greatly expanded at marriage. Adolescent girls are subjected to much more supervision than boys. For boys, athletics becomes important and for girls, the "glamour girl" pattern is a means of seeking to attract the opposite sex. These relatively free and easy youth roles contrast with the adult roles, which are distinctively less "glamorous" for both sexes.

The "normal" adult male role involves a job, by which not only his own status is determined, but that of his family as well. For women, the adult role is radically different, because the majority of wives are not employed. This is a relatively new pattern characterizing the urban middle class, differing from the traditional pattern of rural farm society in which running the farm was the responsibility of the entire family. In that setting, when a husband died, the widow would usually continue operating the farm; this economic continuity is not possible in the urban setting.

For the urban adult woman, the primary available role is that of housewife and mother. The dependence of the family on the occupation of the husband-father alone is a source of significant strain, "since it deprives the wife of her role as a partner in a common enterprise" and she is reduced to the "pseudo-occupation" of household management. This pattern has become unattractive for many women.

Since a woman's status is determined largely by marriage, her marriage is the "single event toward which" her early life is pointed. One source of strain in women's role is the lack of a clear definition of what they are supposed to do, with the various options of glamour, domesticity, and good companionship competing for their attention even after marriage.

The masculine role has its own strains, even though it has better prospects for prestige, achievement, and authority. However, the increasing specialization of occupations often leads to boredom and nostalgia for youthful freedom. Another result of specialization is that the average man has little in common with his wife. This lack of common interest may encourage her to seek other sources of gratification, such as involvement in domesticity, community, or other activities not involving her husband. The differentiation of adult sex roles then leads to strains in marriage itself. "It is notable that brilliance of conversation . . . is not prominent" in our society, notes Parsons.

This article is a good example of functionalist theorizing. Parsons criticizes adult sex roles in terms of "strains" due to specialization, but he never mentions such possible sources of these problems as power differences, exploitation, conflicts of interest, or discrimination, as might a conflict theorist or feminist thinker. The activities women engage in to compensate for the strains in their roles are viewed as an adjustment to the situation produced by system demands.

AGE AND SEX IN THE SOCIAL STRUCTURE OF THE UNITED STATES

In all societies the initial status of every normal individual is that of child in a given kinship unit. In our society, however, this universal starting point is used in distinctive ways. Although in early childhood the sexes are not usually sharply differentiated, in many kinship systems a relatively sharp segregation of children begins very early. Our own society is conspicuous for the extent to which children of both sexes are in many fundamental respects treated alike. This is particularly true of both privileges and responsibilities. The primary distinctions within the group of dependent siblings are those of age. Birth order as such is notably neglected as a basis of discrimination; a child of eight and a child of five have essentially the privileges and responsibilities appropriate to their respective age levels without regard to what older, intermediate, or younger siblings there may be. The preferential treatment of an older child is not to any significant extent differentiated if and because he happens to be the first born.

There are, of course, important sex differences in dress and in approved play interest and the like, but if anything, it may be surmised that in the urban upper middle classes these are tending to diminish. Thus, for instance, play overalls are essentially similar for both sexes. What is perhaps the most important sex discrimination is more than anything else a reflection of the differentiation of adult sex roles. It seems to be a definite fact that girls are more apt to be relatively docile, to conform in general according to adult expectations, to be "good," whereas boys are more apt to be recalcitrant to discipline and defiant of adult authority and expectations. There is really no feminine equivalent of the expression "bad boy." It may be suggested that this is at least partially explained by the fact that it is possible from an early age to initiate girls directly into many important aspects of the adult feminine role. Their mothers are continually about the house and the meaning of many of the things they are doing is relatively tangible and easily understandable to a child. It is also possible for the daughter to participate actively and usefully in many of these activities. Especially in the urban middle classes, however, the father does not work in the home and his son is

not able to observe his work or to participate in it from an early age. Furthermore many of the masculine functions are of a relatively abstract and intangible character, such that their meaning must remain almost wholly inaccessible to a child. This leaves the boy without a tangible meaningful model to emulate and without the possibility of a gradual initiation into the activities of the adult male role. An important verification of this analysis could be provided through the study in our own society of the rural situation. It is my impression that farm boys tend to be "good" in a sense in which that is not typical of their urban brothers.

The equality of privileges and responsibilities, graded only by age but not by birth order, is extended to a certain degree throughout the whole range of the life cycle. In full adult status, however, it is seriously modified by the asymmetrical relation of the sexes to the occupational structure. One of the most conspicuous expressions and symbols of the underlying equality, however, is the lack of sex differentiation in the process of formal education, so far, at least, as it is not explicitly vocational. Up through college differentiation seems to be primarily a matter on the one hand of individual ability, on the other hand of class status, and only to a secondary degree of sex differentiation. One can certainly speak of a strongly established pattern that all children of the family have a "right" to a good education, rights which are graduated according to the class status of the family but also to individual ability. It is only in post-graduate professional education, with its direct connection with future occupational careers, that sex discrimination becomes conspicuous. It is particularly important that this equality of treatment exists in the sphere of liberal education since throughout the social structure of our society there is a strong tendency to segregate the occupational sphere from one in which certain more generally human patterns and values are dominant, particularly in informal social life and the realm of what will here be called community participation.

Although this pattern of equality of treatment is present in certain fundamental respects at all age levels, at the transition from childhood to adolescence new features appear which disturb the symmetry of sex roles while still a second set of factors appears with marriage and the acquisition of full adult status and responsibilities.

An indication of the change is the practice of chaperonage, through which girls are given a kind of protection and supervision by adults to which boys of the same age group are not subjected. Boys, that is, are chaperoned only in their relations with girls of their own class. This modification of equality of treatment has been extended to the control of the private lives of women students in boarding schools and colleges. Of undoubted significance is the fact that it has been rapidly declining not only in actual effectiveness but as an ideal pattern. Its prominence in our recent past, however, is an important manifestation of the importance of sex role differentiation. Important light might be thrown upon its functions by systematic comparison with the related phenomena in Latin countries where this type of asymmetry has been far more sharply accentuated than in this country in the more modern period.

It is at the point of emergence into adolescence that there first begins to develop a set of patterns and behavior phenomena which involve a highly complex combination of age grading and sex role elements. These may be referred to together as the phenomena of the "youth culture." Certain of its elements are present in pre-adolescence and others in the adult culture. But the peculiar combination in connection with this particular age level is unique and highly distinctive for American society.

Perhaps the best single point of reference for characterizing the youth culture lies in its contrast with the dominant pattern of the adult male role. By contrast with the emphasis on responsibility in this role, the orientation of the youth culture is more or less specifically irresponsible. One of its dominant notes is "having a good time" in relation to which there is a particularly strong emphasis on social activities in company with the opposite sex. A second predominant characteristic on the male side lies in the prominence of athletics, which is an avenue of achievement and competition which stands in sharp contrast to the primary standards of adult achievement in professional and executive capacities. Negatively, there is a strong tendency to repudiate interest in adult things and to feel at least a certain recalcitrance to the pressure of adult expectations and discipline. In addition to, but including, athletic prowess the typical pattern of the male youth culture seems to lay emphasis on the value of certain qualities of attractiveness, especially in relation to the opposite sex. It is very definitely a rounded humanistic pattern rather than one of competence in the performance of specified functions. Such stereotypes as the "swell guy" are significant of this. On the feminine side there is correspondingly a strong tendency to accentuate sexual attractiveness in terms of various versions of what may be called the "glamor girl" pattern. Although these patterns defining roles tend to polarize sexually—for instance, as between star athlete and socially popular girl—yet on a certain level they are complementary, both emphasizing certain features of a total personality in terms of the direct expression of certain values rather than of instrumental significance.

One further feature of this situation is the extent to which it is crystallized about the system of formal education. One might say that the principal centers of prestige dissemination are the colleges, but that many of the most distinctive phenomena are to be found in high schools throughout the country. It is of course of great importance that liberal education is not primarily a matter of vocational training in the United States. The individual status on the curricular side of formal education is, however, in fundamental ways linked up with adult expectations, and doing "good work" is one of the most important sources of parental approval. Because of secondary institutionalization this approval is extended into various spheres distinctive of the youth culture. But it is notable that the youth culture has a strong tendency to develop in directions which are either on the borderline of parental approval or beyond the pale, in such matters as sex behavior, drinking and various forms of frivolous and irresponsible behavior. The fact that adults have attitudes to these things which are often deeply ambivalent and that on such occasions as college reunions they may outdo the younger generation, as, for instance, in drinking, is of great significance, but probably structurally secondary to the youth-versus-adult differential aspect. Thus the youth culture is not only, as is true of the curricular aspect of formal education, a matter of age status as such but also shows strong signs of being a product of tensions in the relationship of younger people and adults.

From the point of view of age grading perhaps the most notable fact about this situation is the existence of definite pattern distinctions from the periods coming both before and after. At the line between childhood and adolescence "growing up" consists precisely in ability to participate in youth culture patterns, which are not for either sex, the same as the adult patterns practiced by the parental generation. In both sexes the transition to full adulthood means loss of a certain "glamorous" element. From being the athletic hero or the lion of college dances, the young man becomes a prosaic business executive or lawyer. The more successful adults participate in an important order of prestige symbols but these are of a very different order from those of the youth culture. The contrast in the case of the feminine role is perhaps equally sharp, with at least a strong tendency to take on a "domestic" pattern with marriage and the arrival of young children.

The symmetry in this respect must, however, not be exaggerated. It is of fundamental significance to the sex role structure of the adult age levels that the normal man has a "job" which is fundamental to his social status in general. It is perhaps not too much to say that only in very exceptional cases can an adult man be genuinely self-respecting and enjoy a respected status in the eyes of others if he does not "earn a living" in an approved occupational role. Not only is this a matter of his own economic support but, generally speaking, his occupational status is the primary source of the income and class status of his wife and children.

In the case of the feminine role the situation is radically different. The majority of married women, of course, are not employed, but even of those that are a very large proportion do not have jobs which are in basic competition for status with those of their husbands.[1] The majority of "career" women whose occupational status is comparable with that of men in their own class, at

---

[1] The above statement, even more than most in the present paper, needs to be qualified in relation to the problem of class. It is above all to the upper middle class that it applies. Here probably the great majority of "working wives" are engaged in some form of secretarial work which would, on an independent basis, generally be classed as a lower middle class occupation. The situation at lower levels of the class structure is quite different since the prestige of the jobs of husband and wife is then much more likely to be nearly equivalent. It is quite possible that this fact is closely related to the relative instability of marriage which Davis and Gardner (*Deep South*) find, at least for the community they studied, to be typical of lower class groups. The relation is one which deserves careful study.

least in the upper middle and upper classes, are unmarried, and in the small proportion of cases where they are married the result is a profound alteration in family structure.

This pattern, which is central to the urban middle classes, should not be misunderstood. In rural society, for instance, the operation of the farm and the attendant status in the community may be said to be a matter of the joint status of both parties to a marriage. Whereas a farm is operated by a family, an urban job is held by an individual and does not involve other members of the family in a comparable sense. One convenient expression of the difference lies in the question of what would happen in case of death. In the case of a farm it would at least be not at all unusual for the widow to continue operating the farm with the help of a son or even of hired men. In the urban situation the widow would cease to have any connection with the organization which had employed her husband and he would be replaced by another man without reference to family affiliations.

In this urban situation the primary status-carrying role is in a sense that of housewife. The woman's fundamental status is that of her husband's wife, the mother of his children, and traditionally the person responsible for a complex of activities in connection with the management of the household, care of children, etc.

For the structuring of sex roles in the adult phase the most fundamental considerations seem to be those involved in the interrelations of the occupational system and the conjugal family. In a certain sense the most fundamental basis of the family's status is the occupational status of the husband and father. As has been pointed out, this is a status occupied by an individual by virtue of his individual qualities and achievements. But both directly and indirectly, more than any other single factor, it determines the status of the family in the social structure, directly because of the symbolic significance of the office or occupation as a symbol of prestige, indirectly because as the principal source of family income it determines the standard of living of the family. From one point of view the emergence of occupational status into this primary position can be regarded as the principal source of strain in the sex role structure of our society since it deprives the wife of her role as a partner in a common enterprise. The common enterprise is reduced to the life of the family itself and to the informal social activities in which husband and wife participate together. This leaves the wife a set of utilitarian functions in the management of the household which may be considered a kind of "pseudo-" occupation. Since the present interest is primarily in the middle classes, the relatively unstable character of the role of housewife as the principal content of the feminine role is strongly illustrated by the tendency to employ domestic servants wherever financially possible. It is true that there is an American tendency to accept tasks of drudgery with relative willingness, but it is notable that in middle class families there tends to be a dissociation of the essential personality from the performance of these tasks. Thus, advertising continually appeals to such desires as to have hands which one could never tell had washed dishes or scrubbed floors. Organization about the function of housewife, however, with the addition of strong affectional devotion to husband and children, is the primary focus of one of the principal patterns governing the adult feminine role—what may be called the "domestic" pattern. It is, however, a conspicuous fact, that strict adherence to this pattern has become progressively less common and has a strong tendency to a residual status—that is, to be followed most closely by those who are unsuccessful in competition for prestige in other directions.

It is, of course, possible for the adult woman to follow the masculine pattern and seek a career in fields of occupational achievement in direct competition with men of her own class. It is, however, notable that in spite of the very great progress of the emancipation of women from the traditional domestic pattern only a very small fraction have gone very far in this direction. It is also clear that its generalization would only be possible with profound alterations in the structure of the family.

Hence it seems that concomitant with the alteration in the basic masculine role in the direction of occupation there have appeared two important tendencies in the feminine role which are alternative to that of simple domesticity on the one hand, and to a full-fledged career on the other. In the older situation there tended to be a very rigid distinction between respectable married women and those who were "no better than they should be." The rigidity of this line has progressively broken down through the infiltration into the respectable sphere of elements of what may be called again the glamor pattern, with the emphasis on a specifically feminine form of attractiveness which on occasion involves directly sexual patterns of appeal. One important expression of this trend lies in the fact that many of the symbols of feminine attractiveness have been taken over directly from the practices of social types previously beyond the pale of respectable society. This would seem to be substantially true of the practice of women smoking and of at least the modern version of the use of cosmetics. The same would seem to be true of many of the modern versions of women's dress. "Emancipation" in this connection means primarily emancipation from traditional and conventional restrictions on the free expression of sexual attraction and impulses, but in a direction which tends to segregate the element of sexual interest and attraction from the total personality and in so doing tends to emphasize the segregation of sex roles. It is particularly notable that there has been no corresponding

tendency to emphasize masculine attraction in terms of dress and other such aids. One might perhaps say that in a situation which strongly inhibits competition between the sexes on the same plane the feminine glamor pattern has appeared as an offset to masculine occupational status and to its attendant symbols of prestige. It is perhaps significant that there is a common stereotype of the association of physically beautiful, expensively and elaborately dressed women with physically unattractive but rich and powerful men.

The other principal direction of emancipation from domesticity seems to lie in emphasis on what has been called the common humanistic element. This takes a wide variety of forms. One of them lies in a relatively mature appreciation and systematic cultivation of cultural interests and educated tastes, extending all the way from the intellectual sphere to matters of art, music and house furnishings. A second consists in cultivation of serious interests and humanitarian obligations in community welfare situations and the like. It is understandable that many of these orientations are most conspicuous in fields where through some kind of tradition there is an element of particular suitability for feminine participation. Thus, a woman who takes obligations to social welfare particularly seriously will find opportunities in various forms of activity which traditionally tie up with women's relation to children, to sickness and so on. But this may be regarded as secondary to the underlying orientation which would seek an outlet in work useful to the community following the most favorable opportunities which happen to be available.

This pattern, which with reference to the character of relationship to men may be called that of the "good companion," is distinguished from the others in that it lays far less stress on the exploitation of sex role as such and more on that which is essentially common to both sexes. There are reasons, however, why cultural interests, interest in social welfare and community activities are particularly prominent in the activities of women in our urban communities. On the one side the masculine occupational role tends to absorb a very large proportion of the man's time and energy and to leave him relatively little for other interests. Furthermore, unless his position is such as to make him particularly prominent his primary orientation is to those elements of the social structure which divide the community into occupational groups rather than those which unite it in common interests and activities. The utilitarian aspect of the role of housewife, on the other hand, has declined in importance to the point where it scarcely approaches a full-time occupation for a vigorous person. Hence the resort to other interests to fill up the gap. In addition, women, being more closely tied to the local residential community are more apt to be involved in matters of common concern to the members of that community. This peculiar role of women becomes particularly conspicuous in middle age. The younger married woman is apt to be relatively highly absorbed in the care of young children. With their growing up, however, her absorption in the household is greatly lessened, often just at the time when the husband is approaching the apex of his career and is most heavily involved in its obligations. Since to a high degree this humanistic aspect of the feminine role is only partially institutionalized it is not surprising that its patterns often bear the marks of strain and insecurity, as perhaps has been classically depicted by Helen Hokinson's cartoons of women's clubs.

The adult roles of both sexes involve important elements of strain which are involved in certain dynamic relationships, especially to the youth culture. In the case of the feminine role marriage is the single event toward which a selective process, in which personal qualities and effort can play a decisive role, has pointed up. That determines a woman's fundamental

status, and after that her role patterning is not so much status determining as a matter of living up to expectations and finding satisfying interests and activities. In a society where such strong emphasis is placed upon individual achievement it is not surprising that there should be a certain romantic nostalgia for the time when the fundamental choices were still open. This element of strain is added to by the lack of clear-cut definition of the adult feminine role. Once the possibility of a career has been eliminated there still tends to be a rather unstable oscillation between emphasis in the direction of domesticity or glamor or good companionship. According to situational pressures and individual character the tendency will be to emphasize one or another of these more strongly. But it is a situation likely to produce a rather high level of insecurity. In this state the pattern of domesticity must be ranked lowest in terms of prestige but also, because of the strong emphasis in community sentiment on the virtues of fidelity and devotion to husband and children, it offers perhaps the highest level of a certain kind of security. It is no wonder that such an important symbol as Whistler's mother concentrates primarily on this pattern.

The glamor pattern has certain obvious attractions since to the woman who is excluded from the struggle for power and prestige in the occupational sphere it is the most direct path to a sense of superiority and importance. It has, however, two obvious limitations. In the first place, many of its manifestations encounter the resistance of patterns of moral conduct and engender conflicts not only with community opinion but also with the individual's own moral standards. In the second place, it is a pattern the highest manifestations of which are inevitably associated with a rather early age level—in fact, overwhelmingly with the courtship period. Hence, if strongly entered upon serious strains result from the problem of adaptation to increasing age.

The one pattern which would seem to offer the greatest possibilities for able, intelligent, and emotionally mature women is the third—the good companion pattern. This, however, suffers from a lack of fully institutionalized status and from the multiplicity of choices of channels of expression. It is only those with the strongest initiative and intelligence who achieve fully satisfactory adaptations in this direction. It is quite clear that in the adult feminine role there is quite sufficient strain and insecurity so that widespread manifestations are to be expected in the form of neurotic behavior.

The masculine role at the same time is itself by no means devoid of corresponding elements of strain. It carries with it to be sure the primary prestige of achievement, responsibility and authority. By comparison with the role of the youth culture, however, there are at least two important types of limitations. In the first place, the modern occupational system has led to increasing specialization of role. The job absorbs an extraordinarily large proportion of the individual's energy and emotional interests in a role the content of which is often relatively narrow. This in particular restricts the area within which he can share common interests and experiences with others not in the same occupational specialty. It is perhaps of considerable significance that so many of the highest prestige statuses of our society are of this specialized character. There is in the definition of roles little to bind the individual to others in his community on a comparable status level. By contrast with this situation, it is notable that in the youth culture common human elements are far more strongly emphasized. Leadership and eminence are more in the role of total individuals and less of competent specialists. This perhaps has something to do with the significant tendency in our society for all age levels to idealize youth and for the older age groups to attempt to imitate the patterns of youth behavior.

It is perhaps as one phase of this situation that the relation of the adult man to persons of the opposite sex should be treated. The effect of the specialization of occupational role is to narrow the range in which the sharing of common human interests can play a large part. In relation to his wife the tendency of this narrowness would seem to be to encourage on her part either the domestic or the glamorous role, or community participation somewhat unrelated to the marriage relationship. This relationship between sex roles presumably introduces a certain amount of strain into the marriage relationship itself since this is of such overwhelming importance to the family and hence to a woman's status and yet so relatively difficult to maintain on a level of human companionship. Outside the marriage relationship, however, there seems to be a notable inhibition against easy social intercourse, particularly in mixed company. The man's close personal intimacy with other women is checked by the danger of the situation being defined as one of rivalry with the wife, and easy friendship without sexual-emotional involvement seems to be inhibited by the specialization of interests in the occupational sphere. It is notable that brilliance of conversation of the "salon" type seems to be associated with aristocratic society and is not prominent in ours.

Along with all this goes a certain tendency for middle-aged men, as symbolized by the "bald-headed row," to be interested in the physical aspect of sex—that is, in women precisely as dissociated from those personal considerations which are important to relationships of companionship or friendship, to say nothing of marriage. In so far as it does not take this physical form, however, there seems to be a strong tendency for middle-aged men to idealize youth patterns—that is, to think of the ideal inter-sex friendship as that of their pre-marital period.

Joseph Kirk Folsom (1893–1960) on Wives' Changing Roles

The son of a clergyman, Joseph Kirk Folsom was a family sociologist who authored a number of widely used family textbooks in the 1930s and 1940s, including *The Family* (1934) and *The Family in Democratic Society* (1943). Howard W. Odum includes these books in his list of "Leading Sociology Authors and Texts on Marriage and the Family" in his book *American Sociology* (1951:314–15). Although Folsom was not widely known outside of this field, he had a strong influence on the early development of family sociology through these and other writings.

Folsom received his bachelor of science degree from Rutgers University in 1913, followed by a master's degree from Clark College (1915) and a PhD from Columbia University (1917). During World War I, he was a psychological examiner in the army, with the rank of lieutenant. Following completion of his doctorate, he taught at the University of Pittsburgh, Dartmouth, and Sweet Briar College, where he served as professor and head of economics and sociology.

In 1931 he joined the sociology faculty at Vassar, where he spent the remainder of his career until 1959. Folsom was involved in advocacy and applied work, serving on the boards of the National Council of Parent Education, the American Eugenics Society, and the *American Sociological Review,* which he edited in 1943. Folsom died in June of 1960 after he had just completed teaching a course at Boston University on "The Family." As the reading demonstrates, Folsom was familiar with the history of feminism and was a strong supporter of improving the position of women in the interest of justice, freedom, and democratic values.

MAJOR WORKS

Folsom, Joseph Kirk. *Culture and Social Progress,* New York: Longman's, Green., 1928.
———. *The Family: Its Sociology and Social Psychiatry.* New York: Wiley, 1934.
———, ed. *Plan for Marriage: An Intelligent Approach to Marriage and Parenthood.* New York: Harper, 1938.

SOURCES

Odum, Howard W. 1951. *American Sociology.* New York: Longman's, Green.

New York Times. 1960. Joseph K. Folsom, a sociologist, 66. Obituary, June 4, 23.

THE SELECTION

The following reading, from *The Family in Democratic Society* (1943), is a critical analysis of the changing roles of women and men in the early 1940s and an argument for the continuing need for a feminist movement. Joseph Kirk Folsom argues that women's entry into the labor market is mainly due to economic pressures and that the employment of married women should not be restricted. He outlines the history of "modern feminism" (beginning with Mary Wollstonecraft) and describes the gradual entry of women into work outside the home, criticizing the continuing problems for women workers, such as lower pay for the same work, lack of access to the best jobs, unequal family burdens for women, and the continued economic dependence of women on their husbands. Folsom's comment that "many say feminism has sufficiently served its purpose; we do not need to go farther" sounds familiar today, although we may be surprised that it was written in 1943.

Folsom warns that the gains made by feminism are threatened by conservative trends of the time resulting partly from economic depression and high unemployment. He notes the increasing (unrealistic) claims in various media which assert that women who retreat to the home are happier than those who are employed. "The ominous feature" of this "neo-familism" is that it can be used to suppress the movement toward equal opportunity for women, he asserts.

Folsom goes on to describe sex categories as "castes," the sex division in our society resembling the racial division between blacks and whites. Folsom is skeptical of conclusions that biological differences dictate different occupations and statuses for men and women. Indeed, he claims boldly, backing the claim with evidence, that "socially relevant sex differences are entirely cultural."

Next Folsom discusses the notion of "justice" and "freedom," arguing that these are lacking for women. He believes that much of the resistance by men to women's equality has to do with their sexual conditioning to seek "restricted, dumb, and docile women" as sex objects, a belief he finds unsupportable. Another obstacle to women's equality, he argues, has to do with the fear of women as competitors for positions that traditionally had been monopolized by men.

Finally, Folsom describes the choices for the future as between fascism and democracy: "Shall we, or shall we not, remove discriminations . . . which prevent in practice the equal opportunity we have long espoused in theory?" He describes the theories of Otto Weininger, whose notions of biologically

From Joseph Kirk Folsom, "Of Men and Women," *The Family in Democratic Society* (New York: Wiley, 1943), 613–34.

determined sex differences were incorporated into Nazism, as representing the antithesis of democracy. Folsom then makes a strong plea for women's equality in the postwar period. His purpose in the chapter was to show the fallacies and dangers of arguments for essential sex differences and determinate roles, but in the end Folsom's fears were realized when women's gains of the 1930s and 1940s were eclipsed and erased in the conservative era of the 1950s. By that decade, even the major sociology textbooks contained no such explicitly feminist analysis as we find in Folsom's work. This chapter is all the more remarkable for the relevance of its reasoning to later decades. The resistance to feminism that he describes in the 1940s seems familiar to readers in the early twenty-first century, and the warnings he issued give us pause today.

OF MEN AND WOMEN

ECONOMIC PRESSURE IS THE DIRECT CAUSE OF WOMEN'S LEAVING THE HOME

We have considered the frustrations of homemaking in women's work. At the same time, many women are pulled out of the home regardless of their inclinations and even against them by the need for extra family income. This need may be for sheer adequacy of food and other necessities, or it may be the urge to maintain a higher standard of living. Coit and Harper [1930], asking several hundred married women why they worked outside the home, found that economic pressure far outweighed other reasons such as interest in outside work or being "lonesome at home." Most of them earned because they were obliged to. A study of the family incomes of our country explains this pressure to earn—one-third below $780 per year and two-thirds below $1,450.[1] The majority of earning women occupy jobs to earn food and shelter for themselves and their families. The next largest group strive to raise their families' scale of living beyond the bare essentials: for example, to obtain a better home, to provide a washing machine, or keep an adolescent from having to leave school to earn.

A study of 12,000 women in business and professional life was made in 1937. It revealed that one-half of them were supporting wholly or in part someone besides themselves.[2]

Indeed, advertising, instalment buying and credit economy, and the whole psychological atmosphere created by modern business stimulate the desire for additional luxuries, and impel some childless wives, or mothers of older children, to raise the family living scale through extra money rather than through economies, home production, and self-service. This is in line with the general trend of industrialism, urbanism, and personal specialization of labor, which has made the modern world what it is. This whole trend

---

[1]National Resources Committee, *Consumer Incomes in the United States,* 1938, p. 10.
[2]Public Affairs Committee, *Why Women Work,* 1938, p. 16. Based on a study by the National Federation of Business and Professional Women's Clubs, Inc.

may find its natural limits, or it may prove wise to check and divert it, but Democracy insists that it be controlled without discrimination between the sexes.

Probably, for their own welfare and that of their families, we should have an increased number of business-class wives earning outside the home, either part or full time, and fewer working-class wives than at present. The latter might better be aided to permit them to care for their families at home. Housework, given adequate facilities, is probably better for the physical and emotional health of mothers when there are young children, and gives greater scope for intelligence than most of the jobs women perform in factories, stores, and domestic and personal service. On the other hand, the more educated woman can often find more scope for her abilities outside the home. Society would gain by providing her with greater opportunity. Some educated women, however, have the personality which finds satisfaction, and not excessive tension, in the administration of home tasks. When there are young children, home is the center of their concern, and they are usually happiest there during a large part of every day.

No Sound Argument for Restricting Employment of Married Women

One of the most unsound and prejudicial attitudes found in our society is the protest against the employment of married women. It is claimed that these working wives cause the unemployment of men and single women. This is unsound reasoning. In times of depression the refusal to employ married women may seem to spread employment and keep down the number of families needing relief. Yet it also holds down the purchasing power of those families whose women are not employed but

could be, and the net result is no better. The effects are obvious when the discharge of the married woman worker leads to the discharge of a servant she may be employing at home. If an industry employs a married woman rather than a man, presumably it gets more efficiency that way. In the last analysis the difference lies not in the total amount of relief, but in *which* family shall be on relief and *which* family shall help to maintain employment, purchasing power, and taxable income through its greater purchasing power.

In ordinary times the employment of married women merely helps to provide the needed labor supply of expanding industry. We do not protest against a gradual increase of population on the ground that it creates unemployment. From the economic point of view, married women are the same as any other part of the total labor supply. The industrial nations have grown to several times their population of two centuries ago, and have employed practically their full labor supply at each successive period of prosperity.

Cecile Lafollette [1934] found that her 652 married women home-makers supported 676 dependents and employed 540 servants and other workers. The employment of women outside the home, if it takes jobs which others might have, also *creates* new jobs. Moreover, most of the women who do earn outside the home need the jobs as much as any other competitor might need them.

The protest against giving particular kinds of jobs to married women is unsound for additional reasons. Since they are more limited in their mobility, society might rather give them preference in many jobs, so that it could make use of their services while allowing them also to be with their families. In the case of school teachers, the mother, other things being equal, has a personality and experience better fitted to deal with children than has the unmarried woman. The avowedly married teacher has also a better influence upon the students than she would have if frustrated by the postponement of her marriage because she needs to keep her job, or if worried by trying to conceal a secret marriage or a liaison unblessed by clergy.

The Federal Marital Status Law, which declared that husband and wife may not both work for the government, was charged with encouraging illicit cohabitation. The attacker declared that he personally knew of nine such cases, and that the marriage rate among government employees was falling; but a congressman retorted that "men have been tarred and feathered in this country for saying less than that."[3] Soon thereafter the law was changed.

Lorine Pruette [1924] has recommended the deliberate policy of establishing part-time jobs for married women.

In New York and Philadelphia, bureaus of part-time work for women have been established. The fees from placed individuals cover a little more than half of the expenses of these bureaus. In 1928 the New York bureau had 2,000 new registrations, and 2,400 available jobs were reported to it by employers. The principal kinds of work were stenography, typing, and other clerical work, the care of children, teaching and tutoring, and selling. [Pruette, 1929.]

However, the actual opportunities for part-time jobs are far less than the potential workers because industry resists the idea, as it does the policy of shorter hours in general. The resistance is a complicated one, involving the unwillingness of employers to set a precedent of a short working day even though they have to shut down their plants for whole weeks at a time, and their reluctance to shoulder the extra expense of training a larger personnel per hour of labor performed.

THE "CAREER" IDEOLOGY HAS DECLINED

In a questionnaire to 150 Vassar seniors in 1937, Nancy Phillips asked:

> Under the following conditions would you choose to combine an outside vocation with homemaking, including child raising? If (1) you could earn at least $1,500 a year; (2) make the extra income pay for all additional expenses in connection with the children, e.g., nursery school, governess, etc.; (3) have sufficient time out from your work for child bearing, nursing, etc.; (4) have a six hour day so that you could have several hours a day with your children?

Seventy-three said *yes,* 70 *no.* A personal check-up of the girls who had not answered the questionnaire showed that they too were evenly divided. People who answered no were much more vehement than those who answered yes.

Janet Fowler Nelson noted in 1938 a marked change in the attitudes of young couples in the groups with which she deals. Four years previously the men, with the traditional male pride in being able to support their wives, were reluctant to let them work, and the girls wanted to do so. In 1938, with the same economic need, objections were coming from the girls, who resented the willingness of their fiancés to accept this financial help and were afraid that a situation eagerly embraced for the early marriage years might become permanent.[4]

From Pennsylvania State College in 1936 came the report of a poll of 190 senior women among whom the majority opinion

---

[3]*New York Times,* April 28, 1935.
[4]*New York Times,* November 27, 1938.

was "that a young woman cannot continue her business career after her wedding . . . except in the case of real financial need."[5]

Yet Mary Fisher, in a yet unpublished study of 50 homemaking and 50 professionally occupied college women with children, found that the latter actually spent slightly longer hours per week with their children than did the former.[6] There were no substantial differences between the homemakers and earners as regards health or the problems of their children. The 50 homemakers had 104 children, and the 50 earners 74. Such data are often used to show that working mothers cut down the birth rate, but of course it is equally possible that mothers who for various other reasons have fewer children are the ones most likely to take jobs.

The "marriage versus career" formula is a red herring drawn across the trail of the real issue. Most women will choose marriage, if they must choose. The advantages and disadvantages of both alternatives are well known. Rather it would be humane and democratic if public opinion were to bolster up and support each individual in her own personal and difficult choice, and at the same time support measures making such choice less necessary.

If women in increasing numbers work outside the home, a great deal of this work will be in the same fields in which they worked in the home, but it will be more specialized and organized in a more rational way. The nursery school, the laundry, and the restaurant are examples.

The "career" ideology has declined for men also. No longer are boys brought up on the Alger and Henty books, which suggest that any boy can become President and that only the "right attitude" is necessary to insure a steady rise from office boy to general manager. Men as well as women are learning that vocational life is unpredictable and subject to many forces outside their control. They are learning to seek security and meaning by preparing themselves for some broad group of occupations, and for marriage, parenthood, leisure, and citizenship. [Folsom, 1941, 7.]

Needed: A Continuous Educational Program for Mothers

A most urgent need is for a program of part-time work and education for women during years when their children are young, to prepare them for later years. Such a program should help them to keep in contact with the special field for which they earlier prepared themselves and in which they perhaps engaged before marriage. The Bassett study indicates that the great majority would continue in this same field if they returned to outside work after their children were grown.

A woman before marriage was well on the road to becoming a dean or a college president. After many years of successful marriage, raising of children, and sharing with her husband a career full of rich social contacts and constructive experiences, she became a widow. Now she finds herself limited to a low-paying job in a preparatory school. Her interruption of the established ritual of academic degrees and promotions sets her back in the professional scale in spite of the fact that she may be really better qualified than many who go through the usual sequence.

---

[5] *New York Times,* November 15, 1936.
[6] Earning mothers engage service for cooking, cleaning, and laundry, and this substitution for their own labor does not change the amount of time they have available for children. They are more likely to plan so as to give the children periods when they can enjoy the full attention of their mothers.

A rough analysis of the records of several hundred married college alumnae has shown that at least a fourth of them by the age of fifty have suffered either widowhood, divorce, serious family illness, or financial set-back, or other misfortunes which would not have been economically disastrous if these women had maintained their earning power and vocational contacts. In other words, these women, however personally satisfied, were economically deceived by marriage; and their potential contribution to society in terms of a whole lifetime has failed to be what it might be merely because they trusted too much in "marriage" without "career." We may say that during the child-raising years they rendered the service which society most needed from them; it is regrettable that this fact should prevent them from rendering their best service and getting an appropriate reward during the later years.

These facts commend themselves to the attention of college girls who put their whole faith in marriage and, still more, to our colleges which think in terms of preparing women for "either" marriage "or" career. We need less of this distinction and more preparation for life. The problem of women's education is basically the same for all women and is more complex than that of men's education. It involves training for both marriage and a vocation, which *should* be equally true of the education of men. But with women there is an additional problem: namely, woman's education should arouse inner forces of personality which will enable her to maintain through homemaking and child-raising the mental alertness, the vocational contacts, the continuous and cumulative study of a given field, which will allow her to be a creative and happy citizen after 40 and to contribute in her chosen field.

At Smith College from 1925 to 1928, Ethel Puffer Howes [1928, A, 1928, B, 1929] operated an Institute for the Coordination of Women's Interests. This provided a cooperative nursery group, and a cooked food service adjusted to moderate incomes in order to free the time of mothers and enable them to study or earn.

Many are skeptical of such efforts because, they say, with all these aids a mother of small children cannot carry on a "career" in competition with the men. She may perhaps "work" for money, and she may even hold a "job," in Mrs. Howes' terms, but a "career" requires a ruthlessness toward her family which few women have or want. But mere "work" outside the home may be of great value to the community and to the woman herself.

The world which lies before us may be less a competitive world for men as well as women, and rather a world which will need every person to do whatever he or she can do, whether it be a full-time or part-time job outside the home. Work will be carried on to fill human needs rather than for profit, and "the devil take the balance sheet."

IDEOLOGY IS MORE IMPORTANT THAN JOBS

We may expect that for many years to come women's vocational opportunities will fluctuate and they will drift from the home and back again as economic conditions change. Women in some regions shift seasonally between home and canning factories, or between field work and housework, to a much greater extent than we realize. Men also shift in the same way. They also show large cyclical fluctuations of paid employment. In years of depression, women, adolescents, and men, who would otherwise be earning money, stay home and do what they can by way of repair, construction, and other self-services for which there is not time in periods of brisk employment.

In several European countries, before the war, women were employed outside the home much more than in the United States, and yet they had less of sex equality. The more important question is the ideology or scheme of cultural values which governs the roles and relations of men and women both in and outside the home. What people are actually doing at the moment may be less important than what they have the right to do. The ideology of the social roles and relations of the sexes is of crucial importance. It is both a symbol and an important content of the democratic culture system.

The modern feminist movement is sometimes dated as beginning in 1798, with Mary Wollstonecraft's *Vindication of the Rights of Women*, which opens with these words:

> Contending for the rights of woman, my main argument is built on this simple principle, that if she be not prepared by education to become the companion of man, she will stop the progress of knowledge and virtue.

In 1848 was held the first Women's Rights Convention. Elizabeth Cady Stanton, Lucretia Mott, Jane Hunt. Charlotte Perkins Gilman, Carrie Chapman Catt, and others have carried on the torch. . . .

The nineteenth century was devoted largely to removing political and legal disabilities. Some leaders devoted themselves to getting special protective legislation for women employed in factories, and this was an opening wedge to the securing of similar legislation later for men. These achievements relieved the most crying needs of women; that is, they made some restrictions on hours and wages which helped the groups of poor women with little education, most of whom were carrying the double job of raising a family and earning. Such protective legislation was merely the beginning of a movement to provide some of the most fundamental needs of women. Several legal inequalities were removed during that period. When the Woman Suffrage Amendment came in 1920, many people thought that feminism had now reached its goal.

In the late nineteenth century many women entered lines of earning previously occupied by men only. Some of them remained unmarried in order to do so. These women emphasized their need for independence and opportunity to work in their fields of interest; they had strong influence in the liberal arts colleges for women. Other women developed the home economics movement and thereby sought to give professional status, or at least a professional ideology, to the work of the married woman in the home.

Women slowly drifted into occupations outside the home, and certain occupations, such as elementary school teaching and secretarial work in this country, came to be definitely women's occupations. In World War I the women went temporarily into many occupations formerly alien to them, and then were discharged or withdrew without greatly changing the traditions by their war work. Many occupations are still practically barred to women through custom and at the same time men shamefacedly try to withdraw from vocations which get to be known as feminine. Women, however, are not ashamed of being in men's occupations and do not try to withdraw from them, although they may be forced to do so. This very fact is evidence of the real subjection of women, however much it may be hidden beneath our lip-service to "sex equality" and Democracy.

The major economic limitations upon women are now: (1) lower pay for the same work, (2) the reservation of positions of greater skill and authority mainly for men, (3) the customary family pattern, which is supported by the common law and which in practice limits most mothers of young children to the one occupation of housekeeping, with compensation at the discretion of the husband as long as he provides a certain minimum known as "support," and (4) the economic dependence of the mother upon the ability and life of her husband.

There is still a long distance to go, as we can see when we compare our own or British laws with those of Sweden and Russia. Yet many say feminism has sufficiently served its purpose; *we* do not need to go farther. In the 1920's this let-well-enough-alone school of thinkers could point, although not with logic, to peace, prosperity, and a world made "safe for Democracy."

Yet the threat of authoritarianism and Fascism is causing intelligent women, and the more thoroughgoing believers in Democracy of both sexes, to revive their thinking about the woman problem. The present roles of the sexes in America are ambiguous and confused, and it may be that if we do not go forward to a more outright sex equality, we shall be forced backward.

THE GAINS MADE BY FEMINISM ARE THREATENED

. . . During the 1930's there were many subtle ideological influences working against the democratic trend in the relation between the sexes. The idea was widely expressed that women have gone far enough toward equality and some have held that the situation is now unfair to men. These tendencies may be due in part to depression and unemployment, but they can easily be capitalized for ulterior ends. . . .

A number of articles have appeared in the more serious popular magazines recently, presenting the experiences of women who have had jobs and then retired to the home to live more happily thereafter. [Anon., 1939.] But experiences of the reverse pattern are not so well publicized.

In 1938 the newspapers featured a girl of 17, just entering college, who had been chosen in a contest sponsored by a New York store from a thousand competitors to represent the "Ideal American College Girl." Over her picture was the caption, "Ideal College Girl Puts Marriage before a Career,"

and then it was explained below that this attitude was one of the requirements drawn up by the sponsors.

That college girls should idealize marriage, before marriage, and prefer to make child-raising their main job is in itself highly desirable. There is a good chance that the economic needs of *their* families will be supplied. The ominous feature is that this neo-familism, cultivated by the schools and colleges, can be used through upper class prestige and adroit publicity to bring into disrepute the movement for equal opportunity and thus prepare the way for a resubjection of women.

Let us recall now our discussion of homemaking. We saw that as an occupation it has lagged in development and has acquired features which tend to make it frustrating to a large proportion of persons practicing it, regardless of who they are.

MEN AND WOMEN CONSTITUTE CASTES

Regardless of how far we may be able to reorganize homemaking or make it more satisfying, there is the question of whether and why it should be almost exclusively a woman's job.

Our Western culture, like the great majority of all cultures, embodies a sex-division of labor which is not merely a result of the natural process of interaction in millions of individual situations, but is also definitely crystallized as a value. This is more than a mere division of labor; it is part of a complete pattern of differentiation including dress, personality, social role, and style of living. This, as Margaret Mead [1935] points out, may enrich culture but it often cramps individuality.

It is in the nature of human society to categorize individuals, in terms of sex, age, kinship, economic function, social rank, and other factors. Large civilized societies have additional differentiations according to race, language, and religion. Some of these categories, in some societies, are *castes;* that is, people are born into them to stay. Some societies have relatively few caste lines and the general trend and motive of the democratic movement has been to reduce caste and to give social mobility to the individual. In our American society the only caste lines remaining completely intact are two: the line between White and Negro, and the line between Males and Females.

TO WHAT DEGREE ARE SEX DIFFERENCES BIOLOGICAL?

The persistence of the sexes as castes is of course strongly bulwarked by the fact that they constitute two distinct biological forms. To most thinkers, including even social scientists, this is a finality about which no further thought is necessary. It is only recently that cultural anthropology has become a dynamic force in our social science, and not many of our social scientists have yet seen its full implications. These are two: *first,* the roles of women and men can be prescribed in many extremely different ways as demonstrated by actual practice in various cultures; and *second,* cultural patterns are only indirectly and loosely tied to biological sex-differences. Biology makes patriarchy a more "natural" (i.e., frequent) development than sex-equality, but it does not make it inevitable; it takes only one culture to refute the hypothesis of inevitability. . . .

Therefore, as students of sociology let us free ourselves from one of the deepest surviving prejudices of our culture, and consider objectively how much of the difference between the sexes is fixed by "eternal laws of nature." Briefly stated, women must bear the children, and they must nurse them. (Even the latter can be eliminated but it is not desirable.) Population replacement calls for the average marrying woman to have three children. This, on good health standards, might

require from three to six years of her life to be reserved, without any other demanding activity. Yet woman has three years longer in her average lifetime than does man. . . .

Women through history have surprised men with their ability to perform tasks, when given an opportunity, which have formerly been regarded as beyond their sphere. Women's performance in certain lines of manufacturing at present is an example. . . .

It would be unscientific to deny the possibility of a genuine, inborn, temperamental difference between the averages of the two sexes, although this is less than many such differences between individuals of the same sex. Yet human occupations and social roles are such that a wide range of temperament can fit into almost any occupation or role. . . . Not many occupations in modern society require a narrowly defined personality type to fill them, and when they do, persons can very well be selected according to their personal qualifications unprejudiced by their sex. . . .

However, there remains the question whether the temperamental differences of the sexes might produce desirable cultural changes if large numbers of men and women were to change roles as they well might if we abolished all prejudice. For example, the suffragists argued that women would have a humanizing influence upon public policy and many anti-feminists claim that the "feminine" influence has "softened" the democracies. The "emotional instability" which the psychological tests seem to find in women is, partly, a greater sensitiveness to stimuli which arouse fear, anguish, or disgust. This might cause women to shrink more from inflicting pain and to work harder for measures alleviating suffering. It may also be related to the disapproval of women executives, by many women as well as men, on the dubious ground that an executive needs to be "hard-boiled" and not too sensitive emotionally. If there is a constitutional sex difference of this kind, as many people in both the feminist and anti-feminist camps believe, it would argue for placing women in the majority in our legislative bodies and executive offices dealing with human relations, leaving the men to staff the engineering and military services where some ruthlessness might be useful. However, many who place large stress upon native sex differences will not accept this implication of their theory.

In any event, however, representative democratic government would seem to call for proportional representation of women in legislative and judicial bodies. If women are "more interested in social relationships," as Terman claims, they might well introduce a constructive influence.

SOCIALLY RELEVANT SEX DIFFERENCES ARE ENTIRELY CULTURAL

Margaret Mead [1935] has given us a most significant exhibit of evidence in her study of three primitive societies. Among the Arapesh both men and women are gentle and "feminine" in the Euro-American sense; among the Mundugumor both sexes are harsh, aggressive, and "masculine" in our sense. Among the lake-dwelling Tchambuli, our roles are reversed; the men are artists and graceful dancers, they are coquettish, and they leave sexual initiative largely to women. In a group of men there are strain, watchfulness, and petty quarrels; the women are efficient, comradely, and jolly. The men remain much of the time in the seclusion of the men's house, and they depend upon the women for support, food, and affection.

The Tchambuli are a small tribe, but they are enough to upset a world-wide fallacy.

Let it be said here quite emphatically that no school of thought, so far as this writer knows, wants to make the sexes as nearly alike as possible. But since sex differences are cultural we may consider which ones we might desire to abolish and which to retain and perhaps even intensify. Democ-

racy requires that this decision be made in accordance with three governing principles: justice, freedom, and sexual attraction.

DEMOCRACY AND SEX DIFFERENCES

Few thinkers have fully seen the problem of *justice* between the sexes. One who has is the Russian writer Nemilov [1930]. In *The Biological Tragedy of Women* he points out that biological nature has actually been unjust to woman by giving her the entire pain and bodily risk of reproduction. But nature is not governed by any law of justice. Justice is a value which grows out of human intelligence and even then it does not develop fully until all caste patterns are swept away. A completely democratic culture is completely human and implies Nemilov's principle that women should be compensated for their biological burden. He says: "It is absolutely necessary to go beyond social equality and seek such patterns of life which might alleviate the 'tragedy of sex.'"

Because her body is called upon to carry on the continued life stream of the race, in all fairness woman should have special assistance and protection at times of pregnancy, childbirth, nursing, and other periods when her reproductive organs are making serious demands on her vitality. But it does not mean that she lacks desire for the fundamental opportunities for a full physical, emotional, and mental life. At present there is no rational plan for the life of women. Social justice, which is far from realized among people in general, is still more lacking as among women. A young mother with a few-weeks-old baby and no helper usually has far too much work in relation to her strength, whereas the older woman whose children have left home often has too little. Strong mothers with great ability and health are often led by our cultural influences to a life of petty refinements. Worn and tired women with young children work in our factories.

Burgess and Cottrell [1939, 341] whose marital prediction study had purposes quite other than finding any general relation between the sexes as such, obtained as "an outstanding, if not the most significant finding," that "wives make the major adjustment in marriage." . . . They speculate that perhaps our apparent equality in marriage is superficial, that the domineering wife and "henpecked" husband is a pattern characterizing only a small proportion of marriages. The findings imply that the majority of wives are making concessions and adjustments to please their husbands.

The principle of *freedom* also demands more than a mere balancing or equalizing of the two sexes. It requires that each person be given a choice from the full range of occupations, social roles, and other opportunities of which he or she is *personally* capable. It is not satisfied to give the sexes equally green pastures; it removes the fence between the pastures. The traditional pattern is not only *unfair* to women; it is also *oppressive* to women and in some degree to men.

The principle of *sex attraction* can be left till last because it is able to make use of whatever is left after justice and freedom are satisfied. Like esthetic principles it is exceedingly flexible in its use of methods. Anything which does not seriously hamper or unbalance justice and freedom could be chosen as an erotic value. Differences in dress, perfume, and manners, added to the biological differences of voice and bodily form, admirably satisfy these criteria. If desired, these differences could be made qualitatively even more extreme, while at the same time they might be arranged to provide equality of cost, of comfort, and of dressing time.

SEX DIFFERENCES AND EROTIC FIXATIONS

. . . Perhaps the deepest root of the resistance of men to changing the status of women is their sexual conditioning. Are they unconsciously afraid that the supply of "real women" will decrease, making for serious male sexual competition? The assumption here is that only restricted, dumb, and docile women can be true sex objects. Many educated women know this, and by cleverly feigning a naivete which is not theirs, they help to perpetuate this male attitude.

But we know full well that erotic stimuli are subject to change. In fact they are considerably a matter of fashion and not altogether of long, slow trends. A magazine like *Esquire*, which reflects the current fetishisms, can also subtly guide their changes.

Research should be undertaken to tell us more about these erotic fixations of men as regards the social role and rank of women they prefer. Certainly there is no uniformity or inevitability; and certainly there is no reason so far to regard as unnatural or difficult a widespread erotic fixation of men upon intelligent women who share with them equally positions of social power and prestige. Some of the most admired love affairs have been of this type, such as that of Robert and Elizabeth Browning.

INTER-SEX COMPETITION AND ANTAGONISM

But perhaps the difficulty to be feared lies not so much in women's being "higher" or "lower" than men as in their competing with men for the same positions. Competition naturally leads to more or less conflict, and conflict is not conducive to sex attraction. . . .

Let us grant for the moment [the] thesis that woman's most appropriate role under modern social change is a "projection of home tasks into the larger community." What, concretely, does this mean?

Years ago spinning and weaving were projected from the home into the larger community. Women went with their original tasks into the textile factories. But men took over the management of the industry, and plenty of men were also employed in the laboring ranks. Some of the preparation of food was projected into restaurants. Here men took over very largely as managers and chefs, kitchen workers, and waiters, and women have increasingly been employed as waitresses, but lately many women have come to manage tea houses and the like. Child care was projected partly into the elementary school, the kindergarten, and the nursery school. Here women "followed their occupations out of the home," but men still largely manage the school system. Laundry work was projected; women operate laundries and men manage them. The situation is similar in the food industries.

The rather considerable variety of industries into which women go outside the home tends to conceal their rather uniform subordination within each industry they enter. Men can dominate women not only within the home, but also outside. They are less secure in their domination, however, when women are outside, because there the women earn money and have mobility. Their situation as earners is open to public view. Trade unions and managers of competitive businesses are concerned with women's hours and wages. . . .

It was only by conflict that women obtained the suffrage, which almost everyone today admits to be their logical right. Perhaps a few women will always have to sacrifice their "femininity," whatever that is, for the sake of their fellow women who will thereby benefit. . . .

Democracy will not be served by any policy which limits women to some particular field which is "auxiliary" or "complementary" or somehow contingent upon men's prior choice, whether this field be in the home or outside the home.

THE ALTERNATIVES BEFORE US

If we want to maintain population it is quite possible that we shall be obliged either to subordinate one sex much more completely than now to authority and a limited role (and let us guess which one it would be!), or we must attain some more stabilized level of inter-sex justice, personal freedom, and happiness. The present ambiguous relation between the sexes wobbles dangerously on a divide.

The dilemma is part and parcel of the larger issue between Fascism and Democracy. To say that the question of the roles of men and women can be postponed until that larger issue is settled is to ignore an important part of the strategy which will determine the final outcome. Our practical war policies in regard to the use of women are encouraging. The danger lies in what happens after the war is over and the men come home and look for jobs. But the ideological preparation for that event can begin now.

The question regarding men and women is essentially similar to the question regarding races and culture groups and that regarding social classes. Shall we, or shall we not, remove discriminations—legal, economic, social and moral—which prevent in practice the equal opportunity we have long espoused in theory? Shall we have the courage to use the agencies which form our public opinion, not only to build morale for fighting the foreign enemy, as we are doing, but also to discredit the scientifically disproved ideology on which his whole program is based? If so, we shall wage relentless ideological warfare upon all myths alleging the superiority or the special mental limitations of some race, sex, or other class of human beings. . . .

We in this country have dedicated ourselves . . . to seek to understand all groups, to furnish them with opportunity for life and growth, and to bring about human brotherhood. It is a long and complicated task but the only one which recognizes the sacredness of the individual and the only one which contains the possibility of peace. It offers the greatest hope for the continued life of the human race.

Pearl Buck [1941, 202–203] suggests a companionship of free men and free women working together on equal terms in all the processes of life. Democracy requires justice and equality not only between races, nations, and classes, but between the two most basic divisions of mankind: men and women. Indeed, the prophets have been saying something like this since the days of Mary Wollstonecraft. But, although our social values have been changed in this direction, and sex equality has come to be regarded as *desirable,* the forces of reaction have found new weapons for a last-ditch resistance and possible counter-revolution. These weapons are fashioned in the image of Science. They consist of two pseudo-scientific arguments.

The first is that social sex equality, even if desirable, is *impossible* because of the biological differences between the sexes. The *belief* that something is impossible of course tends to weaken the *value* which asserts that it is desirable. The second pseudo-scientific argument is that we already have sex equality—indeed that we have something like a matriarchate with the women lording it over the men.

The two arguments, of course, contradict each other, but one is used in one setting and with one audience, and the other elsewhere. It has been the purpose of this chapter to expose their fallacy and thus to help clear the way for what we have accepted as our value scheme and our goal—what we call Democracy.

Gunnar Myrdal (1898–1987) on Sex as a Parallel to Race

Gunnar Myrdal was primarily an economist, trained in law and economics in his native Sweden. Born in 1898 in Gustaf's parish, Sweden, he attended law school in Stockholm, earning a doctorate of jurisprudence in 1927. He first visited the United States in 1929 as a Rockefeller Fellow. During that year he published his first book, a study of economic development theory. After he returned to Europe, he held a number of academic posts in Switzerland and Sweden. Apart from teaching, Myrdal was active in Swedish politics winning election to the Senate in 1934 as a Social Democrat.

In 1938, Myrdal was commissioned by the Carnegie Corporation of New York to do a major study of race in the United States, focusing on "the Negro problem," which was published in 1944 as *An American Dilemma: The Negro Problem and American Democracy*. In that book, Myrdal argued that American democracy contained an inherent contradiction as long as it refused to admit African Americans to full equality.

He also criticized many of the New Deal economic policies for their effects on African Americans, especially in the rural South.

After this famous study, Myrdal returned to Sweden (1942) and was again active in Swedish politics: he was re-elected to the Senate, chaired the Post-War Planning Commission, was the minister of commerce (1945–1947), and executive secretary of the UN Economic Commission for Europe, among other outstanding accomplishments. In the late 1950s he led a study of Asian economic trends for the Twentieth Century Fund. In his later years, he continued to work in academia as well as international policy and politics, both in Europe and the Americas. Winner of many prizes and awards, his most outstanding recognition was the Nobel Prize for Economics in 1974 for his contributions to economic theory. He was married to Alva Myrdal, a sociologist and important Swedish and international political figure, herself a Nobel Peace laureate.

MAJOR WORKS

Gunnar Myrdal. *Population: A Problem for Democracy.* Cambridge, MA: Harvard University Press, 1940.

————. *An American Dilemma: The Negro Problem and American Democracy.* New York: Harper, 1944.

————. *Economic Theory and Underdeveloped Regions.* London: Duckworth, 1957.

————. *The Challenge of World Poverty.* New York: Pantheon Books, 1960.

————. *Asian Drama: An Inquiry into the Poverty of Nations and the Challenge of World Poverty; The Political Element in the Development of Economic Theory.* New York: Twentieth Century Fund, 1968.

THE SELECTION

Although *An American Dilemma* is widely recognized as a sociological classic in the study of race, very little attention has been given to Appendix 5 in the book, titled "A Parallel to the Negro Problem." In that brief but cogent chapter, Gunnar Myrdal compares the situation of American women to that of African Americans. His opening statement reveals his feminist orientation:

> In every society there are at least two groups of people . . . who are characterized by high social visibility expressed in physical appearance, dress, and patterns of behavior, and who have been "suppressed." We refer to women and children.

Myrdal goes on to draw parallels between women and African Americans, pointing out that the legal status of women, children, and slaves was historically comparable. The subordination of both women and African Americans to white men was justified historically as being the "will of God" and as necessary to good social order. Myrdal also notes that the rights of women and slaves were similarly restricted, especially the denial of the rights to education, to property, to

political participation, and to the control over their children. Here he quotes Dolly Madison as saying that in the South the plantation owner's wife was "the chief slave of the harem." Myrdal further observes that the fight to end slavery was often associated with the struggle for women's rights as well.

Myrdal argues that both women and African Americans were subordinated under a paternalistic system associated with the agrarian economy, a subordination that became increasingly less feasible with the Industrial Revolution and the move to urban settings. However, in terms of women's status, there were continuing problems to be worked out in terms of family reorganization and ideological change to fit the new urban economic realities. Ideologically, most white men had accepted the idea that women were inferior to men in abilities, and they seemed to prefer personalized, traditional interactions with women rather than professional ones, reflecting certain atavistic elements in the culture. In the end, Myrdal argues that women are hindered by the function of procreation, although he fails to point out clearly that it is the *social organization* of

From Gunnar Myrdal, "A Parallel to the Negro Problem," Appendix 5 in *An American Dilemma: The Negro Problem and American Democracy* (New York: Harper, 1944, 1962): 1073–78 procreation and childrearing that is the issue, not procreation itself. Still, Myrdal's short essay is an interesting and largely ignored analysis of sex inequality in American society. The following selection is a slightly edited version of the original.

A PARALLEL TO THE NEGRO PROBLEM

In every society there are at least two groups of people, besides the Negroes, who are characterized by high social visibility expressed in physical appearance, dress, and patterns of behavior, and who have been "suppressed." We refer to women and children. Their present status, as well as their history and their problems in society, reveal striking similarities to those of the Negroes. In studying a special problem like the Negro problem, there is always a danger that one will develop a quite incorrect idea of its uniqueness. It will, therefore, give perspective to the Negro problem and prevent faulty interpretations to sketch some of the important similarities between the Negro problem and the women's problem.

In the historical development of these problem groups in America there have been much closer relations than is now ordinarily recorded. In the earlier common law, women and children were placed under the jurisdiction of the paternal power. When a legal status had to be found for the imported Negro servants in the seventeenth century, the nearest and most natural analogy was the status of women and children. The ninth commandment—linking together women, servants, mules, and other property—could be invoked, as well as a great number of other passages of Holy Scripture. We do not intend to follow here the interesting developments of the institution of slavery in America through the centuries, but merely wish to point out the paternalistic idea which held the slave to be a sort of family member and in

some way—in spite of all differences—placed him beside women and children under the power of the *paterfamilias*.

There was, of course, even in the beginning, a tremendous difference both in actual status of these different groups and in the tone of sentiment in the respective relations. In the decades before the Civil War, in the conservative and increasingly antiquarian ideology of the American South, woman was elevated as an ornament and looked upon with pride, while the Negro slave became increasingly a chattel and a ward. The paternalistic construction came, however, to good service when the South had to build up a moral defense for slavery, and it is found everywhere in the apologetic literature up to the beginning of the Civil War. For illustration, some passages from George Fitzhugh's *Sociology for the South,* published in 1854, may be quoted as typical:

> The kind of slavery is adapted to the men enslaved. Wives and apprentices are slaves; not in theory only, but often in fact. Children are slaves to their parents, guardians and teachers. Imprisoned culprits are slaves. Lunatics and idiots are slaves also.

> A beautiful example and illustration of this kind of communism, is found in the instance of the Patriarch Abraham. His wives and his children, his men servants and his maid servants, his camels and his cattle, were all equally his property. He could sacrifice Isaac or a ram, just as he pleased. He loved and protected all, and all shared, if not equally, at

least fairly, in the products of their light labour. Who would not desire to have been a slave of that old Patriarch, stern and despotic as he was? . . . Pride, affection, self-interest, moved Abraham to protect, love and take care of his slaves. The same motives operate on all masters, and secure comfort, competency and protection to the slave. A man's wife and children are his slaves, and do they not enjoy, in common with himself, his property?

Other protagonists of slavery resort to the same argument:

In this country we believe that the general good requires us to deprive the whole female sex of the right of self-government. They have no voice in the formation of the laws which dispose of their persons and property. . . . We treat all minors much in the same way. . . . Our plea for all this is, that the good of the whole is thereby most effectually promoted. . . .[1]

Significant manifestations of the result of this disposition [on the part of the Abolitionists] to consider their own light a surer guide than the word of God, are visible in the anarchical opinions about human governments, civil and ecclesiastical, and on the rights of women, which have found appropriate advocates in the abolition publications. . . . If our women are to be emancipated from subjection to the law which God has imposed upon them, if they are to quit the retirement of domestic life, where they preside in stillness over the character and destiny of society; . . . if, in studied insult to the authority of God, we are to renounce in the marriage contract all claim to obedience, we shall soon have a

country over which the genius of Mary Wolstonecraft would delight to preside, but from which all order and all virtue would speedily be banished. There is no form of human excellence before which we bow with profounder deference than that which appears in a delicate woman, . . . and there is no deformity of human character from which we turn with deeper loathing than from a woman forgetful of her nature, and clamourous for the vocation and rights of men.[2]

. . . Hence her [Miss Martineau's] wild chapter about the "Rights of Women," her groans and invectives because of their exclusion from the offices of the state, the right of suffrage, the exercise of political authority. In all this, the error of the declaimer consists in the very first movement of the mind. "The Rights of *Women*" may all be conceded to the sex, yet the rights of *men* withheld from them.[3]

The parallel goes, however, considerably deeper than being only a structural part in the defense ideology built up around slavery. Women at that time lacked a number of rights otherwise belonging to all free white citizens of full age.

So chivalrous, indeed, was the ante-bellum South that its women were granted scarcely any rights at all. Everywhere they were subjected to political, legal, educational, and social and economic restrictions. They took no part in governmental affairs, were without legal rights over their property or the guardianship of their children, were denied adequate educational facilities, and were excluded from business and the professions.[4]

---

[1]Charles Hodge, "The Bible Argument on Slavery," in E. N. Elliott (editor), *Cotton Is King, and Pro-Slavery Arguments* (1860), pp. 859–860.

[2]Albert T. Bledsoe, *An Essay on Liberty and Slavery* (1857), pp. 223–225.

[3]W. Gilmore Simms, "The Morals of Slavery," in *The Pro-Slavery Argument* (1853), p. 248. See also Simms' "Address on the Occasion of the Inauguration of the Spartanburg Female College," August 12, 1855.

[4]Virginius Dabney, *Liberalism in the South* (1932), p. 361.

The same was very much true of the rest of the country and of the rest of the world. But there was an especially close relation in the South between the subordination of women and that of Negroes. This is perhaps best expressed in a comment attributed to Dolly Madison, that the Southern wife was "the chief slave of the harem."[5]

From the very beginning, the fight in America for the liberation of the Negro slaves was, therefore, closely coordinated with the fight for women's emancipation. It is interesting to note that the Southern states, in the early beginning of the political emancipation of women during the first decades of the nineteenth century, had led in the granting of legal rights to women. This was the time when the South was still the stronghold of liberal thinking in the period leading up to and following the Revolution. During the same period the South was also the region where Abolitionist societies flourished, while the North was uninterested in the Negro problem. Thereafter the two movements developed in close interrelation and were both gradually driven out of the South.

The women suffragists received their political education from the Abolitionist movement. Women like Angelina Grimke, Sarah Grimke, and Abby Kelly began their public careers by speaking for Negro emancipation and only gradually came to fight for women's rights. The three great suffragists of the nineteenth century—Lucretia Mott, Elizabeth Cady Stanton, and Susan B. Anthony—first attracted attention as ardent campaigners for the emancipation of the Negro and the prohibition of liquor. The women's movement got much of its public support by reason of its affiliation with the Abolitionist movement: the leading male advocates of woman suffrage before the Civil War were such Abolitionists as William Lloyd Garrison, Henry Ward Beecher, Wendell Phillips, Horace Greeley and Frederick Douglass. The women had nearly achieved their aims, when the Civil War induced them to suppress all tendencies distracting the federal government from the prosecution of the War. They were apparently fully convinced that victory would bring the suffrage to them as well as to the Negroes.[6]

The Union's victory, however, brought disappointment to the women suffragists. The arguments "the Negro's hour" and "a political necessity" met and swept aside all their arguments for leaving the word "male" out of the 14th Amendment and putting "sex" alongside "race" and "color" in the 15th Amendment. Even their Abolitionist friends turned on them, and the Republican party shied away from them. A few Democrats, really not in favor of the extension of the suffrage to anyone, sought to make political capital out of the women's demands, and said with Senator Cowan of Pennsylvania, "If I have no reason to offer why a Negro man shall not vote, I have no reason why a white woman shall not vote." Charges of being Democrats and traitors were heaped on the women leaders. Even a few Negroes, invited to the women's convention of January, 1869, denounced the women for jeopardizing the black man's chances for the vote. The War and Reconstruction Amendments had thus sharply divided the women's problem from the Negro problem in actual politics. The deeper relation between the two will, however, be recognized up till this day. Du Bois' famous ideological manifesto *The Souls of Black Folk* is, to mention only one example, an ardent appeal on behalf of women's interests as well as those of the Negro.

---

[5] Cited in Harriet Martineau, *Society in America* (1842, first edition 1837), Vol. II, p. 81.
[6] Carrie Chapman Catt and Nettie Rogers Shuler, *Woman Suffrage and Politics* (1923), pp. 32 ff.

This close relation is no accident. The ideological and economic forces behind the two movements—the emancipation of women and children and the emancipation of Negroes—have much in common and are closely interrelated. Paternalism was a pre-industrial scheme of life, and was gradually becoming broken in the nineteenth century. Negroes and women, both of whom had been under the yoke of the paternalistic system, were both strongly and fatefully influenced by the Industrial Revolution. For neither group is the readjustment process yet consummated. Both are still problem groups. The women's problem is the center of the whole complex of problems of how to reorganize the institution of the family to fit the new economic and ideological basis, a problem which is not solved in any part of the Western world unless it be in the Soviet Union or Palestine. The family problem in the Negro group, as we find when analyzing the Negro family, has its special complications, centering in the tension and conflict between the external patriarchal system in which the Negro was confined as a slave and his own family structure.

As in the Negro problem, most men have accepted as self-evident, until recently, the doctrine that women had inferior endowments in most of those respects which carry prestige, power, and advantages in society, but that they were, at the same time, superior in some other respects. The arguments, when arguments were used, have been about the same: smaller brains, scarcity of geniuses and so on. The study of women's intelligence and personality has had broadly the same history as the one we record for Negroes. As in the case of the Negro, women themselves have often been brought to believe in their inferiority of endowment. As the Negro was awarded his "place" in society, so there was a "woman's place." In both cases the rationalization was strongly believed that men, in confining them to this place, did not act against the true interest of the subordinate groups. The myth of the "contented women," who did not want to have suffrage or other civil rights and equal opportunities, had the same social function as the myth of the "contented Negro." In both cases there was probably—in a static sense—often some truth behind the myth.

As to the character of the deprivations, upheld by law or by social conventions and the pressure of public opinion, no elaboration will here be made. As important and illustrative in the comparison, we shall, however, stress the conventions governing woman's education. There was a time when the most common idea was that she was better off with little education. Later the doctrine developed that she should not be denied education, but that her education should be of a special type, fitting her for her "place" in society and usually directed more on training her hands than her brains.

Political franchise was not granted to women until recently. Even now there are, in all countries, great difficulties for a woman to attain public office. The most important disabilities still affecting her status are those barring her attempt to earn a living and to attain promotion in her work. As in the Negro's case, there are certain "women's jobs," traditionally monopolized by women. They are regularly in the low salary bracket and do not offer much of a career. All over the world men have used the trade unions to keep women out of competition. Woman's competition has, like the Negro's, been particularly obnoxious and dreaded by men because of the low wages women, with their few earning outlets, are prepared to work for. Men often dislike the very idea of having women on an equal plane as co-workers and competitors, and usually they find it even more "unnatural" to work under women. White people generally hold similar attitudes toward Negroes. On the other hand, it is said about women that they prefer men as bosses and do not want to work under another woman. Negroes often feel the same way about working under other Negroes.

In personal relations with both women and Negroes, white men generally prefer a less professional and more human relation, actually a more paternalistic and protective position—somewhat in the nature of patron to client in Roman times, and like the corresponding strongly paternalistic relation of later feudalism. As in Germany it is said that every gentile has his pet Jew, so it is said in the South that every white has his "pet nigger," or—in the upper strata—several of them. We sometimes marry the pet woman, carrying out the paternalistic scheme. But even if we do not, we tend to deal kindly with her as a client and a ward, not as a competitor and an equal.

In drawing a parallel between the position of, and feeling toward, women and Negroes we are uncovering a fundamental basis of our culture. Although it is changing, atavistic elements sometimes unexpectedly break through even in the most emancipated individuals. The similarities in the women's and the Negroes' problems are not accidental. They were, as we have pointed out, originally determined in a paternalistic order of society. The problems remain, even though paternalism is gradually declining as an ideal and is losing its economic basis. In the final analysis, women are still hindered in their competition by the function of procreation; Negroes are laboring under the yoke of the doctrine of unassimilability which has remained although slavery is abolished. The second barrier is actually much stronger than the first in America today. But the first is more eternally inexorable.[7]

---

[7]Alva Myrdal, *Nation and Family* (1941), Chapter 22; "One Sex a Social Problem," pp. 398–426.

Mirra Komarovsky (1905–1998) on Cultural Contradictions of Sex Roles

Mirra Komarovsky was born in Russia in 1905 to a middle-class Jewish family who saw that she was well-tutored in languages and music. After the Bolshevik revolution her family immigrated to the United States, settling in Wichita, Kansas, where she completed high school in one semester in 1922. Her father, recognizing her abilities and desiring greater opportunities for her, convinced his wife to move to Brooklyn, New York, so that Mirra could pursue her studies at Barnard College. At Barnard, Komarovsky majored in economics and sociology, studying with anthropologists Ruth Benedict and Franz Boas and sociologist William F. Ogburn. When she approached Ogburn with the suggestion that she would like to become a professor of sociology, he discouraged her ambition as unrealistic because she was "a woman, foreign born, and Jewish." Still, because of her outstanding performance in undergraduate work, she was admitted to the master's program in sociology at Columbia with Ogburn as her mentor. After her master's degree in 1927, she held a few different positions, finally returning to graduate work at Columbia in 1929. Among her coresearchers and mentors were Dorothy Swaine Thomas, George Lundberg, and Paul Lazarsfeld. Working with Lazarsfeld, Komarovsky completed her doctoral work in 1940 with an intensive study of 59 families, published as *The Unemployed Man and His Family* (1940).

In the same year, Komarovsky married Marcus Heyman, who encouraged her in her career. She began a part-time lectureship at Barnard College in 1935, eventually moving up the ranks to full professor in 1954. Over time, Komarovsky came to be recognized as an important sociologist, even though she was never admitted to Columbia's graduate faculty. In 1973, she was elected president of the American Sociological Association, only the second woman to be so honored since its inception in 1906. In spite of her retirement, she continued to teach—even chairing the new Women's Studies program in 1978–1979. Honored by many professional awards, including the distinguished career award from the American Sociological Association in 1991, Komarovsky spent the remainder of her life in Manhattan, eventually dying at the age of 93.

One of Komarovsky's consistent themes is that cultural change often lags behind social change, a thesis she adopted from her mentor William F. Ogburn. As social conditions change, they often necessitate alterations in cultural norms and values, but culture usually moves more slowly than social patterns.

Major Works

Komarovsky, Mirra. *Women in the Modern World: Their Education and Their Dilemmas.* Boston, MA: Little, Brown, 1953.
————. *Blue Collar Marriage.* New York: Random House, 1964.

————. *Dilemmas of Masculinity: A Study of College Youth.* New York: Norton, 1976.
————. *Women in College: Shaping New Feminine Identities.* New York: Basic Books, 1985.

Sources

New York Times. 1999. Mirra Komarovsky. Obituary. February 1.

Reinharz, Shulamit. 1991. Mirra Komarovsky. In *Women in sociology: A bio-bibliographical sourcebook,* ed. Mary Jo Deegan, 239–48. Westport, CT: Greenwood.

Rosenberg, Rosalind. Mirra Komarovsky. http://www.columbia.edu/~rr91/3567/sample_biographies/mirra_komarovsky%20black%20board.htm (accessed 28 January 2006).

The Selection

In the following article, Mirra Komarovsky argues that changes in the roles of women associated with economic and demographic change have led to contradictions between cultural norms and social realities for women and inconsistencies in values. The norms may be unsuited to current conditions, having developed under social circumstances that were far different from current ones.

In this analysis, Komarovsky maintains the functionalist understanding that norms and social conditions tend to support each other, but she focuses on the inconsistencies and conflicts that occur as different parts of the system change at different rates. In this, she is more critical than Parsons, who spoke in terms of cultural *strains*. Komarovsky uses the stronger terms *contradictions, inconsistencies*, and even *clash* to describe the relation between cultural expectations and social patterns. While not a conflict theorist, in this article she is already moving in the direction of introducing a more critical lens in her work than was common among social theorists of her time, emphasizing areas of dysfunction and contradictions instead of functional adjustment.

The article analyzes data drawn from a qualitative study of university students during the years 1942–1943. Komarovsky's focus is on contradictions between what she terms the "feminine role" on the one hand, and the

Mirra Komarovsky, "Cultural Contradictions in Sex Roles," *American Journal of Sociology* 52 (November 1946): 184–89. Reprinted by permission of the University of Chicago Press.

"modern role" on the other. Both sets of expectations are promoted within the culture for middle-class women, but they involve contradictory goals and thus set up serious conflicts for many women. The modern role is the newer one—the outcome of social change toward urban, industrial economies that treat individuals as independent actors regardless of ascribed traits such as sex. The feminine role is another set of expectations, more suited to earlier times and socioeconomic realities.

As Komarovsky describes it, the "feminine role" involves the expectation that girls will be less aggressive than boys and will display certain personality traits (sympathy, emotional expressiveness) not expected of males. The role also implies that women will be somewhat deferential to men, that they will avoid competing with men, and that they will take a secondary role in intellectual, family, and romantic relationships. On the other hand, the "modern" role for women implies that women and men can be equals in education, career, and relationships. The conflict comes about when men and women date, but the problem is more acute for women. Komarovsky's data from autobiographical accounts of women and in-depth interviews are fascinating to read and may still ring a familiar bell with some students.

CULTURAL CONTRADICTIONS AND SEX ROLES

Profound changes in the roles of women during the past century have been accompanied by innumerable contradictions and inconsistencies. With our rapidly changing and highly differentiated culture, with migrations and multiplied social contacts, the stage is set for myriads of combinations of incongruous elements. Cultural norms are often functionally unsuited to the social situations to which they apply. Thus they may deter an individual from a course of action which would serve his own, and society's, interests best. Or, if behavior contrary to the norm is engaged in, the individual may suffer from guilt over violating mores which no longer serve any socially useful end. Sometimes culturally defined roles are adhered to in the face of new conditions without a conscious realization of the discrepancies involved. The reciprocal actions dictated by the roles may be at variance with those demanded by the actual situation. This may result in an imbalance of privileges and obligation or in some frustration of basic interests.

Again, problems arise because changes in the mode of life have created new situations which have not as yet been defined by culture. Individuals left thus without social guidance tend to act in terms of egotistic or "short-run hedonistic" motives which at times defeat their own long-term interests or create conflict with others. The precise obligation of a gainfully employed wife toward the support of the family is one such undefined situation.

Finally, a third mode of discrepancy arises in the existence of incompatible cultural definitions of the same social situation, such as the clash of "old-fashioned" and "radical" mores, of religion and law, of norms of economic and familial institutions.

The problems raised by these discrepancies are social problems in the sense that they engender mental conflict or social conflict or otherwise frustrate some basic interest of large segments of the population.

This article sets forth in detail the nature of certain incompatible sex roles imposed by our society upon the college woman. It is based on data collected in 1942 and 1943. Members of an undergraduate course on the family were asked for two successive years to submit autobiographical documents focused on the topic; 73 were collected. In addition, 80 interviews, lasting about an hour each, were conducted with every member of a course in social psychology of the same institution—making a total of 153 documents ranging from a minimum of five to a maximum of thirty typewritten pages.

The generalization emerging from these documents is the existence of serious contradictions between two roles present in the social environment of the college woman. The goals set by each role are mutually exclusive, and the fundamental personality traits each evokes are at points diametrically opposed, so that what are assets for one become liabilities for the other, and the full realization of one role threatens defeat in the other.

One of these roles may be termed the "feminine" role. While there are a number of permissive variants of the feminine role for women of college age (the "good sport," the "glamour girl," the "young lady," the domestic "home girl," etc.), they have a common core of attributes defining the proper attitudes to men, family, work, love, etc., and a set of personality traits often described with reference to the male sex role as "not as dominant, or aggressive as men" or "more emotional, sympathetic."

The other and more recent role is, in a sense, no *sex* role at all, because it partly obliterates the differentiation in sex. It demands of the woman much the same virtues, patterns of behavior, and attitude that it does of the men of a corresponding age. We shall refer to this as the "modern" role.

Both roles are present in the social environment of these women throughout their lives, though, as the precise content of each

sex role varies with age, so does the nature of their clashes change from one stage to another. In the period under discussion the conflict between the two roles apparently centers about academic work, social life, vocational plans, excellence in specific fields of endeavor, and a number of personality traits.

One manifestation of the problem is in the inconsistency of the goals set for the girl by her family.

Forty, or 26 per cent, of the respondents expressed some grievance against their families for failure to confront them with clearcut and consistent goals. The majority, 74 per cent, denied having had such experiences. One student writes:

> How am I to pursue any course single-mindedly when some way along the line a person I respect is sure to say, "You are on the wrong track and are wasting your time." Uncle John telephones every Sunday morning. His first question is: "Did you go out last night?" He would think me a "grind" if I were to stay home Saturday night to finish a term paper. My father expects me to get an "A" in every subject and is disappointed by a "B." He says I have plenty of time for social life. Mother says, "That 'A' in Philosophy is very nice dear. But please don't become so deep that no man will be good enough for you." And, finally, Aunt Mary's line is careers for women. "Prepare yourself for some profession. This is the only way to insure yourself independence and an interesting life. You have plenty of time to marry."

A Senior writes:

> I get a letter from my mother at least three times a week. One week her letters will say, "Remember that this is your last year at college. Subordinate everything to your studies. You must have a good record to secure a job." The next week her letters are full of wedding news. This friend of mine got married; that one is engaged; my young cousin's wedding

is only a week off. When, my mother wonders, will I make up my mind? Surely, I wouldn't want to be the only unmarried one in my group. It is high time, she feels, that I give some thought to it.

A student reminisces:

All through high school my family urged me to work hard because they wished me to enter a first-rate college. At the same time they were always raving about a girl schoomate who lived next door to us. How pretty and sweet she was, how popular, and what taste in clothes! Couldn't I also pay more attention to my appearance and to social life? They were overlooking the fact that this carefree friend of mine had little time left for school work and had failed several subjects. It seemed that my family had expected me to become Eve Curie and Hedy Lamar wrapped up in one.

Another comments:

My mother thinks that it is very nice to be smart in college but only if it doesn't take too much effort. She always tells me not to be too intellectual on dates, to be clever in a light sort of way. My father, on the other hand, wants me to study law. He thinks that if I applied myself I could make an excellent lawyer and keeps telling me that I am better fitted for this profession than my brother.

Another writes:

One of my two brothers writes: "Cover up that high forehead and act a little dumb once in a while"; while the other always urges upon me the importance of rigorous scholarship.

The students testified to a certain bewilderment and confusion caused by the failure on the part of the family to smooth the passage from one role to another, especially when the roles involved were contradictory. It seemed to some of them that they had awakened one morning to find their world upside down: what had hitherto evoked praise and rewards from relatives, now suddenly aroused censure. A student recollects:

I could match my older brother in skating sledding, riflery, ball, and many of the other games we played. He enjoyed teaching me and took great pride in my accomplishments. Then one day it all changed. He must have suddenly become conscious of the fact that girls ought to be feminine. I was walking with him, proud to be able to make long strides and keep up with his long-legged steps when he turned to me in annoyance, "Can't you walk like a lady?" I still remember feeling hurt and bewildered by his scorn, when I had been led to expect approval.

Once during her freshman year in college, after a delightful date, a student wrote her brother with great elation:

"What a wonderful evening at——fraternity house! You would be proud of me, Johnny! I won all ping-pong games but one!"

"For heaven's sake," came the reply, "when will you grow up? Don't you know that a boy likes to think he is better than a girl? Give him a little competition, sure, but miss a few serves in the end. Should you join the Debate Club? By all means, but don't practice too much on the boys." Believe me I was stunned by this letter, but then I saw that he was right. To be a success in the dorms one must date, to date one must not win too many ping-pong games. At first I resented this bitterly. But now I am more or less used to it and live in hope of one day meeting a man who is my superior so that I may be my natural self.

It is the parents and not the older sibling who reversed their expectations in the following excerpt:

All through grammar school and high school my parents led me to feel that to do well in school was my chief responsibility. A good report card, an election to student office, these were the news Mother bragged about in telephone conversations with her friends. But recently they suddenly got worried about me: I don't pay enough attention to social life, a woman needs *some* education but not that much. They are disturbed by my determination to go to the School of Social Work. Why my ambitions should surprise them after they have exposed me for four years to some of the most inspired and stimulating social scientists in the country, I can't imagine. They have some mighty strong arguments on their side. What is the use, they say, of investing years in training for a profession, only to drop it in a few years? Chances of meeting men are slim in this profession. Besides, I may become so preoccupied with it as to sacrifice social life. The next few years are, after all, the proper time to find a mate. But the urge to apply what I have learned, and the challenge of this profession is so strong that I shall go on despite the family opposition.

The final excerpt illustrates both the sudden transition of roles and the ambiguity of standards:

I major in English composition. This is not a completely "approved" field for girls so I usually just say "English." An English Literature major is quite liked and approved by boys. Somehow it is lumped with all the other arts and even has a little glamour. But a composition major is a girl to beware of because she supposedly will notice all your grammar mistakes, look at your letters too critically, and consider your ordinary speech and conversation as too crude.

I also work for a big metropolitan daily as a correspondent in the city room. I am well liked there and may possibly stay as a reporter after graduation in February. I have had several spreads [stories running to more than eight or ten inches of space], and this is considered pretty good for a college correspondent. Naturally, I was elated and pleased at such breaks, and as far as the city room is concerned I'm off to a very good start on a career that is hard for a man to achieve and even harder for a woman. General reporting is still a man's work in the opinion of most people. I have a lot of acclaim but also criticism, and I find it confusing and difficult to be praised for being clever and working hard and then, when my efforts promise to be successful, to be condemned and criticized for being unfeminine and ambitious.

Here are a few of these reactions:

My father: "I don't like this newspaper setup at all. The people you meet are making you less interested in marriage than ever. You're getting too educated and intellectual to be attractive to men."

My mother: "I don't like your attitude toward people. The paper is making you too analytical and calculating. Above all, you shouldn't sacrifice your education and career for marriage."

A lieutenant with two years of college: "It pleased me greatly to hear about your news assignment—good girl."

A Navy pilot with one year of college: "Undoubtedly, I'm old-fashioned, but I could never expect or feel right about a girl giving up a very promising or interesting future to hang around waiting for me to finish college. Nevertheless, congratulations on your job on the paper. Where in the world do you get that wonderful energy? Anyway I know you were thrilled at getting it and feel very glad for you. I've an idea that it means the same to you as that letter saying 'report for active duty' meant to me."

A graduate metallurgist now a private in the Army: "It was good to hear that you got that break with the paper. I am sure that talent will prove itself and that you will go far. But not too far, as I don't think you should become a career woman. You'll get repressed and not be interested enough in having fun if you keep after that career."

A lieutenant with a year and a half of college: "All this career business is nonsense. A woman belongs in the home and absolutely no place else. My wife will have to stay home. That should keep her happy. Men are just superior in everything, and women have no right to expect to compete with them. They should do just what will keep their husbands happy."

A graduate engineer—my fiancé: "Go right ahead and get as far as you can in your field. I am glad you are ambitious and clever, and I'm as anxious to see you happily successful as I am myself. It is a shame to let all those brains go to waste over just dusting and washing dishes. I think the usual home life and children are small sacrifices to make if a career will keep you happy. But I'd rather see you in radio because I am a bit wary of the effect upon our marriage of the way of life you will have around the newspaper."

Sixty-one, or 40 per cent, of the students indicated that they have occasionally "played dumb" on dates, that is, concealed some academic honor, pretended ignorance of some subject, or allowed the man the last word in an intellectual discussion. Among these were women who "threw games" and in general played down certain skills in obedience to the unwritten law that men must possess these skills to a superior degree. At the same time, in other areas of life, social pressures were being exerted upon these women to "play to win," to compete to the utmost of their abilities for intellectual distinction and academic honors. One student writes:

I was glad to transfer to a women's college. The two years at the co-ed university produced a constant strain. I am a good student; my family expects me to get good marks. At the same time I am normal enough to want to be invited to the Saturday night dance. Well, everyone knew that on that campus a reputation of a "brain" killed a girl socially. I was always fearful lest I say too much in class

or answer a question which the boys I dated couldn't answer.

Here are some significant remarks made from the interviews:

When a girl asks me what marks I got last semester I answer, "Not so good—only one 'A'," When a boy asks the same question, I say very brightly with a note of surprise, "Imagine, I got an 'A!'"

I am engaged to a southern boy who doesn't think too much of the woman's intellect. In spite of myself, I play up to his theories because the less one knows and does, the more he does for you and thinks you "cute" into the bargain. . . . . I allow him to explain things to me in great detail and to treat me as a child in financial matters.

One of the nicest techniques is to spell long words incorrectly once in a while. My boyfriend seems to get a great kick out of it and writes back, "Honey, you certainly don't know how to spell."

When my date said that he considers Ravel's *Bolero* the greatest piece of music ever written, I changed the subject because I knew I would talk down to him.

A boy advised me not to tell of my proficiency in math and not to talk of my plans to study medicine unless I knew my date well.

My fiancé didn't go to college. I intend to finish college and work hard at it, but in talking to him I make college appear a kind of a game.

Once I went sailing with a man who so obviously enjoyed the role of a protector that I told him I didn't know how to sail. As it turned out he didn't either. We got into a tough spot, and I was torn between a desire to get a hold of the boat and a fear to reveal that I had lied to him.

It embarrassed me that my "steady" in high school got worse marks than I. A boy should naturally do better in school. I would never tell him my marks and would often ask him to help me with my homework.

I am better in math than my fiancé. But while I let him explain politics to me, we never talk about math even though, being a math major, I could tell him some interesting things. Mother used to tell me to lay off the brains on dates because glasses make me look too intellectual anyhow.

I was once at a work camp. The girls did the same work as the boys. If some girls worked better, the boys resented it fiercely. The director told one capable girl to slow down to keep peace in the group.

How to do the job and remain popular was a tough task. If you worked your best, the boys resented the competition; if you acted feminine, they complained that you were clumsy.

On dates I always go through the "I-don't-care-anything-you-want-to-do" routine. It gets monotonous but boys fear girls who make decisions. They think such girls would make nagging wives.

I am a natural leader and, when in the company of girls, usually take the lead. That is why I am so active in college activities. But I know that men fear bossy women, and I always have to watch myself on dates not to assume the "executive" role. Once a boy walking to the theater with me took the wrong street. I knew a short cut but kept quiet.

I let my fiancé make most of the decisions when we are out. It annoys me, but he prefers it.

I sometimes "play dumb" on dates, but it leaves a bad taste. The emotions are complicated. Part of me enjoys "putting something over" on the unsuspecting male. But this sense of superiority over him is mixed with feeling of guilt for my hypocrisy. Toward the "date" I feel some contempt because he is "taken in" by my technique, or if I like the boy, a kind of a maternal condescension. At times I resent him! Why isn't he my superior in all ways in which a man should excel so that I could be my natural self? What am I doing here with him, anyhow? Slumming? And the funny part of it is that the man, I think, is not always so unsuspecting. He may sense the truth and become uneasy in the relation. "Where do I stand? Is she laughing up her sleeve or did she mean this praise? Was she really impressed with that little speech of mine or did she only pretend to know nothing about politics?" And once or twice I felt that the joke was on me: the boy saw through my wiles and felt contempt for me for stooping to such tricks.

Another aspect of the problem is the conflict between the psychogenetic personality of the girl and the cultural role foisted upon her by the milieu.[1] At times it is the girl with "masculine" interests and personality traits who chafes under the pressure to conform to the "feminine" pattern. At other times it is the family and the college who thrusts upon the reluctant girl the "modern" role.

While, historically, the "modern" role is the most recent one, ontogenetically it is the one emphasized earlier in the education of the college girl, if these 153 documents are representative. Society confronts the girl with powerful challenges and strong pressure to excel in certain competitive lines of endeavor and to develop certain techniques of adaptations very similar to those expected of her brothers. But, then, quite suddenly as it appears to these girls, the very success in meeting these challenges begins to cause anxiety. It is precisely those most successful in the earlier role who are now penalized.

It is not only the passage from age to age but the moving to another region or type of campus which may create for the girl similar problems. The precise content of sex roles, or, to put it in another way, the degree of

---

[1]Margaret Mead, *Sex and Temperament in Three Primitive Societies* (New York: Morrow & Co., 1935).

their differentiation, varies with regional class, nativity, and other subcultures.

Whenever individuals show differences in response to some social situation, as have our 153 respondents, the question naturally arises as to the causes. It will be remembered that 40 per cent admitted some difficulties in personal relations with men due to conflicting sex roles but that 60 per cent said that they had no such problems. Inconsistency of parental expectations troubled 26 per cent of the students.

To account for individual differences would require another study, involving a classification of personalities in relation to the peculiar social environments of each. Generally speaking, it would seem that it is the girl with a "middle-of-the-road personality" who is most happily adjusted to the present historical moment. She is not a perfect incarnation of either role but is flexible enough to play both. She is a girl who is intelligent enough to do well in school but not so brilliant as to "get all 'A''s"; informed and alert but not consumed by an intellectual passion; capable but not talented in areas relatively new to women; able to stand on her own feet and to earn a living but not so good a living as to compete with men; capable of doing some job well (in case she does not marry or, otherwise, has to work) but not so identified with a profession as to need it for her happiness.

A search for less immediate causes of individual reactions would lead us further back to the study of genesis of the personality differences found relevant to the problem. One of the clues will certainly be provided by the relation of the child to the parent of the same and of the opposite sex. This relation affects the conception of self and the inclination for a particular sex role.

The problems set forth in this article will persist, in the opinion of the writer, until the adult sex roles of women are redefined in greater harmony with the socioeconomic and ideological character of modern society. Until then neither the formal education nor the unverbalized sex roles of the adolescent woman can be cleared of intrinsic contradictions.

Robert Staughton Lynd (1892–1970) on Changes in Sex Roles

Robert Staughton Lynd is known primarily for his studies of "Middletown" (1929, 1937, coauthored with his wife Helen Merrell Lynd), describing the nature of life in what was viewed as a typical "middle-America" town. Their discussions of power and bureaucracy in this community of 36,000 was highly influential and led to his entry into an academic career. After receiving a bachelor's degree at Princeton (1914), Lynd studied for a time at Union Theological Seminary in New York. He decided not to enter the ministry and instead was hired as a researcher on religion in a typical American town in what became the Middletown study. He married Helen Merrell at the beginning of that project and she became an important coresearcher and coauthor. Robert Lynd went on to complete a doctorate in sociology at Columbia and became a faculty member there. In 1938 he was invited to give the Stafford Lectures at Princeton University, which resulted in the publication of the lectures as a book, titled *Knowledge for What? The Place of Social Science in American Culture* (1948). In this book Lynd argues against the dominant "objective" orientation of science in favor of a more qualitative and problems-oriented approach. He criticizes the overspecialization and thoughtless precision of much quantitative work that ignores larger questions, interdisciplinary issues, and the relation of minutiae to the cultural context. He also calls into question the assumption that culture is independent of human behavior and motivations, arguing instead for a recognition that culture is a human product and its direction can and should be the object of social scientific critique. Within the context of these principles, Lynd develops an analysis of American culture of the late 1930s and has proposals for social science research aimed at the important problems of the day. Always an activist and social critic, Lynd also participated in labor and civil rights movements.

MAJOR WORKS

Lynd, Robert S., and Helen Merrell Lynd. *Middletown: A Study in Contemporary American Culture.* New York: Harcourt Brace, 1929.

———. *Middletown in Transition: A Study in Cultural Conflicts.* New York: Harcourt Brace, 1937.

Lynd, Robert S. *Knowledge for What? The Place of Social Science in American Culture.* Princeton: Princeton University Press, 1948.

SOURCES

PBS interview with Staughton Lynd (son of Robert and Helen Merrell Lynd). The First Measured Century. Host, Ben Wattenburg. http://www.pbs.org/fmc/interviews/lynd.htm (accessed 28 January 2006). PBS First American Century, FMC Segments 1900–1930. Middletown: A Study in Modern American Culture. http://www.pbs.org/fmc/segments/progseg4.htm (accessed 28 January 2006).

THE SELECTION

Within his analysis of American culture in the book *Knowledge for What?* Robert Staughton Lynd argues that forces are at work that encourage conflict between the sexes. As urbanization has increasingly separated job from home, the separation and division of labor between the sexes has increased. The increasing differentiation of the values of work from those of home and living has created a values gap between men and women as well. Home values consist of sympathy, understanding, mutuality, and cooperation while work values emphasize impersonality, aggressiveness, and dominance. Men are increasingly consumed by their work, while their roles in the family are diminished—more and more they are seen narrowly as "good providers."

In addition, there is pressure on men to be sensitive lovers and competent and involved parents, resulting in an overload that leads to intermittent feelings of inadequacy.

As women demand more equal treatment, the dominance of the male in the home is diminishing; however, women's roles have changed much more than have men's. Many marriages are strained because of men's unburdening of their pent-up needs for intimacy on their wives. Lynd describes important conflicts between the emotional expectations of work and those of the home, which create a sense of isolation and neediness on the part of the male breadwinner and puts pressure on wives to be the emotional support of their husbands.

CULTURAL CONFLICT BETWEEN THE SEXES

The character of the culture *encourages considerable (and possibly increasing) conflict between the patterned roles of the two sexes.* As already pointed out, growing urbanization is forcing a separation of the worlds of job and of home; and the job world tends to run under rules of its own, largely divorced from the rest of living. This entails not merely a division of labor, but a basic split in the structure of values by which men and women live. The fact that many women are going into jobs and professions means less the merging of the patterns of the two sexes than the adoption of a difficult dual pattern by these women; for the demands upon them to be feminine remain, even though they must live during their hours of work by the values of the men's world. Both sexes accept the traditional assumption of the culture that, fundamentally, the values for which the home stands— sympathy, understanding, mutuality, gentleness, treating persons as persons, cooperation rather than aggression—are ultimate and therefore more important. But the job world of the men, operating as it does to such a degree independently of the rest of the culture, demands more and more channeling of the personality into impersonality and aggressive dominance. The rôle of the male in the family is also constricting as the separateness of his job world diminishes his activities as parent. The status of the father as a family member is narrowing to that of "a good provider." At the same time, increased popular awareness of the importance of good, positive sex-adjustment—an awareness heightened by the relaxing of religious condemnations of sex, the rise of mental hygiene, fiction written under the Freudian influence, and the great lovers on the cinema screen—has strengthened the demand on the male that he play an emotionally more subtle rôle as husband and lover. Likewise, new knowledge is making fresh demands of him to be an active, constructive person as a parent; which demands neither his training nor his time and energy resources help him to meet. The result is an intermittent sense of personal inadequacy in a situation from which, biologically and emotionally, he should draw strength and security.

The old, secure dominance of the male in the home is changing. The demand of the wife to be treated as a person has shifted the earlier tandem structure of marriage, with the man confidently in the lead, to a looser, more voluntary partnership, in which—

Though in wedlock
He and she go,
Each maintains
A separate ego.

The changes in woman's rôle in recent generations have been far greater than those in man's rôle. Bound by fewer children and less housework than formerly, women find themselves with greatly increased options. The very presence of wider options entails responsibility to choose wisely and to become "a person in her own right"; and this in turn involves more opportunity but, also, more uncertainty and mutual tension for both marital partners. Even if the man wants his wife to be independent, he is apt to perpetuate, in his busy preoccupation with the demands of his job, the emotional stereotype of his mother as constant helpmate and backer-up of his own father. While on the job, he is conscious of strains and insecurity; and, when he returns home, he is frequently unable to lay aside his 9:00-to-5:00 attitudes like a coat. In his weariness and perplexity he frequently feels inadequate as a person in his own home.

The tacit or open recognition by the male of the superiority of the values for which the home stands, as over against the values to which he perforce devotes his best energies on his job, tends to render him by turns fiercely defensive of his own world and erratically demanding that women outdo themselves in standing for all the "finer" things that the world of business denies. Women are thus made to carry as surrogates for the men wellnigh the entire burden of the subtler values in the culture. Upon the intimate and delicate marital relationship the man unloads most of his pent-up needs for intimacy and understanding at the fagged end of the day, and many marriages break under a load which they would not have been forced to carry in a more integrated culture. Karen Horney[1] describes, as a psychiatrist, this compulsive overweighting of the artificially narrowed love-relationship in our culture.

"All these factors together—competitiveness and its potential hostilities between fellow-beings, fears, diminished self-esteem—result psychologically in the individual feeling that he is isolated. Even when he has many contacts with others, even when he is happily married, he is emotionally isolated. Emotional isolation is hard for anyone to endure; it becomes a calamity, however, if it coincides with apprehensions and uncertainties about one's self.

"It is this situation which provokes, in the normal individual of our time, an intensified need for affection as a remedy. Obtaining affection makes him feel less isolated, less threatened by hostility and less uncertain of himself. Because it corresponds to a vital need, love is overvalued in our culture. It becomes a phantom—like success—carrying with it the illusion that it is a solution for all problems. Love itself is not an illusion—although in our culture it is most often a screen for satisfying wishes that have nothing to do with it—but it is made an illusion by our expecting much more of it than it can possibly fulfill. And the ideological emphasis that we place on love serves to cover up the factors which create our exaggerated need for it.

Hence the individual—and I still mean the normal individual—is in the dilemma of needing a great deal of affection but finding difficulty in obtaining it."

At no point more than in the family are the disjunctions of our culture and the worlds of different values they embody more directly and dramatically in conflict. Rich familial and marital adjustments are at best difficult of achievement because of the subtleties of personality demands. These adjustments are rendered more complex in our culture by the lack of strong, clear institutional structure supporting family life. As a result, family members are thrown back upon each other as a small group of over-dependent personalities who must work out a common destiny in a family situation which has lost many of its functions and, hence, forces them to rely overmuch upon intimacy. When the values of a culture are split into two sharply conflicting systems, with each sex assigned the rôle of carrying one system, the family becomes perforce, as Horney points out, the battleground not merely for the resolution of differences among the individual personalities of family members but also for the attempted resolution of the larger conflicts of the entire culture. Too little stress has been laid upon this toll which the casualness of our culture exacts of persons at the point of greatest potential richness in personal intimacy.

---

[1]*The Neurotic Personality of Our Time* (New York: Norton, 1937), pp. 286–87.

The 1950s

Questioning the Paradigm

Viola Klein (1908–1971) on Feminine Stereotypes

Viola Klein was born in 1908 to a progressive Jewish family in Prague, Czechoslovakia. She studied at the Sorbonne for one year and then transferred to Vienna University, but political unrest forced her to return to Czechoslovakia. There she worked as an assistant editor of a political weekly while pursuing graduate study in languages, psychology, and philosophy, eventually earning a doctorate in French Literature. During a visit to the Soviet Union in the 1930s, Klein developed a keen interest in "the woman question," an interest she maintained throughout her career. Her life was again disrupted in 1938, when, to escape the German invasion of Czechoslovakia, she and a brother moved to England, forced to leave their parents who later died in Nazi death camps.

On arriving in England, Klein had to work as a nanny to survive, but soon she won a scholarship and began work on her second doctorate, studying with Karl Mannheim, the famous sociologist of knowledge. In 1946 she published her thesis, *The Feminine Character,* with an introduction by her mentor. This book was an in-depth and thoughtful analysis of previous theories of femininity, debunking many of them and providing a strongly social-constructionist interpretation in the end. The book was rejected by mainstream psychologists and sociologists, however, who criticized it as a "militant" feminist work. In that book, Klein showed how the notion of femininity changes with cultural expectations, social position, and experience. She also argued that the social and cultural location of social scientists who study this and other problems affects their views, carefully critiquing the notion of objectivity in social science and calling for a more self-critical stance.

Substantively, Klein focused on the negative impacts of stereotypes of femininity on women's own self-image and behavior. She saw women as occupying a "marginal" status, similar to that of minority groups. The arguments in Klein's work have come to be accepted widely in recent decades, but at the time of their publication they met with skepticism and even hostility in the field of psychology, which was still dominated by essentialist ideas of sex-related personality traits. Ironically, the lack of acceptance of Klein's work reinforces her claim that people's ideas are related to their cultural and social location and milieu. More recently, in the 1970s and later, her work has been recognized as theoretically important and ahead of its time.

In spite of her two doctorates and her erudite scholarship, Klein was unable to obtain an academic position, taking various low-level jobs such as editor, translator, government researcher, and teacher. She came to be respected for her research on women in Britain. In the 1950s she was asked by the Swedish sociologist Alva Myrdal to collaborate on a project on women's dual roles in work and family, resulting in a coauthored book, *Women's Two Roles,* in 1956. Finally, in 1964 Klein was appointed to her first academic position as Lecturer in Sociology at Reading University in England, where her papers are now housed. In 1967 she was promoted to Senior Lecturer, and to Reader in 1971. She died suddenly later that year, soon after retiring.

MAJOR WORKS

Klein, Viola. 1946. *The feminine character: History of an ideology.* London: Kegan Paul, Trench, Trubner.

Myrdal, Alva and Viola Klein. 1956. *Women's two roles: Home and work.* London: Routledge & Kegan Paul.

SOURCES

Broschart, Kay Richards. "Viola Klein (1908–1973)." In *Women in Sociology: A Bio-Biographical Sourcebook,* edited by Mary Jo Deegan, 225–30. Westport, CT: Greenwood, 1991.

Giele, Janet Zollinger. "New Developments in Research on Women." In *The Feminine Character: History of an Ideology,* by Viola Klein, xix–lvi. Urbana: University of Illinois Press, 1971.

"Papers of Viola Klein." Archives of Reading Library, Web page: www.Archiveshub.ac.uk/news/04032303.html (accessed January 2006).

THE SELECTION

Reprinted here is an article from the 1950 special issue of the *Journal of Social Issues,* titled "Women in the Professions." Viola Klein's article summarizes many of her arguments in her earlier book *The Feminine Character.* She points out that many types of personalities are attributed to men, but for women one universal "feminine type" is often assumed. This assumption conflicts with reality, but its widespread acceptance limits women's opportunities and leads to their own self-doubts and anxieties, especially when they do not fit the stereotype. Klein refers to the notion of femininity as an "ideology" that helps to maintain women in a subordinate position, leading to double standards of evaluation of the accomplishments of men and women. Her example of the differential evaluation of male and female artists is telling. In the end, Klein argues for changing our ideas of femininity so as to emphasize the common humanity of men and women and to allow for the full development of human capacities, regardless of sex.

From Viola Klein, "The Stereotype of Femininity," *Journal of Social Issues* 6, no. 3 (1950): 3–12. Reprinted by permission of Blackwell Publishing Ltd.

THE STEREOTYPE OF FEMININITY

"Why is there no recount of the personality of woman that you could hand over to undergraduates to read?" I was recently asked by a lecturer in gynaecology who, conscious of the intimate relationship between mind and body, feels he would not do justice to his subject unless he included in his course at least five lectures each year on the Psychology of Woman.

Underlying this question, as, indeed, most thinking on the subject of feminine psychology, is the assumption that Woman represents a psychological type in the same way as "introvert—extrovert," "cyclothyme—schizothyme," "phlegmatic," "sanguinic," etc. are distinct psychological types.

Innumerable attempts have been made to define this type, to describe the mental traits supposed to be characteristic of the human female. They are not matched by equal endeavors to establish a "Psychology of the Human Male." Indeed, the mere suggestion of such a possibility would, rightly, be considered absurd. The Male is not one psychological type: the great variety of differing temperaments, characters, abilities and interests cannot be summarized under one heading if any purpose is to be served by classification at all.

Why, then, should there be this consistent search for a common denominator among the variety of feminine characters, this search for the Essential Woman, the "Eternal Feminine?"

It is, because, although there is no uniform feminine "type," society carries, as part of its ideological baggage, a stereotype of Woman, a sort of rough model purporting to contain the *essential* characteristics, while all the *existential* features are but variations on a basic theme. Stereotypes—defined by

Kimball Young as false classificatory concepts to which, as a rule, some strong emotional-feeling tone of like or dislike, approval or disapproval, is attached—are popular means to simplify, indeed to oversimplify, a complex social reality. They are a device to sum up a strange and thus bewildering situation in one simplified symbol, a kind of logogram which reduces a situation to the minimum necessary to be understood by common consent. One has only to think of the roars of laughter evoked on a music-hall stage by the mere mentioning of the word "mother-in-law" to be reminded of this shorthand function of stereotypes.

It is in the nature of stereotypes as parts of prejudice that they should be applied not to ourselves but to others. While we see ourselves and the members of our own set as individuals, we are apt to generalize about members of the out-group and to label them in sweeping terms. Thus it is not surprising that in our chiefly man-made civilization a situation should have arisen in which woman is thought of as a psychological type while man is not.

The stereotype of woman has two distinct functions: on the one hand it gives a short-cut explanation of all sorts of peculiarities in individual women's behaviour; whether she is strong-willed or meek, single-minded or hesitant, gentle or quarrelsome—she is supposed to possess a particular version of whatever trait she manifests and her stubbornness or submissiveness, her capriciousness or lack of humor will all be found "typically feminine." On the other hand, the stereotype holds up to woman a sort of mirror which has previously been treated so as to show her reflection in a peculiar light or at a particular angle. To see yourself as others see you—what Cooley calls "the looking-glass self"—is a very important part of the educational process concerned with the transmission of attitudes and values. Thus a model is set up for others to imitate. Conformity is at a premium, whereas deviation from the norm is wrought with a variety of penalties, from feelings of frustration and inferiority to social ostracism and outright condemnation.

To be sure, the traditional typology recognized not one but two feminine types, the "good" and the "bad" woman—Eve and Lilith, the Mother and the Courtesan, as Weininger defined them: the woman to whom sex is chiefly a means to produce children, and the woman who seeks it for the sake of the pleasure it affords her by itself. In either case her relationship to the opposite sex is the focal point from which her personality is viewed and both types are characterized exclusively with reference to their attitude to men, not in regard of any mental or temperamental traits. Thus woman is seen as an apendage to man—on whom, in fact, she was socially and economically, as well as emotionally dependent—not as a personality in her own right.

This traditional picture of woman had the appeal of simplicity and was the "ideological superstructure" of a social system in which woman's role was equally narrowly circumscribed. Thanks to its strong emotional tone it has outlived its material basis and has lingered on long after the underlying social structure has been transformed. Today women have assumed a great variety of social functions and responsibilities apart from, and in addition to, their relations to the other sex and claim to be judged on their individual merits rather than by the degree of their conformity to an out-of-date stereotype.

Difficulties, however, arise on a number of levels. For one, the traditional linkage of psychological characteristics with sex and its contrast to the practical realities of everyday life have caused in many women a feeling of uncertainty of their sex role. If women are as active and aggressive as life in a competitive society requires, have they, on that account, become less feminine? Can a woman who is interested in mathematics, or mechanics, or logic, still claim to be a "complete" woman, and is she so regarded by others? Or, she will ask herself, is there anything fundamentally wrong or odd about her? This uncertainty is all the more harassing as in our rapidly changing society the desire to "belong," to be reassured, to conform to an accepted norm, is increasingly gaining weight. The many questionnaires published in all kinds of periodicals, and particularly, it seems, in women's journals, in which the reader is given a chance to rate himself, serve this very purpose: to reassure the individual that he, or she, fits into a set pattern. The tendency for quantitative measurements of personality traits, prevalent in contemporary psychology, also goes to meet this demand for norms and provides the standards of comparison.

A second difficulty arises from the historical circumstances of women's emancipation. It was carried by an *avantgarde* whose aim it was to widen the sphere of economic and political activities open to women and to force a breach into a solidly masculine world of affairs. Thus they had to maintain, and to prove, that woman, as a class, were in every respect "just as good" as man. In the competitive struggle for jobs "equality" was the catchword.

But in the sphere of ideologies, it was maintained, that women had a distinctive contribution to make; that they were possessed of qualities which were not sufficiently represented in public life; that they would add a new facet to it and thereby make it not only more complete, but all the richer and happier.

Many pinned their hopes for greater social justice, national sanity and international peace on the increasing contribution of women, in the same way as many people expected these aims to be achieved by greater participation of the working classes. Both these groups were untried forces, unspoiled by power, and those who were anxious to create a better world looked to either, or to both, for salvation. "As long as man is oppressed and downtrodden, as long as the compulsion of social injustice keeps him in subjection, we are at liberty to hope much from what has not yet had opportunity to burgeon, from all the latent fertility in the fallow classes. Just as we hope much from children who may eventually grow up into quite commonplace people, in the same way we often have the illusion that the masses are composed of a finer clay than the rest of disappointing humanity."[1] Thus writes the disillusioned André Gide after his return from the USSR: "I think they are merely less corrupt and less decadent than the others, that is all."[2] Come to power they show the same faults and vices as the classes which have ruled hitherto—naturally, for they are made of the same fallible human stuff.

The belief, not in the common humanity of all, but in the intrinsic merits of some particular section of mankind which, so far, has not had an opportunity to prove its mettle, has led to disappointment in the case of women as well as that of the "common man." Faith, to be preserved, has to be in something abstract or supernatural. It does not, as a rule, bear confrontation with its object.

Thus, many a keen feminist was disillusioned when women suffrage did not produce peace, abolish militarism, nor in any other way make a marked change for the better in world affairs. The disappointment was, in most cases, not with one's own judgment but with women for not being up to expectation.

In another respect, too, the originators of women's emancipation overshot their mark. Being Victorians in their mental make-up they tended to underrate the force of the sexual instinct. Concerned as they were to create new jobs for women, to prove their equality and to open up roads to independence, they concentrated on careers, and on careers only. "Marriage mortality" was the term applied to those who fell by the wayside in this struggle. They were a dead loss to the "Cause" which demanded whole-hearted and single-minded devotion. Having to choose between marriage and career, being subjected to the rival pulls of love and ambition, imposed a strain on women that was too great for most to withstand.

Among the generation who inherited the spoils of feminism without having to fight for them, there were many who asked themselves whether, in the competitive game, it was not better to "specialize." Were they to put the emphasis—as their mothers had done—on doing the same things equally well with men, or rather to concentrate on the things which they, as women, could do better? But if so, what were the activities for which they were particularly suited? Thus, while preserving the spirit of rivalry between the sexes, many women tried to shirk the issue of "equality" by moving the competition on to another level.

In this way, the conflict of specialization versus universalism, one of the big dilemmas of our time, has also affected the woman's problem. It has led to the peculiar result that, at a moment in our historical development when the range of activities in which sheer physical strength is a decisive factor

---

[1]Gide, André. In *The God that Failed*. Crossman, Richard (editor). New York, Harper and Brothers, 1949. p. 194.
[2]*Ibid.*

has been reduced to such an extent as to make egalitarianism a practical possibility, many women began to doubt its wisdom.

At present, therefore, egalitarianism has arrived at a crossroad and the time is ripe for stocktaking and for a reassessment of the values involved. At this critical point it behooves us to survey, once more, both our potentialities and aims; to ask whether women have achieved what they set out to do and, if so, whether their purpose, and the purpose of humanity, is best served by continuing along the same road.

The problem of women's careers is, of course, closely linked with that of feminine psychology. It hinges on the question whether women, as a group, show distinctive mental or temperamental traits that fit them better for one type of work than for another. *As a group,* they have, of old, been excluded from remunerative work; *as a group,* they tried to enter the economic field. Do they, also *as a group,* show psychological characteristics that collectively mark them off from the rest of humanity? Even if this question be answered in the affirmative it still remains to be decided whether these traits are, like class or national characteristics, the result of upbringing, social and economic conditions and historical background, and therefore bound to change with the alteration of any of these factors, or whether they are linked with the physique and biological function of women.

To this question both practical experience and the various sciences concerned tend to give divergent answers. While the social changes of recent years in our own society and comparison with other patterns of culture weigh heavily on the side of social conditioning, biologists and, on a different plane, psycho-analysts stress the important bearing of the sexual function on mental development.

An interesting example of this conflict of opinions is afforded by Margaret Mead who, by her book *Sex and Temperament,*[3] has done more than anybody else to underline the relativity of the terms "masculine" and "feminine" when applied to psychological characteristics. She has shown in this and other publications the great malleability of human nature and given examples of variations in behavior patterns of men and women which in some societies go as far as the direct reversal of our accepted standards. Recently, in *Male and Female,*[4] however, Margaret Mead has come out in favor of a theory which explains feminine psychology in terms of women's biological function. Though she still maintains, as before, that to assign certain psychological traits and certain social roles to one sex rather than another means forcing Nature into a straight-jacket and causing frustration and neuroses to great numbers of individuals who won't fit into the mold, she nevertheless asserts that from birth on—which itself, in her view, is a different experience for the two sexes—the life and the mental outlook of a girl are shaped by her potential maternity. A boy has to be active and to prove himself through achievement; he has to *"become"* in order to be reassured; a girl simply *is.*

"The life of the female starts and ends with sureness, first with the simple identification with her mother, last with the sureness that that identification is true, and that she has made another human being."[5] This assumption implies a fundamental difference in character structure between

---

[3]Mead, Margaret. *Sex and Temperament in Three Primitive Societies.* New York, W. Morrow, 1935.
[4]Mead, Margaret. *Male and Female, A Study of the Sexes in a Changing World.* New York, W. Morrow, 1949.
[5]*Ibid.,* p. 158.

men and women which would necessarily cut across variations in culture patterns and in individual temperaments and abilities. It is in direct contradiction to the views expressed by the same author in many places even in the same book, e.g.: "Every known society creates and maintains artificial occupational divisions and personality expectations for each sex that limit the humanity of the other sex. One form that these distinctions make is to deny the range of difference among the members of one sex . . . . our failure to recognize the very great variety of human beings who are now mingled and mated in one great mélange that includes temperamental contrasts as great as if the rabbit mated with the lion and sheep with leopards. Characteristic after characteristic in which the differences within a sex are so great that there is enormous overlapping are artificially assigned as masculine or feminine . . . . We may go up the scale from simple physical differences through complementary definitions that overstress the role of sex difference and extend it inappropriately to other aspects of life, to stereotypes of such complex activities as those involved in the formal use of the intellect, in the arts, in government and in religion. In all these complex achievements of civilization, those activities which are mankind's glory, and upon which depends our hope of survival in this world that we have built, there has been this tendency to make artificial distinctions that limit an activity to one sex, and by denying the actual potentialities of human beings limit not only both men and women, but also equally the development of the activity itself."[6] Thus, as a social anthropologist Margaret Mead stresses the variety of culture patterns and the purely conventional coincidence of psychological traits with sex; under the influence of psycho-analytic theory she links the two. The split between the two disciplines manifests itself even within the same mind; it is more outspoken where the conflicting schools of thought are expressed by different representatives.

At this juncture, when the question of psychological sex characteristics and their origin is so undecided, it is probably best to leave the issue in abeyance and to confine ourselves to the statement of two facts: First, that there is, in our society, a stereotype of Woman which has a practical reality. Retail traders—who, after all, know their business—cater for it; advertisers appeal to it; film producers and editors of women's journals direct their activities with this ideal consumer in mind. It represents the lowest common denominator of contemporary womankind as established by mass observation and market research. According to it the majority of women, or rather the abstract Woman, is the homemaker, interested chiefly in domestic affairs: she is fond of babies and devoted to her children's success; she is attracted by "glamor" and longing for "romance"; she is vitally interested in her appearance and pays attention to minute details; her success or failure are measured in terms of marriage and appeal to the other sex, generally, not of a career. To preserve the semblance of youth is therefore her main concern. This is the popular and much publicized stereotype, the Woman to whom radio programs, posters and sales catalogues are addressed, whose instincts are appealed to and whose vanity is flattered by skillful salesmanship. It is the model set up to aspiring young girls by pressure of public opinion and to which they will be eager to conform.

The second fact worth noting is this: There are in our culture notions of femininity

---

[6]*Ibid.*, pp. 372–74. Many more passages in a similar vein could be quoted. See footnote 3 of Dr. Mead's article in this issue.

and masculinity as two contrasting sets of personality traits and, though these terms are by no means clearly defined, the dichotomy as such is well established. It is customary to refer to some qualities of character and behavior as "feminine" and to others as "masculine," though these terms do *not* mean, as the dictionary states: "of female sex, of woman" and "of male sex," respectively. Rather, they are meant to express a kind of tone quality, a subtle nuance superimposed on each personality trait. Every person, it is generally agreed, possesses both masculine and feminine traits, is, in fact, a mixture of the two. L. M. Terman and C. C. Miles, in their *Sex and Personality: Studies in Masculinity and Femininity,*[7] tried to establish a scale by which personalities can be measured in terms of their relative masculinity and femininity and they applied their score—carefully worked out on the basis of questionnaires and tests of attitudes, opinions, interests, emotional response, and so on—to different social groups, classified by occupation, age, education, and other factors. Their very interesting findings show, among others, that high scholarship students score more highly feminine than low scholarship students, or that policemen, as a group, have a higher femininity score than mechanics.

As will readily be seen from these examples, femininity is a quality divorced from sex and possessed in varying degrees by individuals of either. It is impossible to nail down what the term, so widely used and so generally accepted, really means.

At the time of writing, for instance, there is in London an exhibition of paintings by the Impressionist Berthe Morisot. Not one critic failed to mention the feminine charm of her pictures, the "exquisite femininity" of her art, etc. although both in style and in subject matter her paintings are entirely in line with the impressionist school and do not differ in any essential from the works of Renoir, Manet or Corot whose influences are clearly visible. Why, then, are her landscapes, portraits and still-lives "feminine" whereas Renoir's are not—except for the fact that they are known to be created by a woman? Sensitivity and loving attention to detail—which in this connection are possibly meant to be the feminine characteristics—are typical of all the Impressionists, though Berthe Morisot was the only woman among them.

Compassion and devotion to individuals rather than causes have, also, often been called feminine traits, though chiefly when possessed by women. Men who are outstanding in these virtues are on that account not usually labelled feminine.

Absence of aggressiveness has sometimes been characterized as a feminine virtue and much has been made of this notion by those who advocate greater participation of women in public affairs on the ground that this would strengthen the pacifist element in politics. Here again, not only were the chief exponents of "non-violence" men, but the women who have entered politics did, on the whole, not differ from the average male politician. If they did, they would not have been elected by the men and women voters of their constituencies.

Thinking in concrete images rather than abstract ideas has been described by some others as a feminine characteristic. On the basis of this assumption the vast majority of mankind would fall into the category of feminine minds.

Ultimately, femininity has been said—and said with the authority of psychoanalysis—to consist in passivity, or, to use Freud's terms, in a "preference for passive aims." The passivity

---

[7]Terman, Lewis Madison and Miles, Catharine Cox, *Sex and Personality: Studies in Masculinity and Feminity.* New York and London, McGraw-Hill, 1936.

which, in Freud's view, is typical of woman's role in the sexual act, pervades all her personality. Margaret Mead's assertion that at the very start of life, effort, an attempt at greater self-differentiation, is suggested to the boy, while a relaxed acceptance of herself is suggested to the girl is another version, a different interpretation of the same assumption that femininity fundamentally is passivity.

The degree of passivity or initiative, in the sexual act as elsewhere, differs in individuals of either sex; and among the many varying influences on the development of personality, identification with one or the other parent is only one of many cross-currents. Longing for surrender and for a passive drifting-along is a tendency present in many men and women and is, in our competitive society, increasingly difficult to realize for either.

Women today show initiative in matters of sex as well as business. To call them "masculinized" because they have, on the whole, adjusted themselves to modern living conditions—or, on the other hand, to call "feminine" men who prefer the pen to the sword, or domestic felicity to the "struggle for existence"—means stretching the terms masculine and feminine to the limits of their meaning. What is termed "masculine" or "feminine" differs from one society to another, according to the way in which a culture defines the respective roles of men and women. If these roles change as a result of altered social conditions new psychological adjustments of both sexes follow. To refer these changes to a supposedly absolute scale is to minimize the importance of cultural factors in the formation of a personality. Not to mention that, as standards of measurements, the conventional terms masculine-feminine are much too vague and undefined to be useful.

If, admittedly, men and women represent composites of masculine and feminine characteristics in infinite variations it seems pertinent to ask what purpose is to be served by classifying personality traits according to sex altogether. The dichotomy which, as has been generally agreed, does not correspond to any real temperamental division along sex lines, only tends to create uncertainty about the degree of their maleness and femaleness in the innumerable intermediate personality types. It causes doubts, and sometimes anxieties, about their adequacy as members of their own sex in people who differ in some irrelevant characteristics from an, in fact, purely fictitious norm. To unfold freely the potentialities of their personalities both men and women have to think of themselves as human beings first, as males and females afterwards. Their maleness and femaleness will develop all the more fully the less it is hampered by fear lest a deviant taste or interest may mark some fundamental deficiency.

The question, then, whether in the competition for jobs women ought to specialize in fields which suit their feminine abilities and inclinations best, cannot be answered in the affirmative, for women differ in their interests and temperaments as much as men do. To label some occupations masculine, others feminine, means to bar people of either sex from activities for which they may well be temperamentally suited and which they might accomplish with success. This exclusion is done not only at the expense of individual happiness but also to the detriment of human advance.

To free women from the social and economic disqualifications from which they had suffered for centuries was the feminist aim. This liberation was important for them not qua women but qua human beings—just as the liberation of slaves happened for the sake of their humanity.

Today, when so much has been achieved—when so many roads to freedom have been opened and the dividing line between the temperamental characteristics of the two sexes have been blurred by so much overlapping—the time has come to lay aside the battle-axe and to stop the competitive struggle between the sexes. What matters, at this point, is to re-emphasize the value of the individual personality and to call back to mind the common humanity of men and women. The ideals worth striving for, such as truth, justice, freedom, goodness, sympathy, fair play, are unrelated to sex and can be achieved—or aimed at—by both. Peace is an ethical postulate and a necessity for the survival of mankind; there is no point in making it a competitive issue between the sexes by maintaining that pacifism is a feminine virtue. This would only make peace all the more difficult to attain by enhancing the aggressive tendencies in men who would feel they had thereby to assert their masculinity. And the same which is true of peace applies to any other human value.

It will not be easy to give up the age-old struggle between the sexes, to overcome the in-group solidarity of each and its antagonism against the out-group. It may be too deeply rooted, too much ingrained in the relationship between men and women.

But to realize the artificiality of a juxtaposition of masculine and feminine character traits is a first step towards a greater feeling of human solidarity between the sexes. Moreover, the ideology of equality is today sufficiently well established to be, at least, generally paid lip-service to. Finally, the free mingling of boys and girls at school, of men and women in work and sport has substituted a number of new solidarities—"school-tie," club, profession—which may contribute to a lessening of in-group feelings among the members of each sex.

This is a useful preparation of the ground for a philosophy which is not egalitarian, in terms of one sex as against another, but individualist and which stresses common human ideals while allowing the widest range to individual differences.

Margaret Mead on Women, Culture, and Work

We have already presented a biographical introduction to Margaret Mead with the excerpt from her significant and influential *Sex and Temperament in Three Primitive Societies.* In some of her later work, especially *Male and Female: A Study of the Sexes in the Changing World* (1949), Mead takes a more cautious stance toward changing sex roles, raising questions about how the biological fact of maternity and infant care might come into conflict with women's individualistic desires for equality with men in the workplace. Although she did not argue that women and men were differently programmed biologically, she did address the cultural and biological constraints on complete equality, given the necessity of reproduction and child care.

THE SELECTION

In the article presented here, Margaret Mead writes the final entry in a special issue on professional women in the *Journal of Social Issues* published in 1950, in which she evaluates the other articles and raises important questions on women's changing roles. While she argues forcefully for equal access to education and occupation, she leaves open the possibility that women's unique reproductive roles will limit complete integration and equality. She criticizes some egalitarians for not taking these issues seriously enough, and for not considering men's roles or cultural needs. She argues forcefully that without significant changes in men's family roles, married women and mothers

From Margaret Mead, "Towards Mutual Responsibility," *Journal of Social Issues* 6, no. 3 (1950): 45–56.

will not be able to achieve complete equality in the occupational realm. Among other possible solutions, she points to the need to change attitudes mandating that men marry women who will devote their lives to their husbands' careers. Although some points of her discussion bear assumptions that contemporary scholars would not accept, she raises some key issues that have still not been resolved by our society. She admits that, given equal opportunity, there might be a difference in the range of talents and choices exhibited by men and women. Nevertheless, she believes even that possibility would not justify artificial limitations keeping people from pursuing the goals they desire. Mead also wants to make sure that no one sex is "double-burdened" by the social needs of child rearing and household work. In the end she argues for the creation of a world in which the individual gifts and talents of all people, male and female, are encouraged and developed without the cultural obstacles of contemporaneous society.

TOWARDS MUTUAL RESPONSIBILITY

I was enormously struck by how much this series of articles takes for granted, how many assumptions are made without being explicitly stated, how mysterious this discussion would have been to our great-grandparents and possibly will seem to our great-great grandchildren, how oddly it must read even now to educated women from other cultures who still draw deeply on their own tradition. We could take these assumptions one by one: (1) the problem of women in the professions is treated as a problem for women alone, the references being of the order either that competition between the sexes is unfortunate and should be stopped, or that everybody will be better off if women exercise their gifts; and (2) the problem is stated as a problem of choice, in which the individual's choice is not fully implemented by society and should be.

On the negative side, I am particularly struck by those things which are not discussed. (1) The body: a foreign anthropologist combing the pages of this issue would find the statement from time to time that women do have children, but never a sugges-

tion of bodily envolvement in the activity of such matters as bodily rhythms, menopause or lactation. There is no suggestion that a human mind which is mediated by a body which performs such strikingly different activities from those of men might reflect these differences. . . . Marriage is discussed as a kind of job, involving night work of a sort of night watchman character at a specified spot, and combining marriage and a career as a matter of budgets, opportunities for part time work, and social attitudes towards married women. (2) Duty: this may seem odd even to mention, but the placid assumption that what the individual wants must always be good for society, that old fashioned social attitudes which interfere with what the individual wants at the moment should simply be swept aside, the absence of any question about the importance of cultural patterning of the relations between men and women and children is conspicuous.

This contemporary discussion boils down to a question of, if a woman in the United States wants to practice a profession, what external difficulties she will meet in chances to get training, in chances for a job, in combining a job with marriage and child rearing, in getting ahead in her profession, and what are some of the things which she can or ought to do about it. This is the problem as stated so far. As I see it, my task is to place it in a wider context. How does it stack up against the problems which have faced the human race since the Old Stone Age?

In the following discussion I shall not discuss sources and details. I have summarized my best understanding of the available anthropological literature elsewhere and I shall simply attempt here to apply those findings to the current problem. Seen broadly, we may examine known human cultures for two trends: (1) the trend towards the sharing of nurturing responsibilities toward the next generation, which in their widest sense include defense of the group as well as the provision of nourishment, shelter and education, and (2) the trend towards the specialization of some individuals, of one or both sexes, in such a way that they as priests or magicians, artists, intellectuals, physicians and engineers, have added to the elaborate structure of belief and knowledge that we call human culture. The special problem of women in the professions in the United States, 1950, is a subdivision of both problems: how does her professional life fit in with the contemporary division of labor with regard to nurture and how does it fit in with regard to specialization.

The history of the division of labor in regard to the nurture of children has included many oscillations in male and female responsibility, with the major food getting or clothes making or house building role falling now to the men, now to the women, now to both. When the differential in sheer physical strength is not involved as it is when one individual must raise a house post or hunt a large game animal in some way which involves struggling with it, or carrying it a great distance, there seems to have been no particular advantage resulting from assigning any one of these activities to one sex or the other. At certain periods in history, these activities have been patterned in ways which required strength: that is now no longer the case as the tractor replaces the plough, automatic guns the cannon, and derricks human effort in raising house posts. Aside from these matters of strength, each society has a division of labor, and where the division has been strong along sex lines it has been regarded as manly or womanly, as the case might be, to cook or sew, make pots or dress dolls. In most instances the association with strength has been proportionately slight and the role played by the division of labor much more important in defining sex roles for growing children, and in assuring adult sex partnerships in which all the necessary tasks would be performed.

Societies have also differed in the extent to which they have used division of tasks as indices of sex role; activities which are rigorously sex typed in one society—like embroidery or tailoring, weaving or sewing, butter making or house building—will be a matter of indiscriminate cooperation in another. And in every society there are essential economic activities in which both sexes can engage without comment, such as harvesting. However, there is one area in the realm of nurture which has always been regarded as belonging to women, although in some societies fathers play a considerable role and in many societies children are taken away from their mothers' care when they are very small,—that is the care of infants. Since up to very recent times the care of infants involved feeding them on human milk, this association was functional and inevitable. Some woman with milk was essential to the existence of the young infant. This is no longer the case as far as physical survival of the infant is concerned; modern bottle feeding was designed by males and it is possibly better adapted to the male care of infants than it is to females caring for infants since the bottle tends to be an extension of the hand rather than of the breast. From the standpoint of sheer economic necessity—against the backdrop of our long human history—there now seems to be no reason whatsoever why the nurture of children, including hour old infants, should be confined to women. It may be expected that as American men have more experience with very young infants they will find children of the nursery age less inexplicable and deal with them as easily as do men in many other cultures. *Economically,* that is in terms of the present balance between cultural invention and natural sources of livelihood, there is no reason for any specialization by sex in the care of children, and therefore there are no longer any economic reasons why women should not work outside the home within a few days of childbirth while someone else, male or female, feeds and cares for their children. Nor is there any reason why men should not work in the home while someone else, male or female, brings home a pay check.

This is one possible direction in which modern society may go, a complete breakdown of the differentiation of economic roles between men and women, so that in some households it is one parent who cares for the children, in some the other, while in some it is shared, with a comparable rearrangement of working hours outside the home. This trend is already in evidence among young GI Bill student families, where both husband and wife study together and care for the children together. If it is to be carried to a conclusion which establishes an even handed sharing between men and women of the burdens of nurture, which then gives an even handed freedom for the jobs and responsibilities of cultural creativity, it must however be carried all the way, so that it is as expectable and reasonable and honorable for a man to do more than fifty per cent of the domestic tasks involved in home making as it is for the woman.

It is striking that throughout these articles, when marriage is discussed, it is tacitly assumed that a professional woman who marries must plan her life so she still carries the full burden of a home. Such an uneven arrangement in which women are expected to carry two jobs while men carry only one, and a marriage that is still expected to work and meet the very complicated job demands which we make on marriage among educated people, is palpably unworkable. The most outstanding attempt at such a system has been in the Soviet Union where women have been "freed" to work in factories, "freed" from the care of their babies during working hours, but remain saddled with problems of homemaking in a society filled with queues and wearisome shortages. Any forthright facing of the relationship between women in the professions and the division of the nurturing role must involve a revision in the attitudes of both men and women towards the roles of both men and women in the home. Bottle feeding has made it possible for these roles to be interchanged or shared; any talk about how a woman can combine marriage and a career which does not include revision of the husband's role simply obscures the real issue. Even such concessions to homemaking as residence in the suburbs which involves commuting are regarded by men as a heavy stress. No one would expect a man to do as well in his profession if he also had the care of a home and several small children on his mind every minute, nor should they expect it of a woman. Arguments that employers should employ married women have to fall back on the fact that married women are less of a sexual menace, or are more balanced and adjusted, to overcome the perfectly real objection against hiring someone who has another job the other sixteen hours which may at any moment claim priority.

This discussion does not, of course, apply only to women in the professions; it applies to all women who by necessity or preference must take part in an activity which requires many hours of concentrated work, usually located outside the home. But the question of women in the professions must be seen against a background of women who work if we are to assess its full importance in a democratic society. The fact that it is even harder for a professional woman, meeting a high standard of skill and creativity, to combine her work and the full responsibility of a home is at least balanced by the circumstance that in a society which is educationally stratified as our is, it is the professional woman who will set the standards for the working woman of all types. The professional woman who insists that a woman *ought* to be able to combine her career and her family is doing a disservice to the unskilled woman factory worker who, after an eight hour day, comes home to wash and mend and cook and clean—all by herself. It is up to the professional woman in the prestige professions to insist that no one, male or female, should be expected to do two jobs, and that as we redesign our social and economic life in such a way that all women who are not being supported by a husband have to work, we must also redesign it in such a way that women with homemaking responsibilities as wives, widows, divorcees or daughters must not be expected to carry two loads. At the lower income levels this means social services. As far as occupational styling goes it means . . . many more part time jobs. As far as the climate of opinion goes, it means a complete restyling of the attitudes of both men and women. But such a restyling is more than a possibility in the contemporary world, it is in line with our insistence upon achievement rather than inheritance—in biological function as well as in beauty or caste. It is in line with our present style of terminable marriage and with our disapproval of all shared living arrangements except those which involve husband and wife and minor children.

It is congruent with our present insistence on educating boys and girls alike, a situation in which the girls will inevitably demand as much choice as the boys are given, and in which as long as the boy's economic role is phrased as one of choice the girl will tend to rebel against a role which is seen as unchosen. "If a boy's marriage does not dictate how he spends his active working hours, why should a girl's?" is an almost inevitable question in the present climate of opinion. I shall return later to some of the conditions which work in the other direction.

If we turn, then, from the problem of shared responsibility for nurture—which involves, of course, mending one's own sox and doing one's own washing as well as caring for children, spouse, the ill and the aged—to the question of the woman who, among the women who work, has a profession we can narrow our discussion. . . . [P]rofessions tend to mean occupations which can only be practiced by individuals with higher than average gifts, and with special training. They are the economic activities of the specialists and of the specialists with prestige, those who are in a position to utilize the highest knowledge available and to make new contributions to that knowledge. They are the practitioners from whom we can expect most of our advances to come. Even if we were to decide that the present trend which prepares women to be self-supporting and favors their working outside their homes for at least those parts of their lives when they do not have young children were a desirable trend, a trend which made for more rounded human beings, a better relationship between the sexes, and a more democratic way of life, there would still be serious questions to answer as to whether women should enter the professions and, if so, which professions.

I want to pause here for a moment to underline what I mean by *should*. A totalitarian society which places the assumed welfare of the state above the welfare of the individual determines what an individual may and may not, must and must not do. A democracy ideally seeks to create conditions within which individuals will be able to make choices which integrate their own intentions and the welfare of the community as a whole. It is still possible, I believe, to discuss the question of whether women should enter professions, or whether women should plan to combine homemaking and a profession, or whether there are certain professions to which women may be expected to make more of a contribution than others—and yet stand firmly for the position that women should be allowed to *try* whatever they wish to try. When I say "should enter" I mean, with our present knowledge and in the light of our present aspirations, is this a goal we should seek; but I do not mean that, if it does not seem to be such a goal, doors to professional schools should be closed, or women sent back to the home. We know far too little to risk losing the most precious privilege of a democratic society, free experimentation.

The question of whether women should enter the professions boils down first to the biological question of how necessary motherhood is for the individual woman. We, at present, have only the scantiest suggestive evidence on such matters as the incidence of cancer in women who have and who have not born children. Even if we find that the woman who does not have children is more in danger of certain somatic disorders, or has more difficult psychological adjustments to make, we might still find that not having children provides certain rearrangements of the use of energy which makes it possible for the childless woman, like the celibate man, to make certain types of contributions to society or to find certain creative outlets valuable both to the individual and to the community. If this were definitely to be established as true—of at least a given period in history—it might then be necessary to restyle some of our social expecta-

tions in a way which treated these women, and those men, who muted their biological roles in favor of exercising some special gift, or performing some special service to humanity as people who had made an honorable choice. Today, outside the religious orders such men and women are heavily penalized by society, suspected variously of sexual inversion, emotional inadequacy, hostility and the like. If it is not only not necessary to lead a usual biological life—which means for a woman bearing children—but perhaps even desirable that some individuals should not lead such a life, then we are at present doing a very poor job of making it possible for them not to do so.

Aside from the question of the election of a state of celibacy, or childlessness without celibacy, the next important question is whether motherhood and a full professional life really are compatible. (If we are to move towards the sort of society envisaged in the preceding pages, in which many men take on the major responsibility for homemaking, the question will equally be raised as to whether a full professional life and fatherhood, in terms which go beyond mere providing the money to run a house, are compatible either. It may be that the increased unwillingness to marry of certain types of ambitious intellectual young males may be directly related to an unwillingness to devote their energies to the new style of fatherhood as contrasted with the less exacting activities of procreation and "making a living.") This question has several facets. Are we going to move as a culture away from the specialization of women's nutritive role, away from breast feeding, away from individual nurturing of young children under two, away from the associated roles for women, the responsibility for food and shelter and all those aspects of nutritive care which call for sympathy? Are we going to eliminate as peculiarly feminine any of the roles associated with the care of children and limit "motherhood" as differing from "fatherhood" to the nine month pregnancy period and a short post partum readjustment period, to, for the women with three children in all, a period of possibly lowered efficiency of at the most two years? If this is done, and in this way, a woman simply has to plan for a two year handicap, capriciously distributed, in her professional life as compared with a man. Given the different distributions of ability within a sex, it would still be reasonable for professional schools to train women who were a little bit better on the average than the men they admit, compensating for the possibility that they will work two years less by insisting on better preparation, greater drive, or greater ability. The accompanying climate of opinion would involve women ceasing to regard with resentment that "lost two years," whereas present indications are that a woman who is willing to reduce her biological child bearing role to such a minimum is also likely to regard the time that she puts into child bearing as a lamentable handicap in her professional competition with men.

At the next level of discussion, if motherhood is to retain some of the characteristics which it has had through history, with a mother-child relationship, originally deeply symbiotic carried over into the period of lactation, and used as a model of mother and child relationship which is slowly modified in its degree of intimate interdependence as the child grows older, so that assigning to women the domestically located part of the nurturing role is a necessary and congruent part of her motherhood and her self-realization as an individual and her functioning in society, then we may raise the question, Are a home and a profession congruent? Will not such a motherhood role demand so much of strength and imagination from a woman that even those women who have the energy to carry on a profession and psychologically mother their children will always be divided, never able to give the same singleness of purpose to their

work that men—or at least men who have had no new style fathering to do—are able to give? And if this is so, doesn't it mean that women's professional contributions will always be given with a divided heart and mind, and that while it may be necessary to train women, it is unrealistic to expect from married women with children whole-hearted attention to high level work? If this question is answered in the affirmative, a second alternative could be offered to women with professional ambitions or professional training.

This alternative is the frank acceptance of women's biological difference from men, which is a very different thing from accepting her "responsibilities for a family," responsibilities most of which some other woman—or man—could perfectly well discharge, were our social expectations different. Such an acceptance would mean that women who had children would be recognized as different in their whole orientation to life from women who did not have children, and that for the period while they were hoping to have children and bearing and rearing children, their energies would be most appropriately employed by focussing on motherhood, but that before marriage and after their children were reared, they were strictly comparable with men, or with unmarried women, in abilities and interests. It would carry with it an expectation on women's part of choosing between devoting their whole lives to a career, and paying the price of childlessness in order to do work they passionately wanted to do, or devoting their lives to two alternating activities, each of major importance, and with the modest expectation that if they only devoted two-thirds of their lives to an activity to which men devoted their whole active lives they could expect to accomplish less professionally, everything else being equal. Such an expectation on the part of women and of society as a whole is at present emerging in the discussion of reorienting women's higher education so that homemaking is restored to dignity as a full time occupation deserving to be chosen by the gifted and the intelligent, and by the insistent question as to what is to be the fate of the mature woman who, after being educated, did choose homemaking and now has nothing adequate to occupy her time. There are a considerable number of feminine biographies which suggest that there is a marked difference in the creative output of women when they have faced the fact that they will not have children, or will have no more children, whether this conviction comes from closed tubes, a hysterectomy, the death of a loved husband or the menopause; and this differential creativity might be systematically utilized in society by institutions for training women over forty for full time professional roles. Any such development would, of course, produce a corresponding change in higher education for young women, whose college years would include preparation for the homemaking choice they might wish to make preparation for a career to be pursued singlemindedly in case of childlessness, and the expectation that in case they have children they will be going back into some professional work afterwards.

Still without considering the question of which professional work would be most appropriate for women, there is one further important question. Does someone who is to do good work in an exacting professional career need a devoted spouse? The trend among professional women has been to marry professional men, thus perhaps adding one more handicap to their professional competency, not only in terms of the complications which come from rivalry, conflicting institutional demands, inevitable choices as to whose career is to suffer if a move is made, and the like, but also depriving themselves of the kind of singleminded devotion which the good wife of the successful doctor or lawyer, artist or scientist has historically given to men. And here

again the deprivation is double, for the professional woman not only does not have the kind of help which a professional man receives from a woman who lives only for his work and subordinates all personal ambitions and interests to promoting his career, but she also has either to be such a wife herself, or fear that perhaps she is robbing her husband of what he needs. Here again, this double dilemma can only be dealt with by a change in the climate of opinion which makes it as respectable for a woman to marry a man with less ambition or less intelligence or less prestige than she has herself without any damage to either of them in the eyes of the world. As long as we encourage a double standard which makes it perfectly acceptable for men to marry women who are notably less ambitious or less gifted than they, and to have their marriages pronounced good marriages, but makes it perfectly unacceptable for a woman to marry a man who stands in the same relationship to her success and gifts, we are cultivating a cultural expectation which adds an extra strain to our professional marriages. Once this problem is frankly faced, endogamous marriages between two professionals can be seen as what they are—a doubly exciting, doubly dangerous venture—as they have always been recognized to be in the world of the theatre. If all of these problems which I have been outlining became part of our cultural definition of the possibilities of adulthood, young men and young women would have larger areas of clear choice, being able to choose a single life, or a married life, a married life in which parenthood was shared between them or a married life on which either the wife *or* the husband assumed the domestic role of homemaking and child rearing, and in the case of the woman a life in which homemaking occupied her full time for part of her life without compromising her full professional functioning at other periods.

We may now turn to the question of which professions are most appropriate for women. Here we find a condition which accurately reflects the division of labor throughout history; women, when they leave the home, have tended to become specialists in those fields which are extensions of their traditional homemaking role,—teaching, nursing, library work, or clerical work which is an extension of certain traditional types of wifely tasks, including the primitive marketing and record keeping. They have been less numerous and less successful in those activities which are the contemporary extensions of the more traditional male activities,—engineering, politics, law, warfare and wholesale trade—activities which in the past have been closely associated with war. We might regard this merely as an historical accident in which, as activities originally performed by the family become institutionalized and extended, women went into those forms which had been their traditional prerogatives and duties, while men simply elaborated their traditional role. Relative success in the two types of activities would then be explained partly in terms of social prejudice against either men or women entering fields which were regarded as unmanly or unwomanly, and partly by the important role of having models during childhood and youth. . . . The boy and girl in our society are presented from earliest childhood with certain expected behavior; mother dries the baby's tears, father fixes the car, mother cooks the dinner, father understands the income tax form. The preeminence of each sex in the field into which their traditional roles have been extended is, however, badly compromised by another historical trend, that of according the highest demands for achievement and the highest rewards for achievement to men. There are cogent reasons for considering that this male demand for achievement may be so deeply rooted in the genetic experiences of the human male that it

may be an ineradicable psychological element with which every society has to deal; but it may also be argued that in a society where men participated in parenthood to an equal degree with women, it might vanish when both sexes were reared by both sexes and the pressure on the male child to differentiate himself from his mother and prove his manliness was reduced. However this may be, we have at present the spectacle of women beginning to desert the feminine professions such as teaching and nursing for the more impersonal activities of industry, repudiating both the demands for disinterestedness which society has extended as a compensation for poor pay and the hazards of being administratively subject to men of inferior calibre just because they are men. The teacher and nursing shortages point up sharply a crisis in social attitudes, the extent to which women are still penalized as professionally inferior to men, especially in executive and highly paid roles.

If society is to continue to institutionalize as the most appropriate fields for women those fields in which they can draw on their historical roles and utilize the model setting women of their childhood, and—in the case of women who spend part of their lives in full time homemaking—use their experience in homes as daughters, wives and mothers in their professional work outside homes, then radical revisions must be made in the administrative structures of medicine and education particularly.

There remains the question of which profession shall be chosen by the very high level and gifted individual. It can be argued on the basis of present evidence that men and women are equally competent at the routine activities of any of the professions, can be good doctors or good lawyers, good teachers or good members of congress; and that relative lack of success in any of these fields can be adequately explained in terms of opportunity, social tradition, and social expectation. But there still is the question of the exceptionally gifted person upon whose vision and insight, skill and imagination, the progress of society rests,—the poet, the seer, the natural scientist, the great social leader. Here the difference between the great and the merely good is a line which is very hard to draw, as Terman's studies of gifted children only too heavily document. This is no simple matter of a high I. Q. or a measurable sensory threshold, but something much subtler, something for which we at present have no measurements. Here we may properly ask two questions: are women as a group as likely to contribute these specially gifted, absolutely essential breakers of new ground? Are they as likely to contribute them in one field as in another? Appeals to history here have been made by those who espouse both sides of the controversy, and have been proved to be relatively inconclusive. The exponent of feminine gifts can always find an historical "proof" that women never were given a chance, the opponents that they were. The more fruitful approach would seem to be to examine the historical roles and psychodynamic structure of both sexes in the light of what we know about creativity and to begin to form hypotheses about the potential contribution of each sex, and then be sure that we create the cultural conditions within which each hypothetical creativity can have a chance to blossom.

Taking the historical approach first, we find that women have in the arts made their greatest contribution in literature, and in the sciences in the human sciences. Attempting to introduce some sort of order into this finding, it is possible to suggest that women have at present more chance of making contributions in fields in which human relations, unabashed introspection and the recognition of differences between the self and others are important conditions, while men have at present more chance of making contributions in those fields where the perception of

order in the natural world and the imposition of these perceptions is more important. Again this hypothesis can be backed up by minute psychodynamic discussions from the clinic, from the laboratory and from the findings on other societies. Its implications for social action—for our mutual responsibility to build a better world—are, however, clear. Without deterring women from entering any field, for it may well be that the most seemingly masculine fields such as mathematics and music would be the richer if a woman of great endowment devoted herself to it, let us make it possible for women to have every chance to develop in those fields in which they have, hypothetically, a particular contribution to make—the arts and sciences of human relations. Paradoxically, in the present structure of our society, in which many of the possible changes in the climate of opinion which have been suggested in this article are not likely to take place very rapidly, we can only make it possible for women to contribute in these fields by seeing to it that men also have a full chance in them. If they are treated even handedly, and well endowed, if those who plan keep a weather eye on the question of utilizing both masculine and feminine gifts so that it will be impossible for a university to set up a study in human success without a single woman on the research team, or for an investigator of one sex ever to claim to give a full account of a human situation, then there is a possibility that women may have a chance to make a contribution, comparable in importance to the great inventions by which men have built up human culture from the Stone Age to the present day.

Mutual responsibility means in fact creating a world in which men and women's gifts are used mutually, in all their great similarity, in all their possible deep difference, to build a world in which no human gift is disallowed because there are not cultural forms through which it can be expressed.

Mirra Komarovsky
on Functional Analysis
of Sex Roles

For a biographical sketch of Mirra Komarovsky, see the earlier entry "Cultural Contradictions and Sex Roles." The following article is based on a paper Komarovsky read at the December 1949 annual meeting of the American Sociological Association. At the time, Komarovsky was teaching at Barnard College, Columbia University, and in a footnote she thanks her colleague Robert Merton for "his valuable help in the preparation of this paper." This is a more theoretical piece than the one earlier "Cultural Contradictions of Sex Roles" we saw in the previous section, and Merton's influence can be seen in the concepts Komarovsky uses.

THE SELECTION

Mirra Komarovsky begins by noting the wide recognition of strain in urban middle-class women's roles, but she believes the nature of this strain has not been adequately described or analyzed. "Why," she asks, "do sex roles today present such an arena of social and mental conflict?" As opposed to the common psychological (Freudian) responses to this question, Komarovsky suggests that the problem lies in the social and cultural realm. As a functionalist, she wants to examine the contradictions in sex roles introduced by social change, looking at their relation to "kinship, occupational, educational and other social systems to which they are relevant." She

From Mirra Komarovsky "Functional Analysis of Sex Roles," *American Sociological Review* 15 (August 1950): 508–16.

especially sets out to explore the "unintended consequences" of changes in relevant social and cultural systems (the latent functions and dysfunctions, referring to Merton's terms).

Komarovsky's main argument is that boys and girls are socialized differently because of their different adult roles. Boys are given more freedom and independence, while girls are given more family responsibilities. These differences are related to the adult male provider role and the adult female domestic–maternal role. With the nuclear family becoming more isolated structurally from the family of orientation, this differential socialization creates conflicts within marriages, in that men feel less obligated to the parental family than do women. Hence, the "in-law" problems commonly referred to in popular culture are more likely to have to do with the wife's continuing ties with her parents and consequent conflicts with her felt obligations to her husband.

This article is a fine example of a functional analysis illustrating concepts such as dysfunction, latent function, and the problem of adjustment (or lack thereof) between different institutions. Here we can also see, however, the tendency of functionalism to take for granted the status quo. Nowhere does Komarovsky raise the question, for example, of whether it might be problematic that the husband shows such a weak tie to his parents, or that he fails to support his wife's sense of obligation to her parental family. Instead, the problem seems to be framed in terms of the wife's overattachment to her parents. Thus, while the article recognizes strains in the adult roles of men and women, the analysis does not question those roles, nor is there much recognition of power differences between men and women. Finally, the author simply assumes that "the norm" is for women to be married and at-home homemakers while men are the employed providers. Still, this and other sociological discussions of the 1950s indicate that even in this era of "traditional" families that our popular culture represents as being simpler and happier, there was widespread recognition of problems in the roles allocated to women.

FUNCTIONAL ANALYSIS OF SEX ROLES

The concept of social roles with special reference to sex and age roles has been the subject of increasing sociological interest. But the problem of sex roles in various segments of our society requires further systematic empirical study. This paper attempts to outline what is believed to constitute a fruitful theoretical orientation for such research and to illustrate the application of this theoretical approach in a pilot study, involving twenty intensive case histories of middle class urban married women, in the summer of 1949. The study was focused on the "problem" aspects of sex roles, and while the discussion will be thus delimited, the theoretical approach it advocates appears equally applicable to other aspects of this general subject.

That there exists a great deal of strain in women's roles among the urban middle classes is generally recognized but the description and analysis of this phenomenon remain to be developed. The mere diversity of roles that women must play at different ages or in different relations need not in itself create a problem. Many societies show such diversity without causing either social conflict or personal disorganization. Indeed in any society, age, sex, class, occupation, race, and ethnic background involve the individual in a variety of socially sanctioned patterns of interaction *vis-à-vis* different categories of persons. Why, then, to put the question most generally, do sex roles today present such an arena of social and mental conflict?

Probably the most influential and systematically developed answer to this question today is the one found in psychiatric literature. This answer centers upon two explanatory models. The orthodox analysts say with Freud: "Anatomy is her fate." They see women's problem in terms of the psychological dynamics arising out of some biologically determined sexual characteristic, i.e., penis envy or masochism. The individual life history is then taken as determining whether the development of this characteristic will follow normal or neurotic patterns. The other explanatory model takes more account of cultural factors. But, again, the root of the problem is seen in the clash between the biologically determined feminine impulses, on the one hand, and the social roles, on the other, which today, it is alleged, are peculiarly at variance with the biologically set needs of the feminine psyche.

In contrast to the psychiatric, the theoretical approach of this paper is sociological. It seeks to interpret social and mental conflict and the institutional malfunctioning which constitute the social problem in question, in terms of interrelation of elements within and between relevant social and cultural systems. It accepts the general premise that our culture is full of contradictions and inconsistencies with regard to women's roles, that new social goals have emerged without the parallel development of social machinery for their attainment, that norms persist which are no longer functionally appropriate to the social situations to which they apply, that the same social situations are subject to the jurisdiction of conflicting social codes, that behavior patterns useful at some stage become dysfunctional at another, and so on.

If orientation towards social patterns distinguishes our approach from the psychiatric, other features set it apart from some of the anthropological and other sociological approaches. It attempts more deliberately and systematically to place sex roles in their structural contexts. It is only when sex roles are seen in their manifold relations to kinship, occupational, educational and other social systems to which they are relevant, that we can attain three scientific objectives: (1) the functional significance of sex roles becomes apparent, (2) cultural contradictions can be located, (3) possibilities for change can be assessed. Furthermore, though to an extent shared by others, it is the central concern of this orientation to explore the *unintended* consequences of relevant social and cultural systems, not only for personality but for other systems; or, to use the terminology suggested by Merton, to explore the latent functions and dysfunctions of one system for another.[1]

The orientation towards social patterns does not preclude the consideration of psychological factors: personality types as determinants of acceptance or rejection of given social roles, tensions in personality produced by diverse roles, techniques of maintaining an unconventional role, and so on. Indeed, it may be suggested that the consideration of these psychological factors can be all the more incisive and precise when they are set in the framework of social patterns.

So described, the approach will be readily identifiable as the "functional analysis" in sociology but a few further observations are in order. Because this research is oriented

---

[1]Robert K. Merton, *Social Theory and Social Structure,* Chap. 1.

towards "social problems," it centers upon precisely those phenomena which have hitherto been on the periphery of functional analysis: phenomena of maladaptation, of strain, of dysfunction. Furthermore, sex roles are in such flux today that research must also deal with phenomena of change and readjustment, so intimately related to social and psychological strains. A static approach which did not address itself to problems of social dynamics would be patently inadequate for the task in hand.

Functional analysis has sometimes been criticized on the score of method; more specifically, because of its failure to subject its theoretical formulations to empirical tests. If the criticism is deserved, it does not appear to arise from its intrinsic features. In the forthcoming application of the approach, general formulations were redefined into propositions which were actually or potentially testable by empirical techniques.

AN APPLICATION OF
FUNCTIONAL ANALYSIS

It is well known that the family of procreation occupies a dominant position in our kinship system. This is evidenced in a large variety of ways. Typically, the family of procreation is residentially segregated from the family of orientation of either spouse which, of course, is not the case in the joint or stem family systems. The ties to ancestors which obtain in a clan society and the ties to siblings maintained in the consanguine family type are much weaker in our society. Furthermore, all social norms, from those expressed in the legal code to those expressed in the "advice to the lovelorn" column, reiterate the theme that the primary loyalty is to one's spouse and children as against parents or

siblings. The legal expression of this theme is found in our inheritance and support laws. If a man dies intestate it is generally true that his wife and children get *all* of his property. It is only in the absence of direct descendants that parents or collateral relatives share the inheritance with his widow. While statutes are fairly common requiring a son to contribute to the support of an indigent parent, his responsibility is more limited than it is toward his wife and children. These laws are deeply rooted in the mores. As an example, undergraduates have been observed by the writer to be shocked to learn that these cultural norms are far from being universal and that among the Arapaho, to take one instance, a dead man's brother has superior claim to his property even if the widow and his children are left destitute.[2]

In fact, the priority of the marriage relationship over the parental family in our culture has in recent years found expression even in certain intellectual fields of inquiry. As the result of the diffusion of the psychiatric point of view, close ties to a parent are under suspicion as the "silver cord" and, conversely, the emancipation from the family of orientation is viewed as the touchstone of emotional maturity. These presuppositions often find their most explicit and unquestioned expression in textbooks. Thus, for example, a popular textbook on marriage states: "If there is a bona-fide in-law problem the young couple need first of all to be certain of their perspective. The success of their marriage should be put above everything else, even above attachment to parents. Husband and wife must come first. Otherwise the individual exhibits immaturity."[3] Another textbook affirms: "Close attachments to members of the family, whether parents or siblings, accentuate the normal difficulties involved in achieving the

---

[2]M. Nimkoff, *Marriage and the Family,* p. 36.
[3]M. A. Bowman, *Marriage for Moderns,* p. 328.

response role expected in marriage."[4] Again, ". . . there is a call for a new attitude, a subordinating of and to some extent an aloofness from the home of one's childhood."[5] "Do not live with or in the neighborhood of your relatives and in-laws, and do not allow them to live with you."[6]

But although this pattern of the primacy of the family of procreation *vis-à-vis* the family of orientation has been abundantly recognized, it has not been systematically related to the wide range of its functional and dysfunctional consequences. From within this range we may mark out the problem of sociopsychological continuities and discontinuities in the kinship structure. More particularly, we wish to consider to what extent the training in the parental family makes for subsequent adjustment to the well-nigh exclusive loyalty to spouse and children. We are raising two specific problems. Which particular elements of role training in the parental family can be discerned to have byproducts which affect later adjustment of the members in their own families of procreation? Which of the two sexes is enabled to make the shift from the parental family to marriage with the minimum of psychological hazards?

DIFFERENTIAL TRAINING OF THE SEXES IN THE PARENTAL FAMILY

Illuminating material bearing upon differential training of boys and girls in the parental family was collected by the writer in the form of 73 biographical documents prepared by women undergraduates. The documents reveal that despite increasing similarity in the upbringing of the sexes among middleclass families, some sex differences relevant to our problem still persist. The girls who had brothers testified that in various ways the parents *tended to speed up, most often unwittingly, but also deliberately, the emancipation of the boy from the family, while they retarded it in the case of his sister.*

Judging from these documents, there are three different mechanisms through which this is achieved. Interesting as these are in themselves, our main problem is to consider presently their further consequences for the operation of the kinship system. Among these mechanisms is, first of all, the pattern of providing sons with *earlier and more frequent opportunities for independent action.* The boys are freer to play away from home grounds, to return later, and to pick their own activities, movies and books. They are ordinarily allowed the first independent steps earlier than their sisters, such as the first walk to school without an adult, the first unaccompanied movie or baseball game, and later in life, the train trip or the job away from home.

A student writes:

It was thought to be a part of my brother's education to be sent away to school. I was expected to go to a local college so that I could live at home. When my brother got his first job he got a room so that he would not have to commute too far. My sister, at 22, turned down several offers of jobs at a high salary

---

[4]H. Becker and R. Hill, *Marriage and the Family*, p. 349.

[5]E. R. Groves, *Marriage*, 1933, p. 274.

[6]H. Hart, *Personality and the Family*, p. 199. "Psychological" statements of this sort are frequently found in family textbooks. Authors often discharge their obligations to the concept of cultural relativity by an introductory chapter on "Other Family Patterns" and a general statement that the rest of the book deals with our own family system. This general disclaimer of universality does not prevent students from accepting the generalizations cited throughout the text as universal and it certainly does not help them to see sociopsychological processes in relation to the larger social structure in which they occur.

and took a much less desirable one only because she could live at home. She continues to be as much under parental control as she was when in college. Frankly, if anything should happen to my parents, I would be at a complete loss while I know that my brothers could carry on alone very well.

The second mechanism through which the emancipation of sons is speeded up involves a *higher degree of privacy in personal affairs* allowed the boys. One girl writes:

My mother is very hurt if I don't let her read the letters I receive. After a telephone call she expects me to tell her who called and what was said. My brother could say "a friend" and she would not feel insulted.

And again:

My brother is 15, 3 years younger than I am. When he goes out after supper mother calls out: "Where are you going, Jimmy?" "Oh, out." Could I get away with this? Not on your life. I would have to tell in detail where to, with whom, and if I am half an hour late mother sits on the edge of the living-room sofa watching the door.

States another student:

I have a brother of 23, and a sister of 22, and a younger brother who is 16. My sister and I had a much more sheltered life than my brothers. My brothers come and go as they please. Even my younger brother feels that his current girl friend is his personal affair. No one knows who she is. But the family wants voluminous files on every boy my sister and I want to date. It is not easy for us to get the complete genealogy of a boy we want to go out with.

Thirdly, the *daughters* of the family *are held to a more exacting code of filial and kinship obligations.* When the grandmother needs somebody to do an errand for her, or Aunt Jane who doesn't hear well needs help, the girl is more likely to be called upon. The pressure to attend and observe birthdays, anniversaries, and other family festivals is apparently greater upon her than upon the boy.

These patterns of differential training of the sexes in the parental family are generally recognized to be functionally oriented to their respective adult roles. The role of the provider, on the one hand, and of the homemaker on the other, call for different attitudes and skills. Competitiveness, independence, dominance, aggressiveness, are all traits felt to be needed by the future head of the family. Although the girl can train for her adult role and rehearse it within the home, the boy prepares for *his* outside the home, by taking a "paper route" or a summer job away from home. Again, the greater sheltering of the girl may be functionally appropriate in the light of greater risks incurred by her in the case of sexual behavior and also in marriage since, for the woman, marriage is not only a choice of a mate but also of a station in life.

The parents at times explicitly recognize this functional character of their training. One girl, for example, reports that both her parents were more indulgent to her. With a little pleading she could usually get what she wanted. Her brother, on the other hand, was expected to earn money for his little luxuries because "boys need that kind of training." In a couple of cases the girls testified that their brothers were expected to work their way through college, while the girls were supported. A student writes:

My brother is two years younger than I am. When we started going to school my father would always say as he saw us off in the morning, "Now, Buddy, you are the man and you must take good care of your sister." It amused me because it was I who always had to take care of him.

Another student recollects that when her brother refused to help her with her "math" on the ground that no one was allowed to help *him,* her mother replied: "Well, she is a girl, and it isn't as important for her to know 'math' and to learn how to get along without help."

More often, however, the proximate ground for enforcing the proper roles is expressed in terms of what constitutes manly or unmanly behavior or just "the right thing to do." The degree to which the recognition of functional implications is explicit is in itself an important problem bearing upon social change.

But if the differential upbringing of the sexes thus constitutes a preparation for their adult roles, it also has unintended consequences. This role training or, more specifically, the greater sheltering of the girl, has, as unintended by-products, further consequences for kinship roles which are not perceived. And it is to this that we now address ourselves. We are now prepared to advance a hypothesis that the greater sheltering of the girl has what Merton terms a "latent dysfunction" for the woman and for marriage in general. More specifically, we suggest that the major unintended consequence of this greater sheltering of the girl is to create in her such ties to the family of orientation that she is handicapped in making the psychosocial shift to the family of procreation which our culture demands. Our problem is not merely to demonstrate the fact of discontinuities in role training so perceptively discerned in other spheres by Benedict and others. These discontinuities must be related to their structural contexts. We shall show how tendencies created within one social structure react back upon the operation of another structure within the same kinship system without the intention or, indeed, the awareness of the participants.

The hypothesis just set forth requires us to examine the actual mechanisms through which these postulated consequences follow. Essentially it is assumed that to the extent that the woman remains more "infantile," less able to make her own decisions, more dependent upon one or both parents for initiating or channeling behavior and attitudes, more closely attached to them so as to find it difficult to part from them or to face their disapproval in case of any conflict between her family and spouse, or shows any other indices of lack of emotional emancipation—to that extent she may find it more difficult than the man to conform to the cultural norm of primary loyalty to the family she establishes later, the family of procreation. It is possible, of course, that the only effect of the greater sheltering is to create in women a generalized dependency which will then be transferred to the husband and which will enable her all the more readily to accept the role of wife in a family which still has many patriarchal features. In contrast to this, we shall explore the hypothesis that this dependency is specific; it is a dependency upon and attachment to the family of orientation.

For the purposes of testing, this hypothesis may be restated in two steps: first, the alleged greater attachment of the girl to her family of orientation and, second, the resulting difficulties for marriage.

Turning to family studies in the search for data bearing crucially upon this hypothesis, we find the data to be scanty indeed. The comparative absence of materials suggests that the hypothesis requiring this material was not at hand. With regard to the first step, the greater attachment to and dependence of the woman upon her family of orientation, the evidence, though scanty, is consistent and confirming.

SEX DIFFERENCES IN ATTACHMENT TO AND DEPENDENCE UPON THE FAMILY OF ORIENTATION

In a recent study, Winch[7] discovers a contrast between the sexes with respect to

---

[7]R. F. Winch, "Courtship in College Women," *American Journal of Sociology*, Nov. 1949.

attachment and submissiveness to parents. Among the 435 college males included in the study, age correlated negatively with love for both parents and submissiveness to them, whereas among the 502 college women neither of these correlations is significant. The author puts forth and is inclined to support the hypothesis that, at least while in college, women do not become emancipated from their families to the same degree or in the same manner as men do. . . .

The next datum bearing upon our hypothesis has the advantage of having been derived from the study of behavior rather than from verbal attitudes alone though it would have been given added meaning had it also included the latter.

The Women's Bureau (Bulletin No. 138) made a study of two communities widely different in employment offered to women: City of Cleveland and the State of Utah. The report concludes:

> In families with unmarried sons and daughters, daughters supply more of the family supporting income than sons supply, though earning less than their brothers earn (p. 13). In Cleveland twice the proportion of boys as of girls contributed nothing to the family support. With working sons and daughters under 21 years, about a third of the girls compared with a fourth of the boys turn over *all* their earnings to their families.

It would be important to determine whether such a pattern of greater contribution of single daughters to family support is generally true. For if it is, it would have bearing upon a more general problem. It would represent a standardized pattern of behavior *which is not directly called for by social norms, but is a by-product of social roles.* In other words, it would mean that differential training of boys and girls in anticipation of adult sex roles has had, as an unintended by-product, a closer identification of the girl with her family and her greater responsibility

for family support. Tracing this by-product brings out anew how interrelations of institutional patterns operate to produce other ramified patterns which are below the threshold of recognition.

So much for the first step of our hypothesis: the lesser emancipation of the daughter in the middle class kinship structure from the family of orientation. In so far as it is valid, we may expect that the transition from the role of the daughter to that of the spouse will be more difficult for her than for the son. She might find it more difficult, as was suggested earlier, to face parental disapproval in case of conflict between parents and spouse and, in general, to sever ties to her parents and to attain the degree of maturity demanded of a wife in our culture. . . .

WOMAN'S LESSER EMANCIPATION FROM HER FAMILY OF ORIENTATION AS A FACTOR IN MARITAL DISCORD

That marriage difficulties arise as a result of the attachment of the wife to her family was amply illustrated in the pilot study conducted by the writer. In some cases the problem took the form of a mental conflict over the claims of parents and husband. For example, one woman said:

> When I was single, I always helped my family. Now I have just heard that my father isn't well and should have a week's vacation. If only I had some money of my own I wouldn't hesitate a minute to send him a check. As it is, even if my husband would agree to give me the money, have I the right to ask him to deny himself the new radio for the sake of my family?

In other cases, the relation of the wife to her family caused marital conflict. The overt conflicts were sometimes about the excessive (in the husband's view) concern of the wife over her younger siblings. One husband accused his wife of neglecting their children in her preoccupation with the problems of her adolescent brother and sister whom, he maintained, she "babied too much." She telephoned them daily, waiting, however, for the husband to leave for work because the telephone conversations irritated him. The relation of the wife to her mother was the focal point of marriage conflict in still other cases. The husband objected to the frequent visits of the wife to her mother, the mother-in-law's excessive help with the housework ("You are shirking your duties as a wife"), the wife's dependence upon her mother for opinions, the mother-in-law's interference, and so on.

If our hypothesis is valid, we should find that such in-law problems in marriage more frequently involve the wife's parents than the husband's parents.

Given this theoretical expectation we examined the body of relevant opinion and data contained in some twenty texts and other books on the family. Of those examined, the bulk were written by sociologists, a few by psychiatrists and psychologists. As far as the sociologists were concerned, the field is virtually barren of data bearing crucially upon our hypothesis. The reason is simple—the problem was never posed. . . .

The writers have not explored the possibility that the cultural definitions of sex roles may have differential consequences for the adjustment at issue. . . .

If future research is to bear crucially upon the hypothesis that the "overattachment" of the wife to her family of orientation creates marriage conflict as evidenced by "in-law" trouble, it must be so designed as to distentangle various contradictory tendencies. It is possible, for example, that such marriage conflict is much more frequent among women whereas among men, though rarer, it may be experienced more acutely. Excessive ties to parents would be even more dysfunctional for the male role of the family head than for the housewife. Our culture is less permissive towards unusually close son-parent ties. Consequently, the "silver cord" may be more socially visible and better reported even if (and because?) it is a rare occurrence as compared with the daughter-mother ties.

Another refinement suggests itself. The role of in-laws as sources of tension may vary with the stages of the family cycle. We have hitherto stressed the attitudes of the spouses towards their parents as the source of in-law trouble. But the parents contribute their share. And here it is possible that during engagement and perhaps even in the first year of marriage it is the husband's family which creates more trouble for the young couple. As a rule, the girl's family may be more favorably disposed to marriage because a reasonably early marriage is more advantageous to the woman. Furthermore, the very attachment of the girl to her family means, as the folklore has it, that "when your son marries, you lose a son, when your daughter marries, you gain one," or, "your son is your son till he takes him a wife, your daughter is your daughter all her life." Again, the greater control exercised over the choice of mates by the girl's family may mean that the prospective son-in-law is more acceptable than the prospective daughter-in-law because he reflects the family's choice. But whereas in the engagement period the husband's family may figure more prominently in in-law conflicts, it is assumed, in the light of this paper, that as the marriage continues, the basic dependence of the woman upon her family tends to make her parents the principal actors in the in-law drama.

It is hoped that future research may recognize the problem and test further the hypotheses here set forth.

Helen Mayer Hacker on Women as a Minority Group

Helen Mayer Hacker was born into a poor Russian Jewish family who gave her up for adoption as an infant. A studious, bright child, she grew up in Minneapolis, Minnesota, with her adoptive parents, who often struggled to make ends meet. Her parents read liberal/socialistic literature, and at an early age Hacker developed an interest in radical politics. After her junior year, she dropped out of high school and applied for admission to the University of Minnesota, to which she was admitted. In that environment, she flourished in the intellectual excitement of academic life, especially focusing on political theory and social criticism.

In the middle of her second year at Minnesota, Hacker transferred to the University of Chicago, so she could live with her parents and work part-time to help pay the bills. After one quarter at Chicago, she left for a few months to study at Commonwealth College, a labor college in Mena, Arkansas, where she was tutored in radical economics. Soon her money ran out, and her desire for a more intellectually stimulating environment led her back to Chicago, where she changed her major from philosophy to economics. There she studied with intellectual giants such as Paul Douglas and Herbert Simon. She was introduced to sociology by a philosophy instructor who assigned Karl Mannheim's *Ideology and Utopia*.

After graduation, Hacker held several jobs in several cities, after which she moved to New York and entered Columbia University to study sociology, with some tuition support from Robert MacIver, then chair of the department. At Columbia she studied primarily with Paul Lazarsfeld, focusing on public opinion and mass communications. In 1944 Hacker completed her course work for a PhD in sociology, leaving to take a teaching position at Randolph Macon College in Virginia. She found the Southern segregation system to be appalling, and soon got into trouble for her activism against these practices. At the end of her first year there, she married Emanuel A. Hacker, an economics scholar. When he was offered a position at Brooklyn College, Hacker left her job and moved with him, finding a job teaching one course per term at the New School for Social Research.

While at Columbia, Hacker began working on research on women, a focus she kept throughout her career. At Teachers College she developed the paper "Women as a Minority Group," which was later published in the *American Journal of Sociology* in 1951. She landed a job at Hunter College as a lecturer for a while, but when circumstances changed and she needed more money, she joined a private company and took up market research. She and Emanuel Hacker divorced during this period. It was not until 1961, in her forties, that Helen Mayer Hacker finally completed her PhD at Columbia. Even with this prestigious degree, Hacker had difficulty finding an academic position, given the fact that she was a woman in her mid-forties. After a few other jobs, including a stint in Italy for a postdoctoral Fulbright, she finally obtained a position at Aldephi University in 1966. She held that position until her retirement in 1984. Hacker now lives in Manhattan.

Helen Mayer Hacker's interest in women's issues was not just academic: she was active in the rise of feminism in the late 1960s, joining the National Organization for Women in 1966 and offering a course in 1970 on "Women's Liberation" at Adelphi. She was also one of the first members of Sociologists for Women in Society, formed by women in the American Sociological Association to counter the sexism in the organization.

I have always been out of sync: entering graduate school a few years older than was customary at the time, completing my Ph. D. as a middle-aged woman, spouting ideas whose time had not come. . . . Feminism has always been the beacon that I follow even as its trajectory changes. It is difficult now to recollect in tranquility just what propelled me along different paths. Overall, like so many others, I have been concerned with the causes of women's subordination. (Hacker, 1995:247–48)

Major Works

Hacker, Helen Mayer. "Marx, Weber, and Pareto on the Changing Status of Women." *American Journal of Economics and Sociology* 12, no. 2 (1955): 149–62.

———. "The New Burdens of Masculinity." *Marriage and Family Living* 19, no. 3 (1957): 227–33.

———. "The Feminine Protest of the Working Wife." *Indian Journal of Social Work* 31, no. 4 (1971): 403–6.

———. "Homosexuals: Deviant or Minority Group?" In *The Other Minorities*, edited by Edward Sagarin, 65–92. Waltham, MA: Ginn, 1971.

———. *Social Roles of Men and Women: A Sociological Approach.* New York: Harper & Row, 1975.

Source

Hacker, Helen Mayer 1995. Slouching toward sociology. Chap. 13 in *Individual voices, collective visions: Fifty years of women in sociology,* ed. Ann Geotting and Sarah Fenstermaker. Philadelphia, PA: Temple Univ. Press.

The Selection

In this pioneering article, Helen Mayer Hacker points out that little consideration has been given to the idea of women as a minority group, as women's issues are usually treated under "family." She argues that a sociological definition of minority group (a group

---

"singled out from the others in society . . . for differential and unequal treatment, and who therefore regard themselves as objects of collective discrimination") seems to fit the situation of women in its objective aspects (singled out for unequal treatment) but not necessarily in its subjective aspects (regarding themselves as objects of discrimination). Even so, subjective recognition of discrimination is not necessary to the definition of a group as having a minority group status.

Women in the United States, she continues, have little consciousness of group membership, but they do exhibit some characteristics of minority groups, including a tendency toward self-hatred, as exhibited in denigration of other women and their abilities. The fact that women are socialized among men and not within their own group may inhibit their identification as a group. Still, women seem to have something of a subculture of their own, which includes unique language, spaces, and activities.

To the original question of whether the "minority group" concept applies to women Hacker answers in the affirmative, with the assumption that "there are no differences attributable to sex membership as such that would justify casting men and women in different social roles." Among the justifications for this designation is the existence of formal discrimination against women in many areas of life, which Hacker describes briefly. She also points out how usual measures of social distance do not apply when attempting to understand the relation between men and women.

Hacker introduces the notion that sex differences may represent a "caste" system, in much the same way as that term is used to describe racial divisions in the United States. She then shows how Park's discussion of the race relations cycle is relevant to the understanding of sex relations historically, especially in speculation about what assimilation would mean for the sexes. Finally, Hacker discusses the "marginal woman," again drawing on Park, highlighting conflicting expectations for modern women, echoing some of the themes discussed by Mirra Komarovsky. According to Hacker, these problems are likely to be greater among women who are more achievement-oriented and less tied to traditional roles.

WOMEN AS A MINORITY GROUP

Although sociological literature reveals scattered references to women as a minority group, comparable in certain respects to racial, ethnic, and national minorities, no systematic investigation has been undertaken as to what extent the term "minority group" is applicable to women. That there has been little serious consideration of women as a minority group among sociologists is manifested in the recently issued index to *The American Journal of Sociology* wherein under the heading of "Minority Groups" there appears: "See Jews; Morale; Negro; Races and Nationalities; Religious Groups; Sects." There is no cross-reference to women, but such reference is found under the heading "Family."

Yet it may well be that regarding women as a minority group may be productive of fresh insights and suggest leads for further research. The purpose of this paper is to apply to women some portion of that body of sociological theory and methodology customarily used for investigating such minority groups as Negroes, Jews, immigrants, etc. It may be anticipated that not only will principles already established in the field of intergroup relations contribute to our understanding of women, but that in the process of modifying traditional concepts and theories to fit the special case of women new viewpoints for the fruitful reexamination of other minority groups will emerge.

In defining the term "minority group," the presence of discrimination is the identifying factor. As Louis Wirth[1] has pointed out, "minority group" is not a statistical concept, nor need it denote an alien group. Indeed for the present discussion I have adopted his definition: "A minority group is any group of people who because of their physical or cultural characteristics, are singled out from the others in the society in which they live for differential and unequal treatment, and who therefore regard themselves as objects of collective discrimination." It is apparent that this definition includes both objective and subjective characteristics of a minority group: the fact of discrimination and the awareness of discrimination, with attendant reactions to that awareness. A person who on the basis of his group affiliation is denied full participation in those opportunities which the value system of his culture extends to all members of the society satisfies the objective criterion, but there are various circumstances which may prevent him from fulfilling the subjective criterion.

In the first place, a person may be unaware of the extent to which his group membership influences the way others treat him. He may have formally dissolved all ties with the group in question and fondly imagine his identity is different from what others hold it to be. Consequently, he interprets their behavior toward him solely in terms of his individual characteristics. Or, less likely, he may be conscious of his membership in a certain group but not be aware of the general disesteem with which the group is regarded. A final possibility is that he may belong in a category which he does not realize has group significance. . . . The foregoing assume[s] that the person believes in equal opportunities for all in the sense that one's group affiliation should not affect his role in the larger society. We turn now to a consideration of situations in which this assumption is not made.

It is frequently the case that a person knows that because of his group affiliation he receives differential treatment, but feels that this treatment is warranted by the distinctive characteristics of his group. . . . A child may accept the fact that physical differences between him and an adult require his going to bed earlier than they do. . . . A woman does not wish for the rights and duties of men. In these situations, clearly, the person does not regard himself as an "object of collective discrimination."

For the two types presented above: (1) those who do not know that they are being discriminated against on a group basis; and (2) those who acknowledge the propriety of differential treatment on a group basis, the subjective attributes of a minority group member are lacking. They feel no minority group consciousness, harbor no resentment, and, hence, cannot properly be said to belong in a minority group. Although the term "minority group" is inapplicable to both types, the term "minority group status" may be substituted. This term is used to categorize persons who are denied rights to which they are entitled according to the value system of the observer. An observer, who is a firm adherent of the democratic ideology, will often consider persons to occupy a minority group status who are well accommodated to their subordinate roles.

---

[1]Louis Wirth, "The Problem of Minority Groups," *The Science of Man in the World Crisis,* ed. by Ralph Linton (1945), p. 347.

No empirical study of the frequency of minority group feelings among women has yet been made, but common observation would suggest that consciously at least, few women believe themselves to be members of a minority group in the way in which some Negroes, Jews, Italians, etc., may so conceive themselves. There are, of course, many sex-conscious women, known to a past generation as feminists, who are filled with resentment at the discriminations they fancy are directed against their sex. Today some of these may be found in the National Woman's Party which since 1923 has been carrying on a campaign for the passage of the Equal Rights Amendment. . . .

Then there are women enrolled in women's clubs, women's auxiliaries of men's organizations, women's professional and educational associations who seemingly believe that women have special interests to follow or unique contributions to make. These latter might reject the appellation of minority group, but their behavior testifies to their awareness of women as a distinct group in our society, either overriding differences of class, occupation, religion, or ethnic identification, or specialized within these categories. Yet the number of women who participate in "women's affairs" even in the United States, the classic land of associations, is so small that one cannot easily say that the majority of women display minority group consciousness. However, documentation, as well as a measuring instrument, is likewise lacking for minority consciousness in other groups.

Still women often manifest many of the psychological characteristics which have been imputed to self-conscious minority groups. Kurt Lewin[2] has pointed to group self-hatred as a frequent reaction of the minority group member to his group affiliation. This feeling is exhibited in the person's tendency to denigrate other members of the group, to accept the dominant group's stereotyped conception of them, and to indulge in "mea culpa" breast-beating. He may seek to exclude himself from the average of his group, or he may point the finger of scorn at himself. Since a person's conception of himself is based on the defining gestures of others, it is unlikely that members of a minority group can wholly escape personality distortion. Constant reiteration of one's inferiority must often lead to its acceptance as a fact.

Certainly women have not been immune to the formulations of the "female character" throughout the ages. From those, to us, deluded creatures who confessed to witchcraft to modern sophisticates who speak disparagingly of the cattiness and disloyalty of women, women reveal their introjection of prevailing attitudes toward them. Like those minority groups whose self-castigation outdoes dominant group derision of them, women frequently exceed men in the violence of their vituperations of their sex. They are more severe in moral judgments, especially in sexual matters. A line of self-criticism may be traced from Hannah More, a blue-stocking herself, to Dr. Marynia Farnham, who lays most of the world's ills at women's door. Women express themselves as disliking other women, as preferring to work under men, and as finding exclusively female gatherings repugnant. The *Fortune* polls conducted in 1946 show that women, more than men, have misgivings concerning women's participation in industry, the professions, and civic life. And more than one-fourth of women wish they had been born in the opposite sex![3]

---

[2]Kurt Lewin, "Self-Hatred Among Jews," *Contemporary Jewish Record,* IV (1941), 219–32.
[3]*Fortune,* September, 1946, p. 5.

Militating against a feeling of group identification on the part of women is a differential factor in their socialization. Members of a minority group are frequently socialized within their own group. Personality development is more largely a resultant of intra- than inter-group interaction. The conception of his role formed by a Negro or a Jew or a second-generation immigrant is greatly dependent upon the definitions offered by members of his own group, on their attitudes and behavior toward him. . . . But only rarely does a woman experience this type of group belongingness. Her interactions with members of the opposite sex may be as frequent as her relationships with members of her own sex. Women's conceptions of themselves, therefore, spring as much from their intimate relationships with men as with women. Although this consideration might seem to limit the applicability to women of research findings on minority groups, conversely, it may suggest investigation to seek out useful parallels in the socialization of women, on the one hand, and the socialization of ethnics living in neighborhoods of hetereogeneous population, on the other.

Even though the sense of group identification is not so conspicuous in women as in racial and ethnic minorities, they, like these others, tend to develop a separate subculture. Women have their own language, comparable to the argot of the underworld and professional groups. It may not extend to a completely separate dialect as has been discovered in some preliterate groups, but there are words and idioms employed chiefly by women. Only the acculturated male can enter into the conversation of the beauty parlor, the exclusive shop, the bridge table, or the kitchen. In contrast to men's interest in physical health, safety, money, and sex, women attach greater importance to attractiveness, personality, home, family, and other people.[4]

We must return now to the original question of the aptness of the designation of minority group for women. It has been indicated that women fail to present in full force the subjective attributes commonly associated with minority groups. That is, they lack a sense of group identification and do not harbor feelings of being treated unfairly because of their sex membership. Can it then be said that women have a minority group status in our society? The answer to this question depends upon the values of the observer whether within or outside the group—just as is true in the case of any group of persons who, on the basis of putative differential characteristics are denied access to some statuses in the social system of their society. If we assume that there are no differences attributable to sex membership as such that would justify casting men and women in different social roles, it can readily be shown that women do occupy a minority group status in our society.

MINORITY GROUP STATUS OF WOMEN

Formal discriminations against women are too well-known for any but the most summary description. In general they take the form of being barred from certain activities or, if admitted, being treated unequally. Discriminations against women may be viewed as arising from the generally ascribed status "female" and from the specially ascribed statuses of "wife," "mother," and "sister." (To meet the possible objection that "wife" and

---

[4]P. M. Symonds, "Changes in Sex Differences in Problems and Interests of Adolescents with Increasing Age," *Journal of Genetic Psychology,* 50 (1937), pp. 83–89, as referred to by Georgene H. Seward, *Sex and the Social Order* (1946), pp. 237–38.

"mother" represent assumed, rather than ascribed, statuses, may I point out that what is important here is that these statuses carry ascribed expectations which are only ancillary in the minds of those who assume them.)

As female, in the economic sphere, women are largely confined to sedentary, monotonous work under the supervision of men, and are treated unequally with regard to pay, promotion, and responsibility. With the exceptions of teaching, nursing, social service, and library work, in which they do not hold a proportionate number of supervisory positions and are often occupationally segregated from men, they make a poor showing in the professions. Although they own 80 percent of the nation's wealth, they do not sit on the boards of directors of great corporations. Educational opportunities are likewise unequal. Professional schools, such as architecture and medicine, apply quotas. Women's colleges are frequently inferior to men's. In co-educational schools women's participation in campus activities is limited. As citizens, women are often barred from jury service and public office. Even when they are admitted to the apparatus of political parties, they are subordinated to men. Socially, women have less freedom of movement, and are permitted fewer deviations in the proprieties of dress, speech, manners. In social intercourse they are confined to a narrower range of personality expression.

In the specially ascribed status of wife, a woman—in several States—has no exclusive right to her earnings, is discriminated against in employment, must take the domicile of her husband, and in general must meet the social expectation of subordination to her husband's interests. As a mother, she may not have the guardianship of her children, bears the chief stigma in the case of an illegitimate child, is rarely given leave of absence for pregnancy. As a sister, she frequently suffers unequal distribution of domestic duties between herself and her brother, must yield preference to him in obtaining an education, and in such other psychic and material gratifications as cars, trips, and living away from home.

If it is conceded that women have a minority group status, what may be learned from applying to women various theoretical constructs in the field of intergroup relations?

SOCIAL DISTANCE BETWEEN MEN AND WOMEN

One instrument of diagnostic value is the measurement of social distance between dominant and minority group. But we have seen that one important difference between women and other minorities is that women's attitudes and self-conceptions are conditioned more largely by interaction with both minority and dominant group members. Before measuring social distance, therefore, a continuum might be constructed of the frequency and extent of women's interaction with men, with the poles conceptualized as ideal types. One extreme would represent a complete "ghetto" status, the woman whose contacts with men were of the most secondary kind. At the other extreme shall we put the woman who has prolonged and repeated associations with men, but only in those situations in which sex-awareness plays a prominent role or the woman who enters into a variety of relationships with men in which her sex identity is to a large extent irrelevant? The decision would depend on the type of scale used. . . .

In our culture, however, men who wish to marry, must perforce marry women, and even if they accept this relationship, they may still wish to limit their association with women in other situations. The male physician may not care for the addition of female physicians to his hospital staff. The male poker player may be thrown off his game if women participate. A damper may be put upon the hunting expedition if women come along. The average man may not wish to consult a woman lawyer. And so on. In these cases it seems apparent that the steps in the social distance scale must be reversed. Men will accept women at the supposed level of greatest intimacy while rejecting them at lower levels.

But before concluding that a different scale must be constructed when the dominant group attitude toward a minority group which is being tested is that of men toward women, the question may be raised as to whether marriage in fact represents the point of minimum social distance. It may not imply anything but physical intimacy and work accommodation, as was frequently true in non-individuated societies, such as preliterate groups and the household economy of the Middle Ages, or marriages of convenience in the European upper class. Even in our own democratic society where marriage is supposedly based on romantic love there may be little communication between the partners in marriage. The Lynds[5] report the absence of real companionship between husband and wife in Middletown. Women have been known to say that although they have been married for twenty years, their husband is still a stranger to them. There is a quatrain of Thoreau's that goes:

Each moment as we drew nearer to each

A stern respect withheld us farther yet

So that we seemed beyond each other's reach

And less acquainted than when first we met.

Part of the explanation may be found in the subordination of wives to husbands in our culture, which is expressed in the separate spheres of activity for men and women. A recent advertisement in a magazine of national circulation depicts a pensive husband seated by his knitting wife, with the caption, "Sometimes a man has moods his wife cannot understand," In this case the husband is worried about a pension plan for his employees. The assumption is that the wife, knowing nothing of the business world, cannot take the role of her husband in this matter.

The presence of love does not in itself argue for either equality of status nor fullness of communication. We may love those who are either inferior or superior to us, and we may love persons whom we do not understand. . . .

In the light of these considerations concerning the relationships between men and women, some doubt may be cast on the propriety of placing marriage on the positive extreme of the social distance scale with respect to ethnic and religious minority groups. Since inequalities of status are preserved in marriage, a dominant group member may be willing to marry a member of a group which, in general, he would not wish admitted to his club. The social distance scale which uses marriage as a sign of an extreme degree of acceptance is inadequate for appreciating the position of women, and perhaps for other minority groups as well. The relationships among similarity of status, communication as a measure of intimacy, and love must be clarified before social distance tests can be applied usefully to attitudes between men and women.

CASTE-CLASS CONFLICT

Is the separation between males and females in our society a caste line? Folsom[6] suggests that it is, and Myrdal[7] in his well-known Appendix 5 considers the parallel between

---

[5]Robert S. and Helen Merrell Lynd, *Middletown* (1929), p. 120, and *Middletown in Transition* (1937), p. 176.

[6]Joseph Kirk Folsom, *The Family and Democratic Society* (1943), pp. 623–24.

[7]Gunnar Myrdal, *An American Dilemma* (1944), pp. 1073–78.

the position of and feelings toward women and Negroes in our society. The relation between women and Negroes is historical, as well as analogical. In the seventeenth century the legal status of Negro servants was borrowed from that of women and children, who were under the patria potestas, and until the Civil War there was considerable cooperation between the Abolitionist and woman suffrage movements. According to Myrdal, the problems of both groups are resultants of the transition from a pre-industrial, paternalistic scheme of life to individualistic, industrial capitalism. Obvious similarities in the status of women and Negroes are indicated in Chart 1.

CHART 1   CASTELIKE STATUS OF WOMEN AND NEGROES

Negroes	Women
1. High Social Visibility	
a. Skin color, other "racial" characteristics	a. Secondary sex characteristics
b. (Sometimes) distinctive dress—bandana, flashy clothes	b. Distinctive dress, skirts, etc.
2. Ascribed Attributes	
a. Inferior intelligence, smaller brain, less convoluted, scarcity of geniuses	a. ditto
b. More free in instinctual gratifications. More emotional, "primitive" and childlike. Imagined sexual prowess envied	b. Irresponsible, inconsistent, emotionally unstable. Lack strong super-ego Women as "temptresses."
c. Common stereotype "inferior"	c. "Weaker"
3. Rationalizations of Status	
a. Thought all right in his place	a. Woman's place is in the home
b. Myth of contented Negro	b. Myth of contented woman—"feminine" woman is happy in subordinate role
4. Discriminations	
a. Limitations on education—should fit "place" in society	a. ditto
b. Confined to traditional jobs—barred from supervisory positions	b. ditto
Their competition feared No family precedents for new aspirations	
c. Deprived of political importance	c. ditto
d. Social and professional segregation	d. ditto
e. More vulnerable to criticism	e. e.g. conduct in bars.
5. Similar Problems	
a. Roles not clearly defined, but in flux as result of social change	
Conflict between achieved status and ascribed status	

While these similarities in the situation of women and Negroes may lead to increased understanding of their social roles, account must also be taken of differences which impose qualifications on the comparison of the two groups. Most importantly, the influence of marriage as a social elevator for women, but not for Negroes, must be considered. Obvious, too, is the greater importance of women to the dominant group, despite the economic, sexual, and prestige gains which Negroes afford the white South. Ambivalence is probably more marked in the attitude of white males toward women than toward Negroes. The "war of the sexes" is only an expression of men's and women's vital need of each other. Again, there is greater polarization in the relationship between men and women. Negroes, although they have borne the brunt of anti-minority group feeling in this country, do not constitute the only racial or ethnic minority, but there are only two sexes. And, although we have seen that social distance exists between men and women, it is not to be compared with the social segregation of Negroes. . . .

Exemplary of the possible usefulness of applying the caste principle to women is viewing some of the confusion surrounding women's roles as reflecting a conflict between class and caste status. Such a conflict is present in the thinking and feeling of both dominant and minority groups toward upper class Negroes and educated women. Should a woman judge be treated with the respect due a judge or the gallantry accorded a woman? The extent to which the rights and duties of one role permeate other roles so as to cause a role conflict has been treated elsewhere by the writer.[8] Lower class Negroes who have acquired dominant group attitudes toward the Negro resent upper class Negro pretensions to superiority. Similarly, domestic women may feel the career woman is neglecting the duties of her proper station. . . .

RACE RELATIONS CYCLE

The "race relations cycle," as defined by Robert E. Park,[9] describes the social processes of reduction in tension and increase of communication in the relations between two or more groups who are living in a common territory under a single political or economic system. The sequence of competition, conflict, accommodation, and assimilation may also occur when social change introduces dissociative forces into an assimilated group or causes accommodated groups to seek new definitions of the situation.[10] The ethnic or nationality characteristics of the groups involved are not essential to the cycle. In a complex industrialized society groups are constantly forming and re-forming on the basis of new interests and new identities. Women, of course, have always possessed a sex-identification though perhaps not a group awareness. Today they represent a previously accommodated group which is endeavoring to modify the relationships between the sexes in the home, in work, and in the community.

The sex relations cycle bears important similarities to the race relations cycle. In the wake of the Industrial Revolution, as women acquired industrial, business, and professional skills, they increasingly sought employment in competition with men. Men were quick to perceive them as a rival group and made use of economic, legal, and ideological weapons to eliminate or reduce their competition. They excluded women from the trade unions, made contracts with employers to prevent their hiring women, passed laws restricting the employment of married women, caricatured the working

---

[8]Helen M. Hacker, Towards a Definition of Role Conflict in Modern Women (unpublished manuscript).

[9]Robert E. Park, "Our Racial Frontier on the Pacific," *The Survey Graphic*, 56 (May 1, 1926), pp. 192–96.

[10]William Ogburn and Meyer Nimkoff, *Sociology* (2d ed., 1950), p. 187.

woman, and carried on ceaseless propaganda to return women to the home or keep them there. Since the days of the suffragettes there has been no overt conflict between men and women on a group basis. Rather than conflict, the dissociative process between the sexes is that of contravention,[11] a type of opposition intermediate between competition and conflict. According to Wiese and Becker, it includes rebuffing, repulsing, working against, hindering, protesting, obstructing, restraining, and upsetting another's plans.

The present contravention of the sexes, arising from women's competition with men, is manifested in the discriminations against women, as well as in the doubts and uncertainties expressed concerning women's character, abilities, motives. The processes of competition and contravention are continually giving way to accommodation in the relationships between men and women. Like other minority groups, women have sought a protected position, a niche in the economy which they could occupy, and, like other minority groups, they have found these positions in new occupations in which dominant group members had not yet established themselves and in old occupations which they no longer wanted. When women entered fields which represented an extension of services in the home (except medicine!), they encountered least opposition. Evidence is accumulating, however, that women are becoming dissatisfied with the employment conditions of the great women-employing occupations and present accommodations are threatened.

What would assimilation of men and women mean? Park and Burgess in their classic text define assimilation as "a process of interpenetration and fusion in which persons and groups acquire the memories, sentiments, and attitudes of other persons or groups, and, by sharing their experiences and history, are incorporated with them in a cultural life." If accommodation is characterized by secondary contacts, assimilation holds the promise of primary contacts. If men and women were truly assimilated, we would find no cleavages of interest along sex lines. The special provinces of men and women would be abolished. Women's pages would disappear from the newspaper and women's magazines from the stands. All special women's organizations would pass into limbo. The sports page and racing news would be read indifferently by men and women. Interest in cookery and interior decoration would follow individual rather than sex lines. Women's talk would be no different from men's talk, and frank and full communication would obtain between the sexes.

THE MARGINAL WOMAN

Group relationships are reflected in personal adjustments. Arising out of the present contravention of the sexes is the marginal woman, torn between rejection and acceptance of traditional roles and attributes. Uncertain of the ground on which she stands, subjected to conflicting cultural expectations, the marginal woman suffers the psychological ravages of instability, conflict, self-hate, anxiety, and resentment.

In applying the concept of marginality to women, the term "role" must be substituted for that of "group."[12] Many of the traditional devices for creating role differentiation among boys and girls, such as dress, manners, activities, have been de-emphasized in modern urban middle class homes. The small girl

---

[11]Howard Becker, *Systematic Sociology on the Basis of the "Beziehungslehre" and "Gebildelehre" of Leopold von Wiese* (1932), pp. 263–68.
[12]Kurt Lewin, *Resolving Social Conflicts* (1948), p. 181.

who wears a play suit, plays games with boys and girls together, attends a co-educational school, may have little awareness of sexual differentiation until the approach of adolescence. Parental expectations in the matters of scholarship, conduct toward others, duties in the home may have differed little for herself and her brother: But in high school or perhaps not until college she finds herself called upon to play a new role. Benedict[13] has called attention to discontinuities in the life cycle, and the fact that these continuities in cultural conditioning take a greater toll of girls than of boys is revealed in test scores showing neuroticism and introversion.[14] In adolescence girls find the frank, spontaneous behavior toward the neighboring sex no longer rewarding. High grades are more likely to elicit anxiety than praise from parents, especially mothers, who seem more pleased if male callers are frequent. There are subtle indications that to remain home with a good book on a Saturday night is a fate worse than death. But even if the die is successfully cast for popularity, all problems are not solved. Girls are encouraged to heighten their sexual attractiveness, but to abjure sexual expression.

Assuming new roles in adolescence does not mean the complete relinquishing of old ones. Scholarship, while not so vital as for the boy, is still important, but must be maintained discreetly and without obvious effort. Mirra Komarovsky[15] has supplied statements of Barnard College girls of the conflicting expectations of their elders. Even more than to the boy is the "all-round" ideal held up to girls, and it is not always possible to integrate the roles of good date, good daughter, good

sorority sister, good student, good friend, and good citizen. The superior achievements of college men over college women bear witness to the crippling division of energies among women. Part of the explanation may lie in women's having interiorized cultural notions of feminine inferiority in certain fields, and even the most self-confident or most defensive woman may be filled with doubt as to whether she can do productive work.

It may be expected that as differences in privileges between men and women decrease, the frequency of marginal women will increase. Widening opportunities for women will call forth a growing number of women capable of performing roles formerly reserved for men, but whose acceptance in these new roles may well remain uncertain and problematic. This hypothesis is in accord with Arnold Green's[16] recent critical reexamination of the marginal man concept in which he points out that it is those Negroes and second-generation immigrants whose values and behavior most approximate those of the dominant majority who experience the most severe personal crises. He believes that the classical marginal man symptoms appear only when a person striving to leave the racial or ethnic group into which he was born is deeply identified with the family of orientation and is met with grudging, uncertain, and unpredictable acceptance, rather than with absolute rejection, by the group he is attempting to join, and also that he is committed to success-careerism. Analogically, one would expect to find that women who display marginal symptoms are psychologically bound to the

[13]Ruth Benedict, "Continuities and Discontinuities in Cultural Conditioning," *Psychiatry*, 1 (1938), pp. 161–67.

[14]Georgene H. Seward, *op. cit.*, pp. 239–40.

[15]Mirra Komarovsky, "Cultural Contradictions and Sex Roles," *The American Journal of Sociology*, LII (November 1946), 184–89.

[16]Arnold Green, "A Re-Examination of the Marginal Man Concept," *Social Forces*, 26 (December 1947), pp. 167–71.

family of orientation in which they experienced the imperatives of both the traditional and new feminine roles, and are seeking to expand the occupational (or other) areas open to women rather than those who content themselves with established fields. Concretely, one might suppose women engineers to have greater personality problems than women librarians.

Other avenues of investigation suggested by the minority group approach can only be mentioned. What social types arise as personal adjustments to sex status? What can be done in the way of experimental modification of the attitudes of men and women toward each other and themselves? What hypotheses of inter-group relations may be tested in regard to men and women? For example, is it true that as women approach the cultural standards of men, they are perceived as a threat and tensions increase? Of what significance are regional and community variations in the treatment of and degree of participation permitted women, mindful here that women share responsibility with men for the perpetuation of attitudes toward women? This paper is exploratory in suggesting the enhanced possibilities of fruitful analysis, if women are included in the minority group corpus, particularly with reference to such concepts and techniques as group belongingness, socialization of the minority group child, cultural differences, social distance tests, conflict between class and caste status, race relations cycle, and marginality. I believe that the concept of the marginal woman should be especially productive, and am now engaged in an empirical study of role conflicts in professional women.

William H. Whyte Jr. (1917–1999) on the Corporate Wife

William H. Whyte Jr. grew up in West Chester, Pennsylvania, graduating from Princeton University in 1939. After service in the U.S. Marine Corps during the Second World War (1941–1945), he worked as a managing editor for *Fortune* magazine through the mid-1950s. During that time, he wrote his best-selling book, *The Organization Man,* in which he critically details growing conformity within American corporate culture and middle-class suburbia. According to Kaufman (1999), this was the book that "first brought him to wide public attention. . . . Whyte's book challenged and refuted claims of entrepreneurial vigor and daring in business by describing an ongoing bureaucratization of white-collar environments—board rooms, offices, laboratories."

The Organization Man was one of a large number of works of keen and critical observation of American social life. Whyte later went on to have a distinguished career as a scholar and observer of urban life, especially the everyday life of the streets, which he studied through film, participant obser-

vation, and critical qualitative analysis. He also served as an advisor to urban planners in many cities. His goal, often in opposition to those of typical urban planners and developers, was to preserve the vitality of urban life through planning spaces for human needs.

Whyte spent most of his life in Manhattan, where he observed, recorded, and commented on urban life. In 1970 he was named Distinguished Professor of Urban Sociology at Hunter College, City University of New York. Among many other awards, he received the Doris C. Freedman Award from New York mayor Ed Koch in 1984 for his 30 years of research in the public environment. According to La Farge (2000:vii), "His objective research on the city, on open space, on the way people use it, was set within what I think I must call a moral context. [Whyte] believed with deep passion that there was such a thing as quality of life, and that the way we build cities, the way we make places, can have a profound effect on what kinds of lives are lived within those places."

MAJOR WORKS

William H. Whyte, Jr. with the editors of Fortune. *Is Anybody Listening? How and Why U. S. Business Fumbles When It Talks with Human Beings.* New York: Simon and Schuster, 1952.

———. *The Organization Man.* New York: Simon and Schuster, 1956.

———. *The Social Life of Small Urban Spaces.* Washington, DC: Conservation Foundation, 1980.

———. *City: Rediscovering the Center.* New York: Doubleday, 1989.

SOURCES

Fortune. In praise of the ornery wife. (November 1951): 75–76.

Kaufman, Michael T. William H. Whyte, 81, Author of *The Organization Man Obituary. New York Times,* January 13, 1999.

La Farge, Albert, and William H. Whyte, eds. 2000. *The Essential William H. Whyte.* New York: Fordham University Press.

Project for Public Spaces. http://www.pps.org/info/placemakingtools/placemakers/wwhyte (accessed 28 January 2006).

THE SELECTION

In the following article, William H. Whyte describes the conformist and security-seeking "ideal wife" as preferred by representatives of 1950s corporate management, based on 230 interviews with corporate executives and lower-management workers and their wives. In an earlier article in this series (October 1951), he describes his typical female respondent as "resolutely antifeminist," thinking of her role primarily in its relation to that of her husband. A "good wife," in the view of these managerial wives and the corporation executives, is one who doesn't interfere, who "stabilizes" the home, and who is a good entertainer and a good listener. She is ultimately concerned with "fitting in" socially and not hurting her husband's career. The selection reprinted here reveals the corporate attitudes of the conservative 1950s: wives will be called on to accept moves in the interest of their husbands' career advancement willingly and cheerfully. There is universal consensus that a good executive's wife does not have a career, even though a college education is important. Whyte describes how employers often interviewed the wives of job applicants before offering a management position to a man; they likewise assessed subordinates' promotion prospects in part by looking at their wives—their taste in clothing, their manners, their attitudes toward motherhood, and their willingness to "play the game." One corporation even set up a system so that wives of upcoming executives could be "groomed" to high standards of expected behavior. As the editors of *Fortune* summarize in their response to Whyte's research,

> The picture that emerges, in brief, is that of a society in which the individualist, rugged or otherwise, seems to be out, definitely. What

From William H. Whyte Jr., "The Corporation and the Wife," *Fortune* (November 1951): 109–11, 150, 152.

the modern corporation wants is "group integration"; to them, the "good" wife is the wife who subordinates her own character and her aspirations to the smooth functioning of the system; the wife, in short, who "adapts." (*Fortune* 1951:75)

Whyte's piece is ironic and critical. He would prefer that American managers and their wives maintain individuality in spite of the pressures to conform. He is disturbed by the fact that many of the young wives accept uncritically the role as laid out for them by corporate interests and that American society appears to be moving more and more toward a conformist culture. The reader should be aware that this type of complaint about American conformity was a common theme in the 1950s, but it primarily refers to white middle-class values. It is not clear how widespread the values uncovered by Whyte were, but they did seem to be those promoted by many business, media, or political leaders of the day. Certainly these findings would not describe racial minorities or the working class. Whyte's description points to some of the problems decried a decade later by Betty Friedan's *The Feminine Mystique* (1963), an early salvo in the second-wave feminist redefinition of women's roles.

THE CORPORATION AND THE WIFE

The American corporation is rapidly approaching a very large question. Should the wife belong to it? If so, to what degree? In one sense, the question is hardly a new one; for generations business has been aware that executives' wives play a great if imponderable role. What is new, however, is that "the wife problem" is now becoming open, official, and in many cases a matter of regular company policy. There are, let it be noted, many exceptions, but the trend is strong enough to make it not altogether facetious to suggest that business schools may soon find it necessary to include the subject in their curricula. Just how to go about "selling" a wife, making her a constructive influence, and other such tasks is by no means yet mastered. And, as we shall see, the success with which corporations solve these problems may well pose an even bigger one. But in the corporate area of the economy one thing, at least, is clear: the days of the "strictly home wife," as one executive puts it, seem to be numbered.

THE ONCE-OVER

Let's start at the beginning. Increasingly, corporations are interviewing the wife before hiring an executive, and some are not uninterested in fiancées. There are many holdouts ("This railroad picks its executives and lets its executives pick their wives and so far it's been O.K."), but roughly half of the companies on which FORTUNE has data have made wife-screening regular practice and many of the others seem about ready to do so. And the look-see is not academic. Roughly 20 per cent of its otherwise acceptable trainee applicants, one large company estimates, are turned down because of their wives.

Ordinarily the screening is accomplished via "informal" social visits. Many executives, for example, make it a point to call on the wife in her own home. Louis Ruthenburg, Board Chairman of Servel (which never hires an executive without a look at the wife), likes to recall how one college president used to insist on eating breakfast with a candidate's family; the wife who didn't fix her husband a good breakfast, he used to say, wasn't a good risk. To help them spot such key indicators many executives rely heavily on their own wives. "My wife is very, very keen on this," says one president. "She can spot things I might miss. And if the gal isn't up to par with her, it's no go."

If the prospective executive lives elsewhere, companies frequently suggest strongly that he bring his wife along for the interviews. The scrutiny is not all one-sided, and since she is also doing some sizing up of her own, many companies provide a standard tour of the schools, churches, golf clubs, and playgrounds. The visit, nevertheless, can be a harrowing experience for the wife. If the company is a close-knit one, she may undergo what amounts to a community interview in depth. This is particularly the case when the present management group has been long entrenched; since an unwise choice, they feel, can upset the delicate social balance achieved over the years, self-protection demands that everyone be given a chance to look over the couple.

"I've seen a lot of trouble along this line," recalls one management consultant. "Up comes a chief engineer for an interview. He makes a swell impression and is hired. Thirty days later he appears and when the company introduces him around, his wife is the wrong kind of person. I have seen whole organizations get stirred up by this and the company says never again—next time we see the wife first. I know a company that has had to bring in two men in the last two years. They brought the man and his wife to town for the weekend and had all the top people meet them socially to get a line on them. In both instances the men were passed up because of their wives." The company, incidentally, is still looking.

Since the screening is generally a subjective process, some executives remain skeptical of its value—"Who is wise enough," asks one, "to get to know enough about a woman in one or two meetings?" To overcome this difficulty, some companies have supplemented the screening with more objective investigations. One life-insurance company, for example, investigates the wife's credit ratings and, in addition, checks around to determine how popular or unpopular she has been in her community. Similarly, some organizations take pains to find out whether or not the wife has independent capital of her own; if it is sizable, they believe, it tends to mitigate the man's economic drive.

The Seeing Eye

But the initial screening is only the beginning of the corporation's interest. In one way or another the corporation manages to keep an eye on the wife, and more and more the surveillance is deliberately planned. At the Container Corp. of America, for example, it is the duty of all vice presidents to get acquainted with their subordinates' wives, and on their travels they are expected to meet the wives of executives in the field. Thus, when a man's name comes up for promotion the company has the answers to these questions: What is the health of the family? What is their attitude toward parenthood? How does the wife run her home? Does she dress with taste?

Management consultants would like to see even more of same. "In our consulting work on personnel and management problems," says one consultant, "we always recommend to our clients that personnel records of executives include data on the wife. It is a personality appraisal. Does she complement him? Is she a helpmate or a millstone? A nagger? Understanding? Does she resent his traveling? Does she criticize him publicly? Is she loud? Is she a lady? The immediate superior of the man in question fills this out over a period of meetings with the wife."

As in the primary interview, companies generally find this out in a social sort of way. In the case of an impending promotion one company has the wife seen individually by three different people at carefully arranged casual dinners or luncheons. Somewhat similarly, companies occasionally stage parties to appraise wives; seeing them under fire, executives explain, makes for a good short cut.

The effect of all this surveillance on the husband's career is substantial. In the home office of an insurance company, to cite one not untypical example, the president is now sidetracking one of his top men in favor of a less able one; the former's wife "has absolutely no sense of public relations." In another company a very promising executive's career is being similarly checked; his wife, the boss explains, is "negative in her attitude toward the company. She feels that business is her husband's life and no part of hers." Wives who have donated income of their own to raise the family living standard may also call down sanctions on the husband. Says one president, "When a man buys a home he can't afford on his salary alone, we either question his judgment or feel that the wife wears the pants." In either case his career is not likely to profit.

So with alcohol. The little woman who gets tipsy in front of the boss is not quite the joke her celebration in cartoon and anecdote would indicate; indeed, it is almost frightening to find out to what degree executive futures have been irretrievably influenced by that fourth martini. And it need happen only once; recently the president of a large utility felt it necessary to revise his former estimate of two executives. At the last company dinner their wives drank too many glasses of champagne. "They disported themselves," he says, regretfully, "with utter lack of propriety."

Interestingly, divorce rarely disqualifies a man. Because of the phenomenon of the outgrown wife, the regret of most companies is tempered by the thought that the executive's next and, presumably more mobile,

wife will be better for all concerned; one company, as a matter of fact, has a policy of sending executives away on extended trips if they need separating from nagging or retrograde wives. . . .

HOW TO INTEGRATE A WIFE

But something far more important is being brewed for the wife. It is not enough, in the view of many companies, that she merely be "sold" on the company; she should, they believe, now be integrated *into* it. Says one manufacturer: "For years we have been trying to find some means of building a close contact between a man's job and his home life. By our new program we believe we are making an important advance in this direction." Roofing-company president: "We consider the home an integral part of this corporation." William Given, Chairman, American Brake Shoe Co.: "When a man comes to work for us . . . we think of the company as employing the family, for it will be supporting the entire family, not merely the breadwinner." . . .

The drift toward this philosophy is unmistakable; roughly one-quarter of the corporations surveyed by FORTUNE believe the wife should be an organic member of the corporation "family"—and more seem ready to adopt the view. Ways of going about the integration vary tremendously but the end goal, in most cases, is the same: a fairly cohesive social system in which the home and the business life are brought into increasing harmony. . . .

THE WIDOWS

Social integration, however, does not mean that the corporation necessarily *likes* the wife. A great many, as we have seen, do—but in some cases the corporation welcomes her largely as a means of defending itself against her. Amiable as it may be about it, the corporation is aware that the relationship is still triangular—or, to put it another way, if you can't beat 'em, join 'em. "Successes here," says one official, "are guys who eat and sleep the company. If a man's first interest is his wife and family, more power to him—but we don't want him." "We've got quite an equity in the man," another explains, "and it's only prudence to protect it by bringing the wife into the picture."

In fairness to the wife, it follows, she must be recompensed somehow for the amount of time the company demands from her husband. Wives in companies where the term "widows" is a kind of standing joke usually point out that because their husbands work so hard and late they just naturally clan together. Companies recognize the fact and are consequently more and more providing social facilities—from ladies' nights to special clubs—to hypo the sense of identification.

One corporation has gone considerably further. Via the wife of the heir apparent to the presidency, there has been set up, in effect, a finishing school so that the wives can be brought up to the same high standards. As soon as the husband reaches the $8,000-to-$10,000 bracket the wife becomes eligible for the grooming. It is all done very subtly; the group leader drops helpful advice on which are the preferred shops, where to dine, what to wear when doing it, and, somewhat like a good cruise director, has a way of introducing newcomers to congenial people. "Her supervision is so clever and indirect," says one wife, "that the other wives appreciate it probably.". . .

The Nomads

With their talent for adaptability, the younger generation of wives is in most respects well prepared for this new way of life. Most accept it philosophically, and a good many actually prefer it to staying put in one place. "Any time the curtains get dirty," says one wife, "I'm ready to move. I enjoy meeting new people and seeing new places. And it's kind of a vacation sometimes—for the first three or four months at a new place you're not bothered with a lot of phone calls asking you to this luncheon and that meeting and so on."

There are, nevertheless, some very real tensions produced. And for no one more than the wife; it is she, who has only one life in contrast to her husband's two, who is called upon to do most of the adjusting. The move at once obsoletes most of her community friendships, severs her local business relationships with the Bank and the stores, takes her from that house and the garden on which she worked so long, and if the move takes her to a large city it probably drops her living standards also.

It is not this aspect of the sacrifice, however, that wives find most unsettling; and in a compensatory way they derive from it a sense of meaning and achievement that they deeply cherish. It's not the move itself, they say; it's the uncertainty of it. "You can't plan," explains one wife. "You're afraid to put your roots too deeply because it might mean so much disappointment later."

It is the effect on the children that concerns wives most. While the children are very young, most wives agree, the effect is not harmful; they make and forget friends easily. As they reach junior-high age, however, a transfer can become a crisis. Recalls one wife: "Every time my daughter made a place for herself at school with the other kids, we'd move and she'd spend the next year trying to break in at another school. Last year, when she was a senior in high school, she had a nervous breakdown. She was sure she was an outsider." The effect is not often this drastic but, while most children sweat out their adjustment without overt pain, the process is one parents find vicariously wrenching. One executive who recently changed to a non-transferring company did so in large part for this reason, and he has no trouble recalling the exact moment of his decision. One night at dinner his little boy turned to him. "Daddy," he said, "where do you really live?"

Talcott Parsons (1902–1979) and Robert F. Bales (1916–2004) on the Functions of Sex Roles

Background information on Talcott Parsons has been presented in an earlier section. His coauthor in the excerpt reprinted below was Robert F. Bales (1916–2004), a social psychologist and colleague at Harvard. Bales was known for his small-group studies, especially for his model of analysis called Interaction Process Analysis. In 1955, Bales and Parsons coauthored *Family, Socialization and Interaction Process,* a book that combined Bales's interest in small-group interaction with Parsons's functional analysis of roles and family.

Parsons and Bales wrote their book at a time when the dominant family ideology within sociology (and American culture in general) was decidedly conservative. Their discussion can be read as an academic justification of that conservative ideology, but it soon came in for strong criticism from conflict theorists and feminist writers for its justification of women's restricted social roles.

SOURCES

Robert F. Bales (1916–2004). http://www.infoamerica.org/teoria/balesl.htm (Accessed 28 January 2006).

In Memorium. http://www.symlog.com/internet/news/freedbales/freedbales.htm (Accessed 28 January 2006).

THE SELECTION

Talcott Parsons and Robert F. Bales discuss the interconnection between the family and the occupational structure, in a classic functionalist approach. Note the prominence of language of systems and roles, "interpenetration," and balance and adjustment, instead of interests or individual needs or actions. The selection emphasizes the differentiation between the husband-father role as the *instrumental* leader in the family, and the wife-mother role as the *expressive* leader, drawing on Bales's small-group process concepts. The so-called normal male role is seen as primarily that of economic support of the family, just as the "feminine" role is oriented to the socialization and nurture of the family. The authors' explanation for differences in male and female occupational status is couched in notions of system needs and balance and of the "differentiation" of instrumental and expressive roles, ignoring completely any presence of power or discrimination. Indeed, there is a denial of power imbalance in marriage. Throughout the selection there is an explicit assumption that the then-current middle-class gendered division of household labor (with the husband as breadwinner and the wife as homemaker) is an inevitable and permanent aspect of "modern" social organization. The reader will also note the authors' attempts to incorporate Freudian assumptions about socialization and sexuality into the analysis—an attempt that is somewhat unsuccessful. They also apparently view motherhood as necessary to balance wives' tendency to become too emotionally dependant. This argument by Parsons and Bales received much criticism, not surprisingly, from feminists and family sociologists in later decades.

FAMILY AND THE OCCUPATIONAL STRUCTURE

Over much of the world and of history a very large proportion of the world's ordinary work is and has been performed in the context of kinship units. Occupational organization in the modern sense is the sociological antithesis of this.

This means essentially, that as the occupational system develops and absorbs functions in the society, it *must* be at the expense of the relative prominence of kinship organization as a structural component in one sense, and must also be at the expense of many of what previously have been *functions* of the kinship unit. The double consequence is that the same people, who are members of kinship units, perform economic, political, religious and cultural functions outside the kinship context in occupational roles and otherwise in a variety of other types of organization. But conversely, the members of kinship units must meet many of their needs, which formerly were met in the processes of interaction within the kinship unit, through other channels. This of course includes meeting the need for income with which to purchase the goods and services necessary for family functioning itself.

In this type of society the basic mode of articulation between family and the occupational world lies in the fact that the *same* adults are both members of nuclear families and incumbents of occupational roles, the holders of "jobs." The individual's job and not the products of the coöperative activities of the family as a unit is of course the primary source of income for the family.

Next it is important to remember that the *primary* responsibility for this support rests on the one adult male member of the nuclear family. It is clearly the exceptional "normal" adult male who can occupy a respected place in our society without having a regular "job," though he may of course be "independent" as a professional practitioner or some kind of a "free lance" and not be employed by an organization, or he may be the proprietor of one. That at the bottom of the scale the "hobo" and the sick and disabled are deviants scarcely needs mentioning, while at the other end, among the relatively few who are in a position to "live on their money" there is a notable reluctance to do so. The "playboy" is not a highly respected type and there is no real American equivalent of the older European type of "gentleman" who did not "work" unless he had to.

The occupational role is of course, in the first instance, part of the "occupational system" but it is not only that. It is an example of the phenomenon of "interpenetration" which will be extensively analyzed below. In this connection it is both a role in the occupational system, *and* in the family; it is a "boundary-role" between them. The husband-father, in holding an acceptable job and earning an income from it is performing an essential function or set of functions for his family (which of course includes himself in one set of roles) as a system. The status of the family in the community is determined probably more by the "level" of job he holds than by any other single factor, and the income he earns is usually the most important basis of the family's standard of living and hence "style of life." Of course, as we shall see, he has other very important functions in relation both to wife and to children, but it is fundamentally by virtue of the importance of his occupational role *as a component of his familial role* that in our society we can unequivocally designate the husband-father as the "instrumental leader" of the family as a system.

The membership of large numbers of women in the American labor force must not be overlooked. Nevertheless there can be no question of symmetry between the sexes in this respect, and we argue, there is no serious tendency in this direction. In the first place a large proportion of gainfully employed women are single, widowed or divorced, and thus cannot be said to be either

taking the place of a husband as breadwinner of the family, or competing with him. A second large contingent are women who either do not yet have children (some of course never will) or whose children are grown up and independent. The number in the labor force who have small children is still quite small and has not shown a marked tendency to increase. The role of "housewife" is still the overwhelmingly predominant one for the married woman with small children.

But even where this type does have a job, as is also true of those who are married but do not have dependent children, above the lowest occupational levels it is quite clear that in general the woman's job tends to be of a qualitatively different type and not of a status which seriously competes with that of her husband as the primary status-giver or income-earner.

It seems quite safe in general to say that the adult feminine role has not ceased to be anchored primarily in the internal affairs of the family, as wife, mother and manager of the household, while the role of the adult male is primarily anchored in the occupational world, in his job and through it by his status-giving and income-earning functions for the family. Even if, as seems possible, it should come about that the average married woman had some kind of job, it seems most unlikely that this relative balance would be upset; that either the roles would be reversed, or their qualitative differentiation in these respects completely erased.

[After marriage] *within* the new familial collectivity the marital sub-collectivity has the system goal of optimizing "tension-management" or "gratification" of the partners. Since it is a collectivity, however, there must be both a differentiation of roles and the involvement of at least two *primary* need-disposition components on each side. Furthermore, as a system, we suggest its *differentiation* must involve one or both of the two elementary axes of differentiation, power and instrumental-expressive.

Considered as a social system, the marriage relationship is clearly a differentiated system. The fact that sex (as category) is constitutive of it suggests that, of the two "primary" axes, the instrumental-expressive one here takes precedence over that of power. From this point of view, though the general functions of this collectivity in the superordinate systems are expressive, the *more* instrumental role in the subsystem is taken by the husband, the *more* expressive one by the wife. This is to say that externally, the husband has the primary adaptive responsibilities, relative to the outside situation, and that internally he is in the first instance "giver-of-care," or pleasure, and secondarily the giver of love, whereas the wife is primarily the giver of love and secondarily the giver of care or pleasure. The husband role, that is, is prototypically closer to the "mother" role, that of the wife, to the "child" role. But both are both "mother" and "child" to each other.

Compared with the mother-child situation, however, the power relation has been very greatly, if not completely equalized. We suggest that this has happened by a process similar to that analyzed in the last chapter in relation to the attitudes toward rules in connection with the emergence of universalistic orientations. This involves a high degree of internalized superego control in relation to an institutionalized set of universalistic values. It is probably not a matter of chance that this equalization of power has gone very far in the American marriage relationship and that this has occurred in a society with an exceptionally strong general accent on universalistic values (there are of course other factors). . . .

The next set of considerations which is also very important, concerns the fact that institutionally the marriage relationship is a subsystem of the nuclear family. The parties' roles as parents therefore must be integrated with their marital roles. Here, as we have seen in instrumental-expressive and possibly in power terms, there is an important complication. The husband-father has the predominantly instrumental role in connection with the *family* as a collectivity, not only the marriage, he not only "supports" a wife, but a family. The wife, however, in spite of her *more* expressive role in the family as a whole, which we may say above all centers on her acceptance or love complex of motives, in her role of mother of specific children, must for the mother-child subsystems, take the predominantly instrumental role. From this point of view the pre-oedipal child is the terminal member of a *series* of role relationships which combine system-subsystem memberships and instrumental-expressive differentiation.

Because of his principally instrumental responsibilities in his familial as distinguished from his marital role, the husband-father needs a relatively more highly developed instrumental complex of motivational components than does his wife. But in turn it is evident that he must also have this specialization in order to serve his function as a socializing agent at the critical oedipal phase, as the primary symbolic source of the superego. The wife-mother, on the other hand, needs the predominance of expressive motivational elements in her total mother and familial role, in the case of the former because young children do not have highly developed instrumental motive systems and are not capable of responding to them. But because the mother must take relatively instrumental roles in relation to her children, and of course in important ways in relation to the family as a whole, those expressive motives must be balanced by those on the instrumental side. To take only one example, we have seen how essential it is that both parents should present a united front in imposing disciplines on their children. If the mother herself did not have adequate superego control, she would obviously be subject to easy "seduction" by her children. Particularly in our type of society where the father is absent so much of the time, the deleterious possibilities of such a situation are evident.

One further balance is interesting. In the marital relationship, we have argued, the more instrumental role of the husband makes him more the "giver" of "pleasure," from the facilities necessary for his wife and for the marital collectivity to have "nice things," all the way to erotic pleasure. But in the mother role the wife, in turn, is the primary giver of pleasure to her children. This suggests an important relationship of balance in the feminine personality. It follows from our analysis above that the expressive primacy in the feminine personality and her greater difficulty in achieving emancipation from dependency would, other things equal, make for a greater direct vulnerability to the regressive motivational elements comprised in the "nurturance" complex, which, according to our analysis, is the primary location of the Id. If her pleasure needs were allowed to be too greatly turned inward, to become too narcissistic, this presumably would tend to activate regressive needs. The mother role, however, motivates a woman to turn nurturance needs outward to the child. This strongly suggests the importance of the mother role to the personality-equilibrium of the woman.

Alva Myrdal and Viola Klein on Women's Two Roles

Alva Reimer Myrdal and Viola Klein (see earlier discussions of their lives and careers in this volume) collaborated in the 1950s on a book on the problems of employed women. In this discussion they point out the problems both for housewives, who often envy employed women their financial independence, and working wives, who may envy housewives their time for personal activities.

From Alva Myrdal and Viola Klein, *Women's Two Roles: Home and Work* (London: Routledge & Kegan Paul, 1956), xi–xiii, 1–12. Reprinted by permission of Taylor & Francis Group Ltd.

THE SELECTION

In this selection from the Introduction and Chapter 1 of Alva Reimer Myrdal and Viola Klein's *Women's Two Roles,* the history and current status of women's family and economic roles are discussed. The authors argue that there is no longer an issue of whether women *can* work well in industrialized economies, but a question remains as to what they *should* do. They argue that young girls often are presented with false images of the choices they must make for their adult lives, owing to changes in the social world that have not been sufficiently understood in their impact on women. The authors also point to class differences in how women's work and opportunities are perceived and many differences between how women actually live and the roles they are taught to expect to fulfill. One important component of the changes in women's lives, according to Myrdal and Klein, is the increasing longevity of women's lives combined with early childbearing of fewer children, resulting in much longer periods in which women have no children at home to care for. This and other changes have led to "widespread discontent among urban housewives" of the day, a description of middle-class women's roles that anticipates by almost a decade Betty Friedan's "problem with no name" presented in *The Feminine Mystique* (1963).

WOMEN'S TWO ROLES

Whether married women should be employed outside their homes has become the most topical issue concerning women in recent years and the controversy is carried on with much spirit and profound conviction on both sides. Since so many questions of vital concern to individual lives are involved, it is not surprising that the discussion is, by and large, mainly conducted on a level of personal opinions and emotions rather than on the basis of sociological facts. Such facts are, however, essential for a rational assessment of the situation and a sober evaluation of the pros and cons of the case; to supply the relevant data for such an assessment is the intention of this book.

Our readers will be left in no doubt as to the side to which we lean in this controversy; but they will, we hope, credit us with impartiality in the collection of facts and in the presentation of the real issues involved.

The problem of 'women and work', and of women's role in society generally, has completely changed its complexion during the last few decades. It is no longer a question of what women are physically and mentally capable of doing. For experience has settled the long controversy about feminine abilities and has proved that women are fit for a much wider range of activities than merely those compatible with the commonly accepted idea of the 'weaker sex'.

The emphasis has now shifted from the discussion of: 'What *can* women do?' to one of: 'What *should* women do?' Implicit in this question is an interest both in women's individual well-being and in the welfare of society.

What to do with our lives is a problem which poses itself more acutely in regard to women than to men, partly because women are relative newcomers to important sectors of the social scene, partly because their lives are more intricately linked with the existence of the family and the continuation of the race.

At this juncture in our social history women are guided by two apparently conflicting aims. On the one hand, they want, like everybody else, to develop their personalities to the full and to take an active part in adult social and economic life within the limits of their individual interests and abilities. On the other hand, most women want a home and a family of their own. At a time when most social and economic life was carried on at home these aims did not conflict with each other. They appear to do so to-day.

The claims of society on women are, likewise, twofold, and these, too, appear under present conditions of life and work to contradict each other. The need of society to perpetuate and regenerate itself, which puts a relatively greater share of responsibility on women than on men, imposes demands on women which compete with other claims arising from society's need for economic progress. The realization of the latter is to a considerable, yet often underrated, extent, dependent on women's co-operation.

This clash of conflicting interests has stirred public discussion during the last generation or two, and has resulted in varied interpretations of women's 'true' social role. By now, women are becoming weary of listening to contradictory exhortations about their duties. Different cultural traditions make their influences felt, and contrasting political ideologies have clouded the issue. The Catholic ideal is not the same as the Moslem one; National-Socialism presented a theory very different from that of Communism. Yet these, and others, persist side by side in confusing variety.

In the old days, women knew where they stood and their lives were spent in the care of their families. Their world was bounded by the walls of their homes. From there, a resolute minority thrust out into the world of business and public affairs and succeeded in being admitted, largely to the extent that they were willing to turn their backs on home and family.

Those pioneering days are now over. With them has gone the need for women to make a fatal decision between irreconcilable alternatives. The Gordian knot of a seemingly insoluble feminine dilemma has been cut. The technical and social developments of the last few decades have given women the opportunity to combine and to integrate their two interests in Home and Work—if we may thus, in short, characterize the two spheres of interest. No longer need women forgo the pleasures of one sphere in order to enjoy the satisfactions of the other. The best of both worlds has come within their grasp, if only they reach out for it.

To make this a reality for more than the chosen few, something in the nature of a mental revolt will be needed. There is no doubt that society can be organized in such a way as to give practical scope for both feminine roles. But more clear thinking both about ends and means, and a courageous facing of facts, will be required before these two roles will be fused into one harmonious whole.

In discussing this contemporary problem of Women one qualification has to be made: we are speaking here only of women in Western societies. We are fully aware that there is no uniform 'Woman Problem' which equally applies to all countries. Within the limits of this study it would, however, be impossible to include a comparison between the social roles of women all over the world, or to discuss the great variety of difficulties affecting women in different cultures and various stages of social development. . . .

A REVOLUTION IN TWO STAGES

During the present century the social position of women has undergone a series of profound changes, in which we can distinguish two main phases. The first is characterized by the admission of women to an increasing variety of hitherto 'masculine' jobs, provided, on the whole, that the women were unencumbered by family ties. The outstanding feature of the second phase is the endeavour of a growing number of women to combine family and employment. Altogether, this social change amounts to a gradual recapture of positions which were lost when women were squeezed out of the economic process by the Industrial Revolution.

Before that revolution women had at all times played a very active part in the economic life of society, as they do in agricultural communities to this day. Their two roles, raising a family and doing economically productive work, were fused into one way of life, work at home. When industrialization forced these to be separated, it was at first thought that women could carry on only one, namely, the family function. They had, therefore, first to assert their right to work alongside men; and now they have to prove that they can carry on both functions in one and the same lifetime, which is so much longer now than it was.

The process of eliminating women from economically active positions of course affected different social groups in different ways, as does the complementary process of bringing them back into paid jobs. In both the urban and the rural proletariat the latter was an immediate effect of industrialization, and the exploitation of women and children in its early phases was one of the blackest spots in the social history of the nineteenth century. Later, as wages rose, many working-class women left the labour market, since it was felt to be an important element in a higher standard of living that wives and mothers should be able to stay at home, like the women in more privileged social groups.

It eventually fell to the women in the urban middle class to symbolize the more systematic return to economic productivity, by entering paid employment.

The recovering of women's lost territory is a long and uneven process, as yet incomplete. The most painful part of the readjustment is caused by the fact that habits of thought that belong to past phases of these complex developments, and frequently to particular social groups, become established as absolutes in situations where they no longer apply.

Proving Women's Abilities outside the Home

The first lingering misconception which had to be cleared up was that women did not fit into the world of industry, of paid employment, in short, of 'men's jobs'. The sweated labour of women during the early period of industrialization, and their continued employment in several sectors of light industry, was not appreciated as proving their competitive qualifications.

It was left to the pioneers from the middle and upper classes, fighting their way to individual recognition against heavy odds, to demonstrate women's fitness to do 'masculine' work under the same conditions as men. To prove their case the pioneers were mostly quite willing to ignore the fact that they were women, and satisfied that this fact should also be ignored by others. Women's share in the economic life of the past had been forgotten, and it appeared to many that in their claim for a place in the scheme of economic production women had to break completely new ground. Whether hesitant or defiant, every new step seemed to provide a new test case. Every professionally active woman felt herself to be continually on trial.

This, in fact, the pioneers of women's emancipation were, individually and collectively. The period was characterized by the publication of countless comparative studies and measurements testing the relative aptitudes and traits of men and women—from their genius for mathematics to their ability to walk the tight-rope.

These investigations, carried out by psychologists and sociologists, have proved that most women are as good as most men on most scores; that individuals of one sex always vary more between themselves than any averages for the sexes as a whole differ from each other; and that any measurable differences in average performance of one sex in a particular field are balanced by the differences in another. If men show a somewhat greater inclination towards one capacity, such as mechanics, women compensate by excelling in another, such as languages. If men more often excel in physical strength, women correspondingly excel in dexterity.

The issue of comparative performances can be regarded as settled to-day, both scientifically and practically. Though differences in attitudes between men and women still form a favourite topic of drawing-room conversation and popular quiz-programmes, women's abilities are no longer seriously in doubt. These discussions rather seem to be a kind of rearguard action carried on after the main battle has been decided. In a world of so much accepted sex equality they perhaps represent a last unconscious protest against standardization and uniformity.

In the meantime, women's achievements have become evident to anyone. This process was undoubtedly accelerated by the two world wars in which necessity compelled society to use women in occupations which previously were the monopoly of men. At some time during the 1939 war a most impressive poster could be seen all over Britain. It showed the photograph of a young woman in uniform and steel helmet carrying a crying child out of the flames of a bombed house. In her composed and matter-of-fact way she symbolized the courage and determination of Britain under air bombardment, and her attitude had beneath its efficiency just that touch of motherliness and sentiment that made so direct an appeal to the heart. There could be no doubt in anybody's mind that the photograph was genuine. For everybody knew from personal experience that countless women had faced, and were facing, similar dangers with equal courage and equanimity. It was no longer necessary for women to 'protest too much', as the early feminists did in their exaggerated imitation of men.

The first phase of the revolution was concluded and women had met the demands made on them.

It must also be admitted that the demands came half-way to meet women. In our highly complex and diversified economic structure there is scope for all sorts of natural gifts. Physical strength is no longer an essential prerequisite for most jobs. Many operations formerly imposing great strain on the workers are now performed by machines requiring the attendant's skill rather than muscular force; better hygienic conditions and reduced hours of work have made both industrial and clerical jobs less exhausting; and improved means of communication have helped to bridge the gulf between home and workplace. Changed also is the attitude of employers: modern industrial management in Western Europe and North America no longer pursues the short-sighted policy of getting the most out of its workers by methods of sweated labour. Instead, it tries as far as possible to adjust the working conditions to human needs. Good labour relations are considered essential to successful production. Scientific investigations are carried out in the fields of industrial psychology and personnel management, as well as in the sphere of production techniques, in order to discover the material and psychological conditions leading to the highest productivity.

Thus the setting for participation in the processes of economic production is much more favourable to women than at any time since the beginning of the Industrial Revolution. Moreover, our society has begun to accept the fact that women are in jobs to stay.

Defining Women's Family Role

However there is often a lack of clarity in present-day generalizations about women's economic function. We know now that the highly important contribution of women within the old type of home, which was the centre of productive processes, has been changed in a radical way. Nevertheless, this domestic setting as the accepted framework of women's life and work still underlies the pattern of women's 'roles' to an irrationally large extent. Memories of a long obsolete social pattern linger on and as well as colouring our dreams they distort our attempts at rational thinking.

Up to the beginning of the nineteenth century spinning, weaving and making clothes, baking bread, curing meat, making soap, brewing beer, preserving fruit and many other processes now usually carried out in factories, as well as a good deal of teaching and nursing, were part of a woman's household routine. Thus, the importance of a woman's contribution could not be in question. Even the bearing of numerous children, who were not merely a liability as additional mouths to be fed, but also, from an early age, an asset as additional hands to help earning the family's income, enhanced women's economic value and filled them with a secure sense of purpose.

When the equilibrium of pre-industrial society was upset by new technical and social developments the external conditions of women's lives were radically changed. Small-scale family handicrafts decayed and were superseded by large industries employing individual workers, not families. The employment of children in factories and mines had soon to be stopped by legislation, for humanitarian reasons; elementary education became general, and before long the law enjoined on parents the duty to support their children fully, at least up to the age of 10. Thus from the economic point of view children became a burden instead of an asset to the poorer section of the population, while at the same time a large part of the responsibility for their education was taken away from the home. Many working-class wives went to work in factories and, with their ten- to twelve-hour day, neglected their children and homes to a degree which shocked the social conscience of the later nineteenth century. This is the background against which married women's employment outside their homes came to be regarded as a social evil, and their concentration on homemaking as an improvement of their standard of living.

That the workload in the home meanwhile drastically diminished—for a variety of reasons, the most important being the reduction in the size of the family—was never fully recognized. It is still, in some quarters, considered almost blasphemous to point out this historical fact.

Side by side with the ideal of the hard-working housewife another, quite different, feminine ideal, related to the privileges of the aristocracy, became more important as the middle classes grew in size and prosperity, the 'Lady of Leisure'. This ideal, cultivated more in the last century than in the present one, in point of fact put parasitism of women at a premium. The task of an upper-middle-class wife was chiefly to be an ornament to her husband's home and a living testimony to his wealth. Her idleness was one of the prerequisites. Up to this day, the two contrary ideals vie with each other in the columns of every woman's journal. There are on the one hand the domestic virtues with the fragrance of freshly-made bread every day, together with the statistics showing a fourteen- to sixteen-hour working day. But there are also the costly cults of the lily-white hands, of lavish entertaining, and of changing one's highly fashionable clothes oftener and oftener—the much advertised dreams of all that goes with being 'well provided for', once one is married. There is a curious causal relationship (though this is not necessarily appreciated) operating in the advertising columns of modern fashion magazines. While on the one hand more and more gadgets are offered to save time and labour, more and more time-consuming beauty treatments are recommended to keep in control a feminine figure which shows the effects of too little exercise and too much leisure.

There is no use denying that, even today, the twin ideals of the hard-working housewife and of the leisured lady exist in an unholy (and as a rule unrecognized) alliance, jointly circumscribing woman's role as one to be acted out within the home. The worst of this ideology is not that it is irrational and out of harmony with the facts of contemporary life, but that it presents our young girls with a thoroughly false picture of the practical choice they have to make for their lives. An honest scrutiny should be made to differentiate between productive and necessary work in the home and what is only a time-consuming pretext; a distinction must also be made between well-earned leisure and sheer waste of time.

Women become Citizens

Yet, while the nineteenth-century ideal of bourgeois women has been kept alive to this day and has become accepted in all social classes, the futility of feminine existence in the upper middle class was the very mainspring which motivated the social revolution usually called the emancipation of women. This movement was not simply a revolt of the weaker sex against the shackles imposed on it throughout the centuries by the strong, free male—effective though the emotional appeal of this image may be. The fact is rather that women lagged one step behind men in the process of social evolution. This is true both in the fields of economics and politics.

A social group can only achieve representation in parliamentary government when it is strong enough to enforce its demand. The middle classes in France were admitted to a share in political power only after the Revolution, and in England, only after the passing of the Reform Bill in 1832. While in Sweden the farmers, like the merchants, had their place in the 'four estates' from the inception of parliamentary democracy more than 500 years ago, the working class became a partner very late, in the first decades of this century, through gradual reforms. Only in the U.S.A. was universal male suffrage tried out very early on. In Europe, the gradual extension of the political franchise to cover all the adult population except lunatics, convicts, and women, followed after the social changes created by the Industrial

Revolution. Women were not enfranchised until the end of the first world war in the U.S.A., the United Kingdom, and Sweden, and until the end of the second world war in France.

It took women longer than men to achieve political freedom and democratic rights, access to education and opportunity for employment, as women were generally retarded in their adjustment to the Industrial Revolution. In their clamour for the 'Right to Work' their aim was to regain the position of economic productivity and the sense of social usefulness they had lost when the centre of production was moved from the home to the factory. However revolutionary women's demand for the right to work may have appeared at the time, in fact they were not striving for a new thing but for the restitution of their lost share in the scheme of economic affairs. If women now made an articulate and conscious request to go out into the world, they were not driven by a sudden wave of perversity, or fashion, but by the simple logic of economics. The work had been moved from the home, and women wanted to move after it, as men had done not so long before.

Discrimination against women in the field of property rights was another consequence of the new economic developments of the nineteenth century. Among the landed gentry and in the families of independent craftsmen, women had often wielded considerable power, but they were handicapped when it came to the new types of investment in industry and commerce. The servitude against which they now protested was a more recent growth than was generally recognized.

The Right to Education, another important issue in the emancipation of women, was granted to women somewhat later than to men. But here, too, they should be regarded as latecomers in the evolutionary process rather than as one half of mankind kept in subjection by the other half. Education, previously a privilege of the few, was gradually put on a broader basis during the nineteenth century. Beginning with some States of the U.S.A., where a system of free, tax-supported State schools, open to all, was already established in the first quarter of the century and spread to all the Northern States before 1850, compulsory general education was introduced in Sweden in 1842, in Britain in 1870 and in France in 1882 (to confine our examples to the four countries which will provide our illustrations throughout this study).

In some past societies, for instance, the aristocratic culture of the Middle Ages, education, particularly in the 'humanities', was more women's domain than that of men. This situation became reversed as economic developments affected the two sexes differently, for with general education went professional training. While medicine, for instance, was often in the hands of women as long as it was a humanitarian art, women became excluded from its practice as soon as conditions of competence were officially regulated—because women could not get the basic training. Thus it was logical that one of the earliest reforms women fought for should have been the right to higher education. The dates when they won the right to enter universities mark the pioneer victories for the efforts to set the world right again for women.

Conflicting Roles and Ideals

The Woman with a Career is a creation of distinctly middle-class origin, and is symptomatic of the second phase of the social revolution which we have been describing. The acceptance of this feminine role shows that it is possible for women to envisage the idea of work outside the home as a career for life without any feeling of self-denial or resignation, and to plan for it as a positive gain.

Admittedly, the ideal of 'career woman' has until recently been held by women only—and by a very limited number of women at that. To this day the term has such an unpleasant connotation for many people that professional women often hasten to assure you that they are not 'career women'. Men have, for a variety of reasons, found it difficult to adjust themselves to the idea of a wife who so radically differs from their mothers. The other two ideal feminine roles—that of the hard-working housewife and that of the lady of the salon—continue to thrive together in the minds both of men and of innumerable women, and this confusion brings a great deal of unreality into the life plans of young girls. While woman's external conditions of life have changed drastically, the ideal picture of her future is still visualized by the young girl as if these changes had never happened. In this case there is an unusually long time-lag between the emergence of new realities and relationships and the acceptance of their full implications.

It is, of course, neither accurate nor fair to make general statements about women as if they all belonged to one class or one type.

Take, for example, the desire of women to share in productive social processes which we discussed before, and their demands for the 'Right to Work' and the 'Right to Education'. These, clearly, were middle-class ideologies. While to women condemned to the passivity and languor of a Victorian drawing-room the chance of going out to work, like their menfolk, might seem exciting and enriching, work was a necessity, often hardly bearable, for working-class women.

To-day, a few generations later, with women's education fairly well established, the difference in the attitude to work is still quite marked between different strata—which do not necessarily coincide with social classes. Women with higher education or a specialized training who have known the satisfactions of responsibility or of skilled work are, naturally, more loath to give up their jobs on marrying than girls who have done semi-skilled or routine work. Pearl Jephcott, in her studies of factory girls[1], was struck by the absence among them of any sympathetic relationship to their work. She found that employment was considered by these girls as an unavoidable but temporary phase in their lives and the sooner it came to an end the better. Their imaginations having been fed on Hollywood pictures and the weekly magazines which form their chief reading matter, they wait for the day on which they will enter the blissful state of matrimony, happily to live in it ever after. In the same way, most short-hand typists, shop assistants, and women employed in jobs of a similar routine nature, with little prospect of advancement, long to escape into a world in which they will have neither a boss nor a fixed timetable. Though the change may in effect be the substitution of one routine for another, it replaces one which is imposed from outside—either by the impersonal workings of the machinery or by the will of a superior—with another which the woman can to some extent manipulate herself and which therefore gives her the feeling of freedom.

In contrast, the highly skilled or the professional woman who has to give up her career for domestic routine is likely to feel frustrated after some time if she cannot use her abilities. Her frustration may express itself in various forms, the most frequent of which is the complaint about the drudgery of domestic work.

To-day, when families have generally been reduced to manageable size, when public services and factory products have taken over many functions previously performed at home, and when labour-saving devices, even if they have not considerably reduced the number of working hours, have at least taken the backache and sweat out of a good deal of housework, the word 'drudgery' in connexion with domestic duties is more frequently used than ever before. Just as the rising standards of living have made poverty, though generally less acute, psychologically more frustrating, so the availability of labour-saving gadgets on the one hand, and of an alternative way of life as independent income-earner on the other, have made the domestic routine more irksome to the housewife. Housewives, in our time, have become a discontented class and are on that account—and because they have votes, too—constantly courted, appealed to and glorified by governments and politicians.

During the last generation or so, an interesting shift in feminine discontent has taken place. Much of women's envy of men, which undoubtedly was a strong undercurrent in the earlier feminist movement, has changed its direction and turned into envy of one group of women against another: working women begrudge housewives their freedom to do things in their own time and in their own way, and possibly also the prestige that tends to go with greater leisure; whereas housewives envy employed women their financial independence, the greater variety of their social contacts, and their sense of purpose. This is one result of the present stage of partial emancipation in which two feminine ideals, two distinct ways of life, continue uneasily side by side.

There exist, it is true, many individual differences of emphasis and also, more important, varying degrees of consciousness of aims. But on the whole it seems true to say that human beings—women no less than men—need for their happiness both emotional fulfilment in their personal relations and a sense of social purpose. Even to the

---

[1] A. P. Jephcott; *Girls Growing Up,* London, 1942, and *Rising Twenty,* London, 1948.

most ardent feminists it is clear to-day that work is no end in itself and that the past over-emphasis on careers at the expense of marriage and family has done great damage to the women's cause.

On the other hand, the widespread discontent among urban housewives to-day bears witness to the fact that looking after one man and a family of two—however attractive a pattern of life this may seem to the young girl spending her days at the typewriter or behind a shop-counter—is, under present conditions, not enough to fill the many years of a woman's life and to give her the satisfaction of feeling that she is pulling her weight. Although this is unpleasant to accept, many women have begun to wake up to the realization that their children will not remain children all the time and that husbands, however ardent in their courtship, cannot be expected to remain the same for the half-century that their married life is now statistically likely to last. . . .

Certain facts, however, apply universally, and they are sufficient to serve as starting points for a rough analysis of present conditions as well as a basis for a discussion of future possibilities. The following five points will throw the problem into relief:

(1) Women, as the child-bearing sex, present specific social problems. This fact has, in particular, to be taken into account in the evaluation of their creative contribution to society.

(2) As a result of their maternal function women's adjustment to the social changes brought about by the Industrial Revolution, especially to the separation of work from home, has been retarded.

(3) The mental health and happiness of coming generations depend, to an extent which we have to-day only begun to understand, on the love and security which maternal care provides during early childhood. In this sense women bear a special responsibility for the future quality of our people.

(4) The general increase in longevity which characterizes this century has had a more marked effect on women than on men. Women to-day have a longer average expectation of life compared with their grandmothers, and also compared with their male contemporaries.

(5) Under present conditions, with an average family of only slightly more than two children, and reasonable amenities, an average housewife can be considered to be employed full-time on tasks which are necessary for home-making only during a quarter to one-third of her normal adult life.

Helen Mayer Hacker on the Burdens of Masculinity

THE SELECTION

Helen Mayer Hacker's pioneering work in gender was not restricted to the study of women. In one of the rare pre-1970s pieces on men's roles and masculinity, she presents here an analysis of the problematic aspects of masculine roles in the late 1950s. She notes the lack of attention to these questions, suggesting that since "man" has stood for "humanity," it has not occurred to many to analyze their roles, the focus having been on women and how they were "different." The sources of contemporary male problems she identifies as (1) traditional roles that have been made more burdensome by changes in the occupational structure, (2) contradictions in expectations of masculinity, and (3) problems caused by changes in women's roles.

Hacker points out that objective data indicate that "all is not well with men," as evidenced in part by widespread expressions of resentment toward women. Hacker goes on to examine men's roles as men, as husbands, as fathers, and as lovers, pointing out contradictions and difficulties in each of these. Her discussion of homosexuality as a "flight from masculinity" is similar to many such theories of her time, explanations that would not be considered well founded today. However, her overall analysis of how men's self-identities as men are implicated in their economic and leisure activities is a valuable contribution to the early literature on men and masculinity.

From Helen Mayer Hacker, "The New Burdens of Masculinity," *Journal of Marriage and Family Living* 19 (August 1957): 227–33. Copyright © 1957. Reprinted by permission of Blackwell Publishing Ltd.

THE NEW BURDENS OF MASCULINITY

In the field of intergroup relations it has often been ruefully remarked that there is no Negro problem, but only a white problem, no Jewish problem, but a Gentile problem; in short, no minority group problem, but a dominant group problem. And the problem of the dominant group was not only that its attitudes perpetuated the minority group, but also placed limitations on its own development. Amusingly enough, when men are the dominant group, they are quick to admit that their chief problem is women. This answer may be in part defensive, in part facetious, but it is true that inadequate attention has been paid to the sociology of dominant groups, and the strains imposed by the burdens of their status.

Indeed interest and research in changes in men's social roles have been eclipsed by the voluminous concentration on the more spectacular developments and contradictions in feminine roles, and changes in masculine roles have been treated largely as a reaction and adjustment to the new status of women. Possibly one reason why masculine social roles have not been subjected to scrutiny is that such a concept has not clearly emerged. Men have stood for mankind, and their problems have been identified with the general human condition. It is a plausible hypothesis, however, that men, as well as women, suffer from the lack of a generally accepted, clearly defined pattern of behavior expected of them, and that their interpretation of the masculine role varies according to individual personality needs and social situations. The massive social changes initiated by the Industrial Revolution have not only affected the complementariness of the sexes, but posed new problems of personality fulfillment for both men and women.

Analytically, contemporary masculine problems may be viewed as arising from three sources, which may prove difficult to disentangle. First, we may consider those burdens of masculinity which have survived from earlier periods, but which modern conditions may have aggravated. Men in their traditional role of breadwinners have always encountered difficulties, but it may be that recent developments in our occupational structure have added new tensions. Pertinent to this problem would be studies of occupational mobility and the increasing importance of education as both barrier and base to economic success, of vocational adjustment and the new personality traits, such as skill in politicking, needed for high level positions. We will return to this theme later on, when the worker role will be taken up explicitly. Then, too, from Adam on, men have had their troubles with women, but can we distinguish the enduring from the variable in their complaints?

Secondly, it may be useful to distinguish conflicts engendered by feelings of inadequacy in fulfilling role expectations from those stemming from feelings of uncertainty, ambiguity, or confusion regarding role expectations. A man may have no doubts concerning the criteria of masculinity, but feel that he does not live up to them, or he may be unsure concerning the requirements for validating manhood. Preliminary interview materials reveal that the ideal man is considered by men as being, among other things, a good provider, the ultimate source of knowledge and authority, and strong in character so that he may give a feeling of security, not only financially but emotionally, to his wife and children, and it was evident from their further responses that the respondents found themselves deficient in meeting these demands.

The norms of masculinity, however (and, conversely, those of effeminacy) may vary among social groups, and multiple group participations may set up contradictions and inconsistencies in outlook. For example, it was only after several months of counseling that a skilled mechanic developed the courage to dust off some old Caruso records he had stored in the attic, and find that listening to them was no threat to his manhood. The group memberships of a professional man, however, would hardly produce this particular conflict.

The third source or way of examining the problematic aspects of masculine social roles is interpreting them in terms of accommodation to the new freedoms and responsibilities of women. Here again we may look with profit to the minority group literature. Horace R. Cayton has spoken of the guilt-hate-fear complex of whites in regard to Negroes. He says:

> Guilt, because his treatment of the American Negro is contrary to all of his higher impulses. . . . But having such guilt and being unable and unwilling to resolve it, persons learn to hate the object they feel guilty about so the guilt turns to hate and with it the necessity to rationalize and justify their behavior. Finally there is fear, for the white man in all of his arrogance knows that in spite of his rationalizations about racial inferiority he would be resentful and strike back if treated the way he treats Negroes.[1]

Perhaps I would not press this analogy, if several men had not told me themselves that in their eyes men have guilt feelings about

the whole history of male-female relationships, and that while the "emotionally stable" man was attempting to work out a new, more equitable pattern, neurotic men succumbed to the other elements in the complex by striving to stand firm on traditional male prerogatives or going too far in their subservience to women. Again, in the matter of social distance, some men are willing to admit their occasional need of exclusive male companionship, while others are afraid to recognize it. Some find friendship with women enjoyable, while others are as uneasy with "intellectual" women as the white Southerner with educated Negroes.

In fact the chief obstacle so far experienced in efforts to collect data as a basis for the formulation of precise hypotheses has been men's reticence, which may be attributed in part, as mentioned previously, to the lack of cultural focus of attention on men's problems, as revealed in the defensive answer, "women." More important, though, is an element of the traditional masculine role which proscribes admission and expression of psychological problems, feelings, and general overt introspection, as summed up in the stereotype of the strong, silent man. True he may be permitted moments of weakness, some faltering in his self-appointed task, when he falls back on a woman for emotional support, but such support is in the nature of ego-building rather than direct participation and counsel. The ideal American male personality has been described by John Gillin[2] as a "red-blooded, gentlemanly, go-getter" and any confessions of doubts, uncertainties, or insecurities would tarnish this image, any sign of weakness might be taken for effeminacy.

---

[1]Horace R. Cayton, "The Psychology of the Negro Under Discrimination," in Arnold M. Rose, Editor, *Race Prejudice and Discrimination,* New York: Alfred A. Knopf, 1951, pp. 287–88.
[2]John Lewis Gillin and John Philip Gillin, *An Introduction to Sociology,* New York: The Macmillan Company, 1944, p. 172.

Perhaps this is the greatest burden of masculinity our culture imposes.

Nevertheless, there are objective indices that all is not well with men. Most obvious is the widespread expression of resentment toward women in conversation, plays, novels, and films. Modern women are portrayed as castrating Delilahs busily levelling men's individuality and invading the strongholds of masculinity in work, play, sex, and the home. She seems to say, with Ethel Merman, to the man, "Everything you can do, I can do better." She is the female insect who devours her lover ("The Cage"), the shrike who preys on her husband; she is a storehouse of evil desires, she constantly puts men to tests they cannot meet, she compells their submission. In the words of Oscar Wilde, women are seen as a brimming reservoir of all kinds of powers: physical, mental, moral, legal. In the comic strips, husbands and fathers are the guileless tools of their wives and daughters. To change Congreve's phrase in "The Way of the World," many men seem to see themselves as dwindling into a husband or other female appendage. Other indices, to be discussed later, are the increasing social visibility of impotence and homosexuality.

In seeking a conceptual model in which to cast masculine role problems, Kirkpatrick's[3] discussion of cultural inconsistencies in marital roles may be of service. He distinguished among three roles provided in our society for the married woman, each role implying certain privileges and certain obligations, and suggested that conflict might arise from the disposition of the wife to claim the privileges of more than one role without accepting its corresponding obligations, or from the disposition of the husband to expect his wife to assume the duties of more than one role without receiving its corresponding rights. This situation may be ascribed to social forces operating differentially on the American population, thus leading to a multiplicity of roles, no one of which has universal sanction and, consequently, not clearly isolated from the others.

Let us try to apply this notion of ethical inconsistency to some of the main statuses which men occupy in our society.

As a man, men are now expected to demonstrate the manipulative skill in interpersonal relations formerly reserved for women under the headings of intuition, charm, tact, coquetry, womanly wiles, et cetera. They are asked to bring patience, understanding, gentleness to their human dealings. Yet with regard to women they must still be sturdy oaks. As I heard on the radio recently, a woman wants a man to be "big and strong, sensitive and tender, the sort of person on whom you can rely, and who leaves you free to manage things the way you want." This contradiction is also present in men's relationships with men. As Riesman[4] points out in *The Lonely Crowd*, now that the "softness of the personnel" has been substituted for the "hardness of the material" men must be free with the glad hand, they must impress others with their warmth and sincerity (rather than as formerly with their courage and honesty and industry), they must be trouble shooters on all fronts. Yet they are not thereby relieved of the necessity of achieving economic success or other signal accomplishment, nor are they permitted such catharses as weeping, fits of

[3]Clifford Kirkpatrick. "The Measurement of Ethical Inconsistency in Marriage," *International Journal of Ethics*, 46 (1936). pp. 447–48. Also found in Clifford Kirkpatrick. *The Family at Process and Institution*, New York: The Ronald Press Company, 1955, pp. 163–64.

[4]David Riesman. Nathan Glazer, and Reul Denney, *The Lonely Crowd*, Garden City: Doubleday Anchor Books, 1953.

hysterics, and obvious displays of emotionalism. Of course, it may be objected that as women are increasingly allowed male privileges, they, too, are restricted in their emotional expression. Yet in the present era of transition women may still on the basis of the unpredictability of their sex, which is vaguely linked to biological functioning, have greater recourse to moodiness and irrationality.

In the status of husband, a man must assume the primary responsibility for the support of the home. A man who marries for money is exposed to more social opprobrium than a woman, and there is scanty social support for the expectation that the wife should shoulder half the financial burden. The self-respecting male has no choice but to work. Rarely do marriage and homemaking offer an alternative! Yet his responsibility does not end there. Although he should excel his wife in "external creativity" he is also called upon to show some competence in "internal creativity" in developing the potentialities of the husband-wife relationship, and sharing the physical and policymaking burdens of maintaining the home. Or in Parsonian language,[5] his specialization as "instrumental leader" does not preclude the assumption of "expressive" functions, particularly in view of the growing emphasis on friendship between husband and wife.

As a father, he bears the chief responsibility in law for the guardianship of the children, but often in practice plays a subordinate role. He may wistfully long for or stormily demand the respect of his children, but his protracted absence from the home makes it easy for them to evade his authority and guidance. Moreover, he is increasingly reproached for his delinquencies as a father. He is urged to strengthen his friendly, democratic relationship to his family without in any way lessening the primacy of his occupational role, though he is made to feel guilty for his efforts to support the home to the extent that they remove him from it. Indeed, the conflict between home and job is more salient and universal for men than for women. He has lost the security of the old *paterfamilias,* who was the autocrat of the breakfast table, and experiences difficulties in establishing a satisfying new role. That father is hard put to it to find his rightful place in the home is starkly summarized in the comment of the comic strip character, Penny, on the ambiguity of the father role, "We always try to make father feel he is a part of the family."

Father is no longer the chief mediator between the outside world and his family. As Gunnar Dybwad[6] has said,

> While formerly the father carried prestige because he, largely, was the connecting link to community affairs, now radio and TV, women's clubs and school-organized activities have greatly lessened his importance in this respect. Moreover, with increasing mechanization, his maintenance concerns in everyday houshold affairs have decreased.

He may feel outnumbered in PTA organizations where mother is the parent most often represented. His absorption in work cuts him adrift from the new patterns of child development. It is mother who reads the child psychology books, accompanies the child to the guidance counselor, consults with teachers, and participates in community child projects.

---

[5]Talcott Parsons and Robert F, Bales, *Family, Socialization and Interaction Process,* Glencoe, Illinois: The Free Press, 1955.
[6]Gunnar Dybwad, "Fathers Today: Neglected or Neglectful?" *Child Study,* 29, No. 2 (1952), pp. 3–5.

Dr. Leo Bartemeier[7] has pointed to a further conflict in the father role. In accordance with the cultural ideal of the he-man, fathers may feel that to be loving and gentle is consciously or unconsciously regarded as psychological failure, and indeed it may be difficult to make the transition from the attitude of ruggedness and toughness developed in schools, businesses, colleges, teams, and clubs to "the guiding light of paternal solicitude, love, and affection."

The requirements of the father role are further obscured by recent over-emphasis on the mother-child relationship, especially in infancy. (See, for example, Talcott Parsons, *Family: Socialization and Interaction Process.*) Father is relegated to the role of mother-substitute or nursery assistant, and receives little help in becoming an effective member of the parent team.

As a son, he may face more obstacles to emotional maturity than a daughter. The dangers of "Momism" and the female conscience have been much propagandized.[8] Exposed almost exclusively to the influence of women as mothers, teachers, and sisters the growing boy may identify goodness with femininity. Presumably the immediacy and comparative simplicity of the mother's role in the home is more readily grasped by the daughter, but the son finds difficulty in identifying with the largely absentee father and is cut off from his occupational role. His mother wants him to be an all-round boy and is fearful lest he be a sissy, but she can not show him what it is to be masculine. This he must learn in the peer groups of the youth culture so strangely detached from the adult world. Ruth Benedict's[9] comments on discontinuities in cultural conditioning apply with perhaps more force to boys than to girls. The personality traits which are rewarded in childhood do not bring approval in the peer group, nor are the values of the latter always conducive to success in the adult world of college and business. Arnold Green[10] in his much-quoted "The Middle-Class Male Child and Neurosis" shows how the blind obedience and "love" for his parents which brings surcease from anxiety and guilt are ineffective in competitive relationships outside the family in which independent and aggressive behavior is demanded. Integration of the conflicting roles of dependence and submission inside the home with self-assertiveness outside the home is difficult because of the guilt feelings aroused for either violating the initial submissive adjustment or for not making the effort to achieve. So the son may envy his sister's more protected role, because, although he is permitted greater freedom, more is expected of him in the way of achievement, responsibility, emotional control, and autonomy. To the extent that cultural expectations of masculine superiority persist, boys may resent invidious comparisons to their sisters and other girls in the matters of scholarship and

---

[7]Leo Bartemeier, "The Contribution of the Father to the Mental Health of the Family," quoted by Gunnar Dybwid in "Fathers Today: Neglected or Neglectful?" *Child Study,* 29, No. 2 (1952), p. 4.

[8]Cf. Margaret Mead, *And Keep Your Powder Dry: An Anthropologist Looks At America,* New York: William Morrow and Company, 1943. Margaret Mead, *Male and Female: A Study of the Sexes in a Changing World,* New York; William Morrow and Company, 1949. Geoffrey Gorer, *The American People: A Study in National Character,* New York: W. W, Norton & Company, Inc., 1948.

[9]Ruth Benedict, "Continuities and Discontinuities in Cultural Conditioning," *Psychiatry,* 1 (1938), pp. 161–67.

[10]Arnold Green, "The Middle-Class Male Child and Neurosis," *American Sociological Review,* 11 (February, 1946), pp. 31–41.

social skills. Also to be mentioned is the greater social acceptability girls find in being tomboys than boys who incline to interests labelled feminine. One of my students reported that he wanted to skip rope as a child, and finally got social permission by saying he was practicing to be a prizefighter. Additional problems are posed by the earlier maturation of girls.

We turn now to a consideration of men in the status of lover. In one sense this role strikes at the heart of the problem of masculinity. The ability to perform the sexual act has been a criterion for man's evaluation of himself from time immemorial. Virility used to be conceived as a unilateral expression of male sexuality, but is regarded today in terms of the ability to evoke a full sexual response on the part of the female. Men as the dominant group feel the strains of accommodating to the changing status of the minority group, and meeting the challenge presented by the sexual emancipation of women. Much as whites who feel constrained to convince Negroes of their feelings of friendliness and fair play, men seek from women the assurance that they are satisfied, and may become hurt and resentful when women play the part of psychological Lysistratas refusing to admit complete gratification.

The urgency of the problem of impotence may arise also from the psychological need to buttress masculinity in the one area safe from female competition, and it may also be that sexual prowess represents an alternative to economic success in validating manhood. Any deficiencies in this realm, therefore, are much more ego-threatening to men than to women. Sexual adequacy affects the relationship of men not only to women, but also to other men. Sexual contests may be important for standing in the peer group, and boys who have no exploits to recount may feel constrained to counterfeit them.

In general, it can be said that masculinity is more important to men than femininity is to women, and that sexual performance is more inextricably linked to feelings of masculine self-worth than even motherhood is to women. As stated previously, our cultural heritage has identified masculine with human, and both men and women aspire to masculine values. A dramatic corroboration of this hypothesis was made by Terman and Miles[11] when they found in administering their test of mental masculinity and femininity to students at the University of Chicago that the scores of both men and women shifted toward the masculine end of the continuum after the subjects had been informed of the purpose of the test. If a man is not masculine, not a "real man," he is nothing. But a woman can be unfeminine, and still be a person. There is a neuter category for women, but not for men.

The "flight from masculinity" evident in male homosexuality may be in part a reflection of role conflicts. If it is true that heterosexual functioning is an important component of the masculine role in its social as well as sexual aspects, then homosexuality may be viewed as one index of the burdens of masculinity. First, because of confusion of social and sexual role, as Margaret Mead[12] long ago pointed out in *Sex and Temperament in Three Primitive Societies,* in societies which differentiate strongly between masculine and feminine social roles, individuals who manifest personality traits ascribed to the opposite sex or who feel inadequate in fulfilling their part of the

[11]Louis M. Terman and Catherine C. Miles, *Sex and Personality: Studies in Masculinity and Femininity,* New York: McGraw-Hill, 1936.
[12]Margaret Mead, *Sex and Temperament in Three Primitive Societies,* included in *From the South Seas,* New York: William Morrow and Company, 1939.

sexual division of labor may become confused in their sexual identification, and feel that they must also change their sexual object. Thus, the feelings of our mechanic who feared listening to Caruso records may be interpreted as a fear of homosexuality. Abram Kardiner[13] in his *Sex and Morality* has elaborated this theme:

> The difficulty in our society is that role expectations exercise an influence on sexual activity, sometimes in unexpected ways. The association of money, economic power and prestige with sexual potency or bodily stature is notorious. Money is a common form of the vindication of manliness; by the same token, absence of money may crush the feeling of manliness.

Kardiner further suggests that homosexuality represents a rerouting of aggression and hostility perhaps in response to heightened social demands—from women and competitors. He goes on to say:

> These are the men who are overwhelmed by the increasing demands to fulfill the specifications of masculinity and who flee from competition because they fear the increased pressure on what they consider their very limited resources. . . . This kind of man can get no comfort from the female because she is a threat to him, not a solace, because she expected him to be masculine. The best he can do is to settle for a compromise on sensual satisfaction without further commitment.

It would be a matter of empirical investigation to establish a typology of men, perhaps according to family constellation or social class position, in terms of their interpretation of the demands of masculinity and their felt capacity to fulfill them, possibly along the lines that Merton[14] has suggested in his article "Social Structure and Anomie." A greater range of feminine than masculine types seems available in our society, as suggested by such superficial indices as modes of dress and manner. Significantly, no typology of "masculine" personalities has been advanced, such as Helene Deutsch's[15] categorization of women.

By implication, if not directly, in the foregoing we have referred to men's occupational role, and we may now turn explicitly to this area. The problems which men, more than women, experience on the job have already been mentioned: (1) the greater compulsion to success, if not from themselves, then from their wives; (2) the lack of an alternative to gainful employment; (3) the identification of economic success with masculinity—(one woman of my acquaintance has told me that a man's success is an important component of his sex appeal, both directly and indirectly; that men who feel themselves failures lack confidence in their dealings with women); (4) the new need for politicking or using traditionally feminine forms of behavior for ingratiating superiors, customers, et cetera; and (5) the feeling of being threatened by women in industry, who are seen as limiting opportunities for men, diminishing the prestige of jobs formerly held only by men, and casting a cold eye on masculine pretensions to vocational superiority. Also to be mentioned, although not new and not confined to men, are the problems of obtaining recognition, usually phrased in terms of earning more money, and job satisfaction in the sense of feeling that one is making a vital contribution to society.

---

[13]Abram Kardiner, *Sex and Morality,* Indianapolis and New York: The Bobbs-Merrill Company, Inc., 1954, pp. 168 and 175.

[14]Robert K. Merton, "Social Structure and Anomie," *American Sociological Review,* 3 (Oct., 1938), pp. 672–82.

[15]Helene Deutsch, *The Psychology of Women,* Vol. I, New York: Grune and Stratton, 1945.

The presence of women in industry is a disturbing fact on several grounds. First, it is frequently felt that women are not gentlemen, that is, they compete unfairly by using sexual attractiveness and other tactics closed to or beneath men. If the distribution of the sexes in positions of power were more equitable, this objection would lose its basis. Secondly, women who have ample opportunities of observing men on the job are not so likely, in the words of Virginia Woolf, to reflect their image double life-size. The man's occupational role loses its mystery, and women need no longer depend on men as a link to the world outside the home. This problem, too, is one of transition, and should disappear when through habituation to working women both men and women no longer expect masculine superiority and establish casual, workaday relationships on the job. And if through propaganda and education the presence of women in the occupational world, like other minority groups, can be shown to raise levels of productivity and shorten working hours for men, then their competition will not be regarded differently from that presented by other men.

It remains now to gather up the threads of the discussion. The initial problem was posed as to whether men today in fulfilling masculine social role expectations experience difficulties unknown to their fathers, and since such expectations may vary according to social group, class, et cetera—most particularly, urban middle class white men of native parentage. Such difficulties might flow from stepped-up demands of the role itself making it harder to fulfill or from the infusion of ambiguous or contradictory elements into the role, requiring in some cases a double dose of obligation or causing men to cling to a double dose of privilege. Another way of putting this question is to ask whether substantial changes have occurred in the criteria of masculinity over the past fifty years. Everyone thinks he knows what is masculine, and how to recognize a "real man," but no one can give an adequate definition. It is neither money nor muscles. A woman sociologist offered this one: "A real man is one who can take responsibility for a woman and their children." While not probably in the forefront of men's consciousness, this definition is no doubt the traditional one. A male professor of philosophy felt that the mark of a man was the desire to create something original and lasting, although he believed that woman's ideal man was a subtle Kowalsky plus a smattering of the *Saturday Review of Literature*. A popular expression of professional men was that women were concerned with survival and men with honor.

At the present time I am engaged in a research project to uncover how men interpret the masculine role, to get at their feelings about being men, and to find out what personality and social correlates are linked to the various interpretations of the masculine role and the felt points of tension and strain. The underlying assumption will be that social change has introduced certain cleavages between values and behavior, and that the very forces which gave rise to these conflicts will contribute to their alleviation. In the meantime it will be of both practical and theoretical interest to know in what directions masculine roles are changing, and how men are handling these changes, and with what other variables are associated anxiety concerning these changes or an accepting, experimental attitude. If we can return to our dominant group, minority group analogy, we can say that men are paying a price for the past lack of reciprocity between the sexes, and the future solution need not be the reversal of the caste line in a matriarchal society as some men fear, but rather the collaborative effort of men and women in evolving new masculine and feminine identities which will integrate the sexes in the emotional division of labor so that the roles which men and women play will not be rationalized or seen as external constraint but eagerly embraced as their own.